C000247157

THE AUTHOR'S E

Nicola J. Watson trained at Oxford and held posts at Oxford, Harvard, Northwestern, and Indiana Universities before taking up a position at The Open University. A specialist in the literature and culture of the Romantic period, her research focuses on authorial afterlives and the associated histories of literary tourism, literary commemoration, and the literary museum.

Henry Wallis, with additions by Edwin Landseer, Shakespeare's House, Stratford-upon-Avon, c. 1854.

THE AUTHOR'S EFFECTS

ON WRITER'S HOUSE MUSEUMS

NICOLA J. WATSON

OXFORD
UNIVERSITY PRESS

Great Clarendon Street, Oxford, ox2 6DP,
United Kingdom

Oxford University Press is a department of the University of Oxford.
It furthers the University's objective of excellence in research, scholarship,
and education by publishing worldwide. Oxford is a registered trade mark of
Oxford University Press in the UK and in certain other countries

© Nicola Watson 2020

The moral rights of the author have been asserted

~~First published 2020~~
First published in paperback 2023

Published in the United States of America by Oxford University Press
198 Madison Avenue, New York, NY 10016, United States of America

British Library Cataloguing in Publication Data

Data available

Library of Congress Cataloging in Publication Data

Data available

ISBN 978–0–19–884757–1 (Hbk.)
ISBN 978–0–19–888354–8 (Pbk.)

Acknowledgements

All our books carry in them much of our own lives, and it has taken a long time—far too long a time—out of my life to write this one. It began as an exploration of the literary landscapes with which as a young woman I fell in love, turned inexorably with age and promotion into an essay on committees, fund-raising, and ceremonial, and finally changed under the pressure of loss into a book about the extent and ends to which vanished lives and dead houses can or should be reconstructed and revivified. Throughout these various tiresome and time-consuming metamorphoses I have incurred many debts, which it is a pleasure finally to acknowledge, even if this can hardly constitute adequate repayment.

First of all, my thanks to the British Academy, whose award of a Small Research Grant in 2007 enabled me to make a start on this project by making trips in 2008 and 2009 to visit the many writer's house museums situated in New England, along with Mark Twain's boyhood home in Missouri, and other outlying properties. My thanks too to Elmira College for generously providing me with a night's accommodation in Mark Twain's summer home, Quarry Farm, in 2009. Project TRAUM (Transforming Author Museums in Norway) gave me the chance to explore author museums in Norway and provided me with a full month working at the University of Oslo in 2018, which allowed the final write-through of the manuscript as well as providing intellectual company and stimulus. The Open University has also produced all kinds of financial support over the years for various other research trips, including a visit to Abbotsford to study their latest redisplay in 2017, funding research assistance time to help in the final preparation of the manuscript, and paying for image permissions.

Secondly, my thanks to the many, many archivists, librarians and museum curators, officers, and trustees who have kindly answered queries in person, by mail, and by email, and who have on occasion opened museums to me specially. They have included Kirsty Archer-Thompson of Abbotsford, Diana Boston of Hemingford Grey, Jeff Cowton of Dove Cottage, Anthony

Burton of the Dickens House Museum, Kenneth Page of Keats House, Cindy Lovell of the Mark Twain Boyhood Home and Museum, Lesley Morris and Susan Halpert of the Houghton Rare Book Library, Sue Hodson of the Huntington Library, Ruth Degenhardt of the Berkshire Athenaeum, Anita Israel and Jim Shea of the Longfellow National Historic Site, Sarah Laycock of Haworth Parsonage Museum, Bernard Degout of the Maison de Chateaubriand, Stefan Blomberg and Camilla Larrsson of the Strindberg Museum in Stockholm, Sophie Kerrouche of the Chateau Monte Cristo, and Amanda Molcher and Kate Bostock of the Cowper and Newton Museum. Frankie Kubicki suffered a double dose of interrogation first at the Dickens Museum and then at Keats House. Paul Taylor and the staff of the Shakespeare Birthplace Trust spent much time with me in the vaults unpicking cardboard boxes on the vaguest of treasure-hunts. Fru Bente Forberg of the Sigrid Undset Museum in Lillehammer spent a whole afternoon talking with me when the museum was otherwise shut. Ungratefully and disgracefully, I have misplaced the name of the delightful librarian who coped with all sorts of questions about American visitors to Hardy country in the Dorchester County Museum, and the name of the charming man who allowed me to fossick for an afternoon in the Chawton Cottage scrapbooks, and indeed that of the equally courteous man who pulled out Dorothy Wordsworth's boots from a case at Rydal Mount so that I could photograph them. I have even mislaid the name of the manager of the Marks and Spencer branch in Stratford-upon-Avon who let me in to see their relics of Washington Irving's sojourn there when it was The Red Horse inn. I am afraid there will certainly be others whom I have inadvertently omitted, and hope they will forgive me. I should mention here too the many volunteer guides who put up with having their oral presentations part-transcribed, and who were on occasion obliged to swallow my urgently expressed desire to be left well alone; they have included Lori Satter of the Dickinson House, Matthew Waterhouse of the Twain House, Kurt Masdea of Arrowhead, Susan Davidson of the William Culler Bryant Homestead, 'Peter' and Ted Malone at the Longfellow House in Cambridge, MA, 'Annie H' at Sunnyside, Sue Anne Denneby at the Whitman Birthplace, Liz Cohen of 'The House of Seven Gables', Cathy Walsh of the Hawthorne Birthplace, and Tom Beardsley of the 'Old Manse' in Concord, who very kindly took me by exception up into the attic. There have been, of course, many more, of whom I might mention the charming staff of Coleridge Cottage, Nether Stowey, who entertained my mother and myself on the very last day they were open in 2018.

In connection with my trips to New England and beyond, I owe personal debts of gratitude to many people: to Ellen Harvey who put us up in New York, to Alison Brown and Sonia Hofkosh who put us up in Boston, to Jean Marsden and Lane Barrow who put us up in Connecticut (and lent us a tent), to Gail and Susan Arnott of Wessington Springs, South Dakota for their hospitality and to the delightful Ladies' Shakespeare Club of Wessington Springs headed up by Kathy Dean who hosted a memorable tea, and not forgetting the captain of the Mark Twain Riverboat on the Mississippi who insisted that I took the wheel. To Martine Penwarden's perfect French and forceful charm I owe thanks for brokering a visit and permission to take photographs at the Chateau Monte Cristo.

I would also like to thank the many people and institutions across the UK, Europe, and well beyond who have invited me to speak on this subject, or to associate my work with related research projects, including: Silvia Bigliazzi, Lisanna Calvi, Clara Calvo, Gillian Dow, Paul Edmondson, Ina Habermann, Coppélia Kahn, Maureen McCue, Anthony Mandal, Diana Owen, Murray Pittock, Stijn Reijnders, Matt Sangster, Barbara Schaff, Johan Schimanski, Ulrike Spring, Jo Taylor, Marianne Thormählen, Dale Townshend; The Shakespeare Institute; the York Festival of Ideas; the York Centre for Eighteenth-Century Studies; the Dr Johnson Society; the British Council; the National University of Singapore; Nanyang Technical University; the University of Malta; and Project TRAUM. Each and every one of these invitations has shaped this book's interest in literary tourist sites, partly because I have always felt obliged to come up with something of local interest, partly because they have brought within reach all sorts of museums which otherwise I would not have visited. I should also thank all those audiences for listening and asking questions, sometimes with enthusiasm, sometimes with bemusement, but nearly always politely. A small amount of the research contained in these chapters underpins two already published pieces that arose from these invitations: 'Mrs Thrale's Teapot; and other ways of making Johnson at home', *The New Rambler* (Spring 2017), pp. 66–82 and 'Rousseau on the Tourist Trail' in Angela Esterhammer, Diane Piccitto, and Patrick Vincent, eds. *Romanticism, Rousseau, Switzerland: New Prospects* (Houndmills, UK: Palgrave Macmillan, 2015), pp. 84–100.

More personally, Alison Booth, Clare Brant, Mary Favret, Sonia Hofkosh, and Deidre Shauna Lynch in particular have been friendly and congenial sensibilities, and a few colleagues have been especially supportive on particular occasions: Dame Hermione Lee, who produced a room in Wolfson

College when I was being driven mad by the barking of my neighbour's dog; Katharine Scheil, who sent me pictures of replicas of Anne Hathaway's Cottage; Jennie Batchelor, who dug out early references to dressing up as Jane Austen; Allen Reddick, who produced chapter and verse for a Goethe inscription; Michael Dobson, who arranged for me to borrow Marie Corelli's folly in which to write; Emese Asztalos, who suggested Eastern European examples; Tim O'Brien, who agreed to be interviewed at length about the design process of New Place; Johan Schimanski, who tracked down the whereabouts of a snippet of Voltaire's bed-hangings. This, again, is a wholly inadequate list to cover all the suggestions, and with them friendships, that have been made. Sincere thanks are of course due to the two anonymous readers for Oxford University Press who provided much generous and sound advice and admonition. And my warm thanks go also to my three successive research assistants, Sarah Burdett, Olivia Rose Sisley Madin, and Austen Saunders, whose youth, enthusiasm, and vigour over a few weeks spread over three summers drove me on when the project kept stalling for sheer lack of conviction. Finally, I'd like to thank those friends and family who found themselves lingering over-long in literary museums—my daughters, Elizabeth and Rosalind, perhaps the greatest sufferers.

My greatest debt, finally, is to Michael Dobson, who has faithfully accompanied me to most of the over 100 museums visited. Fixer, photographer, and sounding-board, he has patiently dug out errant images and rooted out typos, and has never permitted himself, even once, to wonder aloud whether I would ever finish.

Contents

List of Figures

Introduction

Entrance this way...

Make your way to Stratford-upon-Avon, buy a ticket to Shakespeare's Birthplace, wander through the entry exhibition, and start climbing up the staircase that leads to the first-floor room in which Shakespeare is reputed to have been born. You will find hanging there a small reproduction of the painting I have chosen as my frontispiece. The original, now held by the Victoria and Albert Museum in London, has a remarkable history, calculated to intrigue anyone with an interest in the story and nature of sites of literary pilgrimage, and in particular the writer's house museum, the subject of this book.

In 1854 an aspiring young painter, Henry Wallis, launched his career by exhibiting three paintings at the Royal Academy in London. Entitled respectively 'The Room in Which Shakespeare was Born', 'The Font in which Shakespeare was Christened', and 'Shakespeare's House, Stratford-upon-Avon', all three show silent, unpeopled interiors. All three meditate upon Shakespeare's increasing status as national genius, recently certified by the acquisition of the Birthplace 'for the nation' in 1847 and its ongoing development as a museum under the auspices of the Shakespeare Birthplace Trust.[1] These paintings are evidence of the growth and evolution of the idea that houses associated with a writer provided a fitting habitation for the individual and collective national imagination.[2]

This idea, as I argue at length in *The Literary Tourist: Readers and Places in Romantic and Victorian Britain* (2006), had already begun to emerge as a commercially significant phenomenon across Europe by the late eighteenth century, expressing itself as a widespread fashion for literary tourism. Literary tourism is the practice of visiting places associated with writers and their works to supplement the experience of reading. It materializes and individualizes reading as remembered experience of place. Its emergence was contemporaneous with a new emphasis upon the poet as an exceptional and often exemplary sensibility. It was rendered inevitable by a Europe-wide cultural drive to connect up books and localities in the service of national identities and national literary cultures, and it was progressively enabled by the development of mass readership and mass travel. As a result, by the early 1800s, places associated with writers were regularly being imagined and visited with reference to biographical and literary texts. The 'homes and haunts' of writers, as the Victorians would come to call them, were animated for readers on- and off-site by letters, diaries, and notebooks, illustrated, introduced, and footnoted editions, memoirs and biographies, travel-writing and guidebooks. Whether actually visited or only visited via the armchair, homes and haunts linked up, located, and materialized a writer's often otherwise disparate body of work, so coalescing and co-locating the reader's inevitably disparate experience of reading.[3]

Within Britain, the advantages of pulling this off around candidates for the title of National Poet were evident early. Building on the actor-manager David Garrick's Shakespeare Jubilee of 1769, Samuel Ireland's *Picturesque Views of the Upper, or Warwickshire Avon* (1795) consolidated a Shakespearean tourist repertoire of houses and locations in Stratford-upon-Avon. By the time that Wallis was exhibiting his paintings, the genre was fully established by William Howitt's fat illustrated volumes, *Visits to Remarkable Places* (1840) and *Homes and Haunts of the Most Eminent British Poets* (1847), both of which described visits to locations associated with Shakespeare at length. These were the books that comprehensively fused travel-writing and literary biography into what Alison Booth has called 'spatialised biography', producing the first of many imagined mappings of 'literary Britain'.[4]

All three of Wallis' paintings are characterized by an effort to render Shakespearean place in elaborate physical detail. As the Tate Gallery label to 'The Room in which Shakespeare was Born' comments, 'Every nail securing the floorboards is visible'.[5] The painting describes the room as a once-domestic space in the process of turning into what we would recognize as a museum: documents and engravings are displayed on a number of chairs, the whitewashed plaster is covered with the signatures of admirers, and what appears to be a board identifying the room as the 'Birthroom' (as it had been known since the Jubilee) hangs on one of the walls. 'The House in which Shakespeare was Born' is equally virtuosic, showing every crack in the plaster and every ridge in the rafters. However, it is rather less conventional in what it suggests about the nature of the emergent museum. In its original state, the painting depicted the staircase leading to the 'Birthroom' as empty, lit from above through a window. Documentary, historicist, and materialist in mode, it is nonetheless in its quiet way about anticipation and possibility, evoking the advent of something less bound by the constraints of time and space. There is more than a touch here of the sacred, in keeping with the displaced discourse of pilgrimage that has long been recognized as inform-ing the texts and practices of literary tourism.[6]

Wallis' canvas was subsequently bought by John Forster, who, as chairman of the London committee of the Royal Shakespearian Club, had helped to secure the Birthplace for the nation in 1847. He hung it in his London dining-room. There it caught the attention of his friend, the painter Sir Edwin Landseer. With Forster's permission, Landseer made a number of additions to Wallis' painting and re-exhibited it in 1867. As Sylvia Morris notes, the exhibition catalogue provided an explanatory gloss in the shape of an extract from a letter from Forster to Landseer:

> The picture in its first state—then an ancient stone staircase wonderfully painted by Mr H Wallis...—was purchased by me fourteen or fifteen years ago. You had often said, as you saw it in my dining-room, that you'd like some day to put something from your own hand into it; and last summer, generously indulging my earnest wish to possess some memorial of our thirty years of uninterrupted friendship, you desired me to send this particular picture to you. That the staircase as represented had been copied from Shakespeare's House at Stratford-on-Avon, you did not then know, or had forgotten...Finding, when the picture reached you, whose house it was the staircase belonged to, it had been your fancy to bring about us memorials of the marvellous man him-self,—his dog waiting for him at the door, as to imply his own immediate neighbourhood; and objects so connecting themselves with his pursuits, and even pointing at the origin of familiar lines and fancies, as almost to indicate and identify the Play with which his brain might have been busy at the time.[7]

Landseer's additions engage in a further and rather different museumiza-tion of the Birthplace. Wallis depicts the (to Victorian eyes) poverty-stricken and provincial historical and physical birthplace as incommensurate with the birth of a genius that would transcend time and space. By contrast, Landseer opts for historical fiction, revivifying the house as the ground of imagination. He fantasizes the imminent presence of the author as an adult, through depicting the gun-dog pausing at the not-quite-shut door in expectation of its master. The objects littering the treads of the staircase evoke lines and episodes from Shakespeare's *Hamlet*: the armour conjures Old

Hamlet, the spade and skull Hamlet's encounter with the gravediggers and Yorick, the rat Hamlet's stabbing of Polonius through the arras ('How now! a rat? Dead, for a ducat, dead', III, iv, 24–6), and the two hawks' hoods counterposed with the dead heron recall the conventional Victorian gloss on Hamlet's rebuke to his informer friends Rosencrantz and Guildenstern ('I am but mad north-north-west—when the wind is southerly, I know a hawk from a handsaw', II, ii, 375–7).[8] The modified painting thinks of the house as a theatre of Shakespeare's ever-living imagination, and models a way of visiting it for readers well versed in his works. So while Wallis offers the tourist pilgrimage to a god's humble beginnings, Landseer suggests that admirers should superimpose a mix of biographical and literary allusion upon their destination.[9] Although Wallis and Landseer thus offer different models for the tourist experience, they have in common a sense of the fabric of the writer's house as simultaneously material and immaterial, real and ideal.

Guidebook

Like these paintings, *The Author's Effects* is preoccupied with describing the paradoxical materiality and immateriality of the writer's house museum. It looks at the writer's house museum as a cultural form, enquiring how, why, and when it emerged, what it was and is for, how it has changed over time, and what its future(s) might be. It offers answers to the comically exasperated question put by Julian Barnes' narrator in *Flaubert's Parrot*—'Why does the writing make us chase the writer? Why can't we leave well alone?'—a question that is elaborated by Simon Goldhill's equally irritated cry, 'What would you really learn by staring at Martin Amis' desk or Philip Roth's kitchen table?'[10] *The Author's Effects* begins with a working hypothesis—that the writer's house museum is primarily designed to 'effect' a figure of the author—and investigates how the writer's house, considered as a discursive and narrative construct, produces this figure through the preservation and display of his or her belongings, or 'effects', within quasi-domestic space.[11] The book as a whole traces how habits of visiting and acquiring literary places and objects, the prehistory and penumbra to the formal establishment of writer's house museums, emerged as a compelling impulse in the late eighteenth century and became established in Britain, Europe, and North America in the nineteenth century. It describes the ways that different types of authorial remains, possessions, and spaces came to evoke the simultaneous materiality and immateriality of the author, and how this in turn effected place, most often conceived as national.

Writer's house museums have rarely been thought of as a discrete cultural formation. This is perhaps because hardly anyone, I imagine, looks in their newly purchased guidebook for 'a writer's house museum' as such; they might set about planning a trip by looking at what museums are on offer, and so serendipitously discover that they are in the environs of the Henrik Ibsen museum in Oslo, for instance; or they might be enthusiasts, who go specifically because they are admirers of, and knowledgeable about, Ibsen. But surely few go to a writer's house museum simply because it is 'a writer's house museum'. Rather, they go because of its associations with a particular writer that they have, at a minimum, heard of; at worst because they have been dragged along in the wake of an enthusiastic friend or family member. This is not surprising, for fundamental to the idea of the writer's house museum is the idea of preserving a house because it is, as a result of its asso-ciation with an author, of especial communal importance, possessing the sort and intensity of significance that should not be erased or overwritten, and which is large enough to warrant the considerable expense involved in maintaining a purportedly domestic space for no-one to live in. The writer's house is typically conceived as unique; so to read this sort of house as generic is counter-intuitive. It offends against the idea of the primacy of authorial 'originality', with its emphasis on individual, yet exemplary, artistic self-expression. Similarly, to think about such houses as culturally and his-torically contingent artefacts damages the fantasy that founds them. This may be summed up in the pious tourist fiction that it is 'as though' the writer has just left the room and might return at any minute to pick up the pen laid casually aside. Popular writing on writer's house museums reflects these commonplaces. Coffee-table books like *Writers' Houses* (1995) or *American Writers at Home* (2004), both sumptuously illustrated with photo-graphs by Erica Lennard, proceed on the presumption that each house has a unique story to tell, even though the photographs themselves reiterate the same trope of the temporarily abandoned house over and over. On the shadow-side of this celebration, books such as Brock Clarke's *The Arsonist's Guide to Writers' Homes in New England* (2007) reiterate the same ideology of uniqueness, despite intending to debunk it.

Academic writing has equally often tended to be invested in the unique-ness of the writer's place. Writer's houses have typically been studied, if at all, in isolation, as symptoms and/or explanations of the fame of their former residents, as in such sentimento-poetic exercises as Diana Fuss' *The Sense of an Interior: Four Writers and the Rooms that Shaped Them* (2004) and Nuala Hancock's *Charleston and Monks' House: The Intimate House Museums of Virginia Woolf and Vanessa Bell* (2012). It is equally true of the self-critical and sophisticated exercise in 'homes and haunts' writing presented in Simon Goldhill's *Freud's Couch, Scott's Buttocks, Brontë's Grave* (2011). When scholarship has devoted itself specifically to the history of turning an author's home into a public cultural amenity it has concentrated on individual authors' houses as an aspect of reputation and afterlife, or offered biographies of individual houses, as in the case of Julia Thomas' *Shakespeare's Shrine: The Bard's Birthplace and the Invention of Stratford-upon-Avon* (2012) or Polly Atkin's essay on the history of Dove Cottage.[12] Case-studies of individual houses are warranted because the story of the formation of each individual writer's house museum seems just that, individual: dependent on the author's reputation during their lifetime and at their death; the longevity of that reputation, or sometimes the wholesale revaluation and revivification of an author's ideological importance and usefulness much later; the availability of persons to curate the author's reputation, generally family and friends to begin with, and later regional, national, or global groupings willing to provide a living public face and voice, and willing to fund-raise; and usually, the continuing existence and availability of authenticating objects or spaces that can be used to evoke the author outside the book. Thus previous scholarship on writer's house museums has not on the whole been interested in thinking about them historically, comparatively, or generically, or in considering them as a transnational form native to Britain, Europe, and North America.[13]

There are a few important exceptions to this rule, prime amongst them Harald Hendrix's trenchant introduction to his edited collection *Writers' Houses and the Making of Memory* (2008). Hendrix divides the genre into houses created by writers themselves and houses created as back-formations by admirers, between those arising from the 'self-fashioning' of the author and those serving as a form of 'cultural memory'. In so doing he goes beyond previous thinking about specific houses in terms of conception, mediated iconography, or their conditioning of the author's *oeuvre*.[14] Other relevant work has come from within the field of tourist and heritage studies. Developing seminal work on tourism and literature by Mike Robinson, David Herbert, and others, this work often adopts empirical methodologies drawn from the social sciences: hence Sarah Gothie's dissertation *(Her)itage:*

Literary Tourism and the Popular Legacies of Louisa May Alcott, L.M. Montgomery, and Beatrix Potter (2015), which analyses 'personal interviews with museum staff…tourism promotions, visitor comments, and souvenirs' to make a comparative argument for these museums as founding female future selves.[15] Museologists and museum practitioners are exceptional in treating them generically. The International Committee for Literary and Composers' Museums (ICLCM) defines the literary museum as 'an institution specially about literature considered as cultural heritage' which 'acquire[s], preserve[s], and communicate[s] this literature through museographical codes, in order to promote knowledge about the literature and its role in the society'.[16] ICLCM sub-divides literary museums into 'writers' museums', 'general literary museums', and 'literary landscapes'. Other heritage professionals, however, have regarded the writer's house museum as a subset of the personality-museum, itself a subset of the historic house museum. As a result, they do not make any functional distinction between the preservation of the houses of writers and the houses of artists and composers, or indeed other celebrities.

Nonetheless, the writer's house museum, this 'small genre' (as Linda Young calls it rather in defiance of the sheer number of them), is my focus here.[17] I have chosen to call it the 'writer's house museum', discarding other possible terminology along with the American term 'author house museum' partly because I wish to allow for a crucial differentiation between the 'writer' and the 'author', and partly because, as will become evident, I am concerned with the variable meanings and power of the possessive apostrophe. My approach is essentially comparative. Through looking at features that many writer's house museums have in common, I investigate and describe how the very idea of the writer's house and by extension that of the writer's house museum first emerges and becomes culturally recognizable, and I enquire into what sort of quasi-literary genre the writer's house museum and its cognate forms might be.[18]

Celebrity and commemoration

In studying the writer's house museum in this fashion, *The Author's Effects* intersects principally with recent scholarship exploring ideas of authorship at the end of the eighteenth century. Over the last ten years or so a number of scholars have argued that an explosion of print culture at the end of the eighteenth century produced a sense of estrangement on the part of both writers and readers, and despair in the face of the problem of sifting a supposed excess of print for value. Tom Mole has suggested that in certain instances, notably that of Byron, the problem of distance between writer and reader was solved by the emergence of a new celebrity culture designed to create a 'hermeneutic of intimacy' between writer and reader.[19] In the case of other authors, Andrew Bennett has argued, this distance produced anxiety and a new reliance on the judgement of posterity.[20] Paul Westover argues forcefully that this combination of desire for intimacy and sense of posterity explains the new passion for 'visiting the dead', and I have myself argued that it drove the development of literary tourism as a way of personally encountering authors and works.[21] In like manner, scholars of author cultism, notably Jayne Lewis and Deidre Shauna Lynch, have argued that between about 1750 and 1850 the Enlightenment systems of forensic and antiquarian enquiry that produced taxonomies of genre, literary history, collection and anthology, variorum edition, literary lives, and above all literary canon also produced in dialectical opposition a new practice of 'private and passional' reading. This strove to 'bridge the distance between self and other and now and then' so as to construct intimate relationships with 'kindred spirits of another time'.[22] The result was what Lewis summarizes as 'uselessness, enthusiasm, sentimentalism, literary cultism, author cultism, and amateurism', bound up in what Lynch describes as 'a cultural space of posthumousness'.[23] In consequence, a new culture of authorial commemoration emerged, taking varied but inter-related forms: literary biography, the pantheonization of remains, literary tourism as a leisure practice, and new habits of marking and preserving objects and places associated with writers and their works, from collecting objects and manuscripts to installing plaques, statuary, monuments, and eventually entire museums in significant places.[24] As this list suggests, this impulse could be expressed as thoroughly public, a matter of national pride, or intensely private, a matter of personal 'author-love', as Paul Westover and Ann Wierda Rowland have called it, or both.[25] At around the same time other ways of personalizing reading (and displaying it as such) emerge: annotation, quotation, extraction, album-making, anthologization, the extra-illustration of favourite books, the acquisition of manuscripts and personalia, and indeed the making of manuscript copies of the printed book.[26] Building on these insights, *The Author's Effects* argues that the writer's house museum was precipitated by the same desire to develop intimacy with dead authors on the part of readers around the turn of the eighteenth century. In this view, the writer's house, as a vastly enlarged para-textual apparatus, came into being to host a practice of reading, understanding, materializing, and above all encountering the author as the embodied origin of his or her works. It was not a coincidence that it appeared at precisely the moment when books were reaching unprecedented numbers of people through cheap mass-production—it was both an effect of increased readership and the product of a counter-insistence on the singularity and particularity of the experience of reading. The writer's house museum attempts the wholesale remediation of the book, transforming it into the figure of the author.

Terms and conditions: museum, object, time, space

Looking a little harder at the preliminary problem of defining a writer's house museum, intriguing if inconvenient complexities emerge. As already noted, Hendrix distinguishes between those house museums created by writers themselves as expressions of their lives as writers, houses such as Horace Walpole's Strawberry Hill, Walter Scott's Abbotsford, or James Fenimore Cooper's 'Cooper's Castle', and those created subsequently as a cultural memory, re-assembled or even re-fabricated after the writer's death, so as to express his or her life as a writer, which form the great majority of such museums.[27] Within this second category there are many further distinguishable sub-categories—buildings in which a writer was born, in which they were brought up, in which they lived or wrote, about which they wrote, where they underwent formative experiences, or in which they died. The Mark Twain Birthplace, Louisa May Alcott's childhood home, Lucy M. Boston's The Manor, Anne Hathaway's Cottage, and the Schillerhaus are examples of all these different kinds of houses. Moreover, within writer's house museums there is great variation not only in ontological claim but also in mode. Some houses are displayed explicitly as museums, often with 'themed' biographical rooms (here Dr Johnson's Birthplace in Lichfield would be a notable instance). Others have been naturalized as period homes flanked with substantial and glossy annex exhibitions (an example would be Mark Twain's house in Connecticut). Some hybridize these modes (such as the Brontë home in Haworth Parsonage). Some, like the Maison de Chateaubriand, emphasize biography. Some, like Beatrix Potter's Hill Top, emphasize the works. Some epitomize genteel domestic life of the period, as in the case of the Wadsworth-Longfellow House in Cambridge, MA. Nor are these expressions stable: displays may be expanded, refreshed, or rethought, or the house's cultural status can decay. If a writer's grip on the cultural imagination wanes, the house museum typically begins to change from being shown as characteristic not of their genius but also, or merely, of period and locality. Such houses become general cultural heritage. On research field trips in the USA, I lost track of how much time I was made to spend admiring the kitchen-arrangements in houses pertaining to writers who I suspect never made it into the kitchen.

The matter is further complicated by cognate but lesser expressions of this desire to 'house' or 'home' the writer. Collections of objects and photographs or similar are preserved inside public cafés, inns, or hotels frequented by writers as 'homes from home' (e.g. the display of the Robert Burns chair in the Globe Inn at Dumfries, the display of Longfellow's chamber in the Wayside Inn, Sudbury, MA, or the little room in The Eagle and Child pub in Oxford that hosted the Inklings). There are displays of collections of objects associated with the writer in semi-private houses once inhabited by the writer (one might think here of the displays devoted to Rudyard Kipling in Naulakha, Vermont, or to the Brownings in Florence, both currently Landmark properties for holiday rental). There are objects that form an uneasy but imaginatively important part of the collections of institutional libraries, such as those housed in the Berkshire Athenaeum's 'Melville Memorial Room', or the Houghton Rare Book Library's 'Keats Room'. Literary museums devoted to national or local traditions such as the Writers' Museum in Edinburgh may dedicate single vitrines to individual writers in a beguilingly indigestible mix of dislocated personalia: 'On display are many items, including the swordstick used by Robert Burns while working as an Excise Officer and the writing desk from his house in Dumfries; Sir Walter Scott's chess set, the rocking horse he used as a boy, and his dining table from 39 Castle Street; the printing press on which Scott's Waverley Novels were printed; Robert Louis Stevenson's fishing-rod, pipe, and the riding boots and hat he wore while living in Samoa'.[28] Whole rooms may be lifted, shifted, and preserved in museums (such as Thomas Hardy's study in the Dorchester County Museum or the reconstructed Franz Grillparzer room in Vienna's Wien Museum). Individual items may be set up temporarily as a microcosm of the writer's home in a temporary exhibition, as in the instance of J.R.R. Tolkien's desk and chair mounted in a vitrine as part of the Tolkien exhibition staged at the Bodleian Library in 2018.[29]

Granting all this variation (and if writing this book has taught me any-thing, it is thoroughgoing respect for the inventiveness of curators), all these cultural formations lie along a continuum. They all contain the kernel of museum-hood, and, given time and commercial viability, a small display may enlarge into a museum proper; thus 'Tennyson's study', once displayed rather casually in the corner of a room in the Faringford Hotel, Freshwater, Isle of Wight, turned into a museum in 2009.[30] All are dedicated to display-ing what is not there, although it once was there—the author. They all construct 'a writer' by evoking a writer's life and writings through objects located in pseudo-domestic spaces. Such objects and spaces speak of the absence, or (more accurately) of the once-but-no-longer presence of the author's body 'at home'. Their value lies in the closeness and longevity of their association with the writer's life, the work of writing, and the 'content' of that writing. The driving impulse is to assert the ongoing 'liveness' of the writer by locating him or her in a specific domestic time and space, so enab-ling personal encounter between reader and writer, bypassing the medium of print and short-circuiting the alienated processes of reading. To labour the point, all these ways of (re)housing the writer consistently speak of the reader's need to make and find the writer 'at home'—disregarding (while exploiting) the fact that the writer is dead and that the writer him or herself, were s/he alive, would almost certainly not be 'at home' to the general public.

I take these commonalities as warrant for ranging across various ways of homing the writer, from displaying single objects to preserving entire houses. The history of making writer's house museums shows that even single objects may have functioned effectively to house a writer, well before they were incorporated into a writer's house museum. The question of pre-cisely what sort of objects these are goes to the heart of the nature and ideo-logical work of the writer's house museum. After all, they are not (as they would be in other museums) displayed because they are typical, valuable, or rare.[31] Jean Baudrillard's description of antique objects is suggestive here; he argues that antique objects function in the present to answer particular cul-tural demands, notably the need for 'witness, memory, nostalgia, or escap-ism', and that their power depends precisely on their obsolescence: 'The antique object no longer has any practical application, its role being merely to *signify* . . . time'.[32] For Baudrillard, 'the signifying of time' is at the heart of the 'authenticity' of antique objects: 'that which occurs in the present as having occurred in a former time, hence that which is folded upon itself, that which is authentic'.[33] Baudrillard's remark opens up the usual sense of 'authenticity', as something that is self-identical and 'true' to itself, by installing a 'fold' at the heart of the object perceived as 'antique'. That fold is the sense of time almost collapsing in space, but not quite. He argues that the psychological efficacy of antique objects is that they supply a myth of origins, satisfy an intention to be altogether elsewhere, and offer an escape-hatch for the subject out of modernity.[34]

These arguments are clearly helpful with regard to objects on display within the writer's house museum, and indeed with regard to the problem of describing how time is collapsed within the space of the writer's house museum, but they only get us so far in dealing with the power, say, of Shakespeare's gold signet-ring. It is plainly an avenue to the past, but this is not primarily what confers value upon it. It is the possessive apostrophe that hangs around this sort of antique object which gives it value. It appertained to someone judged to have been important, and its value depends in large part upon narrating it as a relic, something through which to remember that particular body and that particular life. It remembers a life that modernity has agreed to keep in perpetual resurrection through preserving it from the twin oblivion of charnel-house and auction-house to supplement the literary legacy. Its value depends on how intimate, intensive, or paradigmatic the association between writer and object was, and very often on deriving from a finite resource, or on being unique as an item, or unique to an event. The value of a literary relic increases if it can be identified as having a parallel existence within that writer's works, or within writings that describe that writer. Its value then rests upon its ability to summon up, to be inserted in, and to evidence the truth of writing. At the extreme, such relics are felt to have a daemonic power to conjure and make manifest the author and/or their works for the beholder. That power resides in the object's admonitory materiality, but all the same might be best described as super-material in its ability to raise the ghost of the author. This sense of objects as originatory is related to the way they stand in for original genius, conserving part of the original agency of the author.[35] In her essay 'Great Men's Houses' (1931), Woolf would claim that writers had a special capacity for imprinting themselves upon things: 'It would seem to be a fact that writers stamp themselves upon their possessions more indelibly than other people...making the table, the chair, the curtain, the carpet into their own image'.[36] This accounts for the ability of such objects to embarrass, as in the case of Agatha Christie's mahogany loo-seat (see Figure 0.1).

Figure 0.1. Agatha Christie's cloakroom, Greenway, NT. Author's own photograph

Displayed in its original location at her house Greenway in Devon, the loo-seat is used to describe her trips out to Iraq with her archaeologist husband Max Mallowan because, according to the helpful curatorial gloss, she took it along with her. As such, it forms not merely an adjunct to her biography but also to fictions such as *Murder in Mesopotamia* (1936).[37] Despite this, there was more than a faint feeling among my fellow-tourists in 2015 that peeping into the cloakroom violated social decorum. As pseudo-guests of the writer, they clearly felt this to be outside the proper confines of what parts of the authorial embodied life might be regarded as relevant or what forms of authorial agency one wished to imagine or share in. The case of Christie's loo-seat illuminates what sorts of intimacy with the author are (and are not) sought via literary objects by reader-tourists. It is not accidental that Anne Trubek's *A Skeptic's Guide to Writers' Houses* heads up its first chapter ('The Irrational Allure of Writers' Houses') with a sketch of 'Emily Dickinson's chamber pot' which thus serves as a scatological gloss to (one of) her caustic formulations of literary tourism as 'lit porn'.[38] That said, as in the case of Ibsen's bath, rescued in 2006 from its fate as a cattle-trough to be triumphantly restored, the desire for comprehensive and authentic reconstruction may outweigh threatened social indecorum.[39]

It is possible for literary objects to serve more or less as their own museum space—this is sometimes so in the case of the writer's remains (see Chapter 1). More usually, literary objects exist in organized relationship with each other, contextualized within a defined space whether at the scale of the vitrine or of an entire house. The sort of space characteristic of the writer's house museum and its cognate expressions tends to short-circuit most current theory of museum space.[40] Even at the micro-level of the vitrine, the founding fiction of this sort of space is encounter with the author's absent body. At house-scale, the fiction is that the reader-tourist enters and experiences domestic space as the guest of the author. This means that the theorization of the imaginary of domestic space is more pertinent here; hence this study is informed by Gaston Bachelard's *The Poetics of Space* (1958), still by far the most powerful and suggestive model for reading the spaces of a writer's house as spaces of the imagination.

Space within the writer's house museum is not merely space between things. Rather, such spaces function as depictions of air from time-past, as the medium of imagined breath, voice, movement, and vision, working in something of the way that Rachel Whiteread's casts of domestic spaces do. As Adrian Searle, reviewing her show in 2017, remarks, these casts of space 'pick up the imprint of grain on a wooden floor, the muffled contours and planes of a painted door, dinks and dents, spalled plasterwork, soot stains in a fireplace, human and material imperfections' in such a way as to confer upon the space 'character, even a kind of personality'.[41] Searle notes that these details 'are at once forensic and a reminder that everything that was once new gets worn down by time and accident, imprinted by human contact and use', recalling the way in which the fabric of the writer's house has often been felt to have been 'imprinted' by the wear and tear exerted by the now absent life of the imagination. One might cite, for instance, Virginia Woolf's flight of fancy in her essay 'The Mark on the Wall' (1917).[42] This sense of the house-space as 'imprinted' had emerged in Britain as early as the 1770s. In August 1774, a London artist, Thomas Jones, was commissioned 'to paint... a view of the house at Chalfont St Giles, whither, according to tradition, the poet Milton retired, during the Plague of London'. This was the house in which Milton probably finished *Paradise Lost*. Jones describes in some detail how he and his patrons interacted with the space of the house. On arrival,

> I immediately set to work, and as we had brought provisions and wine with us, about 3 o'clock sat down to dinner in the same room in which we fondly imagined that Milton had so often dined. On these very boards, thought we, the great Milton trod. On that very ceiling (for he was not, at that period, blind) 'The Poet's Eye in a fine frenzy rolled', and [we] pitied those poor frigid flegmatic [sic] philosophers who would not have felt the same enthusiasm as ourselves—on the same occasion…[W]e drank many a bumper to the immortal memory of the illustrious Bard.[43]

The diners conjure the body of Milton as co-located with them in real domestic space through presuming that the 'very' boards and ceiling still carry the memory of the pressure of his presence. On the basis of this, they engage in a number of sociable imaginative experiments: they consciously reiterate his daily routine and viewpoint, they promote Milton as a National Poet through allusion to Shakespeare's *A Midsummer Night's Dream*, and they constitute themselves as an all-male dining club of like-minded enthusiasts, very much in the mode of the all-male dinners in honour of Shakespeare recorded from the 1750s onwards.[44] Jones' account suggests that new ideas of private authorial subjectivity, anterior, concurrent, and congruent with the works, once posited, required a private life, and a private life implied a private house, and in this instance, demanded a private dinner. It also suggests that imagining the authorial footprint was as powerful an experience as encountering the authorial imagination through the medium of print.

Although the house in Chalfont St Giles would not be formally opened as a public museum until 1887, there was therefore more than a century's worth of visitor imaginative and affective practice already in place to draw upon.[45] It is not so very far from Jones' dinner-party of enthusiasts to the epigraph William Howitt chose to govern his *Homes and Haunts of the Most Eminent Poets* (1847): 'An indissoluble sign of their existence has stamped itself on the abodes of all distinguished men, a sign which places all kindred spirits in communion with them'.[46] Thus, as in Wallis' original canvases, the spaces of the writer's house museum are deceptively literal or realist in mode. They are not fully manifest, because they house a phantasm conventionally named as the author. The author of the writer's house museum is the feel of the familiar in the unfamiliar, of the past in the present, of the virtual in the physical, of the invisible pulsating within the visible, of the alive in the life-like, of the immortal in the time-bound. No wonder that nineteenth-century writers so often resorted to the language of Gothic to describe the quality of these spaces as 'uncanny' or 'haunted', or that moderns so often resort to the related though euphoric rhetoric of enchantment. A writer's house museum collapses different times into a single space. As a result, there is a real if invisible barrier within it, crossed by the reader in a deliberate act—the act that Harald Hendrix aptly describes as stepping 'through the looking-glass'.[47] This act of imagination does not so much suspend as supplement the real of the present. It is 'sentimental' in Friedrich Schiller's sense of the term. It is not naïve, although it may appear so, but knowing, with a tinge of the elegiac.[48] As writing and reading came to be construed in Romantic terms as the expression of and exploration of the self, so the space of the writer's house would come to retain and record the inner essence of the author, and therefore to offer the promise of a privileged place of encounter across time between two self-exploring subjectivities, writer and reader, an impossible synchrony brokered by the house.

It seems timely to reflect upon the form of the writer's house museum, given current historical, cultural, intellectual, and popular trends. A widespread sense of historical rupture produced by political and cultural developments in the new millennium has both revivified and challenged the cultural value of national heritage. Ever-increasing mass tourism has foregrounded tourist sensibility both in academia and popular culture. The rise of the virtualized global has produced a hunger for walk-in experience, performative liveness, and locality, and critical reflection on all. Anxieties about the future of capitalism and consumerism have produced a scepticism towards addiction to material mass-produced 'stuff' in popular and academic culture alike, coupled with a marked interest in unique and 'lost' objects housed in the recesses of the archive.[49] A generation is now dedicated through Facebook and other forms of social media to 'curating' and exhibiting their own lives online, and their practices are beginning to look a good deal like the habit of making museums of the self.[50] The supposed death-throes of the book have produced thinking about the materiality of print culture and the historical contingency of reading practices amongst book historians and historians of reading. And in the meantime, the business of writer's house museums is booming.[51] Within the UK, for instance, visitor appetite for literary tourism and writer's house museums as a form of experience is strong, although which writer's house museums survive and thrive is heavily dependent on the winds of fashion that blow through the publishing, film, and TV industries and the school and university curriculum.[52]

Where a commonality of culture is perceived as threatened, writer's house museums are increasingly being seen as possible homes for individual and collective imagination and creativity, and as places able to connect up the diversity of present-day reader-tourists to a past conceived as at once local, national, transnational, and (sometimes) global.[53] In nations actively developing national heritage as a political priority—for example, Norway, South Africa, Hungary, the Ukraine, Taiwan, China—writer's house museums are similarly showing signs of being seen as a way of asserting national cultural capital and international visibility.[54]

While *The Author's Effects* is superficially 'about' the writer's house museum, it is more profoundly and ambitiously an exercise in literary and cultural history, an exploration of the history of the idea of the author within the history of reading. The book therefore proposes to contribute to the growing body of scholarship on literary tourism, literary biography, commemoration, and the making of museums and literary landscapes; but more widely, it engages with and hopes to interest those working on the history of authorship, authorial afterlife, celebrity and authorship, literary life-writing, the cult of Romantic genius, fan culture, 'author-love', and literary collecting. It may also be of interest to those charged with managing and interpreting literary heritage through writer's house museums, given that the history of cultural investment in the author is part of the story of such houses, while the future of it is of practical, not to say commercial, import. Perhaps most of all, this book is directed not just to cultural historians and museum practitioners but also to those general readers who, loving authors, books, and the places associated with them, addicted perhaps to the pleasures of 'reading on the very spot', might nonetheless be prepared to interrogate and reflect upon that pleasure.

In trying to write the history of the ways that affective encounters between author and reader have been brokered, I have used all sorts of disparate evidence. I have pressed into service private letters and albums, published travel-writing and guidebooks, auction catalogues and anecdotes of collectors, books of engravings and photographs of objects and places, and such records as exist within collections themselves of acquisition and display. I have pursued the amateur blog as seriously as the high-flown essay by a star intellectual. I may as well frankly confess also that I have taken my own affective reactions as a critical spur. The pricks of nausea, embarrassment, laughter, exasperation, incredulity, disgust, and bewilderment that have occasionally afflicted me in the face of the zombie-author evoked by the writer's house museum are entirely conventional. I am not the only one who has recoiled from the grotesquerie of Dylan Thomas' mother's crutches, or Hans Christian Andersen's dentures, or Charlotte Brontë's knickers. Simon Goldhill has laughed at the imprint of Scott's buttocks on his chair, Brock Clarke has taken the liberty of burning down (albeit in fiction) great numbers of writer's homes across New England, Anne Trubek conducts her sceptical tour of them by reading 'against the grain', and even Liz Workman's book of beautiful photographs is rudely entitled *Dr Johnson's Doorknob— And Other Significant Parts of Great Men's Houses* (2007).[55] But I should stress that although I keep them at arm's length, I also take the sentimental symptoms of entrancement and enchantment seriously, and they have manifested themselves in my own life in the strangest of places and the strangest ways. I was ghost-ridden when sleeping uneasily in Mark Twain's bedroom in Elmira, NY; unnervedly expectant sitting on the bench in the Botanic Gardens in Oxford upon which Lyra could not see Will at the end of Philip Pullman's trilogy *His Dark Materials*. The sentimental in these places and objects is not residual and ineffective, but powerful. With the right words, it can develop in previously ignored objects and spaces in surprising ways. Such, after all, was the destiny of the coal-scuttle sitting in Dove Cottage, transfigured in import by Seamus Heaney's characterization of it in one of his last poems, 'Dorothy Wordsworth's coal-scuttle'.[56]

Tour starts here

As a whole *The Author's Effects* starts in tight focus upon the remains of the writer's body, widens out to consider the affective functions of writers' possessions, expands thereafter to case-studies of whole houses and their grounds, and finally considers the history of tourist affective practices at the site of writer's houses.[57]

In Chapters 1–6 I develop 'biographies' of a series of celebrated literary objects or places. Each chapter is governed by a pairing across time and space designed to illuminate and interrogate each other's ideological statements. I have focused on particular objects representative of categories of things that were essential to nineteenth-century concepts of authorship. Each has long been credited with a special glamour of authenticity—with a special 'aura', as Walter Benjamin put it.[58] Although many of them presently reside in writer's house museums, some do not. Some have wound up in archives across the world because they function as, to adopt Ann Rigney's term, 'portable monuments'; in this context, as portable museums capable of conjuring authorial presence.[59] I am interested in them because they indicate even more clearly than the museum proper the history and variation of sentimental investment in the materiality of the author as ground, supplement, and substitute for text. I also examine objects which have been lost or destroyed through tourist depredation, and a few which have barely existed except in wishful fantasy, pious replicas, or outright forgeries. As a contrast, I look at a number of forgotten objects. Collected because they were once felt to be powerfully auratic, they have been demoted, found to be fraudulent, or simply no longer seem amenable to narration. Their decay in cultural value suggests how ways of valuing the author, or ways of imagining that value, have changed over time. Chapters 7 and 8 are devoted to the spaces of the writer's house museum and its environs. The concluding chapter deals with the history and range of visitor interaction with such objects and sites.[60] Each chapter contains a number of photographic images by way of illustration; they show the objects and buildings that I have taken as governing conceits for each chapter. Inevitably, none of these images are neutral in affect, whether they show objects simply as museum accessions, picture them as they are displayed in situ, or are conspicuously elaborated to interpretive effect by the photographer. But where the presumed aura of particular objects is clearly dramatized by the image, it corresponds with that discussed in the main text.

Chapter 1 explores the smallest-scale expression of the writer's house museum, the reliquary, through considering the history of affective investment in the remains of the authorial body. It frames this discussion with the biographies of Robert Burns' skull and John Keats' hair, but also touches upon ways in which the mortal remains of Ariosto, Petrarch, Shakespeare, and Schiller have been imagined and preserved. The chapter explores the ways in which the mortal likeness of authors was preserved and transmitted by admirers through acquiring authors' bones, making casts of their skulls, taking life and death masks, and taking, gifting, and displaying authors' hair. Chapter 2 considers evocations of the author's body, focusing on how animal-bodies are deployed as surrogates for the author. With reference to Petrarch's cat, Cowper's hares, Poe's raven, Sterne's starling, and Dickinson's hummingbirds, it argues that these animals describe the doubled body of the author, at once dead and alive, mortal and immortal, body and voice. Chapter 3 investigates ways of figuring the author's doubled body, this time as physical and textual, through clothing. It discusses how, for instance, Dorothy Wordsworth's shoes, William Cowper's nightcap, Henrik Ibsen's top-hat, Charlotte Brontë's wedding-bonnet, and Emily Dickinson's white dress describe writing as a textile that takes and preserves the most intimate and truthful form of its wearer, and survives as witness to it. Chapter 4 turns to look at how objects have been assembled into narratives of the scene of writing, conventionally composed in microcosm of the author's chair, desk, pen, ink, and paper. Here I pursue the adventures of Shakespeare's chair, Jane Austen's writing-table, and other examples across Europe and North America, as a prehistory to the more recent display of Daphne du Maurier's desk at Jamaica Inn in Cornwall, paying especial attention to the ways in which this discourse is gendered.

Chapter 5 widens its focus beyond the narration of the immediate scene of writing to consider how a miscellany of individual domestic objects have been made to speak of the writer's life and work through inscription, cap-tion, and representation of the author in life-size effigy or statue. I canvas objects that bear witness to authorial biography such as Johnson's coffee-pot, explore how and why objects may choose instead to materialize the author's writing, as in the Hans Christian Andersen Museum in Odense, the James Joyce Museum in Sandycove, Dublin, and the Mikhail Bulgakov Museum in Kiev, and investigate how life-size representations of the adult author have been used in the Twain Boyhood Home and Johnson's Birthplace to 'remember' childhood homes. Chapter 6 meditates upon the function of glass as a medium of 'enchantment' within writer's house museums. It con-siders how and to what effect objects are co-located and assembled within the vitrine as the basic meme of the museum, and (with special reference to Dylan Thomas' Boathouse in Laugharne, Virginia Woolf's Monk's House in Sussex, Nathaniel Hawthorne's residence in the Old Manse, Concord, and Sigmund Freud's apartment in Vienna) how eye-glasses, windows, and mir-rors relate to tropes of authorial vision and authorial invisibility. It argues that glass is the material by which the museum thinks through, dramatizes, and fetishizes impossibilities: the desire to see the writer in the flesh; the desire to see what the writer once saw; the desire to share the writer's vision. Chapter 7 jumps out of the window of the house proper to foray into visionary spaces beyond the domestic. It seeks out William Cowper in his summerhouse, Jean-Jacques Rousseau in his hermitage at Ermenonville, Henry Thoreau in his cabin by Walden Pond in Massachusetts, Alexandre Dumas in his folly outside Paris, and Vita Sackville-West in her tower at

Sissinghurst to think both about how writers have enabled and dramatized the writing life as led beyond the everyday and the ordinary.

Chapter 8 explores more fully the ways that nineteenth-century writers constructed houses as 'enchanted ground' to display their own mythos as national authors, focusing especially on Walter Scott's self-dramatization at Abbotsford, and the transatlantic transportability of that model in Washington Irving's founding of a distinctively American national culture within his own grounds at Sunnyside, NY. It concludes by looking at a modern iteration of these ideas in the redevelopment of Shakespeare's New Place in Stratford-upon-Avon upon the 400th anniversary of his death in 2016. Chapter 9 turns its attention from museum objects and spaces to museum visitors, tracing how readers have reacted to and interacted with writer's houses and each other from the late eighteenth century onwards, detailing what literary tourists brought, what they left, and what they took away. It completes the book's trajectory from a focus on the author's body to that of the reader, arguing that the writer's house museum may be seen not so much as staging the scene of writing, but as staging scenes of reading which disavow the medium of the book, erasing it in favour of a fantasy of immediate intimacy with the author. When that, as it is liable to, falters, readers expand into other forms of exasperated or empathetic sociability—with guides, with companions, with strangers, or with visitors long-gone and yet to come. The book concludes with a set of hypotheses about the nature of the writer's house museum as form and practice based on the discourse of the postcard, plus a few thoughts on the implications for the future(s) of writer's house museums. Those who would much prefer to disassemble the thematic organization of the book to pursue their interest in specific authors or places will find it easiest to start with the index.

Throughout, I have made a note of the date when I visited museums—this is because museums change and update their displays with what is, from my point of view, dismaying frequency, and from another, commendable energy. I have also occasionally mentioned where I drafted my various chapters. I have done this because no reader will think this of the slightest interest, as a reflection on the way that academic writing conventionally eschews any suggestion that it emerges from a particular body, place, and time, and on the nature of the quite other sorts of writing and reading that do elicit the desire in their readers to date and locate them more fully through searching out writer's houses. Committing such an indecorum tests the proposition neatly put by Diana Fuss that 'A writer's domestic interior opens a window onto both author and text, reminding us that what we may first perceive to be the timeless and universal truth of writing cannot be so neatly extricated from the complex particularities of its spatial and material origins'.[61] Hmm. Well, in a moment, I will take the few steps over the grass into my house, a writer's house as it really tends to be when the writer is actually writing— comfortless, cheerless, foodless, fireless, laundry unwashed, beds unmade, garden unweeded, children untended, cats unfed, flowers dying in every vase, and dust lying on every surface. While naturally I hope my reader will experience this book as an exercise in scholarship that overleaps temporal and spatial contingencies and so will not wish to come visiting in person, I hope s/he will also forgive me a piece of self-reflexive self-indulgence, given that it is unlikely that a suitably worded commemorative plaque will ever appear, when I record that I am putting these last words to this Introduction in my writing-shed in my garden in Oxford on 12 August 2017.

I

Remains

Burns' skull and Keats' hair

One of the odder aspects of the commemoration of poets is the habit of marking their birthdays by solemnly processing to their graves. On 25 January every year a party makes its way to the Burns mausoleum in the graveyard of St Michael's Church at Dumfries to lay wreaths. On 23 April (or on the Saturday closest to that date) the Shakespeare Birthday Procession makes its way to Holy Trinity Church to lay flowers on Shakespeare's grave, and (a recent innovation, this) to replace the feather quill-pen lodged in the fingers of Shakespeare's bust.[1] A little reflection resolves this apparent contradiction; birth marks incarnation, and the remains of that incarnated body lie in a specified place. The death of the poet marks a birth into 'immortality'; the markers of mortality thus act not as memento mori but as paradoxical guarantors of perpetual life, which explains that regularly renewed quill. As Malcolm Bradbury's posthumous novel *The Hermitage* (2000) puts it, the writer's death ushers in 'the necrological sequel…the pregnant scene for which everything in life is staged, the place where literature becomes literary, a show by a dead writer in front of an audience of readers'.[2] Death completes the birth of the poet to posterity.

The writer's house as museum originates in this paradox, and similarly evidences the desire both to memorialize and to disavow the writer's death. It admits and laments mortality while it insists upon immortality. Its drive is to describe the author as dead although living, and living although dead. Thus the writer's house museum is a mausoleum on the one hand, and a reliquary on the other. Both mausoleum and reliquary, however different in inflection, make claims about the import of the writer's body, and to do so, require its presence in whole or in part. Where the grave of the author is closely adjacent and imaginatively adequate, as in the case of Petrarch or Shakespeare or Emily Dickinson, the grave remains an external annex-exhibition to the house. However, where it is less imaginatively adequate, as in the instance of Emily Brontë's grave, which is in the crypt of Haworth Church rather than in a corner of the churchyard consonant with the grave of her heroine Cathy from *Wuthering Heights* (1847), the evocation of the author's dead body is liable to shift into the house to the place of death; hence the fame of the sofa in the Parsonage parlour on which Emily died.[3] The paradoxical death of the author lies at the heart of the writer's house museum; thus actual bodily remains taken at death or after exhumation, or reconstructions of the dead writer's body in the form of casts, will often fetch up within the writer's house museum to evidence the (im)mortal body of the writer. All remember the physical reality of the writer without being exactly representations. Unlike depictions of writers in portraiture or sculpture, they are the real thing, or, if they are not the real thing, then they have taken their form from explicit contact with the real thing. To get at the ways that the death of the author is described within the writer's house museum, this chapter begins by examining the sorts of value increasingly ascribed to authorial body-parts beyond the grave by late eighteenth-century culture, exploring how, in what forms, and to what affective ends such remains and traces have been preserved and circulated. Then it looks in more detail at what they mean when they are displayed within the writer's house museum, with special reference to the museum devoted to Robert Burns in Alloway and those devoted to John Keats in London and Rome.

Valuing the writer's remains

At around the end of the eighteenth century, Europe was seized with what was, in scale and scope, an unprecedented desire—the desire to memorialize dead writers. Part of this may be attributable to larger cultural shifts in the understanding of death. Michael Kammen notes that 'a widespread desire to ensure the perpetuity of graves dates only from the 1790s and early 1800s'— the perpetuity, that is, of the grave itself, its contents, and its associated memorial.[4] Explanations advanced for this have included a new prevalence of the view that bodily life might be all there was; the effects of urbanization and consequent deracination; and the shock of total war and appalling mortality statistics in the Napoleonic era. Such anxiety, it has been argued, is clearly manifest in the school of 'graveyard writing', in interest in recording churchyard epitaphs, and in the acceleration of commemorative practices, private and public, around the end of the eighteenth century.[5]

Contemporaneous with this there was a striking increase of anxiety around the memorialization of the named and celebrated dead around the beginning of the nineteenth century. The eighteenth century had already seen the emergence of a new celebrity of the authorial body conceived as congruent with genius. This was shadowed by a new celebrity of authorial remains, encouraging an acceleration of efforts to identify and memorialize them in a suitable fashion and in a suitable location. This, for instance, drove the expansion of Poets' Corner in Westminster Abbey.[6] In the wake of the ideological upset of the French Revolution and Napoleonic Wars there was a need to find figures to preside over the emergent social, religious, and political national order. Writers' bodies fitted the bill, and they seem to have been newly assigned, to invoke Thomas Laqueur's formulation, their own special kind of 'work'—a kind of national service.[7] The greater the importance of the writer to the sense of the nation, the greater seems to have grown the need to use the physical actuality of the body to locate national memory. In his 'Essay on Sepulchres' (1809), for instance, the radical philosopher William Godwin would call for a new culture of commemoration concentred on dead celebrities of national importance.

One result of this was, as Samantha Matthews has in part shown, that writers' bodies were regularly disinterred, translocated, and rememorialized as their local, national, or supranational status changed.[8] The entry into 'immortal memory' for national poets in particular tended to involve a remarkable amount of 'moving poets' bones', to misquote the curse carved into the stone marking Shakespeare's grave in Holy Trinity Church in Stratford-upon-Avon.[9] This was early evident in the cases of the bodies of Petrarch and Dante, outliers in being so early conscripted in the cause of proto-nation-making. The story of the adventures of Petrarch's remains starts with the desire to possess the relics of genius on the part of private collectors. Petrarch's body was entombed in the church in the town of Arquà in 1374; in 1630 the tomb was famously disturbed by a drunken grave-robbing monk named Tommaso Martinelli with the object of taking bones to sell. The grave was again opened in December 1874, and then again in 2003. At some point Petrarch's skull seems to have been stolen, apparently being replaced with a woman's skull some two centuries older.[10] The struggle over where Dante Alighieri's body should come to rest was also clearly proto-nationalist well before the eighteenth century dawned. From the fourteenth century onwards there had been rival claims made to the body by the city-states of Florence (rescinding his perpetual banishment of 1302 rather late to be of much use to Dante) and Ravenna, the town where he died in 1321 and which therefore actually had the corpse, and which went to great lengths to keep it, erecting a substantial memorial in 1483.

Nevertheless, late eighteenth-century nation-making left its mark even on Dante's remains, which were re-entombed more grandly in Ravenna in 1780. In France, the Revolutionaries expended considerable effort on exhuming and rememorializing the Enlightenment fathers of the Revolution (including Voltaire in 1791 and Rousseau in 1794) in the Pantheon in Paris, the new 'Temple of the Nation'. In his turn, Napoleon, with his usual unerring eye for a PR coup combined with a desire for secularization, a desire to realize the nation through heroic geography, and a desire to bury out-and-out republicanism now that he was Emperor, contemplated the exhumation of Rousseau and the return of the body to its original resting-place in Ermenonville in 1806.[11] That did not in the event happen, but in 1801 Napoleon had been more successful in sponsoring the removal of the poet Ariosto's body (minus a finger from his right hand which is now displayed in the house museum devoted to him on the other side of the city) from its original burial place in a monastery in Ferrara to the local library, where it lies in a vast marble sepulchre to this day.[12] In Britain, the 1790s saw the churchwardens of St Giles, Cripplegate, planning to exhume the poet John Milton with the intention of providing a new and grander memorial to a hero of the English Revolution.[13] In Germany an effort was made in 1826 to abstract the bones of Schiller from the communal vault in which he had been buried in 1805 to celebrate him as a national genius.[14] After abortive attempts to identify the right coffin, the investigators laid out all the skulls they could lay their hands on (twenty-three in the first instance) on a table, and 'Schiller's skull' was identified through comparing it with a cast of the head taken at death. This proceeding was supported by a post-mortem literary salon, in which everyone in Weimar who had been on terms of intimacy with Schiller was 'admitted...to the room one by one': 'Without an exception they pointed to the same skull as that which must have been the poet's...Goethe unhesitatingly recognized the head, and laid stress on the peculiar beauty and evenness of the teeth'.[15] Efforts to recompose the skeleton followed (including further visits to the vault), along with discussions of a suitable place and mode of reinterment, the first of which was in the base of a colossal bust of Schiller in the ducal library, the second in the ducal vaults.[16]

The history of these exhumations tells of the sorts of value and function writers' remains could have in the project of nation-making. So too does the long-standing fantasy of exhuming Shakespeare. That Shakespeare has never been exhumed may be attributed as much to the fact that Ben Jonson's eulogy specifically dismissed the desirability of interring Shakespeare in Westminster Abbey alongside Spenser, that Shakespeare had the foresight and standing to be buried in a local place of honour in the chancel and in the heart of England into the bargain, and that the chancel of Holy Trinity Church was not subject to opportune Victorian restoration, as to the famous curse on the stone slab. However, the notion of such an exhumation has been regularly aired since the mid-nineteenth century. As James Rigney notes, such proposals have been driven by a mix of 'political, hagiographical, archaeological and economic motives'.[17] Arguments for exhumation included the desire to learn whether there was anything left other than 'dust'; the wish to discover whether the remains had already been disturbed; and the hope of finding the skull in order to subject it to phrenological analysis. (Phrenology argued that areas of the brain were variably developed in different types of personalities and professions and that, given that the growth of the brain affected the shape of the skull, it was possible, through making collections of the skulls of the famous and studying them, to work out what the skull of a literary genius would look like.[18]) Others hoped to find the skull to authenticate (or debunk) contemporary or near-contemporary representations; to discover lost manuscripts; to ascertain what he died of, whether he smoked cannabis, or whether he limped like other paradigmatic poets Scott and Byron; or to prove that Shakespeare was not Shakespeare, but actually Marlowe, Bacon, or someone imaginary.[19] By the 1880s, exhumation fever was running high: in Stratford, Clement M. Ingleby actually secured agreement for an exhumation from the then vicar of Holy Trinity Church, the Revd George Arbuthnot. A lively local, national, and transatlantic debate ensued, arguing the case for and against. The public outcry proved too much for the Town Councillors, and the proposal was eventually voted down.[20]

Ingleby's pamphlet *Shakespeare's Bones: The Proposal to Disinter Them, considered in relation to their possible bearing on his portraiture: illustrated by instances of visits of the living to the dead* had appeared in 1879, arguing that exhumation would lay to rest the tradition that the grave had been disturbed in 1796, and ascertain whether or not the skull had been stolen out of 'that combination of curiosity, cupidity, and relic-worship, which has so often prompted and carried out the exhumation of a great man's bones'.[21] His motivation was more purely scholarly and scientific; exhumation would 'find such evidences as time may not have wholly destroyed, of his personal appearance, including the size and shape of his head, and the special characteristics of his living face'.[22] Examination of the skull would allow for the authentication or otherwise of the 'clownish' monument in Holy Trinity Church (long a source of aesthetic and ideological disappointment to Shakespeareans) and of other disputed portraits of Shakespeare, including the Kesselstadt death mask.[23] Ingleby claimed that the skull would have great value within a scientific museum: 'His skull, if still not turned to dust, should be preserved in the Royal College of Surgeons, as the apex of a climbing series of skeletons, from the microscopic to the divine'.[24] But he also adduced a further argument for the power of such remains—the possibility of conversing with the dead:

> I cannot allow that neither dust and ashes, bones, nor teeth, have any intelligence to give us; nor yet that by the reverential scrutiny of those relics the living can neither be benefited nor improved...[25]

In the same year, an article excitingly entitled 'How Shakespeare's Skull was stolen and found. By a Warwickshire Man' was published. This fiction purported to tell how Frank Chambers, a medical student practising in Alcester in the late 1780s and early 1790s, came to conceive and execute the robbing of Shakespeare's grave, spurred on by the thought that 'old Horace Walpole had offered, after the Jubilee, to give George Selwyn three hundred guineas if he could secure Shakespeare's head'.[26] Chambers gets together three men, breaks into the church, raises the stone, and so 'handled Shakespeare's skull at last...'. His verdict: 'It was smaller than I expected, and in formation not much like what I remembered of the effigy above our heads'.[27] Negotiations with Walpole fail, and so Chambers ends up trying to return the skull to the grave through the agency of one of his original associates, with unsatisfactory results. The story generated enough public excitement to warrant a follow-up piece five years later, in 1884, entitled 'How Shakespeare's Skull was Found'. This fiction was scarcely more reassuring, since it asserted that the skull was even so not back *in situ*. Investigating a 'bulky packet, consisting apparently of pages torn from [a] professional day-book, going back to 1798',[28] the antiquarian author discovers 'a rough envelope, made from large-sized note paper, sealed with two common red wafers, eaten away by time':

> I trembled with excitement to see several sheets of manuscript in the well-known hand of Chambers, and within these was another leaflet, out of which dropt a small piece of bone. Yes! A small piece of bone. I declare to you, that I have it before me as I write. Dark on the outside; slightly curved, of irregular outline, measuring two inches by one, and a quarter of an inch in its thickest part...[29]

The interpolated manuscript details Chambers' conversation with one of his labourers: 'I was druv away in affright from Stratford Church before I could bury that old skull; so, thinks I, as Measter Chambers seems so uncommon particular to have him under cover, I'll just pop him into one of them wessels in this ere wault. And *that* I did, I'll swear, last night; clipping this bit out on him to leave a kind of mark, d'ye see, for you to tell him by...'.[30] At this point the manuscript ends. The antiquarian author then details his efforts to discover the crypt the labourer described, eventually settling on a mortuary chapel dedicated to a Catholic family, the Sheldons. This he visits at midnight on Christmas Eve, to find 'an undersized skull, with a prominent forehead marred by a jagged hole. Over that hole I placed the fragment I had brought with me: it fitted *exactly!* THE VERITABLE SKULL OF WILLIAM SHAKESPEARE WAS THERE'.[31] And with that the pamphlet ends.

What are we to make of the fantasized discovery of a misplaced, undersized, mutilated skull, stamped as 'veritable' with a forger's clipper? This story, like *Hamlet*, flirts with the idea of remains as just that, dispersed remains, 'quite chop-fallen', a genuine *memento mori*. The scene of recognition, depending on the locking together of the reader's relic into the possibly fraudulent skull itself, models reading as personal encounter or private collection, illicit and greedy, which threatens the decorums of national pantheonization.[32]

The flipside of Ingleby's optimistic belief in exhumation for the public benefit was Langstone's fantasized loss and relocation of the skull owing to the cupidity of a private collector compounded by the mildly criminal ineptitude of the locals. Similarly, actual Exhumation might result not in the finding of remains but their disappearance—physically, in the sense that exposure to the air would cause the corpse to crumble away, and historically, in the sense that the authentication of Shakespeare might fail. The scholar and archaeologist James Orchard Halliwell-Phillips warned the Town

Corporation of Stratford-upon-Avon that if the skull did *not* correspond to the monumental bust the inference would not be that the bust was an inaccurate representation, but that the skull was not in fact Shakespeare's— thus exhumation might 'lose' the National Poet outright.[33] A dead loss, one might say. The investigation of Shakespeare's remains carried out via ground-penetrating sonar, the subject of a television documentary in 2016, alarmingly to many, seemed to show that the skull has indeed been lost.[34]

The rhetoric of encountering Shakespeare's remains face to face employed by both Ingleby and Langstone throws light on why it was that celebrated writers' remains were coveted as much by private collectors as they were by those concerned with nation-making. Such remains were disconcertingly inclined to vanish, looted and reincarnated as sought-after curios in private collections. This fate may or may not have overtaken Shakespeare's body, but it certainly overtook the body of the philosopher René Descartes. Buried first in Stockholm, where he died in 1650, his body was exhumed sixteen years later to be returned as a national treasure to France. At that juncture the French ambassador Hugues de Terlon took the opportunity of acquiring a finger as a personal souvenir. In 1792 when the aesthete, revolutionary, and conserver of the cultural heritage of the *ancien regime* Alexandre LeNoir acquired the body for his 'Museum of Monuments' in Paris, he took a perk in the shape of another bone which he set into a piece of jewellery. At some point thereafter the skull was filched for a Swedish private collection, sold at auction in 1819, and then sold again in 1821 to Georges Cuvier, who returned it to Paris as a specimen in the Museum of Natural History in Paris. Misplaced in the floods of 1911–12, it was relocated 'to the school at La Fiche where he [Descartes] studied as a boy' in 2009, the nearest it has yet come to being rethought in the more local and biographical terms characteristic of a writer's house museum. Russell Shorto's history of these relics makes it plain that it was possible to re-identify the skull so often because 'in 1666 and subsequently various owners had inscribed their names on the skull and someone else had composed an entire poem in Latin on the top'.[35] The story of Descartes' bones shows how, once outside the grave proper, their meanings could morph between the national and the personal, the monumental and the collectible, and between pertaining to others and pertaining to Descartes' own life. The afterlife of Descartes' skull exemplifies the characteristic hybridity of such relics, which may successively encode personal memory of the dead, family piety, private cross-generational gifts between subsequent admirers, scholarly lust, and frankly commercial transactions, before achieving sentimental monumentalization within the writer's house museum.

These various stories and histories suggest that the value of the writer's physical remains has been fourfold: to remember and authenticate the writer's material existence; to ascertain the body as evidence of 'genius'; to naturalize the writer within a locality provincial or national (sometimes both), providing an occasion for appropriate monumentalization; and to serve as the occasion and vehicle for affective encounter with the writer, an encounter conceived as at once highly personal and yet of public import. The sequence of verification, reconstitution, and relocation characterizes the ways that authorial remains arrive in writer's house museums; there, their effects of enabling personal encounter are if anything intensified.

Burns' skull

One of the more startling exhibits in the entrance exhibition of the Robert Burns Birthplace Museum at Alloway is contained in an opaque mirrored cabinet. Passing by, the visitor sees only his or her reflection unless they press the inviting button which illuminates the interior; whereupon he or she will come face to face and eyeball to eyeball with a life-size, full-colour, 3D forensic reconstruction of Robert Burns' head. A short distance away, there is another cabinet containing a cast of the poet's skull; in 2013 this served as the basis for the reconstruction (Figure 1.1).

That there is such a cast is the result of the second of two exhumations of Burns' remains, both of which were driven by his growing posthumous reputation as national bard. Burns died in Dumfries on 21 July 1796, and was buried in St Michael's Churchyard, Dumfries. This grave achieved some early fame beyond the locality, most famously visited by William and Dorothy Wordsworth in the summer of 1802.[36] Early complaints that the grave did not seem to accord the poet enough importance resulted in a first attempt by a John Forbes Mitchell of Bombay to have a more suitable memorial erected in 1812. This was unsuccessful. In 1813 William Grierson and John Syme, friends of the poet, formed the Burns Mausoleum Committee, launching a fund for the erection of a mausoleum on a different site within the churchyard on 24 November 1814 and soliciting designs. Thomas Frederick Hunt's neo-classical design was inaugurated in a ceremony that featured the burial of a lengthy Latin inscription with the foundation

Figure 1.1. Cast of Robert Burns' skull, © Robert Burns Birthplace Museum, National Trust for Scotland

stone which hailed Burns in the language of Romantic nationalism as 'The Bard', describing his verses as 'distinguished for the strength and fire of native genius'.[37] By September 1815, the work was largely complete, and the body was moved to its new resting-place by night to thwart contemporary efforts to get at the body to examine it.[38] This first exhumation calibrated a change in the poet's status from that of a well-known local to a 'genius' of national and international stature hailed by posterity. The account of the appearance of the body that circulated in 1815 was consistent with an interest in Burns as living memory. It insisted that the body was unusually well pre-served, being 'nearly entire . . . exhibiting the features of one who had newly sunk into the sleep of death—the lordly forehead, arched and high—the scalp still covered with hair, and the teeth perfectly firm and white'.[39]

When Burns' widow Jean Armour died in March 1834, the opening of the mausoleum ahead of the funeral in advance of her interment allowed access once again to Burns' body. Having obtained permission from the family, a party of men, including John McDiarmid, editor of *The Dumfries Courier*, a surgeon, Archibald Blacklock, and James Bogie, who had helped move the poet's coffin in 1815, entered the mausoleum. They located the skull, cleaned it, and took a plaster cast, before placing it in a lead casket and reburying it.[40] This second exhumation was driven ostensibly by scientific curiosity; Blacklock wrote that 'nothing could exceed the high state of preservation in which we found the bones of the cranium, or offer a fairer opportunity of supplying what has so long been desiderated by Phrenologists—a correct model of our immortal Poet's head'.[41] A single cast seems to have been made initially, and then a number of subsequent copies.[42]

The cast served from the outset to give body to biographical narrative. Burns' biographer, George Combe, for instance, examined the cast, concluding: 'The skull indicates the combination of strong animal passions, with equally powerful moral emotions... The combination... bespeaks a mind extremely subject to contending emotions—capable of great good or great evil...'.[43] That judgement might sum up the general tendency of Combe's biography. Subsequent to the craze for phrenology, the cast was used to evidence the reality of Burns' body. It served, for example, together with the portrait of Burns by Alexander Nasmyth, as the model for Sir John Steell's sculpture of Burns made in 1886 that ornaments Central Park, New York as well as sites in Dundee, London, and Dunedin.[44] More recently, as already noted, it was the basis for the forensic reconstruction of Burns' face carried out by the Professor of Craniofacial Identification, Caroline Wilkinson, and her team at the University of Dundee in 2013.[45] Her remarks, reported in *The Scotsman* on 24 January of that year, underscore the ways this exercise reanimated 'Burns in his full living glory', giving him birth again in Scotland on his birthday: 'To be able to reveal the 3D head of Burns to Scotland and the world is an immense privilege for us, and all the team have watched this head develop and take on character over the last year. Finally we can see this charismatic poet as others would have seen him in life and it has not been disappointing'.[46]

Wilkinson's remarks suggest forcibly the imaginative continuity between facing down the skull itself, presumably still lying in its leaden casket below the Burns Mausoleum in Dumfries, and viewing the cast of the skull in the museum. The forensic reconstruction sets up a charismatically lifelike encounter. If the reburial of Burns in the mausoleum was all about national and international status, and imagines a readership conceived as the nation and its diaspora, the cast and the reconstructed head purport to supply privileged access to Burnsian subjectivity and imagine the individual reader as a reanimator of the past within the present.[47] Richard Howitt's thought-experiment on visiting the Burns mausoleum in 1840 is thus realized for us relatively squeamish moderns within the museum:

> Breathe I above his dust who now has long
> Ceased with his musical breath to charm this air?
> Sleeps Burns within this mausoleum fair,
> The peasant-minstrel of the heaven-taught tongue!
> It must be so, for fancy here grows strong,
> So strong we feel him present everywhere...[48]

Keats' death mask

In sharp contradistinction to the Robert Burns Birthplace Museum, founded upon the idea of the birth of a native bard, the Keats-Shelley Memorial House in Rome is remarkable in that it was primarily inspired by the idea of authorial death. The Keats-Shelley Memorial House was purchased in 1906 and opened to the public in 1909, following an initial meeting on the anniversary of John Keats' death in 1903 between an English diplomat and eight American writers. It memorializes Keats' final illness and death from tuberculosis over a matter of weeks spent in rented lodgings overlooking the Piazza di Spagna, an area much frequented by English travellers both before Keats' time and after. In a small first-floor room here, Keats, attended by his friend Joseph Severn, died slowly and agonizingly, a process documented at length within Severn's letters and subsequent autobiographical and biographical writings. The end came on 23 February 1821, after which Keats was buried in the cemetery just within the walls of Rome devoted to foreigners under an anonymous stone bearing the epitaph he had composed for himself, 'Here lies one whose name was writ in water'. Within a few months, Percy Bysshe Shelley, author of the remarkable elegy on Keats' death, 'Adonais' (1821), was also dead, drowned at sea with (so the story went) a copy of Keats' *Poems* (1820) in his pocket. He was subsequently buried (in part—the heart was removed and eventually taken back to England) in the same cemetery. This coincidence twinned Keats and Shelley as poetic exiles, collated their poetic projects under the composite sign of the youthful, misunderstood poet, and reconstructed them both as 'Adonais'. It had a powerful effect first on how the cemetery and then the house in the Piazza di Spagna were conceived. An undated nineteenth-century print of Shelley's grave displayed in the museum is annotated and embellished by visitors Alfred and Emma Novello: a handwritten comment remarks 'Also of John Keats', and pressed plant material gathered from both graves adorns the margins of the print. This includes a 'violet, gathered from Shelley's grave, 1856, by Alfred Novello' and a 'daisy, gathered from Keats' grave, 1851, by Emma Novello'. The Anglophone cult of the poets resulted first in the supplementary marking of Keats' grave with a plaque set on the wall of the cemetery in 1876, and then, at the height of the pre-World War I enthusiasm for transnational Anglophone literary heritage, in setting up the Keats-Shelley House. As the plaque over the front door has it, the building was 'acquired and dedicated to the memory/of the two poets by their admirers/in England and America'. The present-day museum consists of four unequally sized rooms: of these, the smallest is Keats' bedroom and is devoted to Keats' death, and the largest room, a library, is devoted to the afterlives of Keats and Shelley, and to a lesser extent Byron.

There are, naturally enough, many houses in which writers have died, and if these houses have become museums, the places of their deaths are memorialized, often to great effect. (One might add to the example of Haworth Parsonage that I have already mentioned the instances of Petrarch's chair at Arquà, Strindberg's bed in Stockholm, or Scott's sofa at Abbotsford.) But this museum is unique in using the death of Keats to describe the very notion of the death of the (neglected) poet into (reverential) posterity, as per Malcolm Bradbury's remarks above. For Keats, his early death meant that he would fail to make a sufficient mark upon posterity; the museum describes the extent to which he was mistaken. The entire museum functions as an essay on the deaths of writers and the nature of authorial afterlife to a degree unmatched by any other writer's house museum.

At the time of writing (April 2016), as you enter the room in which Keats died, you are first of all encouraged to look out at the Piazza through the window at which, when Keats was well enough, he amused himself by watching the life of the square. Turning towards the remainder of the room which is mostly roped off, you see a death mask displayed within a glass case to the right of the period-correct bed, inclined at an angle of about forty-five degrees.[49] Directly above the mask hangs Severn's sketch of Keats on his death-bed. Above the bed itself hang three contemporary prints of the cemetery depicting Keats' grave. As the visitor reads from left to right, the imagined dead face on the pillow transmutes into the death mask; reading from top to bottom, the death mask describes the last appearance of the poet in death. The prints convert the bed into a substitute grave lying below the ground depicted. The guide, directing visitors' attention to the blue and white ceiling with its trompe l'oeil panelling and daisy-like rosettes, claims that these inspired Keats' self-comforting fantasy of the daisies that he thought would grow above him in the cemetery. This conceit reiterates the bed as grave, describing the ceiling both as blue sky and daisy-studded turf. Swing your gaze round again from left to right, and it comes to rest at the mantelpiece surmounted by a copy of Severn's posthumous portrait of Keats reading in his room at Hampstead, which directly faces the prints of the grave. The room thus counterposes death to revivification and Rome to London. As you finally turn to go out of the door, to the left you see a small painting of 'Keats' bedroom' by Penny Graham (2008); this miniaturization compacts both what you are meant to remember of the room and its importance as the heart of the museum, the sanctum, the culmination of any tour, the dead-end, the room that remains.

Nothing here is anything but a copy, and, despite its unnerving documentary realism, this includes the death mask. Making both death and life masks entailed taking a 'matrix' of the face, but the mask itself was made by pouring plaster into the resulting mould, so converting a negative into a positive; this process meant that as many copies as desired could be generated from the plaster cast.[50] Life masks were made when it was considered a necessary aid to making a portrait sculpture of a celebrity; because they were merely a means to an end, matrices and casts from them rarely survive.[51] In the case of Keats, a life mask was made because his friend the artist Benjamin Haydon conceived the ambition of painting his friends' features into a career-bid canvas, 'Christ Entering Jerusalem'; it survives partly thanks to the early cult of Keats within his circle, and partly because, his death following so soon after, the life mask served as a better version of the death mask.[52] Death masks, used from Renaissance Florence onwards as an aid to posthumous portraiture and funerary effigy and sculpture, were by the early nineteenth century aids to mourning and memorial; Madame Tussaud's career, built in the first instance on making wax models of the living at Louis XVI's court, accelerated when she was commissioned to take masks of those guillotined in the 1790s, and in nineteenth-century Germany it came to be customary to take masks from dead family members, and to hang them in the parlour.[53] The taking of a death mask might be actuated by a sense of the national importance of a dead writer, and be undertaken along with other death-bed practices, including autopsy, to record the last physical state of the author.[54] 'The Mask-seller', a nineteenth-century statue in the Jardin du Luxembourg in Paris, depicts a young boy selling the death masks of famous French authors.

Before the advent of photography the death mask served a fairly simple purpose as a proto-photographic image of the dead; afterwards, it came to be conceived as describing the moment of translation into death. Theorists of the ideological nature and status of the death mask, from Martin Heidegger through Jean-Luc Nancy, Susan Sontag, and Marcia Pointon, have almost invariably treated it as an autonomous object; but much of the meaning of a death mask depends on the context in which it is displayed.[55] Within the nineteenth-century writer's house museum, the death mask was used to authenticate both the actuality of the writer's body and the moment of its paradoxical dissolution into immortality; Shakespeare's death mask, for example, was hung prominently within the Birthplace at Stratford-upon-Avon, although its provenance was dubious at best.[56] But of the many death masks made of famous writers' faces, there are very few if any which approach the historical and contemporary celebrity of Keats' life and death masks, which have, so to speak, shown signs of taking on a life of their own. Robert Browning and Elizabeth Barrett Browning had the life mask prominently displayed in their apartment in Florence.[57] Another forms part of the collection in the Keats Room in the Houghton Library, Harvard University. A modern version is on sale in the gift shop of Keats House in Hampstead, and another at the National Portrait Gallery; it is said that they sell mostly to American tourists and that the film-actor Helena Bonham Carter recently purchased one.[58] Poems, fiction, and travel-writing, including that of the blogosphere, make it plain that these artefacts have exerted a continuing fascination for collectors and the public alike, attributable to the central importance in his mythos of youthful death.[59]

Both life and death masks are given considerable prominence not just in the Keats-Shelley Memorial House in Rome but also at Wentworth Place, the museum devoted to Keats in Hampstead. Early photographs of the Hampstead house show Keats' life mask hung vertically in Keats' Parlour over the mantelpiece.[60] By contrast, from 2009 prior to the 2015 reinterpretation, the life mask was tilted backwards in a glass case in the bedroom, next to the bed in which Keats awoke to find a spot of arterial blood on the pillow-case and recognized it as his death-warrant. The guidebook of 2009 shows it lying down and in profile, a remarkably private and non-confrontational reading of the mask's refusal of the reader's gaze simply as sleep. Since February 2015 it has formed part of a display in a tall vitrine in the upstairs corridor in front of a long window towards which the visitor walks. The corridor was conceived by the interpretation team on the redisplay of the museum as 'themed around [Keats'] final journey and death', and is hung with visual materials describing Rome, his companion Severn, a copy of the funerary plaque made in 1876 for the cemetery in Rome, and a copy of the famous sketch Severn made of Keats on his death-bed.[61] At the top of the case a ghostly young face with closed eyes gleams whitely, like a personification of sleep; below it the same closed-off face appears again, but this time in some dark, metallic material, like a personification of death; and below that again to the right sits, uptilted, a large golden brooch with the representation of a golden lyre set under a face of crystal within a heavy gold frame inscribed simply 'KEATS'. Respectively, these are Keats' life mask in white plaster, Keats' death mask in a bronzed porcelain version, and the brooch that Severn commissioned as a mourning jewel.[62] The journey between life and death is visualized as the contrast and progression between the light and the dark mask, exhibited for the first time in the history of the house; as the curator put it, 'from the combination of them together you get a sense of what the disease did to him, the real physical degrading of him'.[63] The masks are also present elsewhere in the museum. The life mask is mounted as a pseudo-bust in the case in the room leading off to the left, and downstairs, there is a version specifically designed to be touched by children and the visually impaired.

Why bring Keats' death back to Hampstead in the shape of the bronzed death mask in 2015? On the one hand, it is the equivalent of shipping the body back home, a cultural process that has been at work since the installation of the bust of Keats in the local church and the opening of the museum in 1925. Wentworth Place was where Keats lived between 1818 and 1820, the most productive years of his writing career; thus bringing Keats home returns him to life and Englishness. This impulse is realized in the other version of the death mask that is more covertly on show; above the mantel in 'Keats' Parlour' hangs yet another copy of the picture by Joseph Severn painted posthumously between 1821 and 1823 (the original is held by the National Portrait Gallery, London). Painted from the death mask and the casts of Keats' hand and foot taken on Severn's instructions at the same time, it shows the poet reading at home, a posthumous reconstruction that visitors are themselves invited to reiterate by sitting in the chairs arranged in front of the very window depicted by Severn.[64]

This posthumous portraiture is in accordance with one of the principal motivations behind the making of a nineteenth-century death mask; to have a faithful portrait likeness of the departed. Modern deployment of the death mask within the writers' house museum and cognate forms, however, re-purposes the death mask to describe and dramatize the death of the writer. In the case of Keats, the moment of Romantic dissolution is so important to his mythos that the death mask is critically important to both the museum in Hampstead and that in Rome. Thus in the present display in Hampstead, the life and death masks are hung one above each other and their meaning inheres in the moment of death imagined as intervening between them; in Rome, the inclined death mask portrays not so much Keats as Keats-just-after-death. Death delivers the Romantic poet over to the judgement of posterity, turning the writer into the author; admiring tourists 'rescue' him from death.

Keats' hair

The third term in the Hampstead cabinet is the mourning brooch that contains Keats' hair (Figure 1.2). In the early nineteenth century, little enough that was lifelike could be rescued from the grave to remember the physical appearance and actuality of the dead. For both rich and poor it was customary to take a lock of hair as a memento. The sense that hair could transcend death was formulated by Leigh Hunt in a passage much anthologized by the Victorians:

> Hair is at once the most delicate and lasting of all our materials; and survives us, like love. It is so light, so gentle, so escaping from the idea of death that with a lock of hair belonging to a child or a friend, we may almost look up to heaven, and compare notes with the angelic native; may almost say, 'I have a piece of thee here, not unworthy of thy being now'.[65]

This 'piece of thee' would either simply be kept quietly folded away in paper or made it into mourning jewellery. In this mode, the hair itself might be more or less visible. It might be hidden in the back of a brooch or within a locket, or it might be explicitly on display, elaborately worked into highly conventionalized hair-pictures depicting motifs of mourning within bejewelled frames.[66] Around the hair of the dead there was a complicated dance

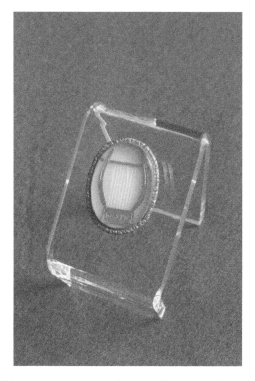

Figure 1.2. Gold brooch containing John Keats' hair, 1822. © Keats House, London

between private and public, intimacy and display, but, almost invariably, hair cut from the dead went in the first instance to intimates, lovers, family, or close friends.

Hence, when it came to the hair of long-dead famous writers, claims of personal intimacy and affection equally accompanied and drove the habit of collection even where there had been no personal friendship. As Hunt had it, possessing the hair of the celebrated could provide 'personal acquaint-ance with people who lived a hundred...years ago' because 'we have *touched* the persons we allude to'.[67] Such a claim of 'personal acquaintance' between author and reader almost certainly drove the attribution of two locks of hair to Shakespeare, now thought to have been concocted as a tourist relic by the then custodian of Shakespeare's Birthplace in the early years of the nineteenth century. This purports to be two samples of Shakespeare's hair, one supposedly taken at the age of fifteen, the other at the age of fifty or so. Bracketing Shakespeare's working life, describing conjecturally his entrance into manhood and his exit into death, this artefact thus connects the Victorian vision of Shakespeare as golden boy with the inconveniently balding bust in Holy Trinity Church. But it also, given that it came into the possession of the poet Samuel Rogers in 1819, served as an intimate token of friendship from one equal to another across the centuries, between National Poet and future contender as Poet Laureate.[68] What exactly the 'personal acquaintance' should be between dead poet and live reader, however, is described in rather different ways by the locks of hair held in the museums devoted to Keats in Hampstead and in Rome. In Rome, the materiality of Keats passes through and describes an Anglophile genealogical connection between men and women of letters, choice spirits far from home. In Hampstead, by contrast, the hair of Keats serves not just to dramatize the value of poetic voice and the sorrow of its loss but also to metamorphose homosocial friendship into heterosexuality and home.

The Salone of the Keats-Shelley Memorial House in Rome features, amongst other relics, an entire case devoted to secular reliquaries containing poetic hair. These include: a frame containing three locks of hair, pertaining to Shelley, Keats, and their friend Leigh Hunt, certified as such, and as presented by Leigh Hunt on 20 October 1850 to the American sculptor, art critic, and poet, William Wetmore; a square glass-topped box containing a large quantity of fairish hair, said to be Percy Bysshe Shelley's childhood hair, presented in November 2013 by Lord Abinger, and captioned 'a tress of Percy Bysshe Shelley's hair, aged 13'; and a silver scallop-shell reliquary that reputedly once belonged to Pope Pius V, containing a lock of hair that belonged to John Milton intertwined with one belonging to Elizabeth Barrett Browning in a special box marked with the name of a famous American collector, Dallas Pratt. The museum's collections include additionally several strands of Shelley's hair, donated by the American writer and poet Harriet Prescott Spofford, which derived from Leigh Hunt's famous collection of the hair of celebrities, including Lucrezia Borgia, Jonathan Swift, Samuel Johnson, Napoleon, Keats, and the Brownings, now held at the University of Texas at Austin; and a further lock of Keats' hair, donated by the New York financier J.P. Morgan.[69]

Whether considered individually or collectively, these items and their histories incarnate the idea of literary inheritance from poet to poet, and nation to nation, although they take the form of personal token or memento. The lock of Milton's hair is part of that which Leigh Hunt showed to Keats in 1818 as having already been possessed in turn by Joseph Addison and Samuel Johnson amongst others, and which he would subsequently give to Robert Browning in 1857. There is controversy as to whether it was combined with Elizabeth Barrett Browning's hair within the reliquary by Robert Browning as an act of mourning or whether this was done some time after Robert Browning's own death by the family; either way, such an action suggests that the celebrity poet rather than the family member was being memorialized.[70] Leigh Hunt's mounting of the hair of his poetic friends is the material equivalent of the then popular genre of paintings of writers and their friends in pubs or their homes. It reads him into an equality of association. Leigh Hunt generally used this collection as a form of flattery, as when he gifted Shelley's hair to Spofford; J.P. Morgan's lock of Keats' hair was similarly divided and subdivided as a form of literary currency; he was, for instance, so taken with the young Beverley Nichols as a beautiful young Englishman abroad that he gave him a single strand, certified and sealed in much the same way.[71] These items would eventually take on the status of national and international capital: on 14 December 1942, locks of Keats' and Shelley's hair were sent from Rome for safety to the Abbey of Montecassino, and, when that came under fire, back to Rome; it was a measure of their global value that they were convoyed there by the Italian curator, Vera Cacciatore, but brought back by 'a German lorry of the Goering division'.[72]

The gold brooch made to Joseph Severn's own design in Rome in the months after the death of his friend, which now sits beneath the life and death masks in the glass case back in Hampstead, serves as a similar statement of Keats' immortality. A brilliant highlight of gold within the cabinet, shifted slightly to the right as though marking the end of a sentence, it constructs a narrative of the cabinet which, read top to bottom and left to right, effectively denotes life, death, and afterlife. The design of the brooch draws on the image of the unstrung lyre to symbolize Keats' unachieved poetic career. Severn used this image repeatedly: Keats House in Hampstead holds Severn's copy of Keats' narrative poem *Endymion* (1818), on the title-page of which he sketched just such a lyre; he chose it for Keats' headstone; and accordingly it also features on the plaque let into the house wall above the Spanish Steps in 1879 which notes (inaccurately) that 'The young English Poet/John Keats/Died in this House/On the 24th February 1821/Aged 25'. Within the crystal of the brooch, the gold frame of the lyre is partially strung with single strands of Keats' hair, thus describing the poet's body itself as the unstrung lyre. Equally, however, the ever bright hair of the poet—and Keats' hair was for Leigh Hunt, as he remarked in 1833: 'a kind of ideal, poetical hair' because he was 'a young man, and manly in spirit as his looks were beautiful'—described not the passage into death but a continuing connection to the living.[73] Originally conceived as a gift for Fanny Brawne, Keats' fiancée, as a mourning jewel, the brooch seems never to have reached her. Instead, Severn gifted it to his daughter on the occasion of her wedding in 1861, converting it thereby from a mourning brooch into a valuable and curious gift. It would metamorphose again once it came into the possession of Keats House, into a museum object. Thus over its lifetime this jewel has changed from personal memento to quasi-personal memorial. What began as a homosocial cult mourning object, failed to become a heterosexual mourning object, was re-scripted as sentimental jewellery within the heterosexual economy of marriage, and was then rethought as a museum exhibit. It now sits within that vitrine as a description of the poetic afterlife, whereby the poet's mortal body is re-conceived as immortal poetic instrument. The death of a writer as conceived by the display of this piece of hair-jewellery within the writer's house museum is a peculiar, ambiguous thing; it is entombed but lifelike, indeed still living.

If both death mask and the taking of hair work, as Marcia Pointon has argued, to separate the memory of the dead person from the corpse itself, preserving memory from impending decay and enshrining it within an enduring structure, this notion needs some refinement and elaboration when it comes to writers and writer's house museums.[74] Keats' death mask comes to mark the precise moment at which the writer dies into the author. It is a mausoleum in miniature. By contrast, the reliquaries containing Keats' hair salvage poetic immortality through offering encounter with undecaying remains. However, while it is possible to distinguish between two aspects of the writer's house museum under the headings of the mausoleum and the reliquary, one might as well concede that these collapse into each other as the museum collects and celebrates authorial remains so as to reconstitute and remember the dead writer as author. Thus Ariosto's finger and Keats' hair sit at either end of the mausoleum–reliquary spectrum, but they are both emblematic of the desire of the museum to house the (im)mortal body of the author. These processes of reconstitution and preservation, however, are not solely activated around authorial remains; as we will see over the course of Chapters 2 and 3, they can extend beyond them to animal-bodies and, yet further, to articles of clothing that equally serve as surrogates for the authorial body.

2

Bodies

Petrarch's cat and Poe's raven

A prickly problem

On the kitchen floor of 48 Doughty Street in London, the house that Charles Dickens and his young family occupied for two years between 1837 and 1839 and which has since 1925 been a museum to the writer's memory, there is, staged in the act of quietly scuttling along the front of the range, a specimen of the art of taxidermy: a hedgehog. This hedgehog is part of the comprehensive redisplay of the museum undertaken in 2012 in honour of the bicentenary of Dickens' birth. Beneath the notice of the souvenir guidebook, it does at least merit a caption on the table nearby. This explains that 'Hedgehogs were sometimes kept in Victorian kitchens to eat insects, as there was a constant war against bugs. Keeping your kitchen clean was seen as both a matter of hygiene and also as a moral duty'. This explanation hardly seems adequate. In my capacity as a fellow householder, I want to know whether it was difficult to avoid stepping on such an animal as one moved around the kitchen, or whether this problem was obviated by the fact that hedgehogs are typically nocturnal, or, at any rate, crepuscular. What happened when it hibernated, or was this also not a problem because infestations of insects would typically only occur in the summer? As a cultural historian, I wonder what the evidence for this practice is, and where it is to be found, and whether hedgehogs were plentiful in this environment of urban walled gardens, or whether there was a trade in bringing hedgehogs in from the country to local markets. But in this context, as a scholar considering the genre of the writer's house museum as a form of literary biography, I wonder what this hedgehog is supposed to say about Charles Dickens, who had the idea of collecting him (or her) from where and when, and how this animal-body works within the context of present-day museum visitor experience.

Dickens' hedgehog, as one might rather mischievously term her (or him), raises larger questions than this, however. She is only one, if one of the more recent, puzzling, and apparently under-motivated, of the various dead–alive animals that make their appearance in museums devoted to writers. In the following year, for instance, the artist and writer Charlotte Cory was commissioned to stage a version of her signature piece, 'Visitoriana', at Haworth Parsonage. This photoshopped images of Victorians, including some of the Brontë circle, with specimens of Victorian taxidermy, giving them all, as the leaflet that accompanied the exhibition put it, 'a new lease of life'.[1] Animals in the form of actual organic remains—entombed, mummified, embalmed, or taxidermied—typically function within the writer's house museum and associated forms of museum-display to allegorize the writer's body in relation to writing, both as act and as output. They have been used to satisfy and to critique the desire to fetishize the authorial body, to describe and comment upon the nature of the writer and writing as imperfectly domesticated, to embody the estrangement of writing from the writer's body through embodying particular texts, and to argue for the unnervingly deathless life of writing.

This chapter tells the story of how celebrated creatures such as Petrarch's cat, Cowper's hares, Poe's raven, Sterne's starling, and Dickinson's hummingbirds have been put to work to produce the author in the writer's house museum. All these individual creatures play an important part in the mythos of the various authors with which they are associated, and for that reason they have been preserved in cultural memory. However, the nature and extent of the import of individual animals derive from very different types of stories told about the authors with whom they are associated. Such animals may owe their celebrity to biographical or autobiographical anecdote, or they may owe it to their appearance within literary texts. Some have made the border crossing back and forth between historical and fictive life. Yet others have achieved emblematic power long after their deaths and that of the author with which they are associated. But one way or another, they have all been imagined as having had a biographical or quasi-biographical authenticity. These case-studies look at the ways in which these animals were used, when alive, within the writer's own mythos, their function within the writer's circle as a way of conceiving or crystallizing personal and professional relationships, how the animals were related by the writer to the writing, how they featured in representations of the author within portraiture, anecdote, and biography, and by extension when and how and in what media these animals come to be realized and reiterated within the writer's house museum. They also explore these animals' variable celebrity within travel-writing and visual representation describing or reacting to writer's houses, both before they become museums and after. These histories may be variable and miscellaneous, but they all have in common the realization of these animals in terms of actual animal remains—paradigmatically, as taxidermy.

Animal-objects derived from particular celebrated creatures are a very specialized and arcane category of taxidermy. Rachel Poliquin's helpful cultural history and taxonomy of taxidermy describes its evolution from Renaissance 'wonder', to early nineteenth-century celebration of 'beauty' in interior decor, into the 'spectacle' and 'order' staged in Victorian natural history museums, 'narratives' of the hunt, 'allegory' in the shape of fabulous or grotesque scenes and post-modern 'animal art', and, finally, 'remembrance' of dead pets.[2] In this schema, the specimens found in writer's house museums appear at first glance to fall into the category of remembering a particular animal for its personality.[3] Staged within the writer's house museum this remembrance is public rather than merely personal; that is to say, the museum visitor is exhorted to remember some sort of personal relationship that once existed between the dead writer and the dead animal. Under scrutiny, this relationship often proves fictive, in that the animal on display is not always or even usually the original animal, but a stand-in. A gap opens between literal and figurative remembrance, the very gap that the hyper-realism of taxidermy endeavours to deny. Nevertheless, as Lorraine Daston has remarked, some things 'speak irresistibly, and not only by interpretation, projection, and puppetry. It is neither entirely arbitrary not entirely entailed which objects will become eloquent when, and in what cause. The language of things derives from certain properties of the things themselves, which suit the cultural purposes for which they are enlisted'.[4] Such animal-objects have become eloquent on the subject and indeed the subjectivity of the author as realized in writing.

Petrarch's cat

'Petrarch's cat' must be one of the most famous writer's pets in the world. It can be found in the house museum dedicated to Francesco Petrarch in the Euganean Hills at Arquà Petrarca, in northern Italy (Figure 2.1). This

Figure 2.1. Petrarch's cat, Casa Petrarca, Arquà. Author's own photograph

house has attracted tourists ever since Petrarch's death in 1374.[5] Invented and reinvented from the fourteenth century onwards as a site of literary pilgrimage, Petrarch's house is probably the oldest such writer's house extant in the world.[6]

Originally displayed freestanding on a classical plinth, this mummified cat was later set behind glass within an ornately grandiose late seventeenth-century baroque wall tablet. It was shown in one of the most important rooms of the house, Venus' room, so-called because a proud previous owner, Giovanni Battista Pellizari, decorated the room with murals featuring the goddess of love. The verse engraved on the stone frame reads, 'Etruscus gemino vates exarsit amore—/Maximis ignis ego, Laura secundus erat./ Quid rides? Divinae illam si gratia formae,/ Me dignam eximio fecit amante fides;/ Si numeros geniumque sacris dedit illa libellis,/ Causa ego ne saevis muribus esca forent./ Arcebam sacro vivens a limine mures,/ Ne domini exitio scripta diserta darem/ Incutio trepidis eadem defuncta pavorem,/ Et viget exanimi in corpore prisca fides'. This may be translated (loosely) as 'The Etruscan Bard burned with twin loves—I was the greater of his loves, Laura was only second-best. Why do you laugh? If it's all a matter of beauty and faithfulness, I should have made a superb lover. The Muse of Poetry offers no reason as to why I should not also eat mice. I guarded the sacred threshold from mice to prevent the frightful destruction of eloquent and inspired writings. I died, but life-like, my lifeless body is faithful to the end'.[7]

The cat is at once a real animal and a long-standing hoax. There was a long tradition of associating intellectuals with pet cats, in part, as the inscription above suggests, because of the necessity of preserving papers from the depredations of mice.[8] (My own cat is presently curled up inconveniently upon my working-notes.) This particular animal-object was a practical joke devised in 1635 by the then owner of the house, in reference to a famous picture depicting Petrarch in his study with his cat, and in response to Petrarch's continuing posthumous ability to attract possibly unwelcome and potentially gullible visitors to the building. It was, first of all, a sophisticated joke on the cultural investment in the rather notional love of Petrarch for the ever unattainable and unattained ideal Laura. A kitchen cat (by tradition and observation flea-bitten and promiscuous) is elevated to flattering comparison with another sort of female untouchability—the married aristocrat. The cat also puts the story of the origin of Petrarchan inspiration under stress. The inscription suggests that poetry is not so much a matter of burning passion conceived while wandering among the beautiful groves and springs of Vaucluse as hard grind at a desk supported by the unsung labour of domestic servants. Most pertinently here, the cat's body may be read as a joke at the expense of the cultural desire to possess and/or encounter the material traces of the author. It functions as a comic meditation on the desire to re-embody the now-disembodied—to re-body Petrarch. It therefore serves as a commentary on the long history of the fetishization of Petrarch's physical remains already touched upon in Chapter 1—the way his skull and bones have been subjected to disinterments, dismemberments, and evacuations.[9] Grotesque and magical, over-embodied, under-motivated, Petrarch's cat perfectly describes the problem of displaying the writer's body and by extension his house as the material condition of writing, commenting sardonically on sentimental investment in the writer's body. It is parodic of both biography and the notion of immortality lived out under the gaze of posterity. Second-best muse and dishonoured housekeeper, its femaleness also represents what the immortality of art supposedly discards: the material and domestic conditions of its making.

Nowadays, the poor cat has been demoted to the kitchen, suggesting not merely that it has been (re)discovered to be spurious, but that the scepticism its spuriousness embodies is no longer welcome. However, throughout the nineteenth century the cat seems to have been widely regarded as genuine. At all events, Teresa Guiccioli's detailed account of her visit in 1819 in company with her lover Byron suggests that it was integral to contemporary literary tourism, without suggesting that it was considered inauthentic.[10] It seems to have sat well within the bounds of sentimental plausibility for literary tourists as material evidence for Petrarch's enviable life of intellectual independence and domestic retirement, now looking like a version of new middle-class ideals of the genteel home, a space set aside as recreation from wealth-production. Pondering Petrarch's cat in its capacity as a nineteenth-century writer's house 'muse-um' in miniature (or, to borrow the spirit of the original jest, a mews-eum) reveals that it had by then come to function as much more than a joke. It served as a surrogate for Petrarch's body, speaking directly to the tourist regarding the poet's life, evoking and arguing for idealized domestic conditions of writing, and expressing and soothing anxiety about the fragility and mortality of paper as the material medium—indeed, the body—of conventionally immortal verse.

Cowper's hares

Olney in Buckinghamshire is marked as a writer's town by a weathervane in the Market Place depicting a quill-pen and a hare, both in silhouette. Although the quill might seem conventional enough, the hare, to those unfamiliar with the life and mythos of the poet William Cowper, might seem altogether more surprising. Through a door opening off the square, inside the house museum devoted to the memory of Cowper and his residence there between April 1773 and the end of 1786, the idiosyncrasy of that hare takes on more substance. A specimen of the taxidermist's art lollops neatly through a hole apparently especially cut through for the purpose between the kitchen and the hall. When I last visited it in September 2018, a volunteer had provided it with a drinking-bowl, and assigned it a name, Tiney.

At the naïvely biographical level, this hare refers to Cowper's particular fondness for the three male hares he acquired as leverets in 1774 and kept as pets until the death of the last in 1786. Puss, Bess, and Tiney formed an important part of his personal life, and make a number of appearances in his letters from Olney. A brief glimpse of Puss (so-called after the hunter's term for a hare) is afforded—'Herself, a House dog and a small Spaniel, were just now basking in the beams of our fire-side, very comfortably in a group'[11]— and Tiney's death was announced with a poetic epitaph.[12] The hares were part of the private sentimental language of his immediate circle, and would appear within the iconography of gifts exchanged between them. As an instance, Cowper received a gift of a snuffbox from his cousin and one-time fiancée Theadora Cowper with the three hares painted on its lid.[13] In Cowper's estimation this representation 'attended particularly to the characters of the three hares...One is sprightly, one is fierce, and one is gentle. The box has done me no small honour in the eyes of the 2 or 3 to whom I have shown it'.[14] The hares also became part of his public mythos; and the extent to which this was so from quite early on is revealed in the first instance by the existence of a seal fob which once belonged to Theadora's sister, Lady Harriot Hesketh, which also depicts the hares. Displayed nowadays in the museum, it is an expensive trifle, consisting of three chalcedony seals, each carved with the name and image of one of the three hares: as Nicola Durbridge describes them,

> The hares have been designed to look pretty much alike: they crouch on the ground apparently grazing grass. But they are named and the stones chosen to depict each one is a different colour to distinguish them further. Bess is carved from bloodstone, that is to say, from a green jasper flecked with red; the red spots are traces of iron. Tiney appears on a rich brown carnelian—the colouring here is again due to trace amounts of iron. Puss is depicted in grey chalcedony...[15]

This fob was given to Lady Hesketh by Princess Elizabeth, the daughter of George III and Queen Charlotte, with whom she had apparently become acquainted at Weymouth. As Durbridge notes, 'For such a gift to have been made, Harriot must have...regaled her at some point with stories of Cowper's domesticated hares'.[16] That the Princess should have made such a gift suggests not merely the intimacy between the two women but also the contemporary attractiveness of the whole idea of being at home with Cowper and his hares.

These days, that idea remains attractive enough to warrant the foregrounding of the hares within the Cowper and Newton Museum. Of the smallish, squarish hole cut in the wall between kitchen and hall with the hare leaping through it, the museum guide remarks: 'The hole is unlikely to have served as a hare passageway in Cowper's day…—it may merely have been intended as a window for light and heat to pass from the kitchen fire into the hall. But…the hall was the hares' indoor resting place and home and this is what the leaping hare commemorates'.[17] It is rare to come across such an explicit description of how a writer's house museum has chosen to realize biography through creative fictionalization of place. Like Petrarch's cat, Cowper's hare did exist; like Petrarch's cat also, this hare is a real animal-object; and as with Petrarch's cat, these are not the remains of the actual animal. However, unlike Petrarch's cat, this exercise in taxidermy is not a hoax, but an admitted representation; and the placement of it in this pose partakes of the downright mythic. Clearly in this case the physical authenticity of the animal-object itself is not precisely the point.

So what is being represented here, exactly, and why is it represented thus? Of course, the stuffed hare stands for Puss, Tiney, and Bess, but this is only to beg the question of what they represented for Cowper's admirers after his, and their, deaths. 'Cowper's hares' were famous throughout the nineteenth and well into the early twentieth century; one might cite as an example a single title, J. Walter West's *Cowper and His Hares* (1904). This fame depended upon four texts. The first was Cowper's long autobiographical letter-essay, published in *The Gentleman's Magazine* in June 1784, in which he described how he came by his pet hares as leverets and how he took them on as a project with a view to curing a bout of the severe depression to which he was subject: he hoped, in rearing them, 'I should find just the sort of employment which my case required'.[18] Part of the appeal of this essay lay in the detail of the habits and diet of the hare generally, and part lay in the description of the different personalities of the untameable Tiney, the gentle Puss, and the courageous Bess. Part of its interest for contemporaries must also have been its then eccentric repudiation of country sports such as hare coursing. Most pertinently here, it provided a beguiling glimpse of a household in which the hares largely lived indoors ('In the daytime they had the range of a hall, and at night retired each to his own bed, never intruding into that of another') and were admitted to the parlour after supper: 'when the carpet afforded their feet a firm hold, they would frisk and bound and play a thousand gambols'.[19] Cowper's essay evoked a Rousseauistic idyll of animal–human equality and sociability; caged birds, a cat, a spaniel, three hares, and a poet living together in mutual domesticated harmony:

I cannot conclude, Sir, without informing you that I have lately introduced a dog to his [Puss's] acquaintance, a spaniel that had never seen a hare to a hare that had never seen a spaniel. I did it with great caution, but there was no real need of it. Puss discovered no token of fear, nor Marquis [Cowper's spaniel] the least symptom of hostility. There is therefore, it should seem, no natural antipathy between dog and hare, but the pursuit of the one occasions the flight of the other, and the dog pursues because he is trained to it: they eat bread at the same time out of the same hand, and are in all respects sociable and friendly.[20]

This letter attracted much interest and admiration over the years of the nineteenth century, when the vogue for keeping pets, including those animals now regarded as wild (such as squirrels) or exotics (such as monkeys), reached new heights amongst a wider section of the population, especially within cities.[21] By the mid-nineteenth century, according to Hannah Velten, vendors in London were selling (in addition to exotics) 'white and yellow mice' and cats, 'owls, hedgehogs, larks, thrushes, blackbirds, rabbits, jackdaws, snails, snakes, hawks, pigeons, turtle doves, starlings, squirrels, guinea pigs...and freshwater and marine fish', all to be kept as pets by persons of all ages and classes.[22] (Velten's list has some explanatory power for the hedgehog in the kitchen of 48 Doughty St, while making it plain that it will have been to some degree a servant's pet.) Reflecting on his boyhood education, the philosopher John Stuart Mill noted that 'nothing in the two volumes [of Cowper's writings] interested me like the prose account of his three hares'.[23]

Cowper's essay was supplemented by the publication in *The Gentleman's Magazine* of December 1784 of his poetic epitaph for Tiney. This reiterated the hare's affective and familiar relationship with the poet:

> I kept him for old Service sake,
> For he would oft beguile
> My heart of thoughts that made it ach [*sic*],
> And force me to a smile.[24]

This poem described the domestic interior as a sanctuary for the wild animal ('His frisking was at Evening hours,/For then he lost his fear') and yet as wilded by the hare at play: 'A Turkey carpet was his lawn,/Whereon he loved to bound'.[25]

In these two published letters, the hares collated a set of meanings that included sentimental sociability, rural retirement as a rejection of the city, and progressive domesticity; when Cowper published his major poem *The Task* in the following year, 1785, the effect was to render the hare a figure for himself as man and as poet. As Baird and Ryskamp point out, as confessedly 'the product of leisure and a record of the thoughts provoked by the situation and the turn of mind of the writer', *The Task* foregrounded the figure of the author:

> Whereas many earlier poets had written about themselves in such a way that the speaker of the poem overlaps in some degree with the historical personality of the author, Cowper was the first to write a long poem which depends entirely upon the mental experience of the speaker, while asserting that the speaker is wholly one with the historical personality of the author.[26]

Book III of *The Task*, 'The Garden', draws an implied comparison between Cowper's own self-defensive retreat as a 'self-sequester'd man' and the sanctuary his pet hare has found in his home:[27]

> They love the country, and none else, who seek
> For their own sake its silence and its shade.
> Delights which who would leave, that has a heart
> Susceptible of pity, or a mind
> Cultured and capable of sober thought,
> For all the savage din of the swift pack
> And clamours of the field? Detested sport,
> That owes its pleasures to another's pain,
> That feeds upon the sobs and dying shrieks
> Of harmless nature, dumb, but yet endued
> With eloquence that agonies inspire
> Of silent tears and heart-distending sighs!
> Vain tears alas! and sighs that never find
> A corresponding tone in jovial souls.
> Well—one at least is safe. One shelter'd hare
> Has never heard the sanguinary yell
> Of cruel man, exulting in her woes.
> Innocent partner of my peaceful home,
> Whom ten long years experience of my care
> Has made at last familiar, she has lost
> Much of her vigilant instinctive dread,
> Not needful here, beneath a roof like mine.
> Yes—thou may'st eat thy bread, and lick the hand
> That feeds thee; thou may'st frolic on the floor
> At evening, and at night retire secure
> To thy straw-couch, and slumber unalarm'd.
> For I have gain'd thy confidence, have pledg'd
> All that is human in me, to protect
> Thine unsuspecting gratitude and love.

> If I survive thee I will dig thy grave,
> And when I place thee in it, sighing say,
> I knew at least one hare that had a friend.[28]

The intimate and parallel relation between the poet's mortal body and that of the hare is still more sharply drawn in the Latin epitaph Cowper wrote for Tiney, '*EPITAPHIUM ALTERUM*':Hic etiam jacet/Qui totum novennium vixit/Puss./Siste paulisper/Qui praeteriturus es,/Et tecum sic repute—/Hunc neque canis venaticus/Nec plumbum missile/Nec imbres nimii/Confecere/Tamen mortuus est—/Et moriar ego. ['Here Puss still rests, after nine whole years of life. Stay a while, you who would pass by, and thus reflect: no huntsman's hound, no leaden ball, no snare, no drenching downpour, brought about his end—yet he is dead, and I too shall die'.][29]

The loose and episodic structure of *The Task* meant that it was easy to excerpt passages and weave them together with other poems, letters, and biographical anecdote. William Hayley's three-volume *The Life and Posthumous Writings of William Cowper* (1803) gives the hares some prominence in the table of contents for volume 1 ('His tame Hares one of his first amusements on his revival [from severe depression])',[30] commenting further that 'These interesting animals had not only the honour of being cherished and celebrated by a Poet, but the pencil has also contributed to their renown; and their portraits . . . may serve as a little embellishment to this Life of their singularly tender and benevolent protector'.[31] The 'embellishment', executed by William Blake as a tail-piece to the last volume, consists of Cowper's 'Motto on a Clock', below which the 'weather-house' mentioned in Book 1 of *The Task* appears, with the muffled-up man representing bad weather with whom Cowper identifies in lines 112–13: 'Fearless of humid air and gathering rains/Forth steps the man, an emblem of myself'. Below again is a tiny representation of the cottage called 'the Peasant's Nest' described in *The Task*, and below that again the three hares variously bounding and couched, clearly adapted from Cowper's snuffbox, and captioned 'Cowper's tame Hare's [*sic*]'. The stated purpose of the volume was to raise funds for a memorial to Cowper in London.[32] Given that the engraving is designed as a proto-memorial to Cowper, it would suggest that anecdotes and illustrations of his hares had already come to be a prominent part of Cowper's posthumous mythos, constructing him as variably gentle, sprightly, and wild, at once domesticated and undomesticated.

Inauthentic though the stuffed hare is, it had a precursor of impeccable provenance. Although none of Cowper's hares were stuffed, one of his spaniels was, and was subsequently displayed in a glass case at the museum when it first opened in 1900. The same conflation between author, pet, house, and domestic pursuits is argued by the frontispiece to one edition of *The Rural Walks of Cowper* (c. 1825) which depicts the spaniel in a glass case with a rose held in its mouth below a silhouette of Cowper's head 'from his shadow taken at Olney'.[33] The spaniel was at some juncture found to be mouldering, retired from display, and lost.[34] While it is possible to imagine that the spaniel might not have been to modern taste, and would have been impossible to replace, given that this was sentimental taxidermy, its significance for Cowper's memory has also been overtaken by that of the hare. The stuffed hare in the museum at Olney is not the only one within the museum; bronze and wicker sculptures of hares are scattered throughout the garden, and in the gift-shop you can buy hares as jewellery and bric-a-brac. The hare references events in Cowper's life and passages in his writings, but above all embodies his distinctive authorial mythos of personal vulnerability safely sequestered within an idyllic domesticity. There is a Romantic statement at work here, a statement of the wildness, shyness, and only partially tamed, partly domesticated nature of writer and writings. Conjecturally, this is what is really on offer in this museum: a seductive and largely unattainable paradigm of the fully expressive life of the modern subject.

Poe's raven

If both Petrarch's cat and Cowper's hare came to embody the country poet for the metropolitan middle-class elite, Poe's raven describes how an animal-object can function both to delineate and to blur the relation between writer and writing and between biography and fiction. Its physical reality has been successively reallocated. It began death as a biographical meme associated with Dickens, shifted to a fictional meme associated with Dickens' works, transformed into a fictional meme associated with the writings of Edgar Allan Poe, and so, finally closing the circuit, morphed into a biographical meme associated with Poe's life. This is the strange story of how 'Dickens' raven' became 'Poe's raven'; how a long-dead pet took flight from London and fetched up in Philadelphia to become an American literary landmark. It exemplifies the variable ways in which an animal-object can remember not just the biographical but the literary; and the ways in which, and reasons why, the writer's belongings can be re-designated.

Perhaps I should say from the outset that the story of Poe's raven involves pursuing a surprising plethora of actual ravens. The first is to be found in the current presentation of the Charles Dickens Museum, 48 Doughty Street, London, in the attic. This attic is themed to childhood and parenthood, displaying objects dating from c. 1790–1854, covering the lifetime of Dickens' parents, his own childhood, and Dickens' own role as a parent. Hanging on the chimney-breast is a large, circular sketch of Dickens' four children made in September 1841 on the eve of his departure with his wife Catherine on his first tour of America. It was something for the couple to take with them for the four to five months Dickens expected to be away from home, and thus away from the children. Made by Dickens' long-time friend, the painter Daniel Maclise, it shows the four children, including the just-born baby. It also depicts, perched in the right-hand quadrant, a large black raven, identified as 'Grip II'. To the right of this picture is a wall-mounted glass-case, containing a stuffed raven. The caption reads: 'RAVEN' and goes on to explain that this stuffed raven belonged to popular Dickens character-actor Bransby Williams (1870–1961), that Williams' interest in ravens probably stemmed from his knowledge of Dickens' pet birds, and describes how Dickens, 'shortly after leaving Doughty Street', acquired a pet raven, upon whose antics and accomplishments he based Grip, the raven in his novel *Barnaby Rudge*, how on the death of this raven Dickens had acquired a second raven, and how 'The first raven was stuffed…and now resides in the Free Library in Philadelphia' (Figure 2.2).[35]

The raven displayed is therefore (unlike Cowper's hare) a particular creature with a documented history of belonging to someone, even if it was certainly not Dickens.[36] A real creature, with a defined individual identity, its own identity is nonetheless not what it here portrays. In that sense it is indeed a character-actor, much like its original owner. What then, is the performance that this raven is putting on? It is, first of all, giving scale and presence to the raven in Maclise's sketch, 'Grip II', and in so doing giving material reality to the history of the child-lives of the nursery in much the same way as the abacus and the card-game scattered on the nursery chair are designed to do. Although there is a fair amount of evidence that ravens were considered suitable pets for children in the Victorian period,[37] Dickens' letters make plain that his pet ravens did not frequent the nursery but lived largely in the garden and the stable-block, with occasional forays into his study, and indeed that the children were less than enthusiastic about the raven, 'which bit their ankles'.[38] One might conjecture that curatorial tact

Figure 2.2. Grip the raven. © Rare Book Department, Philadelphia Free Library

demanded that because this object is *not* what Dickens called 'THE Raven' it should be featured more as children's pet rather than literary inspiration.

This raven, or rather 'THE Raven' for which he serves as body-double, is celebrated because of the place that Dickens gave his pet ravens within his life and imagination. Dickens owned three ravens; the first was called Grip, but we have no record of names for the other two.[39] His letters make it plain that Grip and his doings and sayings served as a source of amusement within his circle of young male friends.[40] Grip's death, which Dickens attributed first to poisoning by an aggrieved butcher, then to influenza, and finally to ingesting 'a pound or two of white lead' paint, occasioned an elaborate account to Maclise in a letter of 12 March 1841 which he enclosed in an envelope embellished with an enormous black mourning seal. It spoofs accounts of family deaths familiar from Victorian letters—'Towards eleven o'clock he was so much worse that it was found necessary to muffle the knocker'—and elicited responses in similarly jocular vein.[41] At Dickens' request Maclise forwarded the letter to their mutual friend John Forster, with additional sketches: 'At the foot of the note is the raven (very black) lying dead on a rectangular slab; from it rises a white raven with eyes upturned. At the head of the note three white ravens, with legs folded across their breasts, look down through clouds... In the left margin Forster has written "apotheosis"'.[42] Maclise's reply to Dickens casts the raven as a suicidal character in the mode of a Byronic hero or Walter Scott's Master of Ravenswood. Dickens would also send similar accounts over the next few months to Thomas Latimer, Basil Hall, Angela Burdett-Coutts, and Angus Fletcher, mentioning his intention of having his pet stuffed: 'The Raven's body was removed with every regard for my feelings, in a covered basket. It was taken off to be stuffed, but has not come home yet'.[43] He mentions, too, that he has a new raven but by June it had proved disappointingly to be 'of comparatively weak intellects',[44] and had been eclipsed by a third raven which gave entire satisfaction; Dickens exulted that

> Some friends in Yorkshire have sent me a raven, before whom *the* Raven (the dead one) sinks into insignificance. He can say anything—and he has a power of swallowing door-keys and reproducing them at pleasure, which fills all beholders with mingled sensations of horror and satisfaction—if I may say so; with a kind of awful delight. His infancy and youth have been passed at a country public house, and I am told that the sight of a drunken man calls forth his utmost powers. My groom is unfortunately sober...[45]

Dickens revelled in his outrageousness; 'Nothing delights him so much as a drunken man—he loves to see human Nature in a state of degradation, and to have the superiority of Ravens asserted. At such time he is *fearful* in his Mephistophelean humour' and 'Good God!—if you could only hear him talk, and see him break the windows! You will be glad to hear—I can only hint at his perfections—that he disturbs the church service, and that his life is threatened by the Beadle. Maclise says he *knows* that he can read and write. I quite believe it; and I go so far as to place implicit reliance on his powers of cyphering'.[46]

Dickens' pleasure in the raven—'sich [*sic*] a thorough going, long headed, deep, outdacious file'—may have derived from fellow-feeling with another anti-social, satirical humourist.[47] At all events, the pet raven and its doings were part of Dickens' self-projection and self-presentation for about four years. It would become associated with him in the public imagination for much longer owing to two decisions. The first was to have the raven stuffed and displayed in the hallway at Dickens' house at Gad's Hill. Combined with the various accounts given of Dickens' relationship with his ravens, notably that in John Forster's *Life* (1872–4) and Mamie Dickens' *My Father as I Recall Him* (1897), this made the raven part of Dickens' public persona.[48] The second was the inclusion of a raven based on Grip in his historical novel *Barnaby Rudge: A Tale of the Riots of 'Eighty*.[49] Appearing in weekly instalments in *Master Humphrey's Clock* between February and November 1841, this followed the adventures of Barnaby, 'a fantastic, half-crazed youth', and his pet raven Grip, 'sharpest and cunningest of all the sharp and cunning ones'.[50] The imaginative force of the pairing depends upon the innocence of Barnaby as contrasted with the comic but demonic force of his pet:

> '*I* make him come?' cried Barnaby, pointing to the bird. 'Him, who never goes to sleep, or so much as winks!—Why, any time of night, you may see his eyes in my dark room, shining like two sparks. And every night, and all night too, he's broad awake, talking to himself, thinking what he shall do tomorrow, where we shall go, and what he shall steal, and hide, and bury. *I* make *him* come! Ha ha ha!'[51]

The long-standing identification between Grip and Barnaby's raven in the public imagination rested principally on the preface Dickens provided to the first Cheap Edition in 1849 which noted that 'The raven in this story is a compound of two great originals, of whom I was, at different times, the proud possessor' and which provided accounts of the deaths of both at length.[52] As a result, the fictitious Grip came to feature prominently in tours of Dickensian fictional locations, including the village of Chigwell and its inn and churchyard.[53] In 1960, he was still recognizable enough to appear in the bas-relief of Dickensian characters installed on the Marylebone Road, London.[54]

The stuffed raven sold at the auction of Dickens' effects at Gad's Hill on 9 July 1870 therefore compounded two real birds and a fictional bird into a representation of Dickens and the Dickensian imagination. It was listed as 'Lot 76 Mr Dickens' Favourite Raven—in a glazed case. (The "Grip" of "Barnaby Rudge")'. It was knocked down to G.S. Nottage for £126.[55] By 1922 it was being listed in the sale of R.T. Jupp's collection as item 17: 'Charles Dickens' Raven, stuffed and mounted in a glass case, 27 × 25 inches, with rustic ornaments. Probably the most famous Bird in the World'.[56] It was famous enough to be bought in due course by a prominent Philadelphia-based collector of literary manuscripts and books, Colonel Richard A. Gimbel, who from his days as a student at Yale University to his death in 1970 poured a fortune amassed from his family's department-store profits into collecting manuscripts and books of special provenance relating to Charles Dickens,

Edgar Allan Poe, Thomas Paine, and aeronautica *inter alia*.[57] Part of Gimbel's collection of Dickens and Dickensiana, including Grip, is now housed and on display in the Rare Books Department of the Free Library of Philadelphia. That meant that in 1971 Grip caught up with Dickens' library desk from Gad's Hill, which had been acquired by another Philadelphia collector, William McIntyre Elkins, as the centre-piece of his collection and for use in his own library. On his death the collection, including the desk, was given to the Library on condition that the room be reconstructed in its entirety.

Removed from London to Philadelphia, the raven has increasingly come to be imagined more as belonging to Poe than Dickens. The ideological mechanism for this is made explicit by one of the four postcards put out by the Rare Books Department; the caption reads: 'Grip, the Raven, which belonged to Charles Dickens, resides in the Free Library of Philadelphia's Rare Book Department. Grip inspired Edgar Allen [*sic*] Poe to write the Raven'. This caption presents the key to the mystery of how Dickens' pet has progressively become Poe's raven in the popular imagination, and how something that once belonged in Britain can be imagined as belonging more appropriately in Philadelphia. This miniaturized narrative is driven by an implied hierarchy between merely 'belonging to' and 'inspiring', between biography and works of the imagination. Largely cutting out Dickens himself as a subject, and entirely erasing the older story of the raven as the inspiration for *Barnaby Rudge*, the raven here embodies a founding text of the American literary canon. The raven, the postcard blurb suggests, has chosen to 'reside' in the Library, exchanging his original owner for a new one. Thus it at once evidences the continuity of Anglophone culture in the nineteenth century, and asserts subsequent American superiority. As such, this animal-object may be viewed as paradigmatic of the entire nineteenth- and early twentieth-century project of founding American authorship through various systems of appropriation of British literary relics, manuscripts, and sites.[58]

The erasure of *Barnaby Rudge* here is the more striking given that for a long time it formed part of the mythology of the genesis of Poe's most famous poem. Poe read *Barnaby Rudge* and had reviewed it in the *Saturday Evening Post* of 1 May 1841, forecasting the outcome of the novel from the evidence of the first few chapters.[59] He had also remarked that, 'intensely amusing as it is', the character of the raven might have been more fully exploited: 'Its croakings might have been *prophetically* heard in the course of the drama'.[60] When Poe subsequently published his poem 'The Raven' in

1845, contemporaries identified it with *Barnaby Rudge*; this is in part the point of James Russell Lowell's hostile squib of 1848: 'There comes Poe with his raven, like Barnaby Rudge,/Three-fifths of him genius and two-fifths sheer fudge'.[61] The association with Dickens was given a little push by Poe's essay 'The Philosophy of Composition' (1846). This took 'The Raven' as a case-study to explain how a poem came into being, and began by citing a letter he had received from Dickens alluding to his review of *Barnaby Rudge*. Indeed, it would be possible to argue that the first appearance of Grip in Dickens' novel has more than a little in common with the first appearance of Poe's raven:

> 'Ah! He's a knowing blade!' said Varden, shaking his head, 'I should be sorry to talk secrets before him. Oh! He's a deep customer... What was that? Him tapping at the door?'
> 'No' returned the widow [Mrs Rudge]. 'It was in the street, I think. Hark! Yes. There again! 'Tis someone knocking softly at the shutter. Who can it be!'[62]

Tapping to gain entrance, the man subsequently revealed to be a murderer is mistaken for Grip.[63] The scene finds echoes in the opening of Poe's poem with the mysterious tapping, which the narrator half-thinks might be the ghost of his lover and actually turns out to be the raven. However, conjectural Dickensian inspiration is by no means the only or even the most important of the many stories that arose concerning the genesis of Poe's most popular and enduring poem. Indeed, Poe informs the reader in 'The Philosophy of Composition' that he first thought of a parrot to embody 'the idea of a non-reasoning creature capable of speech' before settling on a raven (thereby avoiding, mercifully, a potential crossover with another European novelist, Gustave Flaubert);[64] other contemporary sources suggest he may have begun with the idea of an owl.[65] Moreover, Poe had access to many other ideas and realities of ravens. Scholarship has variously advanced the possibilities that Poe saw a raven at the Tower of London or at Stoke Newington when he lived in England as a child between 1815 and 1820, or that he was inspired by his acquaintance Henry B. Hirst, 'a poet who kept a bird store and owned a raven'.[66]

The interest of these stories lies not so much in their plausibility or otherwise, but in their desire to identify a naturalistic original for the raven, despite the poem's emblematic rather than realistic mode.[67] The same impulse lies behind the persistent identification of the first person protagonist of the poem with Poe himself and (in flat disregard of chronological implausibility) its origin in Poe's grief over the loss of his young wife Virginia to consumption. Thus in the view of William F. Gill the poem was like the raven itself, an unsolicited and enigmatic visitant: 'in his silent vigils, enthralled by the imaginative ecstasy which often possessed and over-powered him, Poe conceived and wrought out this marvellous inspiration'.[68] Gill argued that the poem was founded in personal experience: 'with the added factor of some fugitive bird, or domestic pet (the Poes had many pets) breaking in upon his wild reveries with some slight interruption which the poet's distorted fancy exaggerated into some supernatural visitant, an adequate basis for his masterpiece is found'.[69] The famous last stanza brings the encounter between poet and bird into a perpetually freeze-framed present, reminiscent of and congruent with the pseudo-present of both taxidermy and museum:

> And the Raven, never flitting, still is sitting, *still* is sitting
> On the pallid bust of Pallas just above my chamber door;
> And his eyes have all the seeming of a demon's that is dreaming,
> And the lamp-light o'er him streaming throws his shadow on the floor;
> And my soul from out that shadow that lies floating on the floor
> Shall be lifted—nevermore!   (lines 103–8)

This tableau of 'Mournful and Never-Ending Remembrance' transfers read-ily to the cult of the domesticated author; but it is also a montage of writing as deriving from and functioning within a perpetual present.

The desire to find 'an adequate basis' for Poe's masterpiece has produced quite a rush of ravens. In 1908 the newly formed 'Raven Society' of the University of Virginia, at Charlottesville, celebrated the centenary of Poe's birth by opening the room in which Poe had resided during his brief and ill-starred career at the university between February and December 1826. No. 13 West Range was furnished with a 'settee' from his house in Richmond, and 'a real raven, stuffed, [which] looked down from a coign of the room'.[70] Through subsequent refurbishments (including the acquisition of Poe's bed) the stuffed raven has remained a constant, although successive photographs of the room betray its disconcerting mobility, flitting from mantelpiece to chest to bedside table.[71] Thus the opportunity provided by the actuality of Grip was an accident waiting to happen.

On Gimbel's death in 1970, he left his collection of Poe materials, together with the Poe house on N 7th St in which Poe had lived in 1843 and 1844 which he had acquired and refurbished in 1933, to the Free Library of Philadelphia. Grip formed part of the same bequest that included another of Gimbel's acquisitions, the only known entire manuscript in Poe's own hand of 'The Raven'. Inevitably, Grip has been pressed into service as the raven who, 'never flitting', sits alongside Poe's manuscript. The stuffed raven thus comes to be conceived as producing the text, as produced by it, and as thus emblematic of it. It functions to signify the material, temporal, and mortal ground of Poe's inspiration. Its uniqueness and its particular type of 'realness' usefully locates the poem to a place, specifically Philadelphia; and in connecting body to text, Grip turns the manuscript collection into something more like an extension to the Poe House Museum just down the road, nowadays marked by a vast sculpture of a raven installed in 1979.[72] No wonder, then, that Grip was designated as an American literary landmark in 1999 by the American Library Association.[73] It is an odd flight of fancy.

Sterne's starling

The smallish, darkish, panelled room in Shandy Hall looks out onto the road that runs down the hill and past the church in the Yorkshire village of Coxwold. This is the study of eighteenth-century cleric and novelist Laurence Sterne, ridged from ceiling to floor with caged bindings, a square table at its centre, strategically placed between the light from the window and the warmth from the hearth. Above the mantelpiece hangs a portrait of the author himself, marking his primacy in the making of the room's meanings, and just below him, to the right, perches a stuffed starling on a small branch, seeming, with cocked, sardonic head and arrestingly bead-bright black eyes, the very embodiment of the Sternean.

This stuffed bird is not in any simple sense 'Sterne's starling'. It does not make any of the same sort of (admittedly ambiguous) claims to underwrite that possessive as the other creatures I have been discussing. It is not an immortalized pet in the way that Petrarch's cat was supposed to be, or that Grip actually was. Nor is it a stand-in for a real long-dead and vanished pet, in the way that the stuffed hare displayed in William Cowper's house is. Its affinities lie more with the idea of Poe's raven, in that it is generated in the first instance by literary rather than biographical text. It is in fact authored by Sterne.

Like Cowper's hare, the starling's actuality is thoroughly anachronistic—this bird escaped in company with a whole murmuration of stuffed Victorian starlings from any number of disbanded nineteenth-century natural history collections around the country. Glossy and speckled, or moulting and broken-legged, they whirl together nowadays through the ethereal spaces of eBay. This specimen came to rest in Shandy Hall along with many more as part of an imaginative exhibition that the curator, Patrick Wildgust, put together in 2006. 'A Bitter Draught: the Starling and Slavery' used a display of stuffed starlings to materialize and dramatize an influential late eighteenth-century metaphor for slavery, a metaphor born in a famous passage, much quoted and excerpted, from Sterne's best-seller and subsequent classic, *A Sentimental Journey Through France and Italy* (1768). Sojourning in wartime Paris, Sterne's alter ego the narrator 'Mr Yorick' finds himself without a personal passport, and so in some danger of incarceration in the Bastille. He is interrupted while comforting himself as best he can with the thought that 'the Bastile [*sic*] is but another word for a tower—and a tower is but another word for a house you can't get out of' by 'a voice which I took to be of a child which complained "it could not get out"'. This proves to be the voice of a starling 'hung in a little cage', which repeats an English language phrase incessantly:

> 'I can't get out', said the starling—God help thee! said I, but I'll let thee out, cost what it will; so I turn'd about the cage to get at the door; it was twisted and double twisted so fast with wire, there was no getting it open without pulling the cage to pieces—I took both hands to it...'I fear, poor creature!' said I, 'I cannot set thee at liberty'—'No' said the starling—'I can't get out—I can't get out', said the starling.[74]

This encounter overthrows Yorick's 'systematic reasonings upon the Bastile' and prompts him more generally to meditate on the evils of slavery:[75] 'Disguise thyself as thou wilt, still slavery! said I—still thou art a bitter draught; and though thousands in all ages have been made to drink of thee, thou art no less bitter on that account'.[76]

This particular starling is the last of the flock of 2006, but, saved to perch solitary on the mantelpiece of Sterne's study, it has since then begun to develop a rather different affective power and set of meanings. It continues to reference and materialize *A Sentimental Journey*, at least for those who are familiar with the novel, but its singularity also activates some of the other meanings carried by the starling in Sterne's text. 'The bird in his cage' prompts Yorick to meditate on captivity in general, voices English notions of liberty which are equally uncomprehended in Paris and amongst the political aristocracy of London, serves as a double for him as Englishman abroad, is bought by him and brought back to England as a pet, and ultimately perches as crest to Sterne's own heraldic shield. This heraldic device, which puns on the similarity between Sterne's name and the Latin name for a star-ling, is illustrated within the text.[77] Of this possible array of meanings offered by the text, the solitary starling sitting on the study mantelpiece privileges its identification with the author's self-representations, an identification reinforced by a nearby uncaptioned skull which composes an elaborately casual still-life with an hourglass and a stuffed wren, in allusion to the fam-ous engraving of Yorick/Sterne in conversation with the figure of Death, which itself hangs above the mantelpiece.

The starling has also served as a figure for Sterne's writing. When William Howitt recorded his visit to Coxwold to see 'the same pulpit in the church where Sterne preached' and the 'small room, in which Sterne is said to have written', he referenced the starling as a trope for the power of Sterne's writ-ing.[78] In the church, Howitt's attention was attracted by the predicament of 'a solitary swallow, which was flitting about, and giving an occasional twitter as it sought a way out…there was no way for it to escape, and I immedi-ately thought of Sterne's starling, which was always plaintively crying "I can't get out"'.[79] He records his efforts to persuade the sexton to open a window to help it escape, and the sexton's baffled response—'oh, it will die of itself, if we let it alone'. Howitt is driven to indignant reflection upon the moral inefficacy of Sterne's writings on 'the sufferings of animals' in the immedi-ate proximity of the place they were conceived:

> And that was in Sterne's church, in the very front of his pulpit, not very many yards from the place where he probably penned that very pathetic incident of the starling, with its cry, so full of pitiful appeal, 'I can't get out! I can't get out!'…Who could have believed that such an incident could possibly have happened, where Sterne had penned those words which have thrilled so many a youthful bosom, never again to be forgotten?[80]

Although Howitt starts with a real bird, he repeatedly references it to the 'penned' fiction, mentally placing the 'incident of the starling' within the 'small room, where Sterne is said to have written'. As such, his evocation of the starling is a precursor to the one presently perching on the mantelpiece. Uncaged, it functions as a form of extra-illustration to the sentimental argu-ment of the text. Its physical reality in twenty-first-century space directs us back to the eighteenth-century book; its muteness requires the 'voice' sup-plied by memory of the text. Rather than making a claim to materializing the biographical origin of writing, the bird's body points to its origin *in* and *from* the act of writing. And indeed, as Howitt's prose also suggests, its origin in acts of reading and of remembered reading awaiting reanimation within the reader's body—in the never-forgotten thrill in 'the youthful bosom'.

This effect is already predicted and prescribed by *A Sentimental Journey*. What Sterne says of the bird's repeated phrase—'Mechanical as the notes were, yet . . . true in tune to nature were they chanted'—may also be applied to Sterne's mass-produced book and its effect on the reader. Sterne's account of the circulation of the starling on his return to London might just as well be an account of the circulation of *A Sentimental Journey*:

> . . . telling the story of him to Lord A—Lord A begg'd the bird of me—in a week Lord A gave him to Lord B—Lord B made a present of him to Lord C—and Lord C's gentleman sold him to Lord D for a shilling—Lord D gave him to Lord E—and so on—half around the alphabet . . .[81]

Like the starling, the book can only repeat itself over and over again; the sentiment requires to be pointed by each new reader, at each new encounter, and for each new occasion, and its value will fluctuate accordingly. Moreover, although the starling is set up as a celebrated and unique body, it is promptly undercut as such; like a book, a bird whose celebrity consists in repeating a single phrase may itself be re-represented, re-illustrated, pirated, plagiarized, or provided with a sequel by another hand, as Sterne's works notoriously were:

> It is impossible but many of my readers must have heard of him; and if any by mere chance have ever seen him—I beg leave to inform them, that that bird was my bird—or some vile copy set up to represent him.[82]

The Coxwold starling is indeed 'some vile copy set up to represent him', but as with the 'vile copy' Sterne imagines, this pays tribute to the starling's celebrity, and thus is precisely appropriate. Even its muteness and modernity are appropriate, for this bird's body is, surprisingly, all about the fate of authorial voice once it has flown into circulation as print. At the same time, however, perched within Sterne's study, it argues for voice and body as the origin of the book.

Dickinson's hummingbirds

In 2010 the photographer Annie Leibovitz paid a visit to the Emily Dickinson Museum in Amherst, Massachusetts. Out of that trip she put together a book of photographs and accompanying text, which she published subsequently as *Pilgrimage* (2011). This was in part an elegy for her recently dead lover,

Susan Sontag, and, in larger perspective, a virtual museum composed of iconic images derived from meditating upon the nature and power of famous sites and objects, many of them literary, that found the geography of American cultural consciousness. Almost the first photograph in the book is a full-page plate showing in extreme close-up a large Victorian glass dome filled with small, brilliantly feathered birds, including five hummingbirds poised as though in flight. The explanation offered within the caption for the inclusion of these birds within Leibovitz's virtual museum is puzzlingly unhelpful:

> Life in the Dickinson family was complicated by the fact that Austin Dickinson [ED's brother] had a lover, Mabel Loomis Todd. After Emily died, Todd edited her poems and oversaw their publication. She also founded the Amherst Historical Society in 1899 and arranged for a friend of hers to leave her eight-eenth-century house to the Amherst History Museum. A vitrine with stuffed birds from the former owner is in the museum's Todd Room.[83]

This case of birds thus belonged neither to Dickinson nor her family, has never been on display within either of the Dickinson houses, and within the Amherst History Museum functions purely as 'period' marker of local and social history made the more potent by modern unease and fascination in the face of taxidermy as an aesthetic that definitively belongs to the past. Despite all this, the stuffed birds are here constructed by Leibovitz as part of a larger meditation upon Dickinson's life and works. The case of birds appears as a component of a terse and riddling poetic statement in the mode of Dickinson herself, composed otherwise of an opening photograph of a windowless Victorian interior of suffocating respectability, and a closing image of Dickinson's life—led eventually in extreme seclusion, a form of personal erasure, written out in tiny poems recording intense emotion in the finest detail—provided through the camera's insistence on the intricacies of the white-on-white embroidery of the dress-panel that would have covered Dickinson's heart. What, then, is this case of silent and stilled birds being made to say about Dickinson? In what ways (to invoke Lorraine Daston again) does what it has to say derive 'from certain properties of the things themselves' and how does this suit 'the cultural purposes for which they are enlisted'?[84]

One might perhaps begin again with Victorian taxidermy, and more specifically with the Victorian passion for collecting and displaying humming-birds as 'bijouterie' described by both Judith Pascoe and Rachel Poliquin, to the extent that many well-to-do domestic interiors might boast such a vitrine as this one.[85] The oddity of such vitrines is that although they aspire to a lifelikeness composed within formalized naturalism, they actually achieved something impossibly unlifelike: only taxidermy could make the tiny hummingbird visible to the inspection of the human eye as more (or less) than a rapidly moving blur of jewel-like colour.[86] This vitrine was in a sense a precursor to freeze-frame photography. The price of visibility, however, was in this instance particularly explicit: death. The case references despite its best efforts the unattainability of the hummingbird, the impossibility of rendering naturalistically wings 'so rapid in motion, that it is impossible to discern their colours, except by their glittering'[87] or 'the humming noise' 'which proceeds entirely from the surprising velocity with which they perform that motion by which they will keep their bodies in the air, apparently motionless, for hours together'[88] or preserving over time the colours that gave them their species names—'garnets, rubies, sapphire-wings, sun-gems, sparkling-tails, emeralds, and brilliants'.[89] As Pascoe puts it, for nineteenth-century culture 'the hummingbird stationed in flight evoked a resplendent beauty of the most romantically unattainable kind'; the vitrine could only indicate this vision.[90]

Referenced to Dickinson, those hummingbirds take on specificity. Leibovitz's riddle invokes a poem Dickinson originally wrote for a church bazaar as a 'charade', known nowadays by its first line, 'A Route of Evanescence'. In its entirety, it reads:

> **A Route of Evanescence**
> With a revolving Wheel—[renewing/delusive/dissembling/dissolving]
> A Resonance of Emerald—
> A Rush of Cochineal—
> And every Blossom on the Bush
> Adjusts it's [sic] tumbled Head—
> The Mail from Tunis, probably,
> An easy Morning's ride.

The solution was 'A Humming-bird'. Dickinson sent this verse in several variants to a number of friends; this was sufficiently unusual to have prompted the suggestion that it became for her something of a 'calling-card'.[91] Subsequently, it has become one of Dickinson's paradigmatic poems, famous enough to be rewritten, as for instance by Agha Shahid Ali in his elegy for an ex-lover in 'A Nostalgist's Map of America' (1991) and to serve as a point of reference in a poem of 2001 by Jonathan Safran Foer.[92]

For Dickinson, the advent of hummingbirds from Mexico meant the arrival of spring.[93] So far, so conventional, and so suitable for a church bazaar. But the hummingbird also imaged intimate encounter in her writings. It could, for instance, figure conversation:

Dear Mrs Flint
You and I, didn't finish talking. Have you room for the sequel . . .
All the letters I could write,
Were not fair as this—
Syllables of Velvet—
Sentences of Plush—
Depths of Ruby, undrained—
Hid, Lip, for Thee,
Play it were a Humming Bird
And sipped just Me—[94]

Other evocations of encounters with the hummingbird are strikingly sexualized, even when Dickinson is writing to a girl of seven: 'How is your garden—Mary? Are the Pinks true—and the Sweet Williams faithful? I've got a Geranium like a Sultana—and when the Humming-birds come down—Geranium and I shut our eyes—and go far away'.[95]

The two meanings, the arrival of spring and intimate encounter, inform the figuration of the hummingbird as a letter arriving by mail-coach down the post-road, at a speed that makes it all but invisible and which brings it from impossibly far away. Christopher Benfey speculates that Dickinson's fondness for the poem was because it was about 'the miracle of mail for her' because it was 'her major way of "publishing" her poetry to her intimate circle of readers. Letters themselves were like migrating birds, humming with words'.[96] Certainly, the eroticism of the evanescing, resonating rush of encounter as the hummingbird leaves the blossoms 'tumbled' is reinforced by the reference to 'mail from Tunis' which invokes the offstage Claribel of Shakespeare's *The Tempest*:

> She that is Queen of Tunis; she that dwells
> Ten leagues beyond man's life; she that from Naples
> Can have no note, unless the sun were post—
> The man i' th' moon's too slow—[97]

Dickinson's insistence on evanescent encounter as the principal quality of the hummingbird animates an earlier poem of 1862, a whimsical colloquy between poet and dog on whether they had really seen the hummingbird 'Or bore the Garden in the Brain/This Curiosity—', a question resolved by the evidence of the 'just vibrating Blossoms!'[98] Combined with her poetic aesthetic of gap, ellipsis, and riddle expressed typographically by blanks, ruptures, and white spaces, it makes responding to Dickinson's charming invitation to 'accept a Humming-bird' through an encounter with a photograph of a case of stuffed hummingbirds all the more problematic; this is not a simple matter of extra-illustration.

However uncannily literalist the discourse of stuffed hummingbirds in lifelike poses beneath glass might seem to be, and wherever the emphasis falls within this constellation of possible readings of them as 'Dickinson's', the birds are as metaphorical and allegorical as those in Dickinson's own poetic discourse. Leibovitz's enigmatic photograph evokes Dickinson's tiny, occasional poems, glittering with dashes and darting with exotic punctuation, poems that were always much more body than print, hand-sewn together in little hand-written books now known as 'fascicles', or sent as enclosures within letters. The re-imagining of this vitrine by Leibovitz provides a study in how animal-objects can develop new meanings and new life depending not just on their provenance, but also on how they are re-represented. The photograph effectively describes the work of the actual writer's house museum just down the road as a sort of taxidermy. The vitrine displays, as if still alive, things that have been alive, even though they are now dead. As such, it has all the qualities of the writer's house museum: its uncanny and nauseating lifelikeness, coupled with its nagging, disavowed knowledge that everything displayed is only a representation of text. Leibovitz's verdict upon domesticity as the condition of poetic text is, however, notably critical compared to the treatment of domesticity in the cases of Petrarch and Cowper; here the retirement of the poet looks much more like imprisonment. But, while Sterne's house homes the body of the wild starling as the origin of Yorick's fantastical writings, Leibowitz's decision to depict a glass dome full of hummingbirds situated in the Todd room of the Amherst Local History Museum celebrates more than the author. It celebrates the work of the editor, all but invisible in the writer's house museum. That glass dome is pressed into service here to describe the work of Mabel Loomis Todd in preserving, editing, and publishing Dickinson's tiny, brilliant, hummingbird verses. It describes the editor of literary remains as a taxidermist.

Dickens' hedgehog

With which thought, back to the kitchen of 48 Doughty Street and that hedgehog, which, like all these other animal-objects, is to be treated with epistemological caution, as one tourist recognized when she carefully captioned her photograph: 'Stuffed hedgehog in the kitchen. (In Victorian times it would have been a live hedgehog.)'[99] The museum named the hedgehog Bill Spikes, and it was placed in the museum as part of the bicentenary renovation in 2012 in an effort to appeal to younger audiences and render the museum experience more interactive. Of course, it is thoroughly disingenuous to call it 'Dickens' hedgehog'—of all the animal-objects discussed here, in and out of writer's house museums, this is much the least motivated by the writer or his writings. This hedgehog, however, may prove my point: it remains 'a' hedgehog, not in any sense 'the' hedgehog; the cultural notion of a hedgehog does not match our sense of Dickens; in all his writings Dickens hardly so much as mentions a hedgehog.[100] It is not, to adopt a more modern imaginative terminology, a plausible daemon or avatar. Accordingly, it is alone among the animal-objects discussed here in being more cute than unnerving.[101] It is not so much troublingly excessive in its bodiliness as simply surplus to requirements. In this, it is like the stuffed owl that sits in the Old Manse in Concord which could be 'Hawthorne's owl' but simply is not because it does not plausibly set or solve the critical riddle, the riddle of the relation between the lived body and the lifelike written.[102]

By contrast, the animal-objects I have been looking at claim to be 'the' creature, particularized, with greater or lesser levels of plausibility and stability, to an author and/or their *oeuvre*. Conceptually fragmentary, even if they are apparently physically entire, they draw attention to themselves as the text's excess; that is to say, as being the abjected material ground of that strange and ghostly thing we call 'text' for short. They allegorize the author, as we call that lifelikeness produced by the text's operations within the reader. Thus what Poliquin calls the 'impoverished yet resolute immortality' of the taxidermic specimen with its 'strange duality of presence and absence' perfectly embodies the discomforting dead-aliveness of the author and their works performed by the writer's house museum for the literary tourist.[103] Perhaps it is only a matter of time before 'Keats' nightingale' is retrieved from the forlorn lands of internet secondhand sales to perch on the mantelpiece of the room in Hampstead in which he scribbled down his Ode. After all, Philip Larkin's famous but entirely textual toad, his metaphor for the unwelcome pressure of work, having first materialized on his desk in the shape of a ceramic tribute from an admiring reader, recently multiplied into forty toads, colonizing the city of Hull like a plague to celebrate the twenty-fifth and thirtieth anniversaries of Larkin's death in 2010 and 2015 respectively.[104]

Animal-objects within the writer's house museum serve as lifelike surrogates and placeholders for the authorial body, conceived as a volatile mix of biography and literary text. Chapter 3 considers the ways that items of clothing displayed within the writer's house museums serve in like manner to 'body forth' authorial consciousness.[105]

3

Clothing

Brontë's bonnet and Dickinson's dress

Christie's wardrobe

On the first floor of Greenway, the house once owned by Agatha Christie and now cared for as a museum to her memory by the National Trust, the visitor comes across a small room, Christie's dressing-room, off the master bedroom.[1] Safely protected from curious fingers, a fitted wardrobe crammed with sumptuous occasion and evening wear—dresses, furs, ball gowns, and hats—meets the eye. This is shown as evidence of the wealth and social prominence Christie's writing brought her. The clothes that the Queen of Crime once wore prove worthy of any of the many expensively dressed film adaptations made of her fictions as they have slid from contemporaneity into period pieces. Although items of writers' clothing are characteristically scattered throughout writer's house museums, Christie's wardrobe is pretty much unique in the statements it makes about the writer's clothes; these are confined to claiming that these were her clothes, that they evidence wealth and success and Christie's liking for good clothes, and that nonetheless they (and she) were characteristic of their period. They are presented, in fact, as period detail. They are thus, very nearly, presented as just Christie's clothes, even though a moment's recollected thought would remind us that the crime-writer really cannot have spent the majority of her life in evening dress.

Clothes are never, of course, 'just' clothes; historians of dress have taught us that clothes mark status and wealth, class and occupation; historians of portraiture note additionally the critical role of clothing as performative descriptor of personality and subjectivity; theoreticians of fashion have added that clothes design the contours of bodies, enforcing conformity, and giving signification; scholars of theatrical costuming and cross-dressing have argued that perhaps the most critical thing clothes do is to construct gender.[2] Thus, although all writers have undeniably had to own and wear a variety of clothes, and the preservation of any of them is a fairly chancy business, any item of writer's clothing preserved and displayed as such within the writer's house museum will inevitably tend to encode the writer's body, the writer's occupation, the writer's period, and the writer's gender. Marcia Pointon's interest in 'the potential for elision and contiguity between clothing, the body, and acts of creative communication' in portraiture also holds true for the portrayal of the writer that the writer's house museum enacts.[3]

Beyond this, items of clothing held by museums exemplify a general rule: there must have been some reason why they were originally preserved. There are a few instances of clothes serving as relics of death, very much in the spirit of preserving authorial remains discussed in Chapter 1. The last suit of clothes Walter Scott wore, long displayed in the room in which he died, and still shown in the annex exhibition, is a case in point. Even more striking is the blood-stained T-shirt retrieved from the body of the Hungarian poet József Attila following his (conjectured) suicide in 1937 (he fell under a train, probably deliberately), now displayed in the József Attila Memorial House in Balatonszárszó, Hungary.[4] This last precisely describes the interface between the physical life of the author and his posthumous life-as-writing; it is displayed with his writing projected onto the fabric. Both these instances served immediately as public memorial. More usually, however, articles of clothing owe their survival to what was originally private sentiment— memorialization of a life-event or a person by family or friends. Thus baby-clothes may well survive as a memorial of infancy, travelling clothes as souvenir, wedding veils and dresses in remembrance of the short bridal year, and clothes owned at death may serve as a personal memorial for mourners.

Within the writer's house museum, designating and displaying a single item of clothing as, for instance, 'Cowper's waistcoat' involves making an argument as to what the public, sentimental import of that particular item of clothing is. The possessive apostrophe denotes a desire to name the piece of clothing as belonging in perpetuity to someone long dead, and to use the piece of clothing to remember that person. As an illustration, whereas the clothes displayed in the Jane Austen Museum in Bath were once meant to present the bodies of women as young ladies, and now serve as an essay on period costume, the muslin shawl periodically on display in Chawton Cottage is meant to represent Jane Austen's imaginative life.[5] Within the writer's house museum, items of clothing have been understood and used, like the animal-objects discussed in Chapter 2, as surrogates for the writer's body, allegories for the relation of the writer's body to writing, and meditations on the dissemination of that writing across space and time, whether in holograph document or in the multiple reproductions that print makes possible. Writers' clothing has been used to think about writers both as mortal and immortal, embodied and disembodied, of their time and of all time. Sylvia Plath's summary meditation upon her visit to Haworth Parsonage implies the series of questions addressed here: 'They touched this, wore that, wrote here in a house redolent with ghosts.'[6] What does it mean to be in the presence of things the writer has worn, perhaps the most intimate and habitual form of touching things possible? What does this wearing and the material evidence of wear that it leaves upon textile have to say about writing? What might be the proper relation between the writer's clothing and the writer's house? And what role does clothing have in the production of writers' ghostly presence?

Dorothy Wordsworth's shoes

Because it is remarkably difficult to denaturalize the relation between writers and their clothing, to open up and consider the gap that the possessive apostrophe at once indicates and negates, we might start with considering two instances where the ideological connection sparks but sputters out. One such instance is the case of the clothes displayed as having been worn by John Ruskin as a baby at Brantwood, his house on the shores of Coniston.[7] The long white baby-clothes are displayed slightly half-heartedly and apologetically, folded up within a glassed-over half-open drawer in a chest in the bedroom. Although they are therefore displayed definitely and modestly more or less as clothes, much as those in Christie's wardrobe, there remains an imaginative difficulty in conceiving them as 'Ruskin's': these clothes may have been worn, but were not exactly owned, let alone chosen by the infant Ruskin, who must anyway at the time have been closer to being identified with baby endearments than with a patronymic. This is compounded by the even trickier problem that the clothes are doubly in the wrong place. The bedroom is otherwise narrated as the place in which Ruskin suffered a catastrophic nervous breakdown, and Brantwood itself is strongly narrated as a hub and destination of Victorian progressive thinking rather than either being or evoking Ruskin's birthplace. Thus a lurking and persistent sense of the sage's beard, as represented in the various portraits of Ruskin dotted around downstairs, renders the display of baby-clothes and the high-chair next to the chest of drawers impertinently infantilizing.

One might sum this up by saying that because Ruskin's baby-clothes, authentic though they certainly are, predate the self-invention of 'John Ruskin' as writer, they have little imaginative purchase. Something similar may be observed in the case of Dorothy Wordsworth's shoes. The implicit claims made for these shoes are rather more grandiose, in that they are not displayed naturalistically within a plausibly domestic setting—a closet, for example. They sit on a shelf within a glass case at Rydal Mount, the house in which Dorothy and her brother William Wordsworth lived from 1813 until his death in 1850 and her own in 1855.[8] Nevertheless, Dorothy Wordsworth's shoes go almost unnoticed by today's tourists. This seems odd, given how much readers' mental image of the Wordsworth siblings is associated with walking: surely a pair of Dorothy's shoes might powerfully ground Wordsworthian discourse within the female body, the familial, and the biographical? Might not a surviving pair of Dorothy's shoes suggestively insist that poetry exists within the material, the man-made, the domestic, the social, the quotidian, the historically specific, and the indoor? At very least, might such shoes not serve as objective correlative for that seductive literary tourist discourse, so strongly associated with the Wordsworths' Lake District, which speaks the desire 'to walk in the footsteps of...'? But these shoes do not. It is not clear why this particular pair were preserved in the first place, but nowadays they teeter on the edge of solecism or pointlessness, and this is not entirely the curator's fault. It is down to the fact they are doubly in the wrong place: they belonged to a Dorothy aged sixteen or seventeen when she was living in Halifax with her aunt—that is to say, to a time *before* she had joined with her brother to construct Wordsworthian experimental domesticity in the Dove Cottage years between 1799 and 1808; and secondly, they are displayed at Rydal Mount which, for modern readers, is imaginatively post-Wordsworthian—that is to say, it is the house in which the poet lived only after the great years of poetic composition which produced *Lyrical Ballads*, the early complete drafts of *The Prelude*, and associated poetry. It is also down to the fact that they are the wrong sort of shoes: a pair of fancy house-boots in white leather tied up with white grosgrain ribbons. The Dorothy who wore this fashionable footwear indoors was not and could not be the 'Dorothy Wordsworth' of the entries in her famous

Grasmere Journal (1799–1802), which articulate her as housekeeper and gardener, walker in all weathers and all terrains. But if, to engage in a thought experiment, Rydal Mount could instead display the very boots in which she walked up Skiddaw on 3 April 1802, those really would be something, and the gift shop would sell a lot of postcards of them.[9] Perhaps even a line in replicas.

Cowper's nightcap

The instances of John Ruskin's baby-clothes and Dorothy Wordsworth's shoes lay down two rules about writers' clothes: that to be effective/affective such items have to describe the writer's body as that of the writer known to the reader through famous texts and an associated iconography. They have, in short, to be recognizable. At the simplest level, such items may merely form part of a naturalistic display of a particular room as it would have appeared in the writer's lifetime, as in Olney where 'Cowper's waistcoat' may be found by the inquisitive within a chest of drawers built into his original bedroom, or as in any number of writer's house museums, such as Carlyle's house in Cheyne Walk, London, or the Brecht-Weigel Museum in Berlin, or Ruskin's home at Brantwood, Coniston, which use the trope of hat and walking-stick (authentic, stand-ins, or occasionally art-installations) hung on hat-stand or coat-hook or stacked in a corner to suggest that the writer is still imaginatively in and out of the property.[10] Sometimes, such items may be used more explicitly to give scale and dimension to the imagined writer's body, facilitating a quasi-physical encounter. In the Selma Lagerlöf museum at Falun, Sweden, where the writer's shoes lie beneath the desk as though just kicked off to ease a lame foot, the guides explain that the point of displaying the shoes is to show that one foot was larger than the other.[11] This desire to give scale is also in part the purport of Hans Christian Andersen's hat. Displayed suspended in solitary splendour within a glass vitrine in the Hans Christian Andersen Museum in Odense, the caption notes how large a hat it is, befitting the unusual size of the man; it puts the visitor into uncanny encounter with the thin air that apparently supports the hat in lieu of head or face.[12] This is a common strategy in the case of other writers' hats carefully displayed in museums (as though the writer had never owned any other hat!) such as that owned by Henrik Ibsen on display in the Ibsen Museum, Oslo (see Figure 3.1).[13]

Figure 3.1. Henrik Ibsen's hat, coat, and walking-stick in montage within glass case, annex exhibition, Ibsenmuseet, Oslo. Author's own photograph

Ibsen's top-hat, of sufficient iconographic power to merit its own chapter by Anne-Sofie Hjemdahl in *A Thing or Two About Ibsen* (2006), evokes 'the ageing dramatist taking his daily constitutional, walking along Kristiana's Karl Johan, in the 1890s'.[14] It is, as Hjemdahl observes, 'the kind of hat that was virtually synonymous with middle-class affluence and respectability at the turn of the last century'.[15] While the Ibsen museum owns five items of Ibsen's headgear—another top-hat, two collapsible French opera hats, and a German hunting cap[16]—it is this top-hat, made by the foremost local hatter, which is the important one, with its trademark power to conjure the much-photographed Ibsen of the last twenty years of his life, the intellectual 'headworker', the national playwright of international renown. It is accordingly displayed in some splendour in a case at an inter-section of the exhibition rooms, together with Ibsen's coat and walking-stick, disposed apparently in the air to evoke the mass of the dead author himself, all 5ft 4" of him.

The recognizability of this hat, its reiteration of familiar iconography, is what gives it force. Such items are typically displayed alongside representations of the author actually wearing them. These representations may be cartoons, portraits, photographs, portrait sculptures, or even actual dummies. In Ibsen's case, hat, coat, and walking-stick were at one point displayed on a dummy lying on Ibsen's death-bed.[17] Nowadays they are juxtaposed with a ghostly, deliberately blurred projection onto a door of Ibsen's back walking away from the viewer. The effect of juxtaposing such representations with the original item of clothing is characteristic of the writer's house museum. The power of Ibsen's actual hat does not lie primarily in its authentication of past representations through the iteration of evidence; rather, it tends to undo 'representation' itself to reassert the real. Without wishing to get overly tangled up in trying to differentiate the layering of the idea of representation here, one might note that the epistemological shudder in the space between hat-as-original-and-actual and hat-as-represented-on-the-head-of-the-writer puts into play the absence of the body of the writer through the presence of its accoutrements; thus, the very reality of the hat's fabric emanates ghostliness. It re-presents—that is to say, brings into the present—the very absence of the writer's body.

It is inconceivable that these writers ever actually wrote wearing these hats, which were, after all, designed for outdoor wear by gentlemen. This makes it the more remarkable that in the Odense museum, Andersen's hat also serves as a way of giving scale and dimension to his imagination, included within a room themed to the more dream-like aspects of his imaginative life. But the hat as an item of clothing is characterized especially by its quality of theatrical detachability (it can be readily put on and taken off, and different hats are worn according to the proposed role or activity). Most pertinently, it conventionally marked for nineteenth-century culture the border between outside and inside, public and private. As a result, certain sorts of headgear could conventionally figure the intermittent interiority of the writer. Louisa May Alcott's character Jo in *Little Women* (1868/9), when seized by the desire to write, would don a special writing-cap:

> Every few weeks she would shut herself up in her room, put on her scribbling suit, and 'fall into a vortex', as she expressed it, writing away at her novel with all her heart and soul, for till that was finished she could find no peace. Her 'scribbling suit' consisted of a black woollen pinafore on which she could wipe her pen at will, and a cap of the same material, adorned with a cheerful red bow, into which she bundled her hair when the decks were cleared for action.

This cap was a beacon to the inquiring eyes of her family, who during these periods kept their distance, merely popping in their heads semi-occasionally to ask, with interest, "Does genius burn, Jo?" They did not always venture even to ask this question, but took an observation of the cap, and judged accordingly. If this expressive article of dress was drawn low upon the forehead, it was a sign that hard work was going on, in exciting moments it was pushed rakishly askew, and when despair seized the author it was plucked wholly off, and cast upon the floor. At such times the intruder silently withdrew, and not until the red bow was seen gaily erect upon the gifted brow, did anyone dare address Jo.[18]

Neither Jo's writing-cap, nor Alcott's, is extant, but this sort of detachable item of clothing specifically associated with authorial creativity has often survived because celebrated. As illustrated by Frank T. Merrill in the 1896 edition of *Little Women*, Jo's writing-cap is much like a nightcap. Such an article was made of soft fabric to keep the head warm and (in the case of women) to confine the hair, or (in the case of men) to keep the head warm in the absence of hair. This last was especially true in the eighteenth century, when gentlemen's heads were typically shaved to manage headlice, and wigs were popped on over. In fact, writers would often have retired to their closets, where they would have cast off both hat and wig and put on what was called a nightcap. As a result, the nightcap and analogous headgear was something of a conventional marker for the scholar or poet, and was used to denote this occupation in eighteenth-century discourse. Oliver Goldsmith's poem 'Description of an Author's Bedchamber' in his novel *The Citizen of the World* (1760/1), describing the author's squalid living arrangements, notes that 'A night-cap deck'd his brows instead of bay'.[19] In more heroic mode, the nightcap connoted poetic genius in William Hoare's 1739 portrait of Alexander Pope; Germaine de Staël was portrayed by Gérard in 1810 in a variant, the turbanesque cloth-wrappings that in part alluded to Sibylline inspiration;[20] and in the case of Cowper, portrayed in an embroidered and goffered white cotton nightcap in a remarkable painting by George Romney of 1792, it became a brand, indicating his chosen withdrawal from public life and the glitter of the world, as described in the poem *The Task* (1785), and the adoption instead of an informal circle of intimates and a life of country domesticity. Romney's image was often remarked upon as also encoding a certain wildness of nature (Augustine Birrell commented feelingly upon 'that frightful nightcap and eyes gleaming with madness').[21] Beyond this, however, the nightcap and its analogues, whether worn by the female or the male writer, may have had the force not just of unsocializing but unsexing the writer.

Cowper's nightcap became a trademark or even a metonym, much as Ibsen's hat did a century later, although to very different effect. It was constantly reiterated in nineteenth-century iconography as a cultural commonplace. It appears prominently in the quasi-memorial frontispiece to William Hayley's *Life and Posthumous Writings of William Cowper* (1802), and it also features in the much-reproduced plate included there that shows a nightcapped Cowper seated in his study with his favourite hare playing around his feet. Charles Dickens would describe Cowper represented with his nightcap in a charade in *The Old Curiosity Shop* (1841);[22] Robert Browning evoked Cowper's entire cultural import through an imagined display of his nightcap described as 'Poor hectic Cowper's soothing sarsnet-stripe!' amongst others pertaining to Pope, Voltaire, and Hogarth in his poem 'Turf and Towers';[23] G.K. Chesterton notes that in a pageant devoted to eighteenth-century writers, Cowper was rendered instantly recognizable by his nightcap, despite the lamentable lack of his cat and spaniel.[24] Nowadays, within the museum in Olney, the nightcap makes a number of appearances: the authentic artefact (dated to 1788) is displayed in a glass vitrine along with Cowper's hair and other personal effects, and the dummy sitting at Cowper's desk in the parlour, twirling a quill in its hand, is wearing a replica, presumably to encourage afflatus.[25]

Cowper's nightcap encodes certain cultural meanings, but specifies them to his own poetic endeavour, persona, and oeuvre. It makes his absent body look like contemporaneous portraits. Like other writers' headgear, however, it has in common a quality of what Marjorie Garber has suggestively called the 'artifactuality' of the ways clothes produce bodies; artificial and detachable, it suggests that body and writer, writer and writing, and writer and author might not be self-identical.[26] That said, routinely representing the one with the other is a conventional way of constructing the/an author. Unless, that is, what is at issue is the body of a woman author; in which case, the effort of representation is typically troubled by the desire to dress or indeed undress the author in order to recover the woman, with very peculiar results.

Brontë's bonnet

Clothing very often holds a particularly privileged position within house museums dedicated to women writers. Here, Rosemary Hill's exploration of the ways that clothes and body compound to create a dreamed or performed female subjectivity is highly suggestive. Hill picks up Virginia Woolf's musings on 'frock consciousness' to explore 'the conscious frock' from the wedding raiment in Charlotte Brontë's *Jane Eyre* (1847) through to the evocation of clothes in Sylvia Plath's *The Bell Jar* (1963). 'The conscious frock', she argues, 'comes between one state of existence and another, as clothes themselves come between the naked self and the world, and it is also a channel of communication, semi-permeable, existing as an independent consciousness.'[27] Women's clothes are certainly more to do with shape-shifting than men's ever are. They typically work not just to delimit the size and shape of the writer's body, but also to describe its various phases and roles as a woman, metamorphosing through more, and more explicit, cultural/physical stages and states than do the bodies of males—virgin, bride, mother, the menopausal middle years, old age. This, you might think, would be irrelevant to how a woman writer's back catalogue is progressing with publisher and reader, but the relation between a woman writer's clothes and her authorial persona is particularly charged. The museum in Rungsted on the Danish coast devoted to Karen Blixen, known as Isak Dinesen, displays a great number of her clothes alongside photographs of her wearing them; the photographs make plain that she herself conceived her subjectivity as performatively multiple, as multiple as the highly theatrical dresses in her wardrobe. The effect is inevitably intensified in the case of writers who specialized in autobiographical lyric, such as Plath. As Hill notes, 'The extent to which Plath's self is understood to be embodied in her clothes is suggested by the prices some of them fetched when they were included in a sale of Fine Books and Manuscripts at Bonhams [in March 2018]...Lot 315 "a pleated green tartan skirt" with her nametape "in blue lettering" went for £2125.'[28] Hill does not remark on the way in which Plath's clothes appeared in the auction alongside and as analogous to her books and manuscripts, or on the way the nametape, sewn on by Plath herself, clearly functions as an autograph signature, or indeed upon the remarkable photograph in the Bonhams catalogue, which shows three of Plath's costumes, including the tartan skirt, displayed on dummies, standing together behind a desk upon which her typewriter sits, but all of this suggests that it is not just Plath's 'self' but Plath-as-author who is conventionally embodied by her clothes.

In the case of longer-lived writers, conveying a biographical body through a display of clothing presents quite a descriptive challenge. This is tackled inventively by a case in the house museum opened in 2014 in Manchester at 84 Plymouth Grove devoted to the years that the novelist

Elizabeth Gaskell lived there from 1850 to 1865.[29] In the top left-hand corner, dominating the case, stands a marble bust of Gaskell by David Dunbar, depicting her as a young, wealthy, marriageable beauty before her marriage. Gaskell's lace wedding veil occupies the centre of the case, repeating the whiteness, marriageability, and partial disembodiment of the bust, and adding through its transparency a suggestion of ghostliness. In the foreground, a paisley jacket delimits the size and shape of a distinctly middle-aged torso to supplement/support the bust. Each item describes Gaskell's body as woman across time, as child, bride, mother, and middle-aged woman. Presiding over a litter of framed family photographs on the table, an otherwise unexplained doll supplies a surrogate version of a whole female body complete with legs, albeit in rather uncanny miniature.

A similarly composite Victorian female form appears in a display case at the centre of 'Charlotte's room' in the Brontë Parsonage Museum. It is constituted of items once 'worn by' or 'carried by' Charlotte Brontë, as the captions point out. A dress draped with a shawl stands in the centre of the cabinet. Shoes and pattens are displayed on the floor of the right of the vitrine. To the left is propped a half-folded parasol. Above it a pair of stockings are pinned, while above again appear a pair of gloves, and further up, a fan.[30] The head, as it were, is supplied by the posthumously painted portrait by J.H. Thompson hung over the mantelpiece. As in the Gaskell museum, clothes and accessories give scale and dimension to the absent female body, but, as in the instance of Plath's clothes, they are also displayed as having taken her physical impress as a sort of signature; the gloves are noticeably stained and soiled, and, the caption points out, 'the well-darned stockings have the initials CB inked on them'.[31] It is conceivable that many of these items survive because they were not very reusable or repurposable, being too worn. Nowadays, the wear on them describes their import; they preserve the dead owner's once living actuality.

Charlotte's wedding-bonnet and veil are to be found in a separate glass case, located against the bedroom wall (Figure 3.2). This is the only remaining original piece of her wedding outfit. In this, she married the Reverend Arthur Bell Nicholls in Haworth parish church on the morning of 29 June 1854. Brontë's first biographer, Elizabeth Gaskell, noted that locals described her as looking 'like a snowdrop', in a white muslin dress topped off with this pale green-trimmed bonnet and white lace veil.[32] The famously quiet wedding was followed by an unexpectedly happy marriage which was cut short by the bride's death from complications associated with her pregnancy.

Figure 3.2. Wedding-bonnet displayed in Charlotte Brontë's bedroom. © Parsonage Museum, Haworth

Faded and partially dismantled though it is, this bonnet is nowadays—and has been for some considerable time—one of the most celebrated items in the collections of the museum. Its survival was secured in the first instance by Brontë's grieving husband. The museum's holdings of Charlotte's personal belongings (including a large number of dress fragments, her shoes, and the wedding-bonnet) mostly survived because Nicholls kept so many of them as memorials until his death in 1906.[33] Thus many of these personal relics were preserved principally out of Victorian rituals associated with private marital grief. They would only later become the subject of public display when the import of these items became more than merely a matter of personal memory and affection. At that point the wedding veil was lent to Swann, Edgar & Co. of Regent St, London for exhibition in one of their windows.[34] Other items would be shown in the first 'Museum of Brontë Relics' opened in 1889 by the cousins of Martha Brown, above their Refreshment Rooms in Haworth, and then within the Brontë Society's collection, established in 1893, of 'artefacts of whatever nature of the Brontë family' which in turn formed the basis of the museum that opened in 1895, and transferred to the Brontë Parsonage Museum when it in its turn opened in 1928.[35]

The wedding dress itself does not survive. Nicholls requested that it be burnt on his death, but like so many such requests it was not honoured. The wedding dress is so critical to the Brontë mythos that it has been (re)fabricated; the dress periodically shown in the museum is a 'replica made from memory' from the original sold by Nicholls' second wife at auction after his death.[36] Conjecturally, it works not just to construct Brontë as a woman, but to insert her both into the narrative of *Jane Eyre* and into the counter-narrative of *Villette*—'Reader, I married him' and 'Reader, I did not marry him', respectively. It performs her escape from daughterhood, sister-hood, and spinsterhood into the status of achieving 'a home of her own' like her heroine Jane Eyre, while also describing a justified Lucy Snowe-like anxiety about the dangers of marriage.

There is plenty of evidence that the encounter with Brontë's clothing has long carried a considerable affective charge. Virginia Woolf, for example, responded powerfully to the dead woman's personal possessions displayed then in the adjunct Brontë Museum, publishing an unsigned account under the title 'Haworth, November 1904' in *The Guardian* on 21 December 1904:

> The museum is certainly rather a pallid and inanimate collection of objects...Here are many autograph letters, pencil drawings, and other docu-ments. But the most touching case—so touching that one hardly feels reverent in one's gaze—is that which contains the little personal relics of the dead woman. The natural fate of such things is to die before the body that wore them, and because these, trifling and transient though they are, have survived, Charlotte Brontë the woman comes to life, and one forgets the chiefly mem-orable fact that she was a great writer. Her shoes and her thin muslin dress have outlived her.[37]

Woolf would not have seen the wedding-bonnet, since the Brontë Parsonage Museum did not acquire it until 1954,[38] but even so wedding fever perme-ates Woolf's prose; the snow-bound landscape is likened to 'a vast wedding cake' and 'the earth was bridal in its virgin snow'. Keighley is mentioned as where Charlotte made 'her more important purchases—her wedding gown, perhaps, and the thin little cloth boots which we examined under glass in the Brontë museum'. The foregrounding of this language follows from the nervy way in which Woolf effectively describes her experience of Haworth as the site of a struggle between conceiving Brontë as a writer and Brontë as a woman. The writing seems dead, 'pallid' and 'inanimate', reduced to mere 'objects'. By contrast, shoes and dress have 'outlived' the writer, remaining uncomfortably vivid and able to bring the dead woman to uneasy and imperfect life, albeit in a latter-day glass coffin. Woolf thus strongly registers an experience of museum as reliquary. She is troubled by a sense of irreverent prying, something edgily close to prurience, an encounter with things that blots out what they are supposed to be (for Woolf) memorializing— 'the chiefly memorable fact that she was a great writer'. Brontë's 'greatness' sits in a difficult relation to the material constraints of her life; as Woolf puts it, 'The circumference of her life was very narrow', as was, one might remark, her waist. Faced with this, Woolf understandably preferred the notion that it was the moors, rather than the dress or shoes, that best suited Brontë, fitting her 'like a snail its shell'.[39]

The experience of visiting Haworth and encountering Charlotte Brontë's clothing seems to have remained fundamentally the same over the intervening century. In 2005, on the occasion of the commemoration of the 150th anniversary of Brontë's death in 1855, the Brontë Parsonage Museum was once again visited by a *Guardian* journalist, Tanya Gold. Her account is remarkably intemperate and overwritten, but it bears a striking resemblance to Woolf's. She begins by invoking much the same sense of pilgrimage and its promises of remains and relics: 'I decide to visit Saint Central—the parsonage museum at Haworth—to see if anything of the real Charlotte remains. Might a leg, or an arm or a finger be sticking out from under Gaskell's smiling tombstone?' She describes with distaste and embarrassment what she finds: 'relics, pristine and pornographic'. She picks out for comment 'Charlotte's clothing': 'imprisoned behind glass: her ghastly wedding bonnet, covered with lace; her gloves; her bag; her spectacles'. Her reading of this clothing dwells upon the way this evocation of the female body belittles literary achievement: 'I can see from the dress that she was a dwarf. A genius indeed, but a dwarf. . . I can find no remnant of the breathing, brilliant novelist in Haworth.' Her only partially expressed sense of finding domestic imprisonment, disability, gentility, and death instead of 'breathing' brilliance bursts into rage:

> I yearn to . . . torch the parsonage. This shrine needs desecrating, and I want to watch it burn. I want to see the fridge magnets melt, the tea-towels explode and the wedding bonnet wither. Somewhere, glistening in the ashes,

there might remain a copy of *Jane Eyre*. That is all of Charlotte Brontë that need loiter here.[40]

The tension between the tropes of the 'breathing' and the breathless, the escaped and the imprisoned, is played out in the ways that Brontë's corset has recently achieved meaning and celebrity. The corset is not on display within the museum (because this has to date seemed indecorous), but that did not prevent it from being brought out for an airing for the BBC 2 commemorative documentary 'Being the Brontës' (2016). For the presenter, the importance of the corset lay in its harshly constraining power which nonetheless 'speaks...of Charlotte's inner fire'.[41] The real corset, then, was pressed into service to speak of the painful yet necessary embodiment of genius. It was, however, doubled by a fictional one with far more inclination to celebrate female embodiment: the programme concluded with an elaborate re-enactment of Brontë's wedding which featured the lacing-up of Brontë's corset in close-up. Brontë's corset is problematic and provocative because it asks what invasions of personhood and privacy we are entitled as readers and tourists to exact from an admired author. The poet in residence at the museum between 2009 and 2010, Katrina Naomi, apologized in her poem 'Charlotte Brontë's Corset' (2010) for her intrusiveness: 'I'm sorry, Charlotte, for this disservice/...I feel like a tabloid reporter/sniffing around the armholes of your life'.[42] I daresay Nicholls would indeed have sharply reprimanded her for impertinence: his desire that the wedding dress and bonnet be burned reveals a sense that clothing carries more erotic charge than is quite seemly to put on display so openly. Dressing and undressing a beloved wife in public is not entirely, or should not be entirely, the same thing as revealing the author to the eyes of posterity.

The remaining cases in Charlotte Brontë's bedroom endeavour to modify the vision of the woman's body provided by the case at its centre with a sense of the writer. One case is devoted to Miss Richardson Currer, the probable source of Brontë's choice of male pseudonym for *Jane Eyre*; another displays Brontë's portable writing desk, its contents, her spectacles, and a visiting-card. The third, a temporary addition in June 2016 when I last visited, was part of the 2016 exhibition curated by the novelist Tracy Chevalier, for the commemorative season *Brontë200*, entitled 'Charlotte Great and Small'. It effectively constituted an essay on the meanings of Brontë's clothes in relation to literary greatness, and contained what were styled 'Accessories' by the artist Serena Partridge, described as 'new, temporary acquisitions…drawing inspiration from Charlotte's life and personal possessions'. The argument that they collectively made was supposedly that 'despite the restrictive domesticity of needlework chores, Charlotte's imagination took over'. Made at 2/3 life-size, the implausibly tiny items included two pairs of 'Child's boots, c. 1820', a 'Night cap, 1831', 'Doll's miniatures, 1839', a 'Pair of embroidered gloves, 1839', 'Pocket handkerchief, 1843', 'Mourning shoes, 1850', and 'Stocking, 1854'. These objects, read in sequence left to right, provided a fantastical, material, and miniaturized version of Charlotte's biography from early childhood through to her wedding on 29 June 1854. The exhibition that grew more directly out of the creative partnership between the museum and Chevalier was conceived in much the same spirit. It 'explore[d] the contrasts between Charlotte's constricted life and her huge ambition' through showing her 'child-size clothes' and other fragments and miniatures counterposed with 'quotations from her letters and writings…projected onto the walls to demonstrate the scale of her hopes and dreams'.[43] Material objects, that is, were put into dialogue with words represented through the immaterial medium of light, and Brontë's clothing was deliberately scaled as smaller than her words. Chevalier's exhibition thus responded to, and tried to undo, Woolf's conflicted sense of the proper relation between the dead woman and the living novelist, reversioning revulsion and anxiety as wonder at the 'tininess' of Brontë's clothes in contradistinction to the 'greatness' of her works.[44]

Dickinson's dress

Meanwhile, in Amherst, Massachusetts, just outside the bedroom where she died on 15 May 1886, Emily Dickinson is evoked by her famous white dress (Figure 3.3).[45]

This is a house-dress, said to have been worn habitually by Dickinson in the 1870s or 1880s. The inquisitive Mabel Loomis Todd reported in 1881 that the locals had informed her that the poet 'dresses wholly in white, & her mind is said to be perfectly wonderful'.[46] The popular story derived from this stray remark holds that 'In her later years [Dickinson] would wear only white, and as she grew more reclusive, dressmakers fitted her garments to her sister Lavinia.'[47] Whether the colour white had specific meanings within Dickinson's own poetics has been extensively debated, in particular whether it had reference to the poet-heroine of Elizabeth Barrett Browning's

Figure 3.3. Emily Dickinson's dress, displayed in a glass case in Dickinson's bedroom, Dickinson House Museum. © Jerome Liebling and Mount Holyoke College Art Museum, MA. Liebling's photograph uses the reflections in the glass to realize the popular sense of it as animating the ghostly presence of the poet.

Aurora Leigh (1856), but its whiteness has certainly constructed her afterlife, from the moment she was buried in white and enclosed in a white casket, down to the present day. Although there is no firm evidence that this dress actually was her dress, and although there is little documentary evidence for the locals' claim that she insisted on dressing at all times in white, the dress is sufficiently iconic to have been the subject of many postcards, blogs, and artworks, and to have been photographed by celebrity photographer Annie Leibovitz in 2012. In fact, nowadays, it is considered too fragile and too precious to be on display, and what tourists see is actually a place-holding replica. The museum's website remarks that 'the posthumous fame of the dress's owner has given the garment an extraordinary life of its own. For many of Dickinson's fans, the white dress embodies the essence of their beloved writer'.[48] The conscious frock, in short.

The phrase begs the question of what such an 'essence' might be. The positioning of the dress within the museum is sufficiently startling; when I encountered it on my visits in 2008 and 2019, it was standing silently but attentively on the landing.[49] There has always been a frisson borrowed from the American Gothic of Hawthorne or Poe hanging about the house and the story of its inmates. The sense of this Gothic is rather clumsily exploited, for instance, by Brock Clarke's *An Arsonist's Guide to Writers' Homes in New England* (2007).[50] In this novel, the Dickinson house supplies the setting for its opening scene of accidental arson and manslaughter committed by the protagonist. Disappointed of a much-anticipated Gothic frisson during his daytime visit—'after my mother's stories, I expected there to be something exceptional and sinister and mysterious about the house. There wasn't'[51]— he tries to get the proper feeling by making another visit by night. The story of his mother's that he especially hopes to check out is 'the one in which Emily Dickinson's corpse was hidden in one of the house's many secret compartments and came to life (or at least became ambulatory) only when there was a full moon'.[52] Where Plath's exercise in imaginative reanimation at Haworth merely raises ghosts, Clarke produces a vampire, a deadly new Lucy Westenra, clothed in her white night-gown. The two exercises in reanimating the woman writer inflect the immortality of great writers very differently.

Dickinson's white dress serves as a commentary upon the embodiedness of the woman writer. Its whiteness carries overlapping and interrelated meanings to do with constructing the female body as virgin, bride, ghost, and vampire while blanking out such constructions in favour of a purposive poetic idleness signalled, enforced, and enabled by whiteness. Annie Leibovitz's celebrated photograph of the breast of the dress in close-up envisages the female work of the white-on-white embroidery as akin to Dickinson's writing, near invisible to anyone but intimates. Highlighting the signs of lived wear and tear, Leibovitz postulates a powerful relation between wearer and dress and (by analogy) between poet and poem; her commentary imagines a secretive and self-satisfyingly self-contemplative relation between mind, body, and embroidered garment: 'for someone who spent most of her time quietly by herself, the details would have been wonderful to contemplate. And to feel. They weren't meant for anyone else'.[53] The dress can serve by extension too as an idea about women's writing— domestic, secretive, physically intimate. A blog post of 3 April 2013, for example, delightedly and conspiratorially records the pocket built into the sleeve of the dress to hold Dickinson's small notebook; Dickinson's poetry is thus made into the fabric of her dress, and vice versa.[54]

Dickinson's dress demonstrably inspires the desire to read it as measuring or encompassing both the woman's body and the poet's body of work. Whether this is actually appropriate is the subject of the American poet

Billy Collins' poem 'Taking Off Emily Dickinson's Clothes' (1998). The poem nods explicitly to the museum-display and to the desires of its visitors in creating the setting for some sort of seduction:

> You will want to know
> That she was standing
> By an open window in an upstairs bedroom,
> Motionless, a little wide-eyed,
> Looking out at the orchard below,
> The white dress puddled at her feet
> On the wide-board, hardwood floor.

Successively removing tippet, bonnet, dress, and underwear, he comes last of all to the corset:

> I could plainly hear her inhale
> when I undid the very top
> hook-and-eye fastener of her corset
> and I could hear her sigh when finally it was unloosed,
> the way that some readers sigh when they realize
> that Hope has feathers...[55]

Released from her constricting underclothes, Dickinson's body turns out to be neither virginal nor vampiric, but vaporous, merely a sigh. Indeed, it turns out to be a matter of her own poem realized through the reader's body, in a sigh. In a further twist, what sighs through the reader's body is without words at all, the voice of a bird:

> Hope is the thing with feathers
> That perches in the soul,
> And sings the tune without the words,
> And never stops at all...[56]

If writer's house museums are, as they so far seem, to be primarily devoted to turning text (back) into body, then one might assume that displayed clothing works as a substitute for, or a memento of, a writing body. (The vast woollen shawl I've wrapped around myself against the January cold of my writing-shed is just the sort of thing that might make a suitable exhibit.) There is, however, a crucial distinction to be made between the writer's and the author's body. The author's body is what outlives that of the writer while retaining its lived shape; hence it can be appropriately figured by clothing. Items of iconic male clothing, almost invariably already conceived as 'arti-factual', readily allow for this abstraction of author from writer. But such a proposition has proven far less stable within museums dedicated to evoking and celebrating women writers. One instance only comes to mind where a woman writer's clothing looks safely metonymic of the author: in the small entrance exhibition at Sigrid Undset's house, Bjerkebæk, in Lillehammer, Norway, she materializes in company with two fellow Nobel laureates, Bjørnstjerne Bjørnson and Knut Hamsun, in the shape of the well-worn shoes she wore on the occasion of the presentation of the medal in 1928. (Bjørnson appears courtesy of the miniature gold-cased pencil he always carried in his pocket, and Hamsun is realized through a red tie, in a pleasing completion of the Freudian cliché.)[57] But generally clothing belonging to women writers demonstrably teeters closer to the pornographic than the iconic and metonymic, for it tends to insist upon presenting the actual body of the woman writer in its entirety rather than arguing its apotheosis into authorship. Where articles of men's clothing are metonymic of written texts, articles of women's clothing are at best analogous. And while such textiles may be represented as analogous to text, they remain stubbornly in excess of it. It might be rather safer iconographically to conceive the primal scene of writing not as a drama played out within the body, but as a drama played out through negotiation between the twinned surfaces of the writer's chair and the desk, the subject of Chapter 4.

4

Furniture

Shakespeare's chair and Austen's desk

Daphne du Maurier's study

Y ou could do worse, if taking a holiday in Cornwall, than draw off the A30 as it climbs over Bodmin Moor and drop into Jamaica Inn. 'The Daphne du Maurier Room' opened here in 1990, a year after the death of the author of *Rebecca* (1938). The caption to the souvenir postcard of the installation describes it as 'a memorial room' and specifically boasts that amongst other authentic memorabilia it contains Du Maurier's 'Sheraton writing desk top'.[1] The glassed-off room displays a chair drawn up to a desk.[2] On the desk are assembled the mechanics of the twentieth-century writer's trade—an Olivetti typewriter and a telephone. These mass-produced items are given an idiosyncratic twist by a dish of the writer's favourite Glacier Mints and a packet of the Du Maurier cigarettes named after her father Gerald du Maurier. The whole is brought into an imagined present by a half-smoked cigarette perched on an ashtray. There are also a number of photographs, including a photograph of Du Maurier's wedding to Frederick Browning, a photograph of her three children, and a photograph of her last home at Kilmarth, just outside Tywardreath. Above them hangs a portrait of Du Maurier as a sixteen-year-old.

The display therefore remembers Du Maurier as a woman in something of the same way as the vitrine describing Gaskell through a biographical assemblage of her clothing discussed in Chapter 3; as sixteen-year-old, as bride, as mother, and as householder. The desk is what remembers Du Maurier's body as that of a writer, eating, smoking, speaking, and typing. The location of this installation at Jamaica Inn also remembers Du Maurier as a writer; in 1930 Du Maurier and her friend Foy Quiller-Couch had sheltered from the swirling fog and sheeting rain of the moor at the ancient coaching-inn, and this would inspire the novel *Jamaica Inn* (1936).[3] Thus the text that resulted from the encounter between writer and place is metaphorically realized by the presence at the inn of the desk and typewriter upon which the spectator is supposed to assume Du Maurier generated her fiction.

It was possible for this 'memorial room' to come so swiftly into existence after Du Maurier's death not merely because it was evidently in the commercial interests of the owners of the inn but also because this concept of the writer's desk and chair as the microcosm of the writer's actuality is so well entrenched in contemporary culture. These spaces continue to exert substantial imaginative power, perhaps especially since the advent of photo-journalism concentrating on writers and their houses in the late nineteenth century.[4] It became necessary as a novelist to be depicted working at a desk, whether you actually did so or not. Hence although Edith Wharton worked in bed, she was photographed for publicity purposes 'at her desk'; and although Agatha Christie wrote on her portable typewriter without apparently much regard as to where she was, she too was photographed 'in her study'.[5] Nowadays these sites are consumed variously in illustrated articles such as the series 'Writers' Rooms' that ran in *The Guardian* between January and July 2007; coffee-table books such as Erica Lennard and Francesca Premoli-Droulers' *Writers' Houses* (1995) or J.D. McClatchy and Erica Lennard's *American Writers at Home* (2004); in the medium of fine art, as in John Fisher's five one-man exhibitions of oil paintings of writers' rooms, focused on the writer's chair and desk (2001–14); in fictionalized versions in any number of author biopics; and, of course, in the writer's house museum itself in all its variants worldwide.[6]

In the vast majority of writer's house museums, the display of the writer's desk is an essential element—it is, one might say, the writer's house museum in epitome. Thus in defiance of the biographical evidence, Christie's desk is displayed in Greenway as a useful fiction to generate visitor affect; as one tourist wrote: 'The study was the most compelling room for me. An old-fashioned typewriter and desk are set in a prominent place, along with a blotter. On shelves above the desk are first editions of all of Christie's detective novels, and some modern versions too. It wasn't hard for me to imagine her sitting in the leather desk chair and allowing her imagination to flow through her pen and onto the page'.[7] Indeed, where there is no writer's house museum as such, the display of the writer's desk may, as in Jamaica Inn, efficiently stand in for it.

In line with this convention, Alison Booth has remarked that at the core of the writer's house lies 'the act of writing'.[8] One might usefully refine this statement to say that at the core of the writer's house museum one finds not so much the act of writing as the scene that remembers the act of writing. Chapters 1–3 have explored the ways that the body of the writer has been imagined in relation to writing; this chapter considers this scene-setting. What exactly do we have invested in the scene of writing? How does it bear on the construction of the figure of the author and by extension the idea of literature? How have chairs, desks, and desk furniture come to be conceived, valued, represented, and staged as witnesses to the very moment the author 'allow[ed] her imagination to flow through her pen and onto the page'? But before I embark on the fascinating histories of 'Shakespeare's chair' and 'Austen's desk' and other such furniture, a note of caution is in order: I am *not* concerned here with what writer's desks and chairs can tell us about authors' real-life writing practices. Goethe's design of a 'saddle-chair' (displayed in the Garten-haus at Weimar) to protect his back and his digestion from the well-documented ill-effects of writing is fascinating, and A.L. Kennedy's investment in a chair which lifts her feet above her head with a view to improving blood-flow to the brain slightly boggling.[9] There are writers who have done without chairs altogether, writing as I am at the moment in the University of Oslo at custom-built standing-desks (Victor Hugo at Hauteville and Nathaniel Hawthorne at Wayside), or who have lounged luxuriously horizontal in bed or daybed (Marcel Proust at 102 Boulevard Haussmann, Edith Wharton at The Mount, and Rudyard Kipling at Bateman's).[10] Many writers have not themselves bothered with the inky and exacting drudgery of writing themselves, relying on dictation to amanuenses (Milton, Goethe, and Wordsworth were particularly celebrated for this).[11] But it proves easiest to get at what is invested in the figure of the writer at her or his desk by investigating pious back-formations such as forgeries and replicas, and the staging of scenes that never were or could have been. The pressure to stage the writer at his or her desk has regularly produced representations and artefacts that are not warranted by what is known of the writer's working practices; conversely, sometimes the evolving mythos of the author has required creative de-authorization of entirely authentic representations and objects.

Shakespeare's chair

Making a chair into the Writer's Chair proves to be a matter of what Dean MacCannell in *The Tourist* (1976) once called 'site sacralization'.[12] Even if you have the very piece of furniture, it is still only a piece of furniture until it is provided with markers of signification and valuation, and framed within narratives of place and of the nature and moment of creation. These narratives variously conflate stories of 'home', specified to body, time, and locality, with much less embodied or realist ideas of the writer's reach across time and space. In 1783, William Beckford was allowed to sit in 'Petrarch's chair', an experience about which he wrote at some length: 'Who could sit in Petrarch's chair, void of some effect? I rose not from it without a train of pensive sentiments and soft impressions; which I ever love to indulge...'.[13] The 'effect' sought and experienced is vague but powerful, and indeed, entirely conventional; this sort of thrill-seeking was also associated with the idea of Shakespeare's chair. For Beckford, the Petrarchan frisson would have been mostly a matter of love and Laura; the affect constructed by Shakespeare's chair was equally sought after, although the history of its realization betrays altogether more ideological complexity. The hitch was that it was not at all clear that such a chair existed. As John Cam Hobhouse remarked in his notes to Canto IV of Byron's narrative poem *Childe Harold's Pilgrimage* (1819), what was then showing in Stratford-upon-Avon as 'Shakespeare's chair' was of substantially more dubious provenance than Petrarch's chair, which he had just viewed in Arquà: 'The chair is still shown amongst the precious relics of Arquà, which, from the uninterrupted veneration that has been attached to everything relative to this great man from the moment of his death to the present hour, have, it may be hoped, a better chance of authenticity than the Shakespearian memorials of Stratford upon Avon'.[14] Notwithstanding this sort of scepticism, late eighteenth- and nineteenth-century admirers of Shakespeare felt that Shakespeare's chair must have existed, and must still exist. Besides, they ardently desired to sit in it, or, better, to acquire it. Accordingly, it came into being along with other 'Shakespearian memorials'. The history of the various pious frauds known as 'Shakespeare's chair' therefore reveals with especial clarity the cultural work that the writer's chair was required to do from the late eighteenth century onwards.[15]

The first chair recorded as 'Shakespeare's' seems to have been that said to have been borrowed from a Mr James Bacon of Barnet by Garrick on the occasion of the staging of the Shakespeare Jubilee of 1769. Its current whereabouts are unknown.[16] Garrick's desire to borrow it was to do with his self-promotion as the foremost Shakespearean of his time. It was of a piece with his previous commission of a 'mahogany chair, designed by Hogarth, richly carved, on the back of which hangs a medal of the poet' made of wood from Shakespeare's mulberry tree, which he had installed in his 'Temple to Shakespeare' in the grounds of his Hampton villa in 1756.[17] One of the results of the Jubilee's celebration of Shakespeare as a local was that it put Stratford on the national map for the generality of tourists, beginning the process of making it a must-see location in itself, rather than merely a coaching town in which the northward-bound traveller might idle away the hours waiting for his dinner by visiting places of local interest. The Birthplace, as already noted, was made into the centrepiece of the Shakespeare tourist cult for the first time; reports of the Jubilee were illustrated by the first public print of the Birthplace in the *Gentleman's Magazine* in August 1769.[18] Something of a tourist boom ensued, and there was as a result money to be made. As Mary Hart, the tenant who was then living in the Birthplace, said to the Hon. John Byng in 1781 while showing him 'Shakespeare's old chair': 'It has been carefully handed down by our family, but people never thought so much of it till after the Jubilee, and now see what pieces they have cut from it, as well as from the old flooring in the bedroom!'[19] Taking the hint, John Byng seized his opportunity, and hastily acquired the bottom strut of the chair.

It was this second iteration of Shakespeare's chair that was being shown in the kitchen of the Birthplace by the 1780s. Samuel Ireland's *Picturesque Views on the Upper, or Warwickshire Avon* (1795) elaborated Shakespearean biography and oral tradition with illustrations of important locations, and modelled appropriate tourist sentiment in a romantically enthusiastic first-person narrative of Ireland's pilgrimage. The engravings include a view of 'the kitchen of Shakespeare's House' which depicts this chair *in situ*. However, sometime later in the 1790s, the Polish Princess Czartoyska seems to have acquired what was left of it by the likes of John Byng and other enthusiasts, with the exception of the legs which she apparently left as a concession to the sentimental or commercial distress of the daughter of the current tenant, Mary Hornby.[20] Buying it for the extraordinary sum of £300, she took it home to Poland, built it into a quasi-reliquary—an elaborate shell of a new chair ornamented with a lyre—and installed it in her landscape garden in 'the Gothic-House'. It is presently part of the collections of the Polish National Museum in Cracow. (The legs seem to have long disappeared.) The princess's extravagant intervention rethought an old, solid, but otherwise unremarkable kitchen chair into a chair fit for an Apollonian immortal by captioning it with a lyre, and dramatized it as romantically 'gothic', a style which carried with it a flavour of nationalism. A chair that began by certifying Shakespeare as a local boy ended by describing Shakespeare as divinely inspired international treasure and canon-haunting ghost.

The destiny of a third of Shakespeare's chairs forms a strong contrast. This one argued for a version of Shakespeare that was much more clearly biographical, domestic, and sentimental. Ireland's *Picturesque Views* had also included the first ever representation of Anne Hathaway's cottage, complete with a depiction of 'Shakespeare's courting chair' (Figure 4.1). Ireland went to considerable lengths to purchase this item, removed it to London, and then either he or his son William Henry Ireland seems (characteristically) to have paid up to have the initials WS and A carved onto the back to make

Figure 4.1. William Shakespeare's courting chair. © Shakespeare Birthplace Trust

absolutely sure no one missed the point. The Hathaway family subsequently replaced it with a 'courting-settle' to supply the house's resulting sentimental deficit with some considerable success, to judge by the Victorian records of seeing it and the marks of assiduous Victorian plunder still visible upon this much-abused substitute. Nowadays the chair Ireland bought is once again displayed in Anne Hathaway's cottage, having been acquired for £1800 and returned there in 2002 by the Shakespeare Birthplace Trust. The 'courting-settle' has been relegated to inauthenticity.[21]

If Ireland's chair described Shakespeare primarily as local lover, yet a fourth chair known as 'Shakespeare's chair' describes him as local drinker. Gifted in 1865 to the Shakespeare Birthplace Trust as a 'chair from the Falcon Inn, Bidford, where Shakespeare held his drinking club', it is still shown in the Birthplace today.[22] This chair was associated with the eighteenth-century tradition that Shakespeare had indulged in drunken revels to the extent of passing out for the night under a crab-apple tree in Bidford. It did much to assimilate Shakespeare to the model of native bard exemplified by Robert Burns.

None of these chairs conform very precisely to modern ideas of the writer's chair, which appear somewhere around the middle of the nineteenth century. In the eighteenth century, Shakespeare did not do much conscientious sitting down to write. Louis-François Roubiliac's statue of Shakespeare as 'National Poet', commissioned by Garrick (again for his temple at Hampton) and now on permanent display beside the main staircase at the British Library, represents the actor-playwright jotting down loose notes while standing up. For Romantics, Shakespeare's chair risked making him look a bit too much as though he was obliged to drudge for his living instead of being at one with the land. Hence Samuel Ireland had depicted him as 'The Bard of Avon', reclining on the banks of the Avon soaking up muse-delivered inspiration despite the definite risk of catching a chill.[23] Consequently, none of these chairs have much to do with the physical, time-consuming, back-aching grind of professional writing for the metropolitan theatre—this thoroughly local Shakespeare rusticates, kicks his heels by the fire, flirts, and drinks.

It was only the Victorians who came to feel the need to certify Shakespeare as a proper and respectable writer—genteel, closeted, industrious, bookish, desk- and chair-bound. This new sense of the work of the writer is usefully glossed by S. Hicks' painting of Shakespeare, engraved by A.H. Payne for *Payne's Universum* (1847), which shows Shakespeare dutifully scribbling in a room very reminiscent of Horace Walpole's or Walter Scott's well-documented studies, surrounded by an antiquarian litter of armour, halberd, pewter pots, papers, discarded quill-pens, and a globe. Similar in tenor is one of Charles Cattermole's series of thirteen watercolour 'Scenes from the Life of Shakespeare' which includes a depiction of Ben Jonson visiting Shakespeare in London to find him slogging away at a desk by a mullioned window.[24] As a result, another, more satisfactory, Shakespeare chair emerged in 1890. Acquired by the Shakespeare Birthplace Trust in 2015, it is catalogued as 'a 19th century panel-back armchair...made in 1890 by James Plucknett and Co. of Warwick as a replica of the chair in which Shakespeare is said to have sat when he wrote most of his plays'. It may have been made to display in a museum on Sheep Street in Stratford. It bears a brass plaque on the rear which reads:

> Replica of chair in which Shakespeare is said to have/sat when he wrote most of his plays and which was formerly/in the possession of Paul Whitehead the poet laureate/afterwards of John Bacon of Barnet. Then of the Rev. T.J. Judkins/ of St Pancras, then of the Rev. Walter Field, Vicar of Godmersham/Kent & now in 1890 of E. Ledger Esqre of the ERA./Made from oak out of Warwick Castle/with a piece of wood from Shakespeare's Birthplace at/Stratford inserted in the seat of the chair...

The chair thus makes two claims to Shakespearean authenticity—firstly that it is a faithful replica of a chair with serious provenance, possibly a copy of the one Garrick is said to have borrowed, and secondly that it is a memorial associative piece, made of wood from the Birthplace, probably that released from the restoration of 1857.[25] But, most strikingly, it is captioned specifically as a 'writer's chair', as 'a replica of the chair in which Shakespeare is said to have sat when he wrote most of his plays'.[26]

The sheer number of these chairs attests to the enduring power of the idea of 'Shakespeare's chair'. One might return to Beckford's rhetorical question, 'Who could sit in Petrarch's chair, void of some effect?' to ask about the nature of the Shakespearean effect these pieces of furniture were hopeful of producing. There are some clues in John Ferrar's *A Tour from Dublin to London* (1796), which provides an account of the experience of two tourists to the Birthplace. They were shown round by Mary Hornby:

> This poor woman shewed us [Shakespeare's] pedigree in manuscript and we had the supreme satisfaction of handling the old painting box and pencils of our immortal bard. We also got some of his mulberry tree, and his chair is preserved in the chimney corner. Henry sat down in it and received such

inspiration, that we know not what will be the consequence, for he has been writing on every opportunity since.[27]

Ferrar's waggish tone is echoed and amplified in the account provided by Washington Irving of his visit in 1815 when he took Mrs Hornby's tour in his turn:

> The most favourite object of curiosity, however, is Shakespeare's chair. It stands in the chimney nook of a small gloomy chamber...In this chair it is the custom of every one that visits the house to sit: whether this be done with the hope of imbibing any of the inspiration of the bard I am at a loss to say, I merely mention the fact; and mine hostess privately assured me, that, though built of solid oak, such was the fervent zeal of devotees, that the chair had to be new bottomed at least once in three years. It is worthy of notice also in the history of this extraordinary chair, that it partakes something of the volatile nature of the Santa Casa of Loretto, or the flying chair of the Arabian enchanter; for though sold some years since to a northern princess, yet, strange to tell, it has found its way back to the old chimney corner...[28]

Irving knew that the chair he is shown cannot have been the original one, but anyway, inconveniently for those desirous of 'imbibing the inspiration of the bard' and pouring forth literary effusions as a result, not one of these chairs is thought to be any older than the 1630s. The nearest thing to any chair that Shakespeare actually sat in to write is probably the one that was once occupied by a life-size effigy of the bard in the portal exhibition to the Birthplace—whereabouts currently unknown. Still, the enduring desirability of showing 'Shakespeare's chair' in Stratford demonstrated by the Shakespeare Birthplace Trust's willingness to continue to acquire versions of Shakespeare's chair for their collections points to continuing affective investment. From the moment that these chairs start to emerge as a tourist phenomenon, it is plain that they are felt to provide access, if not to Shakespeare himself, then to the possibility of being animated by Shakespearean inspiration.

It is difficult to get at quite what the imaginative mechanics of this fantasy might be. Conjecturally, the desire to preserve, celebrate, and indeed sit in the writer's chair relates first and foremost to the desire to *remember* the writer as embodied and yet *experience* him as disembodied. The chair remembers the impress of the writer's body, or, as Simon Goldhill has comically put it, the very shape of 'Scott's buttocks', but it describes disembodiment because it is now 'empty', a formulation paradigmatically achieved in Luke Fildes' memorial 'portrait' of Charles Dickens after his death, 'The Empty Chair' (1870), which poignantly depicted the writer's now unoccupied desk and chair in the bay window at Gad's Hill just after his death.[29] Irving's passing fancy likening Shakespeare's chair to 'the flying chair of the Arabian enchanter' is true to another aspect of the writer's chair. It is ambivalent about locating the place of writing, connoting both placement and displacement in space and time. Placement, because its dimensions describe the size and posture of the writer's body at a certain historical time, but displacement because it is a disconcertingly small point of departure for the travels of imaginative writing across space and time. The classic visual statement of this idea of the writer's chair as the ground of imagination is again Dickensian, namely R.W. Buss's unfinished painting, entitled 'Dickens' Dream' (1875), which shows Dickens seated leaning back asleep at his desk in Gad's Hill Place surrounded by a cloud of his characters who hover in the air above his head.[30] A modern version of this is the montage of photographs of Roald Dahl working in his armchair with Quentin Blake's depictions of his child characters apparently perched upon the writing-board propped across the chair's arms, now on display in the Roald Dahl Story Museum in Great Missenden.[31] A writer's chair is at once realist and supernatural in that it negotiates between the writer's everyday timebound domestic life and the time of authorial posterity.

The writer's chair, then, may or may not appear to be a chair, it may or may not have been a chair that really belonged to, was used by, or appropriated by a writer, and it may or may not have been a chair in which the writer ever actually wrote or thought about writing. The only thing that makes any writer's chair into one is the act of representing it as such.[32] In the case of Shakespeare's chairs these acts of representation have been many, various, expensive, and ingenious. The case of Shakespeare's chair shows what goes into the making of a writer's chair with particular clarity because all of these chairs are verifiably 'inauthentic'. These same processes of representation also function around the impeccably authentic writer's chair, authenticated both by published autobiographical account describing the writer as sitting in the chair in question, and as the actual material object. Into this category falls the chair in which Washington Irving sat while staying in The Red Horse in Stratford: '"Shall I not take mine ease in mine inn?" thought I, as I gave the fire a stir, lolled back in my elbow-chair, and cast a complacent look about the little parlour of the Red Horse, at Stratford-upon-Avon'.[33] His chair subsequently became celebrated and was marked with a brass plaque as 'Washington Irving's chair'. Its fame having decayed with that of Irving himself, it is presently on show by request only in a private room at the Stratford-upon-Avon branch of Marks and Spencer on Bridge Street which now occupies what remains of the inn.[34]

Given that the writer's chair is a representation of writing, William Cowper's famous sofa, set as a writing task to lever the poet out of depression by a friend, and the starting-point of *The Task* (1785), might be considered the paradigmatic writer's chair: at once inspiring writing and the subject of writing, locus and departure-lounge, homely and Ottoman, epitomizing the domestic situation of writing and marking its exotic reach of imagination.[35] It is almost needless to state that, strictly, it is not a chair at all.

Austen's desk

The writer's chair is a representation of the writer's body in relation to writing. The writer's desk is also such a representation, and, like the writer's chair, is thoroughly clichéd. Any table with a quill-pen laid across it and a caption reserving it to an author may be turned into a writer's desk, as in the curious case of the nondescript table discreetly posed in the 'Shakespeare Corner' of the library at the University of Craiova, Romania—with no fanfare, and no claim to authenticity, a quill left casually on a flat surface does all the iconographic work required. What the writer's desk argues and how it does so may be illustrated by comparing and contrasting the variable claims made by three iterations of 'Jane Austen's desk': a table that briefly impersonated Austen's desk at the Winchester Cathedral Flower Festival of 2013; a writing-table that has for many years been shown as Austen's desk at Chawton Cottage; and the portable writing-desk that belonged to Austen which is presently in the collections of the British Library.

In 2013, as part of Winchester Cathedral's Flower Festival, a large and lavish display of flower arranging was constructed in honour of the 200th year of the publication of *Pride and Prejudice*. Located almost on top of Jane Austen's grave, in the centre of the aisle, the display suggested (amongst other horticultural improbabilities) that the novelist was in the habit of working in the garden on a small round occasional table that, if it had been outside in the summer of 2013, would most certainly have been ruined by torrential rain. At the table which formed the epicentre of a magnificent fantasy of the English country garden was seated a dummy, clothed and bonneted in the style made familiar by the many film and television adaptations of Austen's novels that had appeared over the previous fifteen years or so. The dummy was placed so that its back faced the public, its head inclined attentively over the table, its hand resting upon it, holding a pen poised over a sheet of paper.

This flower-display stated a number of rather conventional things about glimpsing genius in the act of creative writing. The inclusion of a dummy personating Austen insists, for example, on the need to imagine, clothe, and re-animate the volume of the writer's body seated at a desk—here, with unusual and presumably unintentionally macabre literalism, actually appearing like an emanation above Austen's bones. It details not only the body and the bodily position of the author but also the agency of that body, insisting on the importance of the writer's hand by foregrounding it carefully on the writing-table. It also dwells on the materiality of the business of writing, assembling here its furniture and tools—desk, inkstand, quill-pen, and paper. It emphasizes the moment at which writing comes into being on paper, when the attempt at that first famous sentence is just about to be made. It conceives the moment when a quotation is originated, before it knows that it is or is known to be a quotation. Consonant with this, the dummy's positioning—the writer's back turned to the viewer, the face completely hidden—points firstly to the way in which the act of origination is private and solitary and, secondly, to the frustrating indirection of the reader's personal relation with the authorial body which will only come into being when that sheet of paper is filled, and then another, and another. By installing this scene of writing within a fiction of an English country garden, the display re-stated the prevailing popular sense of Austen as a woman writer who composed within and about the confines of the English and the domestic, a mythos which stretches back well over a century. Most striking of all, in this display supposedly celebrating the publication of a book, no book is visible. The tableau renders publication invisible, in favour of visualizing the moment of origination, the primal scene, as one might say.

Nothing included in this tableau was 'authentic'—except, that is, the considerable affect invested in it by enthusiastic designers and viewers alike. Although it looked passably like it, suggesting that the designers expected that visitors would be as familiar with its appearance as with the opening of *Pride and Prejudice*, the table was only a stand-in for the famous twelve-sided walnut table shown in the Jane Austen Museum at Chawton Cottage. It is nonetheless instructive to compare the temporary appearance of Austen's desk in Winchester Cathedral with the permanent one on display at Chawton—not to draw out the differences between the floral fantasy and

Figure 4.2. Jane Austen's writing-table, Chawton Cottage. © Richard Gunn

the real thing, but to identify the continuities between them. For what the fanciful representation suggests in gesturing towards the remembered real thing is that even the real thing is representational.

Battered, undistinguished, and rather rickety, an item of Regency furniture has long been displayed in Chawton Cottage as Jane Austen's writing-table (Figure 4.2). It certainly belonged to Chawton, was inherited by Austen's sister Cassandra, and was bequeathed by her in 1845 to a manservant; thereafter it found its way back to the cottage when it was being set up as a heritage site in the 1920s.[36] The table in Winchester Cathedral required the proximity of gravestone, brass plaque, memorial window, bonneted dummy, writing materials, and apparently discarded 'manuscript' to stage it as 'Austen's table'. By comparison, the installation in Chawton is almost ostentatiously understated—a chair, a table, an empty crystal inkstand, and a single quill, lit by a neighbouring window. There is no claim to provenance, and no manuscript. Nevertheless, protected nowadays by a perspex screen allowing it to be seen but not touched, this table is clearly no longer simply meant to be understood as period furniture. The absence of the writer's body fulfils the same purpose as the dummy seated on Austen's grave—it represents the space of the writer's originating body, while describing its loss. The domestic solitude of the scene of writing in the garden staged in the cathedral is re-described here in terms of the imagined quiet of the sitting-room, which in turn invariably summons the not entirely convincing family anecdote of the door with the creaking hinge that supposedly gave Austen enough warning to conceal the evidence of her writing from all but her close intimates.[37]

The view from that window out into the garden has long been famous as stating the intimate relation of Austen's writing to the English landscape; when Chawton Cottage first came into imaginative visibility with the publication of Jane Austen's *Letters* in 1884, literary tourists began to imagine her looking out onto or walking within the garden, as the best and most natural backdrop to her characterization of English society. Reviewing the *Letters*, for example, the journalist T.E. Kebbel commented on how they had prompted and informed a visit to Chawton: 'the dining-room and drawing-room are still nearly as they were; and we may people the former with the authoress and her little writing-desk, seated at a table by the window, without any effort of the imagination'.[38] After this exercise, he wanders out into the garden, to imagine Austen walking there too 'as the Elliotts and the Musgroves, and the Eltons and the Bertrams grew beneath her hand'.[39] The figure of Austen walking in the garden here both obscures and blends into the woman writing at a table, an effect that the cathedral display also achieved. The modern variant upon this imaginative exercise may be exemplified by Cindy Jones' blog about her literary pilgrimage to all places associated with Austen in 2010:

> Standing in the simple room where the modest writing-table occupied a spot near the window, I felt *my* Jane Austen's presence. Not the celebrity icon, but the unaffected woman... *Jane Austen was the person I had imagined*: physically present at the little table, yet mentally far away, working in a universe of her own creation. And this is what we both understand: being stranded on a desert island is not a problem as long as you have paper, pen, and writing-table. Her writing-table is the most unassuming piece of furniture with the most impressive back-story I've ever met.[40]

Understatement is partly possible simply because the house itself acts as a larger narrative frame; the writer is already at home there. But it also makes a set of still current propositions about the nature of Austen writing, and by extension women's writing, as genteel, amateur, modest to the point of invisibility, and only imperfectly abstracted from her own body and domestic life. Accordingly, the journalist and biographer of Austen, Claire Tomalin, conventionally emphasized the table's smallness: 'This fragile 12-sided piece of walnut on a single tripod must be the smallest table ever used by a writer'.[41] Jones glosses this smallness as a statement of marginal, fragile, resourceful imaginative endeavour and escape.

Although it is not inconceivable that Austen actually sat at this table to write her novels, the surface on which she actually wrote is likely to have been her 'writing-desk'. Gifted by Joan Austen-Leigh to the British Library in 1999, it is now held in the Sir John Ritblat Gallery, together with its contents. A handsome and expensive mahogany portable folding writing-box, it opens into a writing-slope that would have sat on the table itself. It was also capable of storing all sorts of writing equipment and sheets of manuscript if necessary. Its present contents include Jane Austen's eye-glasses and her sewing kit or 'housewife'.[42] This writing-desk is probably the true paraphernalia of literary genius. At the opening of the Millennium exhibition in March 2000 at the British Library ('Chapter and Verse: 1000 years of English Literature') which featured this writing-desk, Tomalin said of it that it demonstrated that 'All you need if you are a writer is a desk, a pencil and of course a great brain'.[43]

Despite its authenticity, so far this writing-desk has exerted surprisingly little purchase on the representation of Austen as an author. This is not because such writing-desks are resistant to carrying cultural charge, especially in relation to women writers. Although many male writers have possessed and used such efficient and versatile desks when travelling, and these have sometimes become celebrated either through their ability to evoke those travels or occasionally because they feature in iconic portraits of the writer, there was and is nonetheless something culturally female about the writing-box.[44] It was compact, portable, ambiguously dutiful (in that it would have dispensed at least as many thank-you letters as wild imaginative fantasies), and personal to the point of secretiveness: 'the writing slope was . . . one of the very few private spaces a school girl, governess or teacher might have . . . Writing slopes could be locked and their keys carried around so they were a rare place to keep items or writings that you might want to keep private'.[45] It was also, on occasion, a highly personal gift.[46] Given this, the relative lack of interest in Austen's writing-desk (as opposed to her writing-table) is surprising; and it makes a striking contrast to the cult status of the writing-slope owned by Charlotte Brontë.

The ways that this desk has been celebrated usefully explain the comparative obscurity of Austen's desk. For many years Brontë's writing-slope has been one of the more famous items displayed in Haworth Parsonage, dressed with eye-glasses, quill-pen, nibs, seal, inkpot, and wafers of sealing-wax. Its meaning is glossed by a caption on a postcard, which uses a quotation from *Agnes Grey* to narrate ownership of it in an autobiographical voice and to give it provenance as 'my precious desk, containing all my letters and papers, my small amount of cash, and all my valuables'.[47] This ingenious use of quotation to narrate the desk is helpful, but what really is important here is the location of the desk in Haworth, 'at home'. In 2011, one of the three other pieces of furniture extant that might be said to be 'Brontë desks', in that they make claims for having been the surfaces on which one or more of the Brontë sisters worked, was donated anonymously to the Parsonage Museum. The write-ups of this event evidence a similar desire to bring writing 'home' through the medium of furniture. 'Brontë writing desk comes home to Haworth Parsonage' ran the BBC headline on 24 May 2011; the then curator Andrew Macarthy was quoted as saying, 'We are delighted that these items are now where they belong, here in Haworth'.[48]

This suggests that the imaginative deficit between Austen's table and Austen's writing-desk is produced by the desire to locate the scene of writing 'at home'; that is, within a simulacrum of the lived domesticity that once generated writing. Siting a writing-desk in a library in the metropolis turns out to be too far from home in its sense of special origin. As Claire Tomalin would remark of Austen's writing-table, 'Today, back in its old home, it speaks to every visitor of the modesty of genius'.[49]

Location, dislocation, translocation

Having begun with Du Maurier's desk as an example of a writer's desk that has emphatically been translocated, it seems rather surprising to arrive at such a powerful articulation of the need to make the writer's desk at home. However, in the instances of translocation touched upon so far, writer's desks and sometimes their entire studies have indeed moved, but they have not moved very far from an idea of 'home'. Many of these translocated desks claim to be at home; Du Maurier's desk is 'at home' in Jamaica Inn because it is the inspiration and setting for her novel, and Thomas Hardy's study is felt to be 'at home' in the Dorset County Museum in Dorchester because

The Mayor of Casterbridge (1886) is set specifically in Dorchester and the bulk of the 'Wessex' novels are set in Dorset. Other instances reveal other mechanisms for making the translocated writer's desk at home. Hans Christian Andersen's study can be transported successfully from Copenhagen to Odense because the museum argues that his career as a writer of fairytales flows directly from his birth and childhood. Knut Hamsun's desk can be transported to the museum devoted to his memory sited in his childhood home Hammarøv on the same basis (with the added advantage that this does something to soften the embarrassment of the older man's Nazi sympathies).[50] The celebrity of Dickens' desk from Gad's Hill has meant that it has been lent around as much as Shakespeare's chair, appearing, for instance, in the Museum of London's 2012 exhibition 'Dickens and London', where it served as a substitute in microcosm for the writer's house museum, 48 Doughty St, then closed for refurbishment.[51] Displayed nowadays in Doughty St, one might say pedantically that the Gad's Hill desk is in the 'wrong' place, but it remains branded to the author through being located in another one of his houses.[52] The Dickens desk displayed as part of the Elkin collection in the Free Library of Philadelphia, or the Brontë desk which surfaced from the collections of the New York Public Library for the exhibition celebrating the centenary of the Library in 2011, or the C.S. Lewis desk at Wheaton College may all seem to someone British to be evidently in exile; even so, they prove to argue that America is the appropriate home for Anglophone literary heritage.[53] On occasion the writer's desk has been reduced metonymically to just one portable and iconic piece of desk furniture to mark the transference of writerly power to a new home. Early instances of this include the gift of Petrarch's inkwell to Maria Edgeworth, and the writers' inkwells that found a home on the poet Henry Wadsworth Longfellow's desk in Brattle St, Cambridge, MA:

> The old-fashioned folding desk on which the poet wrote is opened up on the table in front of his chair. There too is the quill pen which he used and three of his ink-stands. One is a green French china ink-well...Another bears the inscription 'Saml Taylor Coleridge: his inkstand', and beside it is a letter from Longfellow thanking his English friends for having presented him with this inkstand, from which Coleridge had written *The Rime of the Ancient Mariner.* The third ink-well belonged in succession to three poets: the English poet, George Crabbe, the Irish poet, Tom Moore, and the American poet, Longfellow.[54]

These inkwells served to construct Longfellow as worthy inheritor of an Anglophone poetic tradition.[55] The question of where the writer's desk is most 'at home' is re-opened by the recent loan of J.R.R. Tolkien's desk and chair by an American collection for display in the Tolkien exhibition at the Bodleian Library, Oxford, so returning to its old haunts.

The power of the discourse of homing in producing the writer's desk is very great, and may be neatly illustrated by counter-examples where this discourse fails. My first, the Maison de Balzac in Passy, supplies a very striking instance of how a writer's desk of authenticated provenance may not, under certain conditions, function effectively as the cultural formation of 'the writer's desk'. Pushed against the wall of the first room of the museum, there is a plain wooden table. This is a desk that once belonged to François-Réné Chateaubriand. It is, however, culturally inert because it is in Balzac's house; the material artefact is there, but its meaning has been necessarily mothballed. Chateaubriand's desk does not work as Chateaubriand's desk because it is dislocated from its home.

So important is location to the meanings of the writer's desk that on occasion the 'wrong' desk in the right place can be more affectively functional than the authentic piece of furniture. This was borne in upon me the day I discovered, wandering the corridors of the Houghton Rare Book Library in Harvard, a small table stacked with its legs in the air and swathed in dust-sheets. This proved on investigation to be Emily Dickinson's writing-table.[56] That which I had viewed a couple of days previously in Dickinson's bedroom at The Homestead, Amherst, along with other enthusiastic tourists, was in fact a duplicate, made contemporaneously for Dickinson's sister. The question set by this doubled object was where the reality of the writer's desk actually inheres: in the affective experience of reader-tourists produced within the genuine spaces of the writer's house museum? In the form of the table? Or in its material? I very much suspect that my fellow-tourists, had they registered the substitution, would have regarded it as a sort of fraud, because what they wanted to see above all was the place of inscription. The real desk in the wrong place (Chateaubriand's), and the wrong desk in the real place (Dickinson's), mirror each other as versions of the way that the power and authenticity of the writer's desk may be constructed and deconstructed through placement.

The desire to enhome the act of inscription to a desk bespeaks an unspoken, almost unthought, belief that the writer's desk retains an organic and precious memory of the pressure of the writer's pen, much as paper most certainly and demonstrably does. It is possible to illustrate this by looking at a third example, the curious history of the desk once displayed in Victor

Hugo's house, Hauteville, in Guernsey,[57] which is presently on display in the Victor Hugo Museum in the Marais in Paris.[58] An account of the display of this desk in Hauteville can be found in an issue of the *Every Saturday* journal, published in 1869:

> The most interesting...of all the curiosities in these apartments is a small octagonal writing-table; on four sides of the octagon are four inkstands and pens, underneath each inkstand is a small drawer, and a name is inlaid round each inkstand. The four names are, Lamartine, George Sand, Alexandre Dumas, Victor Hugo. In the drawer under each inkstand is an autograph of the author; these inkstands (most of them of the plainest description) and pens being originally the property of each author.[59]

The journalist then transcribes the letters from each author sent in response to the request to provide pen and inkstand for this expensive object of vertu. This article of furniture was conceived by Hugo's widow as a fund-raiser. It proved entirely unsaleable, conjecturally because despite displaying the real thing in the shape of pens, inkstands, and autograph letters, nothing had ever actually been written on it. It was not, and never had been, the original location of writing.[60]

Origin and elegy

For writers, the desk may enable and even dramatize the origination of inscription; for the writer's house museum it fantasizes, memorializes, and elegizes that act of origination. Writers, as already noted in the case of Longfellow, have not been above deploying this range of effects themselves. The best-selling and publicity-conscious novelist Marie Corelli deployed them in her ultra-feminine music room at Mason Croft in Stratford-upon-Avon. Filled with musical instruments, flowers, caged birds, and objets d'art, it was also, according to Maureen Bell, embellished with 'books...artfully displayed, left open at particular passages' and 'manuscripts—with ink pens carefully laid across them—...placed on desks to catch the eye of visitors'.[61] Visitors, that is to say, were to be allowed to feel close to the moment of creation through looking at the conjecturally unfinished and not-yet published.

The desire on the part of those who come visiting dead writers to experience a similar access to the moment of the unfinished has driven the habit of preserving or reconstructing writer's desks in the state that they were when the writer was alive. This impulse may be seen at its most extreme at small scale in the display of August Strindberg's desk in his last home in Stockholm; here, everything inventoried by a grief-stricken friend as left on the desk at Strindberg's death is carefully affixed to a false surface overlaid on the desk, and the whole assemblage covered in an acrylic sheet.[62] At larger scale, there is the instance of Roald Dahl's writing-hut at Great Missenden. Originally located at his home in Gipsy House, Great Missenden, in 2011 it was relocated to the Roald Dahl Museum and Story Centre in the High Street. Here the original ground-plan was drawn out on an interior floor and upon that the interior of the study itself was reconstructed behind glass. An extensive display of mementoes (postcards, photographs, children's drawings, handwritten notes, hand-made gifts, geological curiosities, souvenirs, fragments picked up on travels, joke items, and surgical left-overs—the ball joint of Dahl's femur, shavings from his spine) are assembled along with the writer's more mundane equipment (indigestion pills, pencils and rubbers, pencil-sharpener, a paper-weight, cigarette lighters, an ashtray, spectacles, spectacle-cleaning fluid, a highlighter pen, yellow sticky notes, pads of paper, reference books, an armchair, a writing-board, a brush to clean the board, an anglepoise lamp, a waste-paper basket, a rug, a footstool, and so forth). The argument made by this reconstruction of stuff talismanic and mundane is threefold. It argues for the importance and idiosyncrasy of this as a place of creative origin constructed by the writer—as Dahl put it, 'my nest, my womb' (by which he meant a place of genesis rather than regression). It states, too, the unglamorous, punishing and make-it-up-as-you-go-along nature of creative work through the anglepoise lamp balanced just so by a golf-ball and a pink towel, and the hole cut in the back of the famous armchair to ease Dahl's back-pain. Finally, it argues for authorial presence in a macabre fashion that would have appealed to Dahl; what sets the Dahl reconstruction apart from all previous such inventoried reconstructions of the author's desk is that, having carefully killed all the vermin that were thriving in the rotting paper, wood, and upholstery, the conservators hoovered up the dust of thirty years, sterilized it, and then sprinkled it across the reconstructed and relocated whole as the final touch of authenticity. With this rather ghastly gesture, a fiction of perpetually living origin converts into an elegy for the dead.

Indeed, effects of origin and elegy typically co-exist on the writer's desk. The pathos and frustration of interruption by the writer's death, the equivalent of discovering that the last pages of your engrossing book are actually missing, is a long-standing trope of writer's house museums: one thinks of the display of Friedrich Schiller's desk in the Schillerhaus in Weimar that shows the unfinished manuscript-page of *Demetrius*, a composition interrupted by the author's death from a sudden fever on 9 May 1805; or the way that Dickens' writing-chalet emphasizes the way the manuscript of *Edwin Drood* was left unfinished when Dickens succumbed to a last stroke; or the display at the Gaskell Museum in Manchester of the last pages of the unfinished *Wives and Daughters* in facsimile manuscript lying on the writing-slope as they ought to have been abandoned on Elizabeth Gaskell's death. But irrespective of whether the writer actually died mid-sentence, the aesthetic of work interrupted, whether in euphoric or elegiac mode, is fundamental to almost all fictions of the writer's house museum.

Surface, trace, signature

In 2000, when the British Library borrowed from a private owner the table 'that witnessed the creation' of *Wuthering Heights, Jane Eyre*, and *The Tenant of Wildfell Hall* for its 'Chapter and Verse' exhibition, it designed 'a literary coup [by which] manuscripts from all four siblings will be reunited with—and displayed on—the table for probably the first time in over 150 years'. This was making an analogy between the memory of wood and that of paper. The curator Chris Fletcher remarked, 'To be able to reunite the manuscripts with the table upon which they were created—and which seemed to play such an essential part in their creation—is a remarkable and powerful thing'. The write-up additionally picked out the traces of wear on the table for especial comment: 'Made from Cuban mahogany on an oak base, the table is a real writer's work-place, stained with ink spills and scarred in the centre with a large candle burn. At one end a bold letter E is carved into the surface, almost certainly the work of young Emily, whose initial can also be seen in the notebook of her poems that will be displayed on the table'.[63] The table doubly signified acts of writing, once through displaying the manuscripts, and once though displaying its scars, most especially Emily's conjectured graffito.[64] This is an unusually compressed demonstration of the idea that the act of writing leaves a material 'trace'—a surviving mark, sign or evidence of the former existence, influence, or action of some agent or event, some sort of vestige, through which, indeed, it is possible to trace and find someone or something that was lost. The trace of whatever is really meant by 'the act of writing' is read through its effect on the physical surface of the desk as much as marks on the paper.[65] The desire to do this derives from the desire to home the text—to rewind it from a mass-produced book back to a unique place, and from thence into a unique manuscript. Thus the surface of the desk can be read as at once the place of origination and as the memory-trace of successive acts of signification. It coalesces all the acts of writing achieved upon it, much like a palimpsest. Probably the most elegantly simplified expression of this meaning of the desk as conscious surface is provided by one of Annie Leibovitz's remarkable photographs of Virginia Woolf's desk at Monk's House. Leibovitz takes a view of the desk impossible to achieve in any ordinary relationship to this piece of furniture. She positions the camera directly above the surface, so as to photograph it as perfectly flat, like a page of paper. Then she lights it brilliantly, so that every scar, chip, and ink-stain stands out as clear, intended, and idiosyncratic as handwriting.[66]

Writers themselves sometimes succumb to this need to record the act of writing upon a unique material object. Thomas Hardy labelled his pens with the titles of the novels he had written with them and then put them aside. Rudyard Kipling, a believer in the 'Daemon' of writing that sat upon his pen, kept 'an outsize office pewter inkpot, on which I would gouge the names of the tales and books I wrote out of it' amongst the other 'little fetishes' on his desk.[67] A particularly telling instance of this is furnished by J.K. Rowling's minor but celebrated act of vandalism in the Balmoral Hotel in Edinburgh. Reviewing the hotel for *The Times* in 2007, the journalist Laura Knight paid especial attention to the room in which Rowling was supposed to have written parts of the *Harry Potter* series of children's books:

> It was in this room that J.K. Rowling finished *Harry Potter and the Deathly Hallows* in January. I sit at the modern desk where, presumably, she put an end to either Harry or He Who Must Not Be Named. Then I plump down on the beige sofa, the dark leather chairs, and the soft bed with its leather headboard, just in case she doesn't write at a desk.[68]

In rehearsing the sense that such a site of writing must have existed, and that it offered privileged access to the book, Knight was reiterating practices that, as I have shown, have been in place since at least the eighteenth century; she was, however, in the wrong room, trying out the wrong chairs, desk, and bed. According to Rowling herself, the room she finished the novel in was a floor down, room 552. To mark what she must have assumed was the moment of release from the entire project, she left a memorial inscription on the back of a plaster bust of Hermes: 'J.K. Rowling/finished writing/Harry Potter and the Deathly Hallows/in this room (552)/on 11th Jan 2007'. Following her confession to this piece of graffiti in a tweet of 11 January 2016, the room was promptly transformed into the J.K. Rowling Suite, complete with a new owl knocker, which may either be read as merely twee or as a rather nicely judged reference to the way that Rowling's owls carry correspondence between writers and readers. The desk—'the very same one used by J.K. Rowling to write those crucial last chapters'— was staged and represented as such, the bust protected by a glass cabinet, and a framed replica of Rowling's inscription displayed on the wall behind it.[69] (Sitting in a room in the Grand Hotel in Lund, Sweden, as I am presently doing, I consider and dismiss the notion of scratching my name and the date somewhere in imitation, if only because I have not as yet finished up this project and, because, sadly blind to the obvious cultural value of the gesture, the management might bill me for the damage.) By locating, dating, and signing the text upon a material surface, Rowling's inscription does for the scene of writing exactly what the staging of all the other writer's desks I have been describing is meant to achieve: it confines the immaterialities and the temporal and spatial vagaries of text to material reality, to a place, a time, and an authorial hand.

In the case of women writers, the writer's desk shown 'at home' may remain ambiguous about the constraints and pleasures of domesticity, but it does not typically activate the anxieties of conceiving writing as professional work. However professionalized and driven by the need to earn money these women writers actually were, their desks if displayed 'at home' will argue that their writing was of a piece with domestic life; this is the argument made by the inclusion of the photograph of Kilmarth on Du Maurier's desk at Jamaica Inn, which collapses her own home with the setting for her novel *The House on the Strand* (1969). In the case of male writers, however, asserting a domestic setting for the work of writing can be trickier. It may usefully argue for non-alienated and amateur self-expression, connoting feminized retreat (as in the case of Cowper) or gentlemanly status (as in the case of Longfellow). On the other hand, it may uncomfortably import the professional grind of book-making into the home, whether the ten years of shuffling of paper-slips in an attic that went into the making of a dictionary (as in the case of Samuel Johnson) or the vast, meticulous labour of correcting and revising sheet after sheet of novelistic proofs (in the case of Honoré de Balzac).[70] The domestic bureaucracy of the desk especially threatens national bards, as in the case of the poet Robert Burns, whose chief advantage as a national bard has been his 'wildness'. This is illustrated neatly by comparing the presentation of two desks: that of Longfellow in Portland, Maine; the other of Burns in Alloway. 'The Den', Longfellow's study in his onetime home in Portland, Maine, is presented today much as it ever was. The iconic visitor view is summed up by a postcard of 1904. To the left is a window, facing which is a sloping desk. Beyond it, there is a door, and pinned on the door, a sheet of black paper with a poem written on it in white. This is Longfellow's famous poem 'Rainy Day', written, as the postcard explains, at 'The Rainy Day Desk'.[71] There is a cheerful security about this depiction of writing a poem (still sold in reproduction at the house museum today) that contrasts sharply with the recent display of Burns' desk in the entrance exhibition to the Birthplace at Alloway. As a civil servant (an excise man) Burns owned a number of desks; such was his celebrity during his lifetime that on his death many of them were preserved and are now scattered between the Burns properties in Alloway and Dumfries, and the Writers' Museum in Edinburgh. However, the idea of the ploughman poet inspired by the Muse of Coila did not and does not sit very easily with the idea of a desk. Accordingly, in the Birthplace 'Burns' desk' is exhibited against a backdrop suggesting a field of wheat. It is slightly tilted up, as though flying away, and all the papers on it are cunningly displayed on invisible wires as though caught by a great gust of wind. Burns, that display says, may have worked at a desk, but he wrote in a Caledonian gale of inspiration generated from his native landscape. Writing lyric poetry is not clerical or genteel work but raw native effusion. Hence arguably the most powerful imagined scene of Burns writing does not feature pen and paper, chair and desk, or indeed home at all, but the diamond stylus he used in the local pub to etch his verses on the pane of a window and a glass tumbler.[72] And in case one is tempted to dismiss Burns' desk as a one-off instance of curatorial ingenuity, a glance across Europe is arrested by an exhibition staged in 2017–18 at the Petöfi Museum, Budapest, that swept the desk and chair of the national poet János Arany along with the floor upon which they stand up to a ninety-degree angle to the actual floor, so that impossibly they 'stood' on the wall.[73] Opposite, there were a series of sound and light displays, chiefly of the national landscapes of Arany's poems. Both displays evince an impatience with a realist staging of the scene of writing via the abandoned desk and empty chair, preferring to stage poetry as emanating from the land.

5

Household effects

Johnson's coffee-pot and Twain's effigy

Austen's flagstones

The list of items that the retired London solicitor T.E. Carpenter put together from 1948 onwards through purchase, donation, and loan with a view to rendering Chawton Cottage once more a suitable home for Jane Austen reads uncomfortably like a reverse house clearance project: it comprised the predictably valuable, including a portrait, locks of hair, letters, manuscripts, and early editions, along with a miscellany of household effects of much less stable or evident literary value. These included 'the back of a looking-glass said originally to have been in Jane Austen's house', a dinner service that Austen chose and mentioned in her letters, a donkey-cart known as 'Jane's cart', Mrs Austen's patchwork quilt, and some flagstones said to have been originally laid in the kitchen.[1] Carpenter acquired these items in an endeavour to realize in material form the imaginative acts performed by the travel-writing of Constance Hill and others that had formed the necessary prehistory to the imagining and setting up of Chawton Cottage as a writer's house museum.[2] In aggregate, these writings had described the house and its Hampshire setting both as private homeliness (a peaceful all-female domestic retirement) and national homeliness (a timeless English rural idyll, far from the stresses of global politics). The problem would be how to make this opportunistic collection of objects tell that story within the spaces of Chawton Cottage itself.

It's a common problem for house museums reconstructed well after the death of the author. They are typically made up of a miscellany of things with variable claims to 'authenticity', which in this context turns out to be a matter of how close they are to the author's life and work, something which in turn measures their power to reanimate that life and work in the present of the museum.[3] Thus in addition to objects designed to evoke the author's body (the remains, animal-objects, or items of clothing discussed in Chapters 1–3), the museum may display objects once owned or used by the author. These will have an increased hold on the reader's imagination if they are associated with the work of writing (such as the desks and chairs discussed in Chapter 4) or if they are mentioned in diary, letters, or autobiographical writings, or even better, if they inspire or 'appear', provably or conjecturally, in the imaginative writings. Such items may be fleshed out with objects probably familiar to the writer (e.g. once owned by the writer's family), objects and representations of objects/environs contemporaneous with the writer's lifetime, replicas of things once owned by the writer, and contemporaneous and modern objects and artworks interpreting the author and his/her works. This type of miscellany can be illustrated in epitome using the very sparse contents of the house museum devoted to Ludovico Ariosto in Ferrara. In the two rooms and a landing devoted to the poet are displayed, *inter alia*, Ariosto's finger-bone, Ariosto's chair, a bronze cast of Ariosto's inkstand made sometime in the late eighteenth century after an enterprising English tourist purchased the real thing, a number of portraits and busts of Ariosto, an early copy of the *Orlando Furioso*, a couple of landscape paintings supposed vaguely to be evocative of Ariosto's romances, and a good deal of information on the celebrity of the poet and the house from Ariosto's death to the present day.[4]

So far, in considering the ways in which the author's body has been remembered and the ways that the scene of writing has been staged as an extension of that bodily existence, I have been considering objects imagined as somehow carrying or at least dramatizing authorial subjectivity. This chapter looks at a miscellany of much more mundane and everyday household objects. Few household items carry powerfully pre-determined cultural meanings in and of themselves, and they are therefore unlikely to produce pre-determined cultural effects. Julian Barnes' narrator in *Flaubert's Parrot* (1984) expresses baffled exasperation at the enthusiasm of collectors such as T.E. Carpenter for 'Austen's flagstones': 'What makes us randy for relics? Don't we believe the words enough? Do we think the leavings of a life contain some ancillary truth?'[5] I am similarly driven to ask why, and how, the authorial possessive apostrophe takes such objects out of use to be treasured and repurposed as repositories of what Barnes calls 'ancillary truth', capable of revealing the author's life and art. As the guide to the Hans Christian

Figure 5.1. Samuel Johnson's coffee-pot. © Houghton Rare Book Library

Andersen museum in Odense puts it: 'The pen does not write anymore and the scissors do not cut. The rope was never used, and the bed is no longer slept in. And yet these treasures live on as a reminder of [an] amazing life and art'.[6]

So here I address myself to the questions raised by the idea, desire, reality, and deployment of the unlikelihood of Austen's flagstones. What motivates such an attribution, what *sorts* of objects attract such attribution, and how is that possessive apostrophe constructed and maintained between author, household objects, and the form and fabric of the house itself?

Dr Johnson's coffee-pot and Mrs Thrale's teapot

The collection of materials relating to Dr Samuel Johnson now held at the Houghton Library in Harvard University, formerly the personal collection of Donald and Mary Hyde, includes 'Dr Johnson's teapot' (Figure 5.1). This item was certainly used at 17 Gough Square in London, and certainly belonged to Johnson, and is almost certainly a coffee-pot, made by John Parker and Edward Wakelin and dating from c. 1765.[7] This is probably the 'large silver coffeepot' which was willed by Johnson to his long-standing black manservant Francis Barber 'in recognition of his care and labours', either as a valuable item in itself or as a memento of their relationship. In the event, Johnson's will was in this respect quite outrageously ignored: far from passing to Barber, the coffee-pot was briskly sold by Johnson's executor, Sir John Hawkins, immediately following Johnson's death, on the basis of the weight of silver contained within it.[8] Purchased by Henry Constantine Newell in the first instance, the item was acquired by the American collector and Johnson enthusiast A. Edward Newton in 1927, at the height of Anglophile literary collecting in the States. By this time, the coffee-pot seems already to have been identified as a teapot, because it was used at a tea-party to recreate the Johnsonian Literary Club at Newton's home, Oak Knoll, Boston, on 11 December 1932, complete with servants in eighteenth-century costume. It continues to be described as a 'teapot' in the Houghton Library's online exhibition, despite the fact that the exhibit also includes the manuscript in which, as already noted, Johnson wills it as a coffee-pot to Francis Barber.

Whether designed for making tea or coffee, the pot evidences with unusual explicitness the processes this antique item of household equipment has had to go through to become a valuable literary relic, suitable for inclusion in an enthusiast's collection. The body has been engraved with an extensive inscription, and then the entire pot has been mounted on a plinth complete with a further inscription. Less evidently, the story told in the inscription depends on, but elides, a crucial moment of revaluation, the moment when the coffee-pot fell first out of being valued as a useful household object into a gift describing the value of a relationship with a servant, then into a more commonplace valuation on the basis of its weight of silver, and was then rescued from being melted down on the basis of a quite different sort of valuation. The story is told at length in the inscription on the body of the pot:

> It was weighed out for sale, under the inspection of Sr. Jno. Hawkins, at the very Minute when they were in the next Room closing the incision through which Mr Cruikshank had explored the ruinated Machinery of its dead Master's thorax—so Bray (the silversmith conveyed there in Sr. John's Carriage thus hastily! to buy the Plate) informed its present Possessor Henry Constantine Newell by whom it was, for its celebrated Services, on the 1st of Novr. 1788 rescued from the undiscriminating Obliterations of the Furnace.

(The reference to 'the incision' is to the autopsy conducted on Johnson's body the day after his death despite his vehemently stated wishes to the contrary.⁹) The wonderfully macabre story the coffee-pot tells suggests that for its proudly prolix new owner it stood in as a substitute for the 'ruinated Machinery' of Johnson's body. It is, as it were, the cosmetically whole version of the autopsied corpse. Unlike the dead body, it was something that could be 'rescued' from 'undiscriminating Obliteration'. It could serve as the remains of the mortal wreckage of genius, and as an eyewitness to the moment of death and ruin could be saved to evidence and narrate Johnson's continuing cultural importance to posterity. That indignant exclamation mark effectively describes the greater discrimination of the discerning, even heroically sentimental, collector.

The question as to whether this item is a tea or coffee-pot is instructive, because arguably it points to another purpose that it was made to serve. One might account for the mistake by noting the apparent variant spelling in the manuscript of the will of 'coffea'. It is possible, reading the manuscript at speed, to construe this as a crossing-out, followed by the word 'tea', but this is arguably far-fetched. It is more likely that the coffee-pot ought to have been a teapot. It ought to have been a teapot because, as any reader of James Boswell's *Life of Johnson* (1791) knows, Johnson and Boswell drank coffee at the Turk's Head Coffee-house, and not at home. Perhaps in 1927 tea seemed more English, quite independently of Johnson's well-known and self-confessed addiction to it; it certainly associated better with American temperance culture, and with a reading of Boswell who mentions Johnson taking tea some thirteen times in the *Life* and famously opens his *Journal of A Tour of the Hebrides with Samuel Johnson LLD* (1785) with a vignette of Johnson drinking tea with Boswell and his wife on Johnson's arrival in Edinburgh in August 1773.¹⁰ This scene was imaginatively important enough for contemporaries to be illustrated by Thomas Rowlandson in 1786; after all, it describes the way in which the intransigently English Johnson could be domesticated in a foreign country. Reinvented as a teapot, the coffee-pot thus functioned very efficiently as what one might call a portable writer's house museum—it travelled across the Atlantic to act as precursor and facilitator of a transatlantic version of the Johnsonian salon.¹¹ Its power inhered in its 'celebrated Services'—that is to say, in its ability on the one hand to act as eyewitness to Johnson's life, times, and circle, and on the other to be used to repeat and sanction similar intellectual and sociable transactions in the present. Its especial value lay in its ability to make Johnson at home across the Atlantic, and in allowing his American admirers to be at home with him, indeed to become him by force of proximity. As one American collector of Johnsoniana piously reflected in 1929: 'Such is the force and charm of Dr Johnson that one sometimes seems to see certain of his personal qualities mysteriously conveyed through his relics, and reappearing in those who preserve them'.[12] Possession of Johnson's relics turns into being possessed by Johnson. The coffee-pot is given value by being turned into a witness of the very moment when Johnson turned from a live celebrity into a canonical author; but it is also given value by being the mechanism through which Johnson's writings successively turn back into Johnsonian biography, into Johnsonian body, and so into Johnsonian encounter. The mechanism by which this is achieved is the anecdote. The coffee-pot effectively materializes Boswellian biographical anecdote, bringing it sharply and immediately into the present.

Other household items are similarly converted to authorial effects by withdrawing the object from its original function, and then deploying inscription, caption, and display to develop the item's powers. The apparent inadequacy and fragmentariness of such things belies their force; they are the material equivalent of the simultaneous irreducibility and incompleteness of the biographical anecdote which Helen Deutsch has described as 'the smallest possible version of narrative'.[13] Johnson's own definition of 'anecdote' in the Dictionary as 'something not yet published; secret history' and 'a minute passage of private life' further points to the charm of developing the minute, private, and secretive in an otherwise banal object which crucially expresses 'the not yet published'—that which the lover of Johnson cannot read in his printed works, and which is available only to those who are privileged to encounter it in person. All such items-cum-anecdotes thus ultimately function as metonymic stand-ins for the author's presence. They serve as short-circuits between past writer and present reader; or rather, they serve as short-circuits between the reader's life and the writer's life. Johnson's coffee-pot catches him at once in the quotidian act of drinking coffee (or rather, tea), and as a once-only and never-to-be-repeated exhibition, slashed open on the autopsy table.

The coffee-pot is unusual, though not unique, in being made into 'Johnson's coffee-pot' by an inscription that alters the original material. It is more usual to provide a detachable caption, whether screwed on as a plate (as here on the later plinth) or merely a pasteboard card laid next to the item within a museum case. The detachability of caption underscores its status as supplementary to the object; it develops the affective agency of the object by providing an otherwise invisible and unguessable narrative that mediates the object to the viewer.[14] (One might argue mischievously that the object itself is really the caption, merely supplementary to authorial biography; it is diverting to imagine a writer's house museum as all captions and no objects.) Writer's houses and their contents have always been glossed: first by the writer, the ideal tour-guide, then by whoever showed the house subsequently, then by travel-writers who repeated, corrected, amplified, compressed, or tried to side-step the guide's patter. The caption is a short-form version of this, encompassing a range of site-specific marking practices from inscription (where captioning invades or reshapes the material), through small plaque (where captioning is affixed), to short, proximate description (whether delivered on a written or printed card, or via touch-screen technology or phone app). Caption enables objects to tell their secret history of the author: thus the Andersen museum narrates the writer's study (a reconstruction of that in Nyhavn in Copenhagen) by allowing access to objects through touch-screen technology: 'Click on the different items in the room to get a closer look. Most items have a small story which tells what they are, and what significance they had to Hans Christian Andersen'.

Back across the Atlantic, 'Johnson's teapot' has a rival that pulls off a similar set of tricks. The teapot presently on display in a glass case in the Parlour at the Dr Johnson House Museum, 17 Gough Square, London is, however, Mrs Thrale's teapot. Made by Meissen in Germany sometime between 1755 and 1760, it is porcelain, with a silver spout. Both it and the matching equipage of a sugar bowl, two cups and saucers, a spoon tray, and a tea canister are painted with three figures reminiscent of Watteau: two gentlemen standing, and a seated woman. The whole is what is known as a 'tête-à-tête' set for two.

Of recent years, this tea-set has begun to achieve minor celebrity, appearing prominently on the museum's website as one of the more notable items in the collection. 'Mrs Thrale's teapot', however, can never have been at home at 17 Gough Square. Mrs Thrale did not meet Johnson until 1764 at the earliest, some five years after he had moved out from Gough Square.[15] And anyway, it was not considered good form to bring your own tea-service when you came calling. In itself, then, the teapot is 'authentic' and even 'unique' through its association with Mrs Thrale, but the authenticity of its presence in Gough Square is more questionable. This suggests that the teapot's materiality is somehow necessary to the story of Gough Square.

Noting that the 'pastoral figures' with which it is painted reflect 'the feminine, domestic nature of the tea-ritual', the caption then expands into biographical anecdote: 'Johnson was a frequent house-guest of the Thrales at their country house, Streatham Park, where he would suffer the mistress of the house to sit up and make . . . [tea] for him, until two or three hours after midnight'.[16]

The presence of Mrs Thrale's teapot in 17 Gough Square thus reverses the true state of things, whereby Johnson drank tea made for him by a series of women in their own houses. But, displayed along with the other pieces of porcelain owned by the museum, including a teacup belonging to Boswell, and a whole tea-set belonging to Sir Joshua Reynolds, Mrs Thrale's equipage places her as a member of Johnson's circle within an imaginary tea-party, serving as a metonym for the absent body of its once-owner. Equally, it gives material immediacy to a biographical narrative that it conjecturally initiates, and subsequently epitomizes and evidences. As the imagined intermediary of encounter and transaction, witnessing, describing, and potentially re-imagining and even re-enacting the material conditions of contemporary intellectual and sociable exchange, it possesses the power to revivify and relocate a relationship that was conducted in other places and at other times to the present-day Gough Square. The celebrity of Mrs Thrale's teapot is therefore related to the continuing popularity of the fantasy of drinking tea with Johnson. The house regularly offers tea in the Parlour in the summer, and once you have taken tea with Dr Johnson in this fashion, the gift shop will sell you a range of tea-themed gifts, ways of taking Dr Johnson back home with you.[17] In September 2011, Out of Joint staged a three-hander show entitled 'A Dish of Tea with Dr Johnson' in the garret of 17 Gough Square; its governing conceit was, as you may have guessed, the notion that the audience had been invited to drink a dish of tea with Johnson. The show collapsed many past moments and lost spaces of sociable domesticity within the house into one imagined evening.[18] This is the native and characteristic effect of the Johnson house museum. The presence of Mrs Thrale's teapot allows the house to stage, using objects as actors, what no biographer ever recorded, and what cannot have happened, but what visitors would like to have happened—a happy evening when Mrs Thrale served tea to Dr Johnson tête-à-tête in the parlour at 17 Gough Square till after midnight—and we might have found them both there and sipped our tea by candlelight, chipping in with our own bon mots.

Mrs Gaskell's fire and James Joyce's butter-cooler

Both Johnson's coffee-pot and Thrale's teapot are microcosmic of the endeavour of the writer's house museum as a genre to insert the visitor into authorial presence. What that 'presence' means, however, depends very much on the literary genre in which the author in question typically worked. Johnson's home genre may be said to be the biographical, and hence the way in which both coffee-pot and teapot can successfully evoke him. In the case of a novelist such as Mrs Elizabeth Gaskell, the house museum devoted to her in Manchester has to solve the problem of evoking her at the centre of the world of the Victorian realist novel.[19] Opened in October 2014, the house contains a mix of the representative (this is a period table of the sort that Mrs Gaskell would have used as a writing-table), the replica (this is a copy of the valuable piece of memorabilia/manuscript presently locked up in an archive in the USA), and the relic (this really is Mrs Gaskell's sewing-box). The 'authenticity' of all these things is based on familiar but very different thesis statements—this is really Victorian, this is a faithful replica of something regarded as important and valuable in the author's mythos, this is something that really belonged to the author, even if it might seem a bit beside the point otherwise. These very different forms of authenticity are made to syntactically reinforce each other so as to produce a 3-D working model of 'Mrs Gaskell's life' into which we can walk.

To an unusual degree, the museum has adopted the aesthetic of Victorian realism. One might take as an example the two open fires, one in the dining-room and the other in the drawing-room. These are one of the technical feats of which the curator of the Gaskell house is reputedly most proud. They flicker and glow in their Victorian grates, and although they give out very little heat and absolutely no smell, they appear to give off smoke. Enquiry reveals that this 'smoke' is in fact steam, rising from a cunningly hidden reservoir, filled by the volunteers with water every morning. The technical cleverness is evident. Still, one might well ask, why bother with representing the fires at all? It is not as though we believe that a servant-girl has gone on her knees to light them that very morning, in spite of the artful disposition of the fire-tongs; equally, we are capable of believing that the house was heated by open fires without seeing a 'real' fire. Moreover, the almost excessive cleverness by which the fire is made 'real' through the engineering of 'smoke' betokens a very strong investment in the lifelike, while the pleasure in 'lifelikeness' seems related to the pleasures of completeness, compendiousness, and uselessness represented by the doll's house. Indeed, in case one should mistake this doll's house quality as fortuitous, the table is laid neatly not just with Victorian china, silver, and glass, but with plastic bread rolls, recalling Beatrix Potter's *Tale of Two Bad Mice* (1904) and the angry discomfiture of Hunca Munca when faced with the fraudulent and unyielding plaster ham.

In the face of irritated curatorial responses to this question (it is too risky to include a real fire and real food for conservation reasons) it is instructive to take a brief diversion here to the National Trust's interpretation of Coleridge Cottage at Nether Stowey. On the last day of opening in 2018, on a cold and wet day, there were two open fires burning, and a quantity of real food—including a scattering of flour—visible in the kitchen, conservation risks notwithstanding. The real fire was central to the meaning of the cottage as the place of composition of Coleridge's poem 'Frost at Midnight' with its opening lines on the fire:

> the thin blue flame
> Lies on my low-burnt fire, and quivers not;
> Only that film, which fluttered on the grate,
> Still flutters there, the sole unquiet thing.
> Methinks, its motion in this hush of nature
> Gives it dim sympathies with me who live,
> Making it a companionable form,
> Whose puny flaps and freaks the idling Spirit
> By its own moods interprets, every where
> Echo or mirror seeking of itself,
> And makes a toy of Thought.[20]

The fire in Nether Stowey is necessarily real because it is designed as 'a companionable form' to evoke the poet's thinking body. By comparison, the Gaskell house is made up primarily of a mass of things designed to summon or simulate the original fabric of period domesticity. The artificial fires and bread rolls are suitably congruent with the social realist aesthetic of Gaskell's fiction. They are the unnecessary realist details that serve to describe reality through material objects frozen into a domestic scene at once specific to Gaskell and generic to the Victorian novel.[21] The fact that these material objects are on closer examination representational rather than 'real', and all but immortal rather than ephemeral, is only appropriate in a type of house that is itself a representation, immortalization, and fictionalization of a house rather than its reality.

Beyond this sort of realist formulation of the household object as period décor, objects can be persuaded to function as explicitly paratextual to realist fiction. Charles Dickens' novels, for instance, produced a strong desire on the part of his contemporaries to materialize his texts, giving rise not only to inventive literary tourism, but also to extensive efforts on the part of his admirers to rescue the materiality of 'his' London first from the ravages of Victorian development and then the destruction of the two world wars.[22] A biographical impulse to save the London that Dickens lived in, for instance, must have prompted the preservation of 'A Genuine Dickens Relic. The window of the little attic in 14 Bayham Street, Camden Town, occupied by Charles Dickens as a boy of 11 years of age in 1823, when the Dickens family came to London from Chatham'. But 48 Doughty Street also houses a number of objects that may be thought of as not merely biographical but as paratextual to the novels. These include the 'Goldbeater's Arm' from Manette St, Soho, 'the original sign mentioned by Charles Dickens in his *Tale of Two Cities*' as the Victorian brass plaque claims, the 'Little Wooden Midshipman' from Leadenhall St, 'model for one outside Solomon Gills' shop in *Dombey and Son*' as an old postcard has it, an iron grille from the Marshalsea Prison, 'a stone step, once part of a flight ascending to the West Door of St George's Church, Southwark…where the heroine and her bridegroom pause at the end of *Little Dorrit*', and 'the window from Pyrcroft House, Chertsey, through which Oliver Twist is said to have been pushed by Bill Sikes on the occasion of the burglary'. This habit of co-locating the biographical and fictitious extends to objects that Dickens at one point actually owned, notably Catherine Dickens' engagement ring, which (according to a museum postcard currently for sale) 'resembles the ring presented to Dora by David Copperfield'.

A more recent, and more comprehensive, instance of the practice of annotating realist fictional texts with material objects within the museum is presented by the display at the James Joyce Museum, housed at Sandycove south of Dublin on the east coast of Ireland and opened on Bloomsday, 16 June 1962. Squat at the end of a long curve of sand rises a Martello Tower, *the* Martello Tower one might say, the Martello Tower associated with the youthful James Joyce. Amongst writer's house museums, this must commemorate one of the shortest and most precarious residences ever, a scant six nights in 1904 during which Joyce briefly moved in with fellow writer

Oliver St John Gogarty. This proposed writers' idyll came to an abrupt and unseemly end before dawn on 14 September when, waking from a drunken nightmare-ridden sleep, another guest, Samuel Chevenix Gore, seized up a pistol and fired it at random. The second time his two companions were woken, Gogarty grabbed the gun and fired at the pots and pans above Joyce's head, the bullets ricocheting round the small circular tower room that served equally as living and sleeping area for the three men. According to Gogarty's account of the incident, 'This was too much for the sensitive soul Joyce who rose, pulled on his frayed trousers and shirt...and in silence left the tower forever'.[23] Within the month Joyce would gather up his lover Nora Barnacle and take the next boat for Europe, and then travel yet further east, fetching up via Zurich in Trieste. Although it was in Trieste that he began his masterwork *Ulysses* (1922), the action of *Ulysses* begins with the emergence of 'Stately, plump Buck Mulligan' onto the roof of the Martello Tower to shave in company with Stephen Daedalus after a disturbed night.[24]

The tower then has a double claim to the origination of the novel—biographical and fictive. It consists of three floors—the roof itself enclosed with ramparts, the tower room a floor down, described in *Ulysses* as 'the gloomy domed living room', and the entrance hall. Nowadays, the tower room is laid out with objects designed to evoke the living arrangements of the memorable night that drove Joyce to depart—featuring a hammock, a table, a half-cut loaf, a butter-cooler, and on the table, a pistol—a sparse and naturalistic stage-setting.[25] What is really arresting, however, is the life-size figure, ceramic and glossily black, of a panther which seems to have escaped straight out of the décor of some sort of urbanite boutique hotel, and crouches incongruously and incomprehensibly on its haunches by the hearth. This figure is a reference to the imaginary animal that so terrified Gore's dreams that he caused mayhem, and which appears again in the opening pages of *Ulysses*:

> —Tell me, Mulligan, Stephen said quietly.
> —Yes, my love?
> —How long is Haines going to stay in this tower?...He was raving
> all night about a black panther, Stephen said. Where is his guncase?
> —A woful lunatic! Mulligan said. Were you in a funk?
> —I was, Stephen said with energy and growing fear. Out here in the
> dark with a man I don't know raving and moaning to himself about
> shooting a black panther...If he stays on here I am off.[26]

The panther thus serves to footnote both Joyce's biography and a passage from *Ulysses*. The butter-cooler proves to be similarly composite, but this time of fiction and local history. The museum-caption identifies it as a reference to a passage in *Ulysses* ('Stephen fetched the loaf and the pot of honey and the buttercooler from the locker'), adding that it was 'donated Bloomsday 16 June 2013 by Sean A. Maebh O'Regan in memory of Frances O'Regan... 1928–2005 from whose childhood home it came'.[27] This gesture is reiterated in a wide array of other items associated with other places and motivated by quotations from *Ulysses* and others of Joyce's works. These include a 'fragment of Nelson's Pillar' as featured in 'Parable of the Plums', a 'photograph of the shop where Bloom bought lemon soap, and package wrapped by Sweny, given by Miss M.P. Quinn, 1982', three pennies captioned 'Three pence, please. His hand accepted the moist tender gland and slid it into a side pocket. Then it fetched up three coins from his trousers' pocket and laid them on the rubber prickles', 'a photograph of Davy Stephens, news vendor, referred to in *Ulysses*—given by John Osman of the Gallery of Photography, Wellington Quay, Dublin, 1990', and a 'Pot given by Eamon Morrissey, who felt that without it the museum would be incomplete, Bloomsday 1982', which references the quotation of the advertising slogan 'Plumtree's Potted Meat. What is home without Plumtree's Potted Meat? Incomplete. With it an abode of bliss'.[28] The hyperrealism and all-pervading expatriate nostalgia of *Ulysses*, which documented a city already lost to time, is surely responsible for this sense on the part of the local community that the museum should be 'complete', and that the museum (as a repository of the Dublin of the past) is needed to provide material witness to the opening of Joyce's classic.

The instances of the museums devoted to Johnson and Gaskell argue forcibly that the 'natural' discourse of the writer's house museum is overwhelmingly biographical, and with it, realistic. The presumption is that the act of writing can be delimited by describing the site of writing as a density of physical objects. This is fine around authors famous primarily for their 'lives' (as in the case of Johnson) or their realist fiction (as in the cases of Austen or Gaskell). These modes are necessarily domestic, time-bound, and topographical, meaning that the idea of materiality is hard-wired into them. Indeed, in the case of the Dickens and Joyce museums, this realist aesthetic is catching, beginning to tip into a desire to annotate not just the writer's biography but also his or her fiction with material objects, in an effort to preserve what was once (supposedly) unproblematically present to the writer. But there is and always has been something that threatens to be inconveniently over-material about a writer's house, meaning that the house may not adequately account for writing conceived as dream or vision. Accordingly, in the case of the museums devoted to the more evidently fantastical writers Mikhail Bulgakov and Hans Christian Andersen, the biographical and the material begin to dissolve much more elaborately in and out of the fictional and visionary in an effort to force material objects to bear witness to the author's imaginative life.

Bulgakov's stove and Andersen's rope

The museum in Kiev devoted to one of the masters of magic realism, Mikhail Bulgakov, author of such novels as *The Master and Margarita* (published posthumously only in 1966, twenty-six years after the author's death), tackles the question of how objects within the writer's house may bear witness at once to biographical fact and visionary fiction. The house in which Bulgakov lived between 1906 and 1919 in Kiev was opened in 1989, and the main museum exhibition was completed and opened in 1993. Its central conceit is that 'two different families lived in the house at 13 Andriivsky Uzviz: the Bulgakovs and the Turbins, the heroes of *The White Guard*'. *The White Guard* (1925) is a historical novel about a White Russian family, set in this house and describing events that took place in Kiev in 1918–19. The museum dramatizes both the biographical realities of Bulgakov's life and the fictional uses to which he put the real house: 'The museum contains the personal belongings of the Bulgakovs, as well as a variety of white objects that are symbolically representative of his novel'.[29] The intended effect is, as the leaflet accompanying the exhibition puts it, that 'This white field involves visitors in an intricate game consisting of their own associations, impressions and memories', including, presumably, their memories of reading the novel. Hence the house and all the objects it contains are ambiguously fictional and historical. Because little remains of Bulgakov's original furniture and personal belongings, everything that is not original, along with everything he fictionalized as the possessions of the family of 'Whites', is painted white (Figure 5.2).[30] The house is shown by a guide, who as part of the tour operates the two lighting states installed in each room, a UV state which transforms the real house into something hallucinatory and fictive, and a daylight state, which returns it to a historical artefact. The two most theatrical coups are when visitors are invited to step through a white wardrobe into the next room, a trick door native to the

Figure 5.2. Mikhail Bulgakov's stove. Mikhail Bulgakov museum, Kiev. © Dolf Verlinden

novel, and the climactic denouement of the tour when visitors are invited to peer into 'the fifth dimension' which dramatizes part of the novel's visionary last chapter, the protagonist's dream: as the website puts it (inaccurately, as Turbin only dreams of dying):

> ...the most interesting and mysterious room, pushing the limits of space, is the 'fifth dimension' that can be seen through the mirror from the dining room. In reality, in this room Bulgakov's father died, and in the novel—Alexei Turbin. The created illusion is impressive: bright stars, which appeared to the hero... before death, shine here, and restless flames try to burn up the manuscript lying on the table. And above all these, fluffy snowflakes circle in bizarre dance.[31]

This house museum has chosen to abandon captions—at any rate, captions that are texts rather than the tour-guide's patter. Instead, it uses colour and light to indicate the ontological status of the objects that it displays as alternately biographical or fictive, as matter of fact or matter of the imagination. Thus the Bulgakov museum argues that the real 'events' of a writer's life are as much the solitary, invisible, and interiorized, transformative events of the imagination.

The case of Hans Christian Andersen, a man who framed even his autobiography as a fairy-tale, publishing *The Fairytale of My Life* in 1847, raises the question of how a house museum can fully realize the author of fantasy through material objects.[32] The museum dedicated to Andersen first opened in Odense, his birthplace, in 1908 on the centenary of his birth. The display has since extended well beyond the original building (the cottage in which he was not born but spent his early years), and at present includes a remarkable room as part of the annex exhibition entitled 'Imaginations: expressions and impressions of the artist's mind and creative urge'. This room is composed of a series of vitrines placed within the space to present the possibility of walking through a roughly chronological narrative from Andersen's youth through to his death. Within each vitrine are placed no more than three objects, lit for theatrical effect. Displays include Andersen's hat, his pen and inkpot, some of Andersen's paper-cuts and a pair of his scissors, a decoupage screen made by Andersen, the rope which Andersen insisted on travelling with for fear of fire, a manuscript in his handwriting, some of his hair, and a bouquet of leaves plucked from his grave. These items were evidently preserved out of a familiar Victorian reverence for the biographical 'leavings' of the author's life. However, the way that they are displayed and lit de-familiarizes and de-natures the materiality of these objects so that they serve as a series of surprises, riddles, and conundrums. The aesthetic is not realistic but that of dream, with its insistence on all-but-unreadable associations and conjunctions, distortions of scale, metamorphic space, and narrative rupture or inconsequence. Taken together, the displays argue for the incommensurate relation of the real material object to its imaginative power. The hugeness of Andersen's hat is given additional uncanniness by being suspended on invisible wires at just above eye-level, emphasizing the absence of the head but also denying gravity. By contrast, the writer's chair is reduced to a tiny paper-cut chair and juxtaposed with Andersen's huge paper-cutting scissors, and then lit to throw vast shadows. The pen and ink-pot are lit from beneath so as to appear to be on fire. The portraits of other admired authors so characteristic of writers' libraries here appear in the shape of a screen ornamented with cut-out scraps of Shakespeare, Scott, Byron, and other luminaries, interspersed with fairies and other images that had caught Andersen's fancy between 1873 and 1876, an exercise in wild fluctuations of scale and improbable juxtapositions. The writer's manuscript appears in unreadable form as one of those Victorian jokes that requires you to squint at a slant to decipher apparently meaningless squiggles, and as a fan which snaps shut to conceal the writing. The writer's grave appears grotesquely miniaturized in the shape of a sample of hair laid alongside what is captioned as a 'Fairy-tale book with leaves from Hans Christian Andersen's grave and grave bouquet'.

In strong contrast to the types of third-person biographical anecdote that characterize Johnson's coffee-pot, these objects are made to function as part of Andersen's dream-life and to 'speak' themselves in the first-person voice of his private diary: the pen and inkpot are captioned: '"I dreamt I was writing and the letters set the paper on fire". 1 May 1856'. High above the visitor's head is a blank window set in the wall with a rope dangling from it to the floor, captioned: '"I went to the Grand Hotel, the whole place full, I had to take a room on the fourth floor overlooking a narrow street, the height made me dizzy, no fireplace, I was afraid of a fire breaking out at night". 26 Nov 1869'. Even the grave bouquet is captioned with an entry from Andersen's diary: '"Dust and ashes he is, dead, burnt out like the candle, there is nothing left! Oh Lord may you let us disappear completely". 5 Mar 1872'. Objects are consistently made to speak with the writer's voice generally without much warrant from biography: thus both a bed piled with seventeen mattresses recalling 'The Princess and the Pea' and a vast and rather menacing mirror flanked by a tailor's dummy which captures the visitor's image and inserts it within the tale of 'The Emperor's New Clothes' are captioned with passages from the diaries that record Andersen's struggles with unhappiness, loneliness, and his perception of his own over-sensitiveness. The obsessive and private quality of these confessions is emphasized by unconventional typography set on long narrow banners, thus:

My ardent
imagination
surely
leads me
to the
bedlam, my
vehement
feelings
will turn
me into a
self
murderer...

Speaking stones: effigy, statue, plaque

From detachable captions, then, to the incorporation of words into the fabric of the museum itself. Of recent years the interior and exterior walls of an increasing number of writer's house museums have broken out into inscription, in an effort to make the house more conscious of the writer. Houses have been made to 'speak' in the person of the writer, through using quotations from letters, diaries, or poems. This in itself is not an especially new strategy. Ariosto's house in Ferrara, for example, is firmly ascribed to Ariosto through the use of a Latin epigram he himself authored, 'nella loggetta di questa sua casa' [in the loggia of this his house], carved into what is conjecturally a late nineteenth-century marble wall-plaque fixed to the garden-wall.[33] The house where the Shelleys were staying in Lerici when Shelley was drowned similarly carries two wall-plaques quoting his diary entries on the pleasures of living in the bay on the north- and south-facing side-walls, respectively, and another at the door in Italian, put up for the bicentenary of the poet's birth in 1992, which alludes to Shelley's famous manifesto for poetry, the *Defense*.[34] More recently, the Gaskell museum has broken out into inscription on the interior walls, as has the Burns Birthplace museum, which has, in addition, carved quotations from the poems set into the exterior walls of the exhibition hall. A similar strategy has been adopted in the Twain museum in Connecticut. In Dove Cottage in Grasmere, a variant has been developed; Dorothy Wordsworth's Grasmere Journal has been used to provide a set of rolling captions that are changed according to the date, so that in imagination the house is always at once living in the present, and in a day in the late 1790s, a museum variant on time-slip fantasy. At Nether Stowey, lines of Coleridge's verse and prose curl in silvery smoke-like drifts across the wall above the desk, along the bedroom wall, and elsewhere. In Vita Sackville-West's tower at Sissinghurst, her lines are inked in black on a whitewashed wall above a vintage typewriter, while her recorded voice echoes in the room, reciting other lines.

The practice of indicating the writer's house and its core meaning(s) with supplementary figuration of the author may also be regarded as a way of making the house more conscious of its owner. For this reason, displaying multiple portraits and busts of the author (and less usually dummies) within the museum is a core convention and may be regarded as a form of captioning.[35] More extreme is the tactic adopted in the house that was both Samuel

Figure 5.3. Mark Twain's effigy, Hannibal, Missouri. Author's own photograph

Clemens' boyhood home and the setting for his two semi-autobiographical works *The Adventures of Tom Sawyer* (1876) and *The Adventures of Huckleberry Finn* (1884) in Hannibal, Missouri. The Mark Twain Boyhood Home and Museum, restored in the early 1990s, houses some six life-size white plaster figures of an elderly Samuel Clemens, each in a different room (Figure 5.3).[36] Their presence is warranted by Twain's five visits to Hannibal, the last of which, in June 1902, is documented in photographs of him standing in front of his boyhood home. The whiteness of these figures alludes to Twain's trademark habit of wearing a white suit, visible in the famous autochrome by Alvin Langdon Coburn in the collection of the Mark Twain House and Museum, Hartford, Connecticut, and materialized there in the shape of Twain's white jacket.[37] But the whiteness also renders Twain's figure ghostly, or at any rate, as inhabiting a different ontological state of being to the house itself, pulling off a trick analogous to that staged in the Bulgakov house. Each room in the boyhood house is inhabited by one of these figures sitting or standing, posing in front of lengthy captions derived from his letters and autobiographical works. In these, Twain meditates upon his relation to his own boyhood home, fluctuating between a sense of its 'lostness' ('Nothing remains the same. When a man goes back to the house of his childhood, it has always shrunk; there is no instance of such a house being as big as the picture in memory or imagination calls for'), the liveness of the lost within the imagination (his evocation of 'the procession of the dead' through his mind and his assertion that 'After all these years I can picture [it] just as it was then: the little white town dreaming in the sunshine of a summer's morning'), and an insistence on the ability of the place to revivify boyhood ('The things about me and before me made me feel like a boy again—convinced me that I was a boy again, and that I had simply been dreaming an unusually long dream...').[38] Most striking is the scene in the bedroom in which the seated daydreaming figure of the elderly author glossed by this last caption seems to 'remember' a figure of Tom Sawyer, rendered in colour, climbing out of the window behind him. This alludes to the famous scene in *The Adventures of Tom Sawyer* when Tom escapes from his aunt's house:

> The raising of a neighboring window disturbed him. A cry of 'Scat! you devil!' and the crash of an empty bottle against the back of his aunt's woodshed brought him wide awake, and a single minute later he was dressed and out of the window and creeping along the roof of the 'ell' on all fours. He 'meow'd' with caution once or twice, as he went; then jumped to the roof of the woodshed and thence to the ground.[39]

This mise-en-scène neatly captions Twain as Sawyer and vice versa, and the house as the product equally of Twain's life and imagination; as the welcoming interpretive board has it: 'Like all of us, Mark Twain told stories about his childhood in order to understand who he had become as an adult'. The inclusion of Twain's figure in white pinpoints the central tease of the writer's house museum, which is that the materiality of the house and all the objects authentic or inauthentic that it may or may not contain are not really the point. Rather, these materialities are at once the obstacle to and the point of departure into the immaterial worlds of imagination. The house is represented as remembered, both in that it is the point of departure for Twain's own spinning of stories in adulthood, and in that it is used by tourists to remember their own reading, whether they are adults or still children.

These multiple figures of 'Mark Twain' solve the tricky problem of how to construct the meaning of the birthplace and/or the childhood home, the problem that the author was not yet a writer when he lived there, and so the house can hardly be conscious to the writing. Surprisingly, this is not quite such an innovation as it might appear. It is foreshadowed by the statue erected to Dr Johnson in Lichfield opposite his birthplace and childhood home some fifty years after his death. In 1838, Richard Cockle Lucas was commissioned by James Thomas Law, Chancellor of Lichfield Cathedral, to design and erect a statue in the town in which Johnson was born and grew up. The figure sits on a Greek revival chair surrounded by books in the classic pose of the philosopher. The stone plinth is decorated with three bas-reliefs depicting scenes from the writer's life with especial relevance to the locality. These show Johnson as a three-year-old on his father's shoulders 'listening to Dr Sacheverel preaching', Johnson's schoolfellows carrying him 'from school' on their shoulders; and the 'Penance in Uttoxeter market', depicting the moment that Johnson stood bareheaded in the market after his father's death in penance for having once arrogantly refused to lend a hand at his father's market stall.[40] The figure is thus conceived as the sum-mation of a series of anecdotes famous from Boswell's biography; the American Samuel Gross understood it as 'his statue illustrative of events in his early childhood'.[41] Most striking, however, is the way that the statue is placed so as to contemplate the house in which Johnson was born and brought up. This simulacrum of autobiographical reflexiveness at a birth-place is unique for its period. It is absent in other writers' birthplaces then developing their profile as celebrated places at the time, such as those of Shakespeare and Burns, even though in the case of Burns, he had made his birthplace famous through writing verse about it, and in the case of Shakespeare, Garrick had done the honours. Only in Lichfield is the author himself credited with autobiographical agency in this fashion.

For all the Victorians' well-documented enthusiasm for erecting com-memorative statues, the statue's ability to evoke the author adequately in the age of literary biography was always problematic. No-one expresses this more elaborately and subtly than the American writer Nathaniel Hawthorne, who published his account of visiting Lichfield in the 1850s as part of his collection of travel-writing essays on England, *Our Old Home* (1863). This account is remarkable for describing both actual and imaginary statues as though they were alive. Hawthorne tells of trying in vain to gain access to Johnson's Birthplace and then his experience of encountering 'Dr Johnson himself, who happened, just at that moment, to be sitting at his ease nearly in the middle of St Mary's Square, with his face turned towards his father's house'. Such is Hawthorne's whimsical description of turning away from the door of the Birthplace to be confronted by the statue in the Square.[42] Hawthorne's take on this statue may be glossed by his equally whimsical admiration of an entirely imaginary statue of Johnson at the very centre of Uttoxeter marketplace:

> The picturesque arrangement and full impressiveness of the story absolutely require that Johnson shall not have done his penance in a corner...but shall have been the very nucleus of the crowd—the midmost man of the marketplace—a central image of Memory and Remorse.[43]

Standing therefore in the very middle of the marketplace as a sort of substitute statue, and unsurprisingly stared at by the townspeople, Hawthorne chooses to impute their curiosity to a 'singularity' shared with Johnson: 'I felt as if my genuine sympathy for the illustrious penitent, and my many reflections about him, must have imbued me with some of his own singularity of mien'.[44] Having thus embodied a living statue of Johnson, he calls for a more permanent memorial, remarking that it might almost grow of itself: 'Such a statue, if the piety of the people did not raise it, might almost have been expected to grow up out of the pavement of its own accord on the spot that had been watered by the rain that dripped from Johnson's garments, mingled with his remorseful tears'.[45] (In due course, the pressure of this sort of sensibility did indeed produce a memorial, even though it is as Hawthorne feared situated in a corner of the marketplace.) Both actual and imagined statues of Johnson come alive through Hawthorne's power to locate and embody familiar biographical anecdote. But his accounts of both also construct the statues as images of the author remembering, a model for the reader's belated act of remembrance.[46] Nor was this merely a conceit that Hawthorne indulged; it clearly informs an oil painting by Harry Godwin of 1876, presently owed by the Dr Johnson Trust, which shows the back of the statue of Johnson contemplating at twilight the lamplit house in which he was born.

Both the Twain childhood home and the Johnson birthplace are in this fashion constructed as 'remembered' by the author, and so rendered worthy of remembrance by subsequent readers. Acts of remembering authors' houses may not always be warranted by authorial reminiscence. But they often manifest a similar desire to celebrate the past homes of an author as both explanatory and generative. To illustrate this, let's return to Chawton Cottage. In 1917, Constance Hill and her sister were the moving spirits in the funding and design of a plaque to be put up on the cottage to mark the centenary of Austen's death. However, the plaque, and the ceremonial speeches given at its unveiling, made it plain that Austen was to be remembered 100 years on because her novels evoked and so guaranteed the continuities of English life in the face of historical change. The speeches set up a series of important interconnected meanings for the cottage: as a site of continuity, a place of refuge and source of consolation in wartime, as the classic literary ground of England connecting Mary Russell Mitford, Jane Austen, and Gilbert White, and as a national and supranational site that connected the Anglophone cultures and allies Australia, North America, and England.[47] As one dignitary put it:

> It is perhaps a remarkable thing that, in these days of war, we can turn aside, even for a day, from the sterner demands of the moment to come together to pay this homage to the genius of Jane Austen, and may we not take from this thought a new hope of the civilisation that we are fighting together to save?[48]

It would take World War II finally to elevate Chawton to exemplifying everything that yet another generation of now dead young men had been fighting for when, in 1948, T.E. Carpenter would buy the house in memory of his son killed in action, as the plaque that he subsequently erected alongside the original 1917 memorial states.[49] Chawton Cottage, like so many other writer's house museums, is remembered as a foundational, generative place of national culture. As to the riddle of why one might collect Jane Austen's kitchen flagstones—the answer turns out to be that, in rescuing them, Carpenter felt himself to be recovering the bedrock of an older, politer, quotidian England from the appalling wreckage of war.

I began by asking why Carpenter collected 'Austen's flagstones', about how this possessive association between author and mundane object was produced and maintained, and to what ends. That type of association will generally have been originally constructed through narrative, through tradition handed down among family or friends, published writings, letters, autobiography or biography. It finally develops in the house museum through inscription or caption dramatizing objects as materialized anecdote or quotation which conceives them as quasi-subjects in possession of bodies and voices that bear witness to the authorial life or works and can animate them in the present. What those bodies and voices say in the present, however, seems to be at least as much about loss as about endurance—here are only the traces of the lost worlds of Johnson's London, Gaskell's Manchester, Joyce's Ireland, Bulgakov's Kiev, Austen's England.

6

Glass

Woolf's spectacles and Freud's mirror

Glass

As I write this, my gaze flicks between reading the messages rising within the glass of my mobile phone, the glass computer screen within which text is slowly appearing (I am old enough still to find this a magic and improbable dissociation), and then up over the rims of my reading glasses and out, through one of the high windows of the Upper Reading Room of the Bodleian Library in Oxford, whose dark-rimmed rectangular panes, regular as graph-paper, divide sky and stone, weather vane and dome, spiked pinnacle and pot-bellied urn, balustrade and gargoyle into flattened and discrete pictorial detail. Confined, constrained, and constructed by window struts, the view is further abstracted towards the flatness of a hyperrealist painting by the interposition of glass, a surface at once visible and transparent, near, fragile, thin (and today, raindrop-spattered), and yet offering access to the far and the large scale, depth and height. It floats as a meniscus upon the real, a lens introducing distance, distortion, and a scattering of allegorization through the superimposition of a number of enigmatic emblematic roundels of antique painted glass. Accordingly, this chapter has turned out to be all about the rhetoric of glass in the writer's house museum. It sits right in the middle of this book because glass may serve as the governing conceit for the not quite invisible divider that runs right through the writer's house museum and its cognate forms, dividing past writer and present reader. In the same way that literary objects such as Mrs Gaskell's inkstand are de-naturalized, de-materialized, and imaginatively energized by the interposition of glass, so too is the figure of the writer more generally. Glass is the material by which the writer's house museum thinks through, dramatizes, and fetishizes impossibilities: the desire to see the writer in the flesh, the desire to see what the writer once saw in the here and now, and the desire to share in the writer's visions for real. It enables—and disables—these ambitions. In the domestic and material context of the writer's house museum, glass talks of vision and the visionary in the shape of vitrine, spectacles, window, and mirror.

Vitrine

Glass as a material is critical to the genre of the museum—in fact, it might not be too much to say that the aesthetic of the modern museum originates in miniature in the vitrine as a many-sided glass showcase.[1] The importance of the glass case to the writer's house museum, however, is not primarily because it serves as a way of displaying an object or objects in clear view while protecting, presenting, positioning, contextualizing, and interpreting them—although of course it often performs those acts of ordering, albeit to very different ends and with variable levels of plausibility or persuasiveness.[2] The common-sense explanation for the vitrine would be that, whether in a shop or a museum, the objects, and the value of the objects, are at risk, either through being damaged through handling or through theft, both of which certainly happen (as in the case of the theft of George Eliot's portable writing-desk in 2012); moreover, even the most circumspect handling would risk upsetting the import of the carefully composed display of isolation or relationship within which the object sits.[3]

All of this is undoubtedly true, but it is by no means the whole story. Rather, as Anna Woodhouse has argued, following Walter Benjamin, the interposition of glass, even when it is apparently and merely clear and transparent, changes the way we look at things behind it, having a 'creative and imaginary function'.[4] Whatever is put on display in a glass case changes its nature and cultural status—think of the instances of Keats' hair and Dickinson's hummingbirds considered in Chapters 1 and 2. In the context of the writer's house museum, glass works to produce 'aura'; and, however forcefully transparent and non-auratic clear glass supposedly is *in itself*, and however much it claims to display the object in question to full view, it also describes it as inaccessible. As James Putnam points out, 'The act of placing an object in a vitrine immediately focuses attention on it and suggests that it might also be both precious and vulnerable. The vitrine reinforces the notion of the unique, untouchable, and unattainable ... The glass creates not just a physical barrier but establishes an official distance between object and viewer'.[5] A pair of shoes in a locked glass case is plainly not simply a pair of shoes: it may be, as Benjamin noted in the *Arcades Project*, that they are displayed as a luxury commodity in a department store window, and are thus as, one might put it, *not yet* or only shoes, but rather objects of desire; within the writer's house museum, they are displayed as having *once been* shoes, and more than that, the shoes that someone in particular once wore or wore once, as in the case of Dorothy Wordsworth's white leather boots, or Sigrid Undset's black leather shoes. A glass case says, like Snow White's glass coffin, 'look, but don't touch'. Such objects are at risk from being handled because such over-familiarity would erode the object's value by eroding its function. Handling would subtly interrupt the statement of the object's supposed power despite mortality to connect its original owner, by which is specifically meant its original user and handler, with the literary tourist, who is nonetheless specified by the glass casing as a non-user and non-handler. One might add, too, that neither glass nor perspex (despite its name) are perfectly transparent from the viewer's perspective. A photograph of something in a glass case invariably risks showing merely a reflex of light cutting across the object in question, often enough the reflection of the viewer. Looking through glass is surprisingly problematic in practice.

This use of glass, or its modern equivalent, acrylic glass, to produce aura and distance within the writer's house museum is evident at both small and large scale. At small scale, it may be used to distinguish between the authentic and the replica; in the Gaskell house only things that once belonged to Elizabeth Gaskell herself, her inkstand, her tape-measure, and her needlework box, are sequestered under glass. At larger scale, one might adduce a number of writers' rooms that have been moved and enclosed in glass cases in their entirety (as in the instance of Thomas Hardy's study originally at Max Gate and now displayed in the Dorchester County Museum), or sealed behind glass *in situ* (as in the instance of Ralph Waldo Emerson's study in his house in Concord, Massachusetts). A particularly instructive example is provided by Dylan Thomas' 'writing-shed' at the Boat House in Laugharne, which is preserved, sealed off, the interior visible only through glassed peepholes. This was the shed mythologized in 'Poem on His Birthday' (1944), in which Thomas describes himself as 'the rhymer in the long tongued room' of the 'word-splashed hut', and the shed as 'this house on stilts high among beaks/And palavers of birds'.[6] There are crumpled papers on the floor.

On the desk there are empty chocolate wrappers, a beer bottle, cigarette butts, matches, a shell, a stripy coffee-mug, and word-lists. Books are heaped on shelves, and pictures pinned askew to the walls. A jacket is slung on the back of a chair, and the rug's corner is flipped over and caught under the chair's leg as though the chair had been carelessly shoved backwards. Beyond the detritus of work, a window above the desk offers an uncluttered view of a wide sky and below it, the confluence of four estuaries, their waters changing with the tide's ebb and flow.[7] The mendacious claim is that this is simply how things were left some unspecified day; this claim underpins an inexplicit argument that what the visitor sees is the poet's work, still in progress, apparently temporarily abandoned mid-task for the pub. In short, here glass purports to offer access to a perpetually present past. The story of how Henrik Ibsen's study in his apartment in Oslo comes to be glassed-in, told as part of the standard guided tour, serves as a further useful gloss. Although the study was shown to the public after Ibsen's death in 1906 for some years until his wife Susanna died in 1914, and was then moved to the Norwegian Folk Museum where it resided until being returned when the Ibsenmuseet was set up in 2006, it is glassed-in in accordance with the wishes of the widow, who stipulated that no-one should be allowed into the study for fear of disturbing the ghost that continued to inhabit it. Whether or not the ghost has been discouraged by so many moves, the interposition of glass carefully preserves the fiction of its continuing presence.[8]

The importance of the glass case within the writer's house museum is as a way at once of describing the writer's value and constructing the tourist view—as Jeannette Winterson puts it, 'Here is the writer behind glass, mummified, invented'.[9] The mystified relation between mummifying the authorial relic and inventing the author suggested by Winterson's remark was acknowledged and exploited by the rather sardonic art installation mounted in Charlotte Brontë's bedroom at Haworth Parsonage in February 2016 in commemoration of her death, already visited in Chapter 3. The artist Serena Partridge simply added an extra vitrine to those already present, and filled it with subtly impossible objects. One might cite (since we have already touched on the subject of hair, shoes, and needlework boxes) the implausibly small 'mourning slippers' supposedly embroidered by Charlotte with human hair. The installation served as a sceptical essay not just on the tourist desire for relics of the author, but also on the efficacy of the vitrine in conferring aura. This ability of glass to hoax the ignorant and credulous, as I observed happening at Haworth, has not been what has troubled museum practitioners over recent years; rather, the museum case as a viewing apparatus has attracted a significant amount of critical commentary, sometimes amounting to hostility, because it is said to be synonymous with turning off visitor interest. The result has been a museum-wide move towards enabling more sensory engagement, and an especial interest in haptics; that is to say, in making objects 'touchable'.[10] But the whole point of the glass case in the writer's house museum is precisely to produce frustration. This frustration epitomizes—no, more, it is constitutive of—the entire experience of the writer's house museum. The nearly but not quite invisible glass of the vitrine marks the limit of permitted readerly impertinence and intrusion; more particularly, it signifies absolute and impermeable difference between the genius of the past and the tourist of the present. The writer's house museum is not really about access to the writer's body but about experiencing it as inaccessible.

Woolf's spectacles

The act of peering into glass cases thinks of the authorial body as spectacle. Surveillance of this kind is one-way reading, a complicated process of collating objects and captions to rouse an authorial phantasm. Mostly, these objects do not threaten to survey the viewer in their turn. The writer's spectacles are an exception to this rule. Although, like so many other objects, they might be described as giving shape to the writer's body, they are more properly thought of as relics of an event that happens sometime or somewhere between the writer's body and the act of writing, the moment of uniquely idiosyncratic authorial vision. Representative of, but detached from, the writer's body, they take on an uncanny life of their own as quasi-eyes; they become not the looked-at or even the looked-through, but the crystalline personification of a particular mode of looking. As Nathaniel finds in E.T.A. Hoffmann's novella 'The Sandman' (1816), encountering spectacles in this mode may be thoroughly unnerving: the maker of optical instruments, Coppola, offers spectacles for sale to Nathanael as 'occhi' or 'eyes':

> . . . reaching into his capacious coat-pockets, [he] brought out lorgnettes and pairs of spectacles and laid them on the table. 'Here, here: glasses, glasses to put on your nose; they're my *occe*, lovely *occe!*'
>
> And with that he fetched out more and more pairs of spectacles, so that the whole table began to sparkle and glitter in an uncanny fashion. A thousand

eyes gazed and blinked and stared up at Nathaniel, but he could not look away from the table, and Coppola laid more and more pairs of spectacles on to it, and flaming glances leaped more and more wildly together and directed their blood-red beams into Nathaniel's breast. Unmanned by an ungovernable terror, he cried: 'Stop! Stop!'[11]

Hoffmann's story is primarily concerned with the seductions and the dangers of the sorts of vision conferred by the Romantic imagination, but his interest in the uncanniness of spectacles as having their own ability to see is reiterated in Edgar Allan Poe's story 'The Spectacles' (1850) and again in Henry James' story inspired by it entitled 'Glasses' (1896); these stories hint at some of the cultural meanings of spectacles once off the writer's nose.

Not all writers have owned spectacles, although reading, writing, and age take their toll on eyesight, and a remarkable number of writers have been portrayed wearing eye-glasses or spectacles (the distinction is between those with and those without hooked ear-pieces), from Benjamin Franklin through Rudyard Kipling to Alan Bennett. Not all documented writers' spectacles have been the same sort of spectacles: they have corrected for short-sight or mitigated age-related long-sight; they have masked celebrity from view, shaded inflamed eyes from glare, or lent experimental rose or blue tints to the view. Individual pairs of writer's spectacles have enjoyed a degree of celebrity derived from their power to evoke or explain the author. Thus the real thing may be displayed within the writer's house museum, to serve as a long-standing code signifying the professional writer, often conjecturally temporarily laid aside on a desk on top of loose paper or a book in an imagined break from work—such are Walter Scott's spectacles laid out in a glassed-off desk-drawer in Abbotsford—or laid down owing to the advent of death itself, or so Marina Warner fantasizes in the Freud Museum in London: 'time had been stilled by Anna Freud when she did not move any of her father's things, not even his spectacles on the desk'.[12] So prevalent is this cliché that Erica Lennard's choice of image for the cover of *American Writers at Home* (2004) foregrounds William Faulkner's spectacles 'still on the desk in his old study' while everything else is out of focus.[13] Authentic enough in provenance, these spectacles generally exert no further hold on the readerly imagination, because they cross-reference neither with portrait, nor with biographical anecdote, nor with the central preoccupations of an author's work. Contrast Charlotte Brontë's spectacles, displayed on her portable writing-desk in Haworth Parsonage, used to narrate how her sight was ruined by working in miniature, according to her first biographer Elizabeth Gaskell, on copying engravings from annuals line by line:

> the way she weakened her eyesight was this: she copied niminipimini copper-plate drawings out of annuals...After she had tried to *draw* stories, and not succeeded, she took the better mode of writing; but in so small a hand, that it is almost impossible to decipher what she wrote at this time.[14]

The smallness of the hand restates the rhetoric of the tiny, constrained, and provincial that continues to be characteristic of Brontë's popular image.

On the other hand, the absence of the real thing is no barrier to producing the spectacles for display if they are essential to the author's image. James Joyce's spectacles, evidence of a lifelong struggle with eyesight disorders, were repeated across photograph, portrait, and caricature during his lifetime and defined his persona and image both in his lifetime and after his death. The question of Joyce's eyesight was prominent in his biographer Richard Ellmann's account of the seven ophthalmic operations Joyce was forced to undergo, and in a long series of related critical readings of Joyce's fictional alter-ego Stephen Dedalus as short-sighted in *Portrait of the Artist as a Young Man* (1916).[15] Thus, although only one of the (presumably) many pairs of Joyce's spectacles is extant, and is kept in the James Joyce Collection at the University at Buffalo, New York, two further pairs of period or replica glasses representing them (or rather him) are on display in the Writer's Museum, Dublin, and the James Joyce Centre in Dublin.[16] Yet more telling is the problematic status of Henrik Ibsen's spectacles in the Ibsenmuseet. There are in total three pairs of spectacles claiming to have been Ibsen's—in the Ibsen Centre in Oslo, in the Telemark Museum in Skien (Ibsen's birth-place), and at the Ibsenhuset in Grimstad (Ibsen's childhood home). The rhetorical opportunity is that questions of sight and insight symbolized by the various lenses of the eye, of spectacles, and of the camera feature heavily both within Ibsen's mythos and within his work, most notably in the case of the failing sight of Hedvig in *The Wild Duck* (1884). The difficulty is that the prescriptions of the three pairs of spectacles suggest that they are unlikely to have belonged to the same person, and the Oslo pair are the least likely to have belonged to Ibsen. While Hjemdahl and Aasland admit this in their essay on the Oslo collection, they point out that it may not matter very much:

> This pair of spectacles has been exhibited at the Ibsen Museum in Oslo for some considerable time, and the museum's display case, walls and name have

imparted an ostensibly secure identity as Henrik Ibsen's spectacles...[T]his story illustrates that objects are always 'coloured' by their surroundings, and serves to emphasise that what we see is not necessarily what we think we are seeing.[17]

The spectacles are brought into existence as Ibsen's by the necessity of providing an objective correlative to authorial mythos and oeuvre, and through the framing mechanisms of the vitrine, the building-as-vitrine, and the caption that names them as such.

What then, is it 'that we see' in the writer's spectacles? A pair of glasses laid open on a desk in the museum, whether authenticated or representative, stands symbolically and metonymically for the author's presence; but they also stand for the idea of the specialness of authorial vision. As such, they are not unambiguous. Spectacles evidence imperfect or even failing eyesight, but they also describe the ability to see differently and allow for the desire to record what is seen differently, indeed almost indecipherably, to return to Gaskell's remarks, to the ordinary eye. This relation between the nature of the writer's sight and the nature of the writer's vision perhaps explains the haunting quality of the photographs of Joyce wearing a black eye-patch over his left eye under his spectacles, or the use of an image of Freud's spectacles for the guide leaflet for the Freud Museum at 20 Maresfield Gardens, London. The idiosyncrasy of personal vision is at the heart of Romantic thinking upon the nature of the imagination, and this is neatly described through prescription spectacles which make you feel giddy and sick, if they are not prescribed for your own eyes. As Hoffmann's story insists, spectacles are therefore other, and others', eyes. The special, insightful blindness of the writer would half-blind the reader. Thus, the fantasy of 'seeing with the writer's eyes' which underlies much of the promise and the frustration of the writer's house museum is epitomized by the lens that promises the reader a window into the otherwise invisible world that the writer saw, but which in practice would actually obscure the reader's view.

Hoffmann's story plays with the idea that spectacles are detached and detachable eyes; nowhere are these possibilities more interestingly explored than in the case of Virginia Woolf's glasses. Despite the fact that there are only two photographs of Woolf extant showing her wearing glasses, one as a child, and one as a middle-aged woman, they have taken on undoubted iconic power.[18] The gift shop at Monk's House at Rodmell, the museum devoted to Woolf and her husband who used it as a country retreat from London life between 1919 and 1941, sells a porcelain coffee-mug. This constellates three pictures into a composite portrait of Woolf as an author: a photograph of Woolf as a young and marriageable socialite, the head turned away from the viewer in near-profile, hair and neck overwritten with the titles of her various works; a facsimile of her signature; and above it, a depiction of her folded spectacles. Although the woman herself does not meet the viewer's eye, the confrontational spectacles do, and, set over the signature, they redescribe the society beauty as an author.

This pair of spectacles, gifted to the National Trust by Professor and Mrs Bell in 1980, are presently on display at Monk's House. The meanings they are capable of constellating are usefully suggested in the writing of Nuala Hancock on the *second* pair of Woolf's spectacles extant, presently stored in the archives of Charleston, the house that belonged to Woolf's sister Vanessa a few miles away, now managed by the National Trust. Exhuming them from store, Hancock puts the spectacles through all their currently possible affective tricks, reiterating in the process much of the arc of this book's argument so far. She begins by dramatizing them as bodily remains: 'weightless; exquisitely fragile; inordinately narrow; impossibly ephemeral'. 'The lenses are gone', which means that gone too are 'the content, the substance, the interstitial matter'—in a word, the soft tissues—'leaving only the skeletal frame—the lightweight, empty vestiges of the original object'. Further speculation on small signs of damage converts this mass-produced object into a type of contact-relic and witness-object that can 'bring us into close contact with Virginia Woolf' through an invitation to 'consider her materiality; the physicality of her head; the surface of her skin; the bony integuments of her skull', and then (backing off a little from the necrophiliac quality of this enthusiasm): 'Handling these spectacles, we are brought in touch with the intimate rhythms of Woolf's daily living... Through this tangible relic, Woolf's habitual body ballets become haptically felt; more vividly knowable'.[19] From this sort of 'knowability', it is not far to further familiarities aligning the processes of Woolf's reading and writing with our own:

> Through this enduring artefact, then, we can intimate her process; actualize the agency through which she accessed other worlds through reading; reached into the spaces of another's mind; entered the internal processes of others. Through a flimsy material frame such as this, she transcribed—externalized—her own artistic processes into visible, tangible, communicable form.[20]

It turns out to be possible to look through these glasses in two ways: they can be turned back on Woolf to bring her 'more clearly into view; into focus;

allowing us to see her in close-up' and they equally allow 'us' to occupy Woolf's own position, 'to imagine seeing as she saw'. The arc of Hancock's essay, then, falls into the rhythm of Keats' 'Ode to a Nightingale', from asserting the possibility of inhabiting this other vision, through to a certain discomfiture at being caught pawing through someone's private effects, to a melancholy attributable to 'a felt disequilibrium; between the survival of the object and the distant evanescence of the life it commemorates', and so to the re-entombing of the object within its 'paper skins' in the Charleston vaults.[21] It is not accidental that this pair of spectacles languishes there out of sight; offered at auction at Sotheby's in 1980, they conjecturally failed to sell because they lack the lenses, and with them their Hoffmannesque quality of imaginative transformation. 'Fled is that vision: do I wake or sleep?'

There is, in addition, something decorously evasive about glass. It does not allow us to force the object into mere objecthood. It is not accidental that Woolf's spectacles, displayed on a virgin blotter on the table in Woolf's writing lodge, lie at the heart of what is effectively a large vitrine (Figure 6.1).[22] The summerhouse window and door, apparently standing wide, are in fact glassed-over and the flickering light and shade, as the overhanging tree moves in the light wind from the Weald, combine, as Annie Leibovitz's photograph celebrates, and as Alison Booth laments, to frustrate full vision:

Figure 6.1. Virginia Woolf's spectacles, Monk's House, Rodmell. © National Trust

'When I got home to the United States I realized that the photograph I had taken of the writer's desk was largely a portrait of the pilgrim reflected in the glass, the camera where my face might appear'.[23]

Hawthorne's window

If it proves tantalizingly impossible to inhabit the writer's sight through borrowing their spectacles, looking through the writer's window might work instead. The photograph of the window in the coffee-table book devoted to literary tourism is something of a cliché: as an instance the window of Dove Cottage, viewed from within and with leaves pressing upon the panes, serves as frontispiece to the collection of essays by modern writers on their precursors' houses, *Writers and Their Houses* (1993).[24] The painter John Fisher, meditating on his interest in writers' houses as 'sites of significant dreaming', remarks especially upon his longing to 'sit in these houses . . . and look out of their windows, to observe their peculiar angle of vision on the outside world'.[25]

Behind this idea of a 'room with a view' lurks an anachronism. Our sense of 'a room with a view', to borrow E.M. Forster's appropriation of Baedeker language apropos the grades of hotel room, derives from notions of genteel purpose-built holiday accommodation, from the Victorian gentleman's house in the Lake District such as that rented by Wordsworth in the shape of Rydal Mount or that developed and extended by Ruskin in Brantwood, to the Victorian gentleman's villa in Fowey, Cornwall that Arthur Quiller-Couch and others of his social status inhabited in the summer. Older housing stock, with the exception of that built by wealth for show, often turns its back upon the wind, and therefore upon the view, and chooses smaller over larger windows for the sake of snugness. Nowadays, too, I reflect, as I watch with regret yet another undergraduate pull down a blind over a window in the Upper Reading Room so that she can continue to stare into her computer screen free of the glare of natural light, the real purpose of windows has been forgotten; for most of history, as far as the writer was concerned, windows were not primarily desirable for the view they offered (which must frequently have come with a nasty draught), but for the natural light they offered to read and write by. They were not, in short, for looking out of, but for letting light in. John Joseph Enneking's canvas *Interior with Figure* (1892) shows a man reading with his back to the window to make the best use of the light.[26] It is not accidental that Thomas Hardy is said to have written his youthful poems, *Desperate Remedies* (1870), *Under the Greenwood Tree* (1872), and parts of *Far from the Madding Crowd* (1874) in the deep window embrasure of his room in the cottage in which he was born at Higher Bockhampton in Dorset.[27]

Nevertheless, a few windows in writers' houses have exerted imaginative power, although not, generally, because of the beauty of the view. The view may actually be ideologically inconvenient; guides to Herman Melville's house Arrowhead near Pittsfield, Massachusetts, 200 miles from the coast, show the room containing the desk at which he wrote *Moby Dick* (1851), and then, gesturing to the left out of the window at the local saddleback mountain Graylock, make the counter-intuitive assertion that it was the profile of this inland mountain which inspired Melville to conceive his white whale.[28] The inward eye was thousands of miles out to sea, while the man himself was land-locked; this window effectively describes the dislocation of imagination from body, a dislocation that the writer's house museum as a genre generally works strenuously to undo.[29] In fact, and counter-intuitively, the writer's window, conceived not as aperture but as struts interrupting the view, at least as often describes confinement and threatens ambition. Thus, one of the earliest visitors to Haworth Parsonage, the American Charles Hale, took the opportunity in 1861 of carrying off 'the whole lower sash of the window of the bedroom of Charlotte Brontë', in anticipation of the powerful narrative of Gothic confinement within the parsonage that would become dominant.[30] The many-windowed turret that gives off John Ruskin's bedroom in Brantwood, built to Ruskin's order as a working-space and to give more access to the astonishing view of Coniston lake, is shown and depicted very largely in relation to his breakdown in February 1878. Perhaps the most involuted version of the idea of the writer-at-the-window is the window at the exhibition of J.M. Barrie's birthplace at Kirriemuir, where until recently a figure of Peter Pan was to be seen flying in through the window of the cottage next door to that where Barrie played as a child.[31] Perhaps the most celebrated statement of the idea is found in the Goethehaus in Rome, which displays a reproduction of a sketch made in 1787 by Johann Heinrich Wilhelm Tischbein of his friend and travelling-companion Goethe 'am Fenster seiner Wohnung in Rom' [at the window of his apartment in Rome]. This depicts Goethe in shirt-sleeves leaning out of the window on the first floor overlooking the Via del Corso. The sketch has come to epitomize Goethe's influential take on Rome in his *Italienreise*

(1786–8, published 1816–17). The window itself has consequently become so celebrated that in addition to showing the actual window, the museum shows a life-size photograph of the window directly next to it, emphasizing the way that the real thing is iconic.[32] And perhaps the most plaintive statement of the idea of the vision of the writer-at-the-window is to be found in lines pencilled onto the window-shutters of Cowper's bedroom in Olney, bidding the house goodbye: '22 July 1795. Farewell dear scenes,/forever closed to me:/Oh for what sorrows must I now/Exchange ye'.

All this said, probably the most celebrated instances of writer's windows dramatize the writer writing on the windowpane itself. This superior form of graffiti (a relatively common amusement from the eighteenth century onwards) may think about the writer within the room, or about the writer within the room looking out, but it has the peculiar effect of engraving the writer's presence in a particular space, at a particular moment in time, and caught in the act of explicitly imagining themselves within that space and time as a writer.[33] Alexander Pope's inscription on the tower window at Stanton Harcourt caught Nathaniel Hawthorne's imagination strongly enough to feature in his collection of essays on England, *Our Old Home* (1883).[34] Of these types of windows within the writer's house museum, certainly the most famous is in the grey clapboard house known as The Old Manse, Concord, Massachusetts.[35] The Old Manse is central to American Romanticism, and to the actual and symbolic inception of American literature more generally. It was built in 1770 by Ralph Waldo Emerson's grandfather, then minister in Concord. It was here in 1834 that Emerson wrote his seminal essay 'Nature', and here that on 9 July 1842 Hawthorne and his new wife Sophia Peabody came to take up a tenancy on their wedding night. They lived here for the next three years, leaving in 1845. Although merely renting it from Emerson's cousin, Hawthorne was responsible both for re-christening the building 'The Old Manse' and for conceiving it as a tourist site/sight central to the birth of American culture. This work was achieved primarily through the introductory essay to his collection of tales, *Mosses from an Old Manse* (1846). This essay consciously mythologized Hawthorne as a writer at home, situating his artistic project variously: as a continuation of the sermon-writing of the old ministers who had once lived in the house; as a dialogue with Emerson's essays, written in the same 'delightful little nook of a study'; and as a conversation with the experimental living of his neighbour Henry Thoreau.[36] So successful was this exercise in self-mythologization that it was commented upon as pretty much equally imaginatively convincing and biographically inaccurate only a few years later, by George William Curtis writing for Putnam's *Homes of American Authors* (1853):

> It seems so fitting a residence for one who loves to explore the twilight of antiquity—and the gloomier the better—that the visitor...could not but fancy that our author's eyes first saw the daylight enchanted by the slumberous orchard behind the house, or tranquillized into twilight by the spacious avenue in front. The character of his imagination, and the golden gloom of its blossoming, completely harmonize with the rusty, gable-roofed old house upon the river side, and the reader of his books would be sure that his boyhood and youth knew no other friends than the dreaming river, and the melancholy meadows and drooping foliage of its vicinity... [T]he reader, however, would greatly mistake if he fancied this...[37]

Most particularly, Hawthorne sited himself as a writer in relation to the view from the first-floor study-window:

> The study had three windows, set with little, old-fashioned panes of glass, each with a crack across it. The two on the western side looked, or rather peeped, between the willow branches down into the orchard, with glimpses of the river through the trees. The third, facing northward, commanded a broader view of the river at the spot where its hitherto obscure waters gleam forth into the light of history. It was at this window that the clergyman who then dwelt in the Manse stood watching the outbreak of a long and deadly struggle between two nations; he saw the irregular array of his parishioners on the farther side of the river and the glittering line of the British on the other bank. He awaited in an agony of suspense the rattle of the musketry. It came, and there needed but a gentle wind to sweep the battle smoke around this quiet house.[38]

The view from this window is of North Bridge over the Concord River where the American War of Independence officially broke out, marked by the graves of two British soldiers and a granite obelisk. As it happens, Hawthorne actually sited his home-made desk (a simple hinged board that could be raised or lowered by a brace set in scaled notches) facing away from the view towards the opposite wall next to the fireplace, possibly for the warmth, as he wrote only in the winter.[39] This did not prevent him from mythologizing this window for his friends well after he had moved out: James T. Fields wrote in his collection of essays *Yesterdays with Authors* (1871) that they had 'strolled round the house, where he spent the first years of his married life, and he pointed from the outside to the windows, out of which he had looked and seen supernatural and other visions'.[40] The result would

Figure 6.2. Nathaniel Hawthorne's inscription on a windowpane, The Old Manse, Concord. © Lisa McCarty

be a cultural formulation of house and environs that is epitomized by Helen Archibald Clarke's description of it as 'the spot where a great nation was born, and where its literature put forth some of its most beauteous manifestations. Here…seem to be centered its brave, stern, historical moment and its gracious literary memories'.[41]

In one of these study-windows is probably the most notable thing in the house (Figure 6.2). A single pane is incised with alternating inscriptions that form a conversation between wife and husband about the view:[42]

Man's accidents are God's purposes
Sophia A. Hawthorne 1843
Nath. Hawthorne
This is his study
1843

The smallest twig
leans clear against the sky
Composed by my wife
And written with her dia
mond
inscribed by my
husband at sunset
April 3d, 1843
In the gold light
Sun S.A.H

Famous by at least 1897 when Theodore Wolfe recorded this inscription (inaccurately) in his homes and haunts book *Literary Shrines*, Shirley Hoover Biggers' gazetteer of 2000 comments that this inscription is 'the main attraction' and that 'It was the study … where the Hawthornes left their most indelible mark, both figuratively and literally'.[43] The power of this inscription lies first in this supposed 'indelibility'. The glass is imagined as more enduring than paper and more integral to the house-structure. Physically and historically this is mistaken; glass is more fragile, and, as the history of panes of glass inscribed by Alexander Pope and Robert Burns proves, panes of glass can readily be lifted from their frames.[44] Its power lies too in the way it dramatizes writing and reading in the historical moment: it captures writing forever within the glass; imagining hand and writing in a defined instant of lit time, it is a vitrine that displays the act of writing. Moreover, the inscription converts the glass-pane into an eye-glass. Hawthorne himself imagines it as the transparent membrane of his study, Sophia as a medium through which to look out at the sky at the 'smallest' twig and to catch the light by which to see to write. But above all, this inscription dramatizes Hawthorne putting his signature to the house and everything it and its environs stand for.

On my own visit in 2007, we saw this inscription, the further two by Sophia Hawthorne in the dining-room downstairs, and another, at the time much less celebrated because much less accessible, being in the attic, accessed by narrow and slightly rickety stairs. Adventuring with a curator frustrated with the lack of custom and anxious to show the haunted rainy-day back-spaces of the house celebrated by Hawthorne, we were shown a pane in one of the attic windows bearing Hawthorne's signature.[45] If the study-window inscription stakes a claim at once to the study as a space of the visionary and the view as Hawthorne's imaginative heritage and territory, the signature in the attic lays claim to the whole house's history, for the attic is full of graffiti and writings by older hands than Hawthorne's, upon which he comments as he describes himself in *Mosses from an Old Manse* hunting among the old books heaped up there for 'any living thought which should burn like a coal of fire, or glow like an inextinguishable gem'.[46]

Although little noticed by literary critics other than biographers, the inscriptions have proven to have a special ability to capture the imagination of tourists. They feature on one of the postcards on sale celebrating Sophia: 'She left her mark on the house by inscribing her thoughts on a window pane with her diamond ring'. This sense of the liveliness, immediacy, and ephemerality of the writer's thoughts fires enthusiastic, if often inaccurate, entries on TripAdvisor and in travel blogs: 'Sophia's diamond writing is finer and more delicate than the loveliest frost pattern. But, whereas frost vanishes when touched by the sun, these tiny silver etchings have survived 167 years. It was the only aspect of The Old Manse that still felt alive'.[47] The appeal of these inscriptions depends on the way they bypass print culture. The Old Manse inscriptions are heavily invested in a version of writing as visionary and the transformative, wishing to capture the very moment when the light turned gold. They describe the desire to transcribe the real onto the interposing glass, 'the smallest twig/leans clear against the sky'. They are occasional, elliptic, fugitive, and fragmentary; sometimes broken, sometimes illegible, always insufficiently self-explanatory. They try to be the 'living thought' that might burn 'like a coal of fire or glow like an inextinguishable gem'.[48] They seem at once immediately present in the effort to fix a definite moment in time and the vision that inhabited it, and yet, although the ground of the vision remains, the vision itself is wholly lost except what remains in the shape of the ghostly writing. Moreover, personal, unique, and located rather than a reproducible and portable commodity, window inscription reanimates the difficult moment of writing within the difficult moment of reading. It is a form of writing and reading that is visibly slow, sharing to a lesser degree something of the way that, as Wordsworth remarked, epitaph exhibits the mere labour of writing: 'the very form and substance of the monument which has received the inscription, and the appearance of the letters, testif[ies] with what a slow and laborious hand they must have been engraven'.[49] Wordsworth thought this should act as a reproach to the prolific author, but these inscriptions act rather as a reproach to the greed of the ordinary reader.[50] They require a sort of reading and reader quite foreign to that constructed by print, standing there, in the right light, to decipher scratches that defy the eye of human and camera alike.

If these inscriptions on glass do much to point up the extent to which the writer's house museum is in paradoxical ways not merely anti-book, but anti-text, they also suggest the extent to which a writer's house museum might itself be thought of as vitrine or even as spectacles. Hawthorne's inscriptions and more generally his mythologizations of the house show him thinking of it in exactly this way, as an enabler and organizer of vision inward, outward, and backward through time. No wonder that Theodore Wolfe's essay describing The Old Manse notes that it seems to look at the visitor: 'From above the door little convex glasses, like a row of eyes, look out upon the visitor as he applies for admission'.[51]

Freud's mirror

A window renders the outside world unreal even as it offers a view of it. It frames, imagines, and distances. Even so, it may tempt the writer to partici-pate in the rhythms of real life rather than continue to live in imagined worlds. This, at any rate, is one of the preoccupations of Alfred, Lord Tennyson's poem 'The Lady of Shalott' (1881), in which the artist, using the light from the window over her shoulder to work by, glances into her mir-ror to see Lancelot riding by, and looks out of the window to verify her vision with fatal consequences. If the window thus describes the possibility of a view outwards into reality, the mirror describes inwardness and the dream-like or even ghostly reversals, transpositions, and distortions of mater-ial reality it achieves. For this reason, mirrors have a peculiar status within writer's house museums.

Following Prince Hamlet's famous remarks on 'the purpose of playing' ('to hold as 'twere the mirror up to nature'), the effects and ambitions of writing have often been conventionally compared to a mirror held up to reality; it is not accidental, then, that writing-spaces often seem to play with, or represent themselves in terms of, reflections.[52] Sometimes this takes its origin within the writer's lifetime, sometimes within curatorial choice, and sometimes within the tourist's own sensibility. The trope of glimpsing the dead author in a mirror has had a long history; the Museum Tassiano in the Church and Friary of Sant'Onofrio in Rome, which commemorates the site of Tasso's death there in 1595, inscrutably preserves, along with memorials of his death (an urn that once contained his ashes and a death-mask) and his work (an armchair and inkstand), his mirror.[53] The fish-eye mirror set on a surface in Woolf's bedroom at Rodmell, a room in part separate from the house proper with an outside door, originally intended as a study and where she would sometimes write in bed, is, and clearly always has been, useless as a looking-glass.[54] An artist's mirror, compressing the room into a slightly distorted version of itself, it's a nervous breakdown in glass. Less obliquely motivated is the display of mirrors associated with Dickens. A dressing-mirror from Gad's Hill Place, the house he purchased in 1856, is presently shown in 48 Doughty St; the caption recommends it to the visitor's attention as a way of simultaneously glimpsing the author at work and reiterating the viewpoint of the author: 'Dickens was known to impersonate many of his fictional characters in front of mirrors so that he could "see" them'.[55] Mirrors might reveal Dickens in otherwise lost Dickensian spaces: prior to the redisplay in 2012, the basement of Doughty St also showed a mirror from the offices of *All the Year Round*. The sense of the possibility of finding the author within a mirror has been a persistent theme in collecting and showing Dickensiana, aided by Dickens' documented passion for mirrors at Gad's Hill, and his acquisition of a pre-fab two-storey Swiss chalet that served as a summer study from 1864 onwards:

> I have put five mirrors in the Swiss chalet (where I write), and they reflect and refract, in all kinds of ways, the leaves that are quivering at the windows, and the great fields of waving corn, and the sail-dotted river. My room is up among the branches of the trees; and the birds and the butterflies fly in and out, and the green branches shoot in, at the open windows, and the lights and shadows of the clouds come and go with the rest of the company. The scent of the flowers, and indeed of everything that is growing for miles and miles, is most delicious.[56]

These mirrors were made to order in London and Dickens took particular pains to have them installed properly 'in order that they may reflect and refract truly'.[57] This letter to Mrs James T. Fields, quoted at length in John Forster's *Life of Charles Dickens* (1874) to support an illustration of the chalet embosomed in trees, would be regularly reiterated. It reappears in James T. Fields' *Yesterdays with Authors* (1871) and in travel-writing by, amongst others, Theodore Wolfe, conjecturally because this evocation of a space of sensory saturation that confounded window and mirror, outside and inside, animal and glass powerfully described something of what contemporaries experienced as Dickens' hyper-reality.[58]

The chalet was (and is) important in the Dickens mythos, in part because it was here that he left unfinished the manuscript of *The Mystery of Edwin Drood* on the day before he died. The Lady of Shalott-like mirrors may have resonated for contemporaries as connoting the end of art and the coming of death. At all events, the chalet seems to have rapidly become a museum of his death: 'when the room in the chalet in which he wrote his last paragraph was opened, sometime after his death, the first thing to be noticed by those who entered was this register [of the date/month], set at "Wednesday, June 8"—the day of his seizure'.[59] In 1874, according to Forster, 'it remains to this day as it was found'; by 1891, the chalet was important enough to have been packed up and preserved at nearby Cobham Hall: nowadays it is under restoration in the grounds of the original for Satis House in Rochester, complete with its mirrors, although, as Alison Booth remarks, it seems 'eyeless', now that it is removed from the view it commanded.[60]

Perhaps even more powerfully, mirrors serve as a special form of witness-object. As Hawthorne's remarks on the books in the attic of The Old Manse suggest, old writing may serve as 'bits of magic looking-glass' within which later readers may view 'the images of a vanished century', and one might say the same of the writer's house museum, which typically promises sight of the 'vanished', offering walk-in access for the reader-tourist out of modernity and into a 'through the looking-glass' space.[61] It is not accidental that mirrors in writer's house museums are often written up as 'having once shown such and such's face to herself', or as prone to showing the author's ghost. Nor does the mirror stop at showing lost bodies. It may shadow lost spaces. Perhaps the most remarkable instance of a mirror functioning as a witness-object in this respect is the one that usually hangs against the window of the study that Sigmund Freud used in his apartment on the Berggasse in Vienna (Figure 6.3). At first glance it is plainly an oddity: it is small, rectangular, and inexpensively framed; its positioning on the window is unorthodox and provides no surface for toiletries or shaving equipment, and anyway, it hangs just behind Freud's desk, a position that would have put it just behind the doctor's left shoulder. A photograph of 1938 confirms this positioning. Enquiry elicits that the mirror had a clinical purpose, designed to force patients to watch themselves rather than the doctor as they related their life-stories—it thus has a kind of celebrity implicated heavily in Freud's

Figure 6.3. Sigmund Freud's mirror. © Freud Museum, Vienna

revolutionary clinical practice.[62] For Freud the reflection in the mirror is also a self-portrait projected onto the outside world.[63] But it also has a less visible exceptionality. It proves to be almost the only 'authentic' thing in the study. Everything else on display, including the consulting couch, is a faithful replica of the original furnishings. Freud fled Vienna for London under the threat of Nazi persecution in 1938, taking the entirety of his effects with him; the set-up of his study was replicated in 20 Maresfield Gardens, London, including this mirror, in 1939.[64] In 1982, it was gifted by his daughter Anna Freud to the new museum in Vienna, to hang in the room that had once been his study, and which otherwise is in large part phantasmal, realized through a photographic wall-mural showing the study as it had been before the move. Freud's mirror, then, describes more poignantly and eloquently than most mirrors one of the peculiar qualities of mirror-image. The authentic mirror, in reflecting the photographs, speaks of what it should but cannot reflect: the reality of what it once witnessed. It speaks, too, of the aesthetic of replication and reversal that determines both the study in London and that in Vienna, mirroring each other, and both ambiguously the real thing rather than the reflection.[65] It opens a window through time and space in an unnervingly counter-factual way, making both studies dream each other.

The mirror in the writer's house museum has one further quality: the ability to position the tourist within the writer's space, real and imaginary. Unlike the frustrations of seeing one's own reflection in the glass of the vitrine, this is one way in which the writer's house seems to fantasize and to be haunted by the tourist in its turn. This effect of the mirror makes it akin to Michel Foucault's heterotopias, spaces, or 'counter-sites', as he puts it, 'outside of all places, even though it may be possible to indicate their location in reality', that 'have the curious property of being in relation with all . . . other sites, but in such a way as to suspect, neutralize, or invert the set of relations that they happen to designate, mirror or reflect'. Foucault speculates that the mirror offers an experience of the 'placeless place', that mixes 'an unreal, virtual space that opens up behind the surface' with 'a sort of counteraction': the mirror 'makes this place that I occupy at the moment when I look at myself in the glass at once absolutely real, connected with all the space that surrounds it, and absolutely unreal, since in order to be perceived it has to pass through this virtual point which is over there'.[66] The mirror, to put it another way, is at once hyperrealist in its faithfulness to immediate space and time, and fantastic, in that it displaces everything, including the viewer, to the virtual. One might say, then, that the mirror does much to describe the central experience of the writer's house museum for the tourist—seen through glass, everything is at once there and not fully here, real and yet not quite real. This is the effect that the Bulgakov museum pulls off in the final reveal of 'the fifth dimension' of the writer's imagined spaces through what has until then appeared to be a mirror. The writer's house museum, for all its rhetoric of vision and the visionary, houses the invisible; the view it offers is in the end that of the inward eye, writer's and reader's both.

All this said, the writer's house museum, and forms of writing associated with it from guidebook through to travel-essay, is heavily invested in the idea of the view, as a space enabling imaginative escape. This is neatly exemplified in the two photographs by Erica Lennard chosen to frame the essay on Woolf in Francesca Premoli-Droulers' *Writers' Houses*. The first shows a view through barred glass, the last a view of the lawn outside Woolf's summerhouse.[67] While this is designed to reiterate a narrative of Woolf's purchase of the property followed by her last walk to the nearby river to drown herself, it also describes Woolf's escape. Jeanette Winterson's essay on Monk's

House, after recording dismay at the summerhouse ('you will be propelled into a dull antechamber to stare through a piece of glass into the original study. Her desk is there, and her blue writing paper and one or two other bits and pieces, but she is long gone ... Here is the writer behind glass, mummified, invented'), turns away to the view:

> The only thing to do, when you have ogled into the goldfish bowl ... is to go and stand in the garden and look at the view. To see what she saw. If you concentrate, then gradually the present will fade ... and you, with the peas and beans on your right and a pear tree beside you, will be able to narrow your eyes across the flats ... How often she saw this view; saw it every time she raised her eyes from her writing block, saw it and never saw, as the mind can do when wrapped in thought. But it was what she wanted, that long far stretch with no man-made interruption to qualify her gaze.
>
> It was to be the last thing she saw ... [68]

Within this celebration of the opening and enabling view nests the conventional idea of the writer's ability to escape from ordinary life, and the seductive possibility for readers of reiterating that escape, however briefly. In Chapter 7, accordingly, we're going to visit some of the anti-domestic spaces which so often characterize the writer's house, places borrowed, commandeered, or built by writers specifically for writing outside the home: huts, garden sheds, summerhouses, garages, hermitages, chalets, and towers—re-purposed or purpose-built. In sum, outhouses.

7

Outhouses

Thoreau's cabin and Dumas' prison

Escaping

A
ll writers need somewhere undisturbed to write. I note this with some feeling, as presently my neighbour's new dog is howling at five-minute intervals not ten feet away from my garden-office, and it is a moot point whether she or I will have a nervous breakdown first.[1] William Cowper's wistful lines envisaging a possible cottage retreat run in my head: 'Here … at least I should possess/The poet's treasure, silence, and indulge/The dreams of fancy, tranquil and secure'.[2] Nearly all writers have had a tendency to place their writing-spaces as far as possible from the demands of domesticity because of its tiresome habit of breaking in upon 'the dreams of fancy'.

These anti-domestic retreats have typically been mythologized by writers themselves, and in turn by their admirers, as 'escapes'. Despite the celebration of writerly domesticity that characterizes the writer's house museum as a form, it is surprising how little traction is exerted by stories of how writers have actually managed to write in comfort at the epicentre of the domestic hurly-burly. One might well admire—one should admire— Elizabeth Gaskell's ability to write at her table in the bow window which provided panoptic command over her entire household through the bell that communicated with the kitchen below, the windows allowing for supervision of the gardener outside, and the positioning of her desk commanding various communicating doors and corridors—but still, this story has yet to achieve the power of the comparable vignette of Jane Austen writing in her living room.[3] The story goes that Austen ensured that a particular door to the sitting-room continued to creak (as it does to this day), so giving her enough warning to allow her to hide the manuscript on which she was working before anyone entered. A staple of the narrative at Chawton Cottage, this originates in James Edward Austen-Leigh's musings on how 'between February 1811 and August 1816, she began and completed *Mansfield Park, Emma,* and *Persuasion*':

> How she was able to effect all this is surprising, for she had no separate study to retire to, and most of the work must have been done in the general sitting-room, subject to all kinds of casual interruptions. She was careful that her occupation should not be suspected by servants, or visitors, or any persons beyond her own family party. She wrote upon small sheets of paper which could easily be put away, or covered with a piece of blotting paper. There was, between the front door and the offices, a swing door which creaked when it was opened; but she objected to having this little inconvenience remedied, because it gave her notice when anyone was coming... I have no doubt that I and my sisters and cousins, in our visits to Chawton, frequently disturbed this mystic process, without having any idea of the mischief that we were doing...[4]

Setting aside improbabilities, including that of managing the entire manuscript of a three-volume novel in this fashion, this story has regularly served to describe not just the difficult conditions for a woman writing in the early nineteenth century (as Virginia Woolf would put it, 'stealthily under cover of a creaking door'), but also the way that writing is secretively opposed to the domestic.[5] Austen's escape, conducted at the heart of the house itself, has become celebrated for its daring and brazen improbability, and its seductive force depends on (almost) catching her in the very act of evading our surveillance.

More usually, 'the mystic process' of imagination will be associated with time outside the public hours of the day, and space behind, above, or beyond the public spaces of the house. The tour of eight period rooms devoted to Giacomo Casanova in Duchcov Castle—where he worked as librarian, wrote an autobiography, and died in 1798—moves through a sequence of public rooms into ever more private spaces, including a bedroom complete with wig and chamberpot, before a faux library shelf swings open to discover a secret chamber, in which a dummy of Casanova is revealed writing by candlelight at his accustomed desk.[6] Other spaces of the imagination may be located high above in the attic, reached by a narrow staircase, perhaps so steep and difficult of access that it is only open to the public by exception, as in the case of The Old Manse, or hidden so cunningly within the chimney, as in the case of The House of Seven Gables or the Manor at Hemingford Grey, that only a guide will know the secret.[7] Attics, which

Gaston Bachelard argues are full of the magically generative disorganization of dream, are all well and good, but an outhouse is better, if probably chillier.[8]

The passage from ordinary domestic life to that of the imagination may be established by hardly more than a threshold and a draught; such is the space, identified and celebrated by the guidebook to Monk's House, that Woolf put between herself and her husband through obliging herself to step out of the kitchen door into the garden, round a corner of wall, and in through another door to the sanctuary of her bedroom where she kept paper and pencil by the bed to write down night-time thoughts and inspir-ations.[9] Or it may entail more of a walk across the garden to some sort of outhouse, repurposed from existing buildings at the furthest bound of the property, such as those used by the likes of Francois-René de Chateaubriand, George Bernard Shaw, Marie Corelli, Virginia Woolf, and Philip Pullman, or purpose-built, as in those devised by Emilia Pardo Bazán, Alphonse de Lamartine, Emile Zola, and Jules Verne.[10] Either way, writers have a habit of enthusiastically mythologizing themselves through their outhouses.

From the point of view of posterity, such outhouses, together with their associated landscapes, serve as usefully purified descriptors of 'the dream of fancy'. These places in which writers have felt able to indulge in dreaming and to do nothing else are imagined by writers and their admirers alike as enviable escapes from the everyday. This envy has in turn produced and reproduced these buildings as iconic tourist destinations, and they have been as a result reinscribed, represented, reiterated, or reconstructed by others in the service of escaping for real into the writer's dream. This chapter pursues symptomatic case-studies of six writer's outhouses, some commandeered, some purpose-built, all situated at the epicentre of variably national land-scapes compounded of the imagined and the real. I pay visits in turn to Cowper's summerhouse, Rousseau's hermitage, and Thoreau's cabin, make an excursion to Dumas' prison as a counter-conceit to their shared fantasies of escape, and finally come back to the question of the woman writer's vexed relation to domesticity through peeping into the towers that served as studies for Marie Corelli and for Vita Sackville-West.

Cowper's summerhouse

Right at the back of the garden of William Cowper's house in Olney stands a rickety little white-painted wooden summerhouse. It has three windows and a solid door, and can be little more than four or five feet square. Inside there are two wooden benches, and through the window-glass it is possible to see that the whitewashed walls are scored with signatures. This is the summerhouse where Cowper wrote much of his poem *The Task* (1785), and it has been celebrated ever since.

The summerhouse was not purpose-built: but, while acknowledging this, Cowper's letters work hard to repurpose it as 'a poet's retreat':

> I write in a nook that I call my boudoir. It is a summerhouse not much bigger than a sedan-chair, the door of which opens into the garden, that is now crowded with pinks, roses, and honeysuckles, and the window into my neigh-bour's orchard. It formerly served an apothecary (Mr Aspray) now dead, as a smoking-room; and under my feet is a trapdoor which once covered a hole in the ground, where he kept his bottles; at present, however, it is dedicated to sublimer uses. Having lined it with garden-mats, and furnished it with a table and two chairs, here I write in summertime...It is secure from all noise and a refuge from all intrusion...[11]

A rapid sequence of images and metaphors—'nook', 'boudoir', 'sedan-chair', and 'refuge'—reversions the summerhouse; elsewhere Cowper describes it as a 'bandbox' or a 'nutshell'.[12] Imagining sitting in there with a close friend, he comes up with an even more whimsical image—'We shall be as close packed as the wax figures in an old-fashioned picture-frame'[13]—scaling his 'verse manufactory' to his body and characterizing it as small, tight, intimate, old-fashioned, and, crucially, hospitable.

The celebrity of the summerhouse immediately following the publication of *The Task* may be accounted for by the way it allowed visitors access to the originating space and sensibility of the poem. Cowper's summerhouse, read as epitomizing *The Task*, signifies withdrawal from 'the world' and the cultivation of the inner life within a domestic setting:

> How various his employments, whom the world
> Calls idle, and who justly in return
> Esteems that busy world an idler too!
> Friends, books, a garden, and perhaps his pen...
> He, that attends to his interior self,
> That has a heart, and keeps it; has a mind
> That hungers, and supplies it; and who seeks
> A social, not a dissipated life,
> Has business; feels himself engag'd t'achieve
> No unimportant, though a silent, task.[14]

The Task's attraction for contemporaries depended upon its 'informality' and 'wandering' nature, its evocation and valuation of personal subjectivity, its investment in reverie, day-dreaming, and memory, its moral musings, and its validation of domestic happiness and retirement. The poet's subjectivity is narrated through a long-standing personal relationship with a minutely described house, garden, and landscape; the poem often reads like a guide-book which includes the reader within the poet's present tense: 'Descending now (but cautious, lest too fast)/A sudden steep, upon a rustic bridge/We pass a gulf....'.[15] The poem as a whole lends itself admirably to extraction and illustration of both sentiments and places, and as a result admirers wanted to try out being Cowper by visiting the places he loved and described.

As early as 1800 the summerhouse was represented in the headpiece to William Hayley's *The Works of William Cowper: His Life and Letters*. By the edition of 1835, Cowper's letter crowing about his new work-space was accompanied by a long footnote:

> Humble however as [the summerhouse] appears, it is approached with those feelings of veneration which the scene of so many interesting recollections cannot fail to inspire. There he wrote 'The Task'... No traveller seems to enter it without considering it to be the shrine of the Muses, and leaving behind a poetical tribute to the memory of so distinguished an author.[16]

The building would become famous enough to be depicted well beyond the confines of literary biography, appearing, for instance, as the frontispiece to volume IV of Thomas Dugdale's *Curiosities of Great Britain, Ireland and Wales Delineated: Historical, Entertaining and Commercial* (1854). From very soon after Cowper's death in 1800, the locality drew visitors desirous first of seeing the summerhouse and then of retracing Cowper's favourite walk as described in *The Task*, up to 'The Alcove', and then back through the 'Wilderness' and the 'Grove' belonging to Weston Park.[17] Designed to facili-tate just this exercise, *Cowper, illustrated by a series of views in, or near, the park of Weston-Underwood, Bucks, accompanied with copious descriptions and a brief sketch of the poet's life* (1803), was formatted to be slipped into a pocket and organized as a series of views glossed by the relevant passages drawn from the poem.[18] More than forty years later, in 1847, William Howitt began his essay on the homes and haunts of Cowper by remarking, 'There is scarcely any ground in England so well known in imagination as the haunts of Cowper at Olney and Weston... There the beautiful but unhappy poet seems to have created a whole world out of unknown ground...'.[19] Even in the 1840s, it was possible to feel a little surprised at how tame Cowper's haunts actually were ('When we follow his footsteps there, we somewhat wonder that scenes so unambitious could so enrapture him').[20] Nowadays, what with the decline in the reputation of Cowper and the increase in local housing development, the once-available raptures of the poetic landscape are yet further eroded. But for nineteenth-century admirers, a walk in the locality allowed access to Cowper's mental and physical landscape: 'every step here shows you some picture sketched by Cowper...; every scene, and every spot of ground which presents itself here, is to be found in Cowper's poetry, particularly the first book of his Task'.[21] *Cowper, Illustrated by a Series of Views* had initiated a long process by which the poem was progressively alienated from the medium of print, disassembled, and dispersed instead across the landscape. Following the walk described in *The Task* from summerhouse to Alcove and back allowed readers to see with Cowper's eyes, to escape with him into a paradigmatically 'English' landscape, which nonetheless once originated in the scene of writing that the summerhouse still memorializes. It is not a coincidence that when it came to preserving Cowper's house as a memorial, well-wishers purchased the summerhouse 'for the nation' in 1919.

While Cowper's escapes were conducted across a fairly restricted country, Rousseau's took him across Europe. Nonetheless, the same cultural investment in their shared intention and ability to escape the world through their poetic imaginations into specified precious landscapes meant that just as Cowper's summerhouse was celebrated, so too was Rousseau's brief refuge on the Île St Pierre. In fact, the idea of refuge was so attractive with respect to Rousseau that it would produce the desire to replicate it as the centre of an entirely artificial landscape altogether elsewhere.

Rousseau's hermitage

Much of Rousseau's life might be said to have consisted of escapes; in later life he found it necessary to flee from one Swiss canton to another according to whom he had annoyed most recently. This was the case in the summer of 1765 when, having offended local religious sensibilities, he was harried out of the house in the village of Môtiers-Travers where he had lived since 1762 with his mistress Thérèse Lavasseur. He took refuge in the sole farmhouse on the Île St Pierre in the lac de Bienne, where he spent six weeks before a

further forced departure for England, living in a couple of rooms on the first
floor, and writing up his experiences as an idyll in the Fifth Essay of *Rêveries
du promeneur solitaire* (1782).[22] The rooms became a celebrated tourist destination, attested as such by the admiring signatures and effusions inscribed on
the walls and window-frames by famous and less famous alike, the remains
of which are still on view.[23] One description will serve to epitomize many:
Louis Simond rather sourly noted that 'A portly Swiss beauty, our landlady,
introduced us to Rousseau's room, in the state he left it, very scantily furnished, and the bare walls scribbled over with...enthusiastic rhapsodies
about the Genevan philosopher', and he added the information that the
farmhouse was now 'a house of entertainment for curious travellers' who
had recorded their names in a visitor-book along with further 'sentimental
effusions about Rousseau'.[24]

The room where, according to one (unfriendly) commentator in 1814,
'the bed of the philosophic Rousseau is now at the command of any of his
admirers who may wish to repose in it', achieved its imaginative purchase as
an emphatically private space.[25] This privacy was exemplified and protected
by the trapdoor through which Rousseau escaped unwanted visitors.[26] This
trapdoor first appears in a brief mention in an account of a visit to Rousseau's
room written in 1777 by a man called Desjobert, and his description was
elaborated eleven years later when it was first said that this was Rousseau's
way of avoiding 'd'importuns' ['the importunate']. Sigismond Wagner's
account, authored first in German in 1795 and extended and translated into
French in 1815 by Madame Steck, is still more circumstantial; having
described the view from the single window it observes that:

> Outre de l'agrément de cette vue, un avantage particulier avoit décidé Rousseau
> à donner la preference à cette chamber sur toutes les autres de la maison, c'étoit
> un escalier dérobé qui conduisoit, au moyen d'une trappe, dans une chamber
> du rez-de-chaussée et de-là dans la campagne. Rousseau s'échappoit souvent
> par cette issue, quand le bruit qui se faisoit dans le corridor l'avertissoit de
> l'approche de quelque visite importune, et se hâtoit de se soustraire à leur vaine
> curiosité, en se réfugiant dans les endroits les plus solitaires du bois...[27]

> [Besides the attraction of this view, one advantage in particular decided
> Rousseau's preference for this room over all the others in the house, a secret
> staircase which led him, by way of a trapdoor, into a ground-floor room and
> from there into the countryside. Rousseau often escaped by this exit, when the
> noise in the corridor alerted him to the approach of some importunate visit,
> and he hastened to escape their vain curiosity by taking refuge in the most
> solitary places of the woods...]

Such an anxiety about securing the means of escape would have been well founded in Rousseau's previous experience at Môtiers-Travers; but whether the story is true or not, for Rousseau's admirers this trapdoor came to represent the writer's notorious disinclination to society's surveillance and his preference for solitary reverie. This is summed up in the engraving included in *Vues de différentes habitations de J. Rousseau* (1819), which shows Rousseau vanishing down through the trapdoor in the bedroom floor in order to escape the well-dressed visitors coming in through the door to pay their respects. The fantasy of the Île St Pierre was of idyll achieved through exile—a trapdoor exit from the pressures of the world. 'Here might I dwell, forgetting and forgot', as Samuel Rogers was to write in an uncharacteristic moment of pseudo-Rousseauism.[28] Tourists, such as the young Marianne Colston on her honeymoon tour, would make considerable efforts to visit Rousseau's refuge: 'Such a scene, so beautiful, so secluded, is calculated to inspire those sentiments, "not of earth", which his writings breathe . . .'.[29]

Rousseau's continued wanderings across Europe after his stay on the Île St Pierre culminated in a few weeks spent, just before his death, as the guest of a long-standing admirer, Réné-Louis de Girardin, on his estate at Ermenonville in 1778. One of the manifestations of the Marquis' admiration for the writer was a *jardin philosophique*. In 1762, Girardin had inherited a pretty chateau which stood in a large estate at the centre of a chain of lakes set along the deep-sided Oise valley, some miles north-east of Paris. He set about improving this natural landscape as a 'jardin anglais', a politically progressive statement.[30] It would become one of the most celebrated gardens of the late eighteenth and early nineteenth centuries, visited by anyone who was anybody, from Marie Antoinette to Gustavus III of Sweden to Joseph of Austria to Paul I of Russia, Benjamin Franklin, Thomas Jefferson, Germaine de Staël, Robespierre, Danton, Chateaubriand, and Bonaparte, and many others who came after.[31] It was designed as a landscape for serendipitous wandering and personal reverie, ornamented with 'fabriques' which the visitor was invited to discover, and which he or she would find embellished with poetic inscriptions to provoke and guide their sentiments. As such, it offered an aesthetic and intellectual walk of between three and four hours through the scenery of Enlightenment thinking and Romantic sentiment.[32] It encompassed places of an explicitly literary kind, often imaginary or semi-imaginary, including 'Laura's tomb' (in reference to Petrarch), and the 'tombeau de l'inconnu', the burial place of a young suicide identified by the inscription as another Werther. No fewer than four of these literary installations referenced Rousseau. They included 'the altar of reverie', a place where the walker could indulge in the Rousseauistic dreaming modelled in his *Rêveries*, and the 'mother's bench' which recalled the celebration in *Emile* (1762) of the tenderness between mother and child. His novel, *La Nouvelle Héloïse* (1761), was evoked at landscape scale in an entire quarter of the garden known as 'Le Désert', a recreation in miniature of Rousseau's choice of setting on the shores of Lake Geneva. The fame of this novel had already transformed that locality into, as S. W. Orson would put it in 1903, 'a fairyland peopled with creatures whose joys and sorrows appealed irresistibly to every breast', producing shortly after publication a 'stream of tourists and travellers' keen to locate the traces of Julie and her lover St Preux, and most especially the graffiti carved into the rocks of Meillerie which recorded their thwarted love, 'le monument des anciennes amours'.[33] Girardin's garden accordingly recreated this graffiti, thus satisfying a demand doomed otherwise to frustration, as *The Traveller's Guide to Switzerland* (1835) sardonically remarked: 'Many travellers have sought for the objects described by the fascinating pen of Rousseau—many still seek them'.[34] There was also a building known as 'Le Chalet de Jean-Jacques Rousseau', surrounded by an orchard recreating that described in *La Nouvelle Héloïse* as belonging to Julie. The oldest feature of this Romantic landscape also identified Rousseau as its presiding genius. This was a 'cabane', a thatched hut made of wood on the outside and raw stones on the inside, which commanded one of the best views. An inscription over the lintel read 'Jean-Jacques est immortel'.[35] Its environs were equally over-written: 'En parcourant les environs de la maison, on trouve gravés, sur plusiers quartiers de rocs, différens passages des Ecrits de Rousseau' [Wandering in the environs of the cottage, you find inscribed on a number of rocks, different passages from Rousseau's writings].[36] These inscriptions included Rousseauistic exhortations to the visitor in praise of solitary contemplation: 'C'est sur la cîme des montagnes solitaires que l'homme sensible aime contempler la nature' [It is at the summit of lonely mountains that the man of sensibility loves to contemplate nature].[37]

Perhaps it was therefore not surprising that when Rousseau was looking for somewhere out of Paris and in the country to bring the ailing Thérèse, Girardin should have offered him the use of a cottage on the estate. Indeed, it seems he actually offered the 'Chalet de Jean-Jacques Rousseau', although Thérèse refused, sensibly enough, to be lodged in it. Here Rousseau spent some six weeks peacefully botanizing in the mode of the Seventh Walk of his *Rêveries*, before succumbing to a sudden apoplexy on 4 July 1778. Being a Protestant, he could not be buried in the local cemetery, but was instead interred by night on the small island within the 'petit lac', the first lake visitors to the garden would have encountered.

Ermenonville was thus accidentally authenticated and further mythologized by the presence of the man within a landscape designed specifically to follow the contours of his imagination. Alive, he inhabited the garden as a recreation of real places that his writings had imagined. Dead, and entombed, he embodied and concentred the meaning of the landscape; as the contemporary guidebook to the garden put it, 'Ce monument imprime un grand caractère à tout le paysage' [This monument imprints a lofty character upon the whole landscape].[38] The removal of Rousseau's body in 1794 to be reinterred in the newly deconsecrated Panthéon in Paris as a father of the Revolution spoiled the perfection of the argument. Napoleon's subsequent unrealized scheme of 1800 to return Rousseau's body to the tomb on the Ile des Peupliers understood the extent to which the entire point of the garden was to provide an immersive Rousseauistic experience within a revolutionary landscape, without having to read anything more than a few inscriptions. Today this is still recognized in the naming of what remains of the garden as the Parc Rousseau.

Thoreau's cabin

Rousseau's writings enabled the Marquis to imagine Rousseau wandering by the shores of a lake and finding a final refuge on an island within one. The American Rousseau, Henry Thoreau, came to imagine himself in something of the same way. As radical political philosophers, proponents of the experimental life, practitioners of confessional-style autobiography, founders of new modes of subjectivity, lovers of nature, and founders of national ways of thinking, Rousseau and Thoreau have much in common. This extends to the celebrity of their exilic sojourns, for Rousseau enforced, for Thoreau chosen. Thoreau's book-length essay *Walden; or, Life in the Woods* (1854) records his decision in early 1845 to 'live deliberately, to front only the essential facts of life, and...learn what it had to teach', and details the building of a one-room cabin on the shores of Walden Pond on land owned by Ralph Waldo Emerson outside Concord, Massachusetts (Figure 7.1). Mostly built of a second-hand wood shanty and reclaimed brick, it was 'a tight shingled and plastered house, ten feet wide by fifteen long...with a

Figure 7.1. Interior of Henry Thoreau's cabin, Concord, MA. Author's own photograph

garret and a closet, a large window on each side, two trap doors, one door at the end, and a brick fireplace opposite'.[39] There Thoreau observed nature, surveyed, farmed, boated, fished, bathed, and wrote for two years and two months. Interweaving accounts of Thoreau's daily routine with meditations upon human existence, society, and government, together with detailed observations on natural phenomena, *Walden* would become a founding classic of American literature.

As Thoreau's choice of an engraving of the cabin as the frontispiece for the first edition suggests, building the cabin was central both to his philosophical and his poetic project:

> There is some of the same fitness in a man's building his own house that there is in a bird's building its own nest. Who knows but if men constructed their dwellings with their own hands...the poetic faculty would be universally developed, as birds universally sing when they are so engaged?[40]

This, then, was a 'poetic' sort of house.[41] As somewhere Thoreau supposedly lived in as well as merely worked within, this building might seem something of an interloper among the outhouses that writers have used or been imagined as using. But Thoreau's cabin was always and deliberately rather less than a house and rather more than merely a writing-space; it both embodied and housed the writing of polemic, and to that extent is an essay in itself about writing and the writer's life, both actual and ideal. Thoreau's friend Ellery Channing described it aptly as a 'wooden inkstand', the place where Thoreau drafted not just *Walden* but also *A Week on the Concord and Merrimack Rivers*.[42] Its textual life, too, has the same freshness and immediacy that writer's outhouses typically take on through the potent combination of describing a creative routine and the type of writing-close-to-the-moment characteristic of journals, letters, and the familiar, digressive essay. One example of Thoreau's virtuosic alternation of the present tense with the habitual, attributable in part to his habitual use of his journal as a source, will serve both to explain and delineate the power that the cabin would come to have as a tourist destination:

> This is a delicious evening, when the whole body is one sense, and imbibes delight through every pore. I go and come with a strange liberty in Nature, a part of herself. As I walk along the stony shore of the pond in my shirt sleeves...all the elements are unusually congenial to me...Sympathy with the fluttering alder and poplar leaves almost takes away my breath; yet, like the lake, my serenity is rippled but not ruffled...

This sort of writing would suggest to the generations of tourists to come that a visit to the cabin would offer access to the very sensorium of Thoreau's idyll, even if there was no one evidently home, and it suggested further the appropriate way of 'leaving a card' by leaving natural offerings:

> When I return to my house I find that visitors have been there and left their cards, either a bunch of flowers, or a wreath of evergreen, or a name in pencil on a yellow walnut leaf or a chip. Those who come rarely to the woods take some little piece of the forest into their hands to play with by the way, which they leave, either intentionally or accidentally. One has peeled a willow wand, woven it into a ring, and dropped it on my table. I could always tell if visitors had called in my absence, either by the bended twigs or grass, or the print of their shoes, and generally of what sex or age or quality they were by some slight trace left, as a flower dropped, or a bunch of grass plucked and thrown away...or by the lingering odour of a cigar or pipe...[43]

It is not surprising that the Thoreau Society has adopted the frontispiece illustration of the cabin as their logo, although Thoreau would certainly have been scathing about the way that this logo is now used to advertise the 'Shop at Walden Pond'.[44]

Yet the cabin did not immediately exert cultural pull, and the story of its fate subsequent to Thoreau's occupation says much about how slowly it accrued iconic power. In September 1847, Thoreau gave it to Emerson (as the landowner), who sold it to his gardener; two years later it was bought again by two farmers who moved it to the other side of Concord where they used it to store grain, and then in 1868 dismantled it for scrap lumber and put the roof on an outbuilding.[45] As a disappointed contemporary Wilson Flagg wrote on visiting in 1872, 'Not a stone marks the place which is sacred to his genius and immortalized by his works'.[46] This cannot have lasted long; it is said that in 1872 Bronson A. Alcott took a visitor out to the site and placed a stone at what he remembered as the site of the cabin; subsequently the cairn became immense.[47] At some point in the later 1870s and 1880s the then landowner 'placed a series of tin stars on trees to lead visitors to the house-site'.[48] By 1895, when Theodore Wolfe published his popular and influential account of 'The Concord Pilgrimage' in *Literary Shrines*, it was possible to visit 'Thoreau's cove', cairn, and beanfield, and to bathe, like the writer, in the waters of Walden.[49] The original site was only formally rediscovered in November 1945, when Roland Wells Robbins, amateur historian and Thoreau enthusiast, discovered and excavated the foundation of Thoreau's chimney.

Nowadays, not much is to be seen on the original site; there are granite posts marking out the ground plan and a cairn built of stones regularly left by admirers. That said, the place is and has been since 1947 marked with a plethora of signs and plaques: one, dedicated in July 1947 by the Thoreau Society, still marks the hearth site; a stone indicates 'the site of Thoreau's cabin', and another the site of the woodshed; a wooden plaque quotes Thoreau's most famous lines from *Walden*, 'I went to the woods because I wished to live deliberately...'; and an information board provides an image of the house, a brief history of the formation of the Thoreau Society, and the discovery of the foundations. The emptiness of the site proper, however, belies (or perhaps underscores, on the evidence of the counterfactual insistence of contemporary postcards on the solitude of Walden Pond) the import of the cabin.[50] Since the 1980s tourists less imaginative, less well read, or just less fit have been offered the chance to view a replica of the cabin nearer the car-park. This is based on a drawing done by Thoreau's sister Sophia and the archaeological excavation carried out by Robbins. Furnished with three replica chairs, bed, table, writing-desk, utensils, books, clothes, a flute, an umbrella, a broom, and a cast-iron stove, it has been further embellished with a visitor-book recording visitors' variously rapturous and bemused reactions, ranging from 'we should all strive to be more like Thoreau' to the more TripAdvisor-style of the waggish 'where's the TV?'.[51] Rather like Ermenonville, this installation is captioned with the writer's body, in this case a modern statue of Thoreau, eyes cast down in thought, apparently caught hastily leaving the cabin for the woods to evade unwelcome visitors. Nor is this the only replica cabin around: there is one rather coyly standing in the backyard of the Thoreau Lyceum in Concord. This proves to have been produced by Robbins himself, and is only one of a production line that he developed in the 1960s, selling kits for the 'Thoreau-Walden cabin' on the promise that 'if it is your wish to live deliberately and make a place in your life to house your dreams, your privacy, or your own personal life style . . . then the Thoreau-Walden cabin is your happy answer'.[52] Given this dreamlike and queasy repetition, it is unsurprising that, at first glance, the Concord Museum's Thoreau Gallery appears to house yet another replica, albeit merely of the interior—until one realizes that this is a different sort of reconstruction, and these really are the chair, bed-frame, sloping desk, snowshoes, walking-stick, and wooden flute celebrated in *Walden*, all displayed under the frontispiece of *Walden*.[53]

For all their evidently different histories, Cowper's summerhouse, Rousseau's hermitage, and Thoreau's cabin present some notable ideological continuities. Each describes and inscribes the search for solitude and the value of the inner, imaginative life. Each originates and locates acts of self-making through writing—all three writers were celebrated for their autobiographical writing and for their exemplary experimental lives. By extension, each is figured as anti-domestic, an escape from the ordinary spaces and functions of the contemporary house which verges upon critique. Countering the documented facts of each writer's life—that Cowper's rea-sonably cosy house was just a step away across the small garden, that Rousseau stayed in a cottage in the village of Ermenonville in preference to either chalet or cabane, that Thoreau walked most days into the village of Concord for company, food, and amenities—the acts of self-making that these out-houses enable and describe are conceived in relation to a natural and 'wild' landscape, whether the artificial 'Wilderness' of Weston Park, Ermenonville's 'Le Désert', or the woods around Walden, even though they were more woodlot than wilderness even when Thoreau was making his experimental sojourn. As a consequence, these landscapes in due course materialize the author and their writing. Running counter to this sense of Romantic location, however, is a persistent undertow of replication that conceives these outhouses as 'mobile', to do with the persistent sense that, for better and for worse, writer's outhouses are not quite fixed appropriately within the ordinary and everyday.

Dumas' prison

Exceptionally, the specially isolated, extra-domestic site of writing may be conceived not as idyllic escape but as imprisonment. A little beyond Paris, it is possible to visit the so-called Chateau Monte Cristo which offers a very different model of the writer's solitude; not as wandering alone in nature but as clapped up in solitary confinement in a thick-walled prison.[54] The Chateau Monte Cristo was built by Alexandre Dumas *père*, one of the most successful novelists of the nineteenth century. Begun in 1846 and finished in 1847, the Chateau's design was commissioned from Hippolyte Durand, the leading architect of the day, as something reminiscent of the Renaissance: 'Vous allez ici même me tracer un parc anglais au milieu duquel je veux une maison Renaissance' [You will lay me out here an English garden at the centre of which I want a Renaissance mansion].[55] The exterior of the main building is indeed putatively 'Renaissance'. The towers are surmounted by Dumas' initials carved in stone, together with his personal motto; the head of Dumas himself appears amongst the series of heads of other famous writers representing a world canon (Shakespeare, Virgil, Goethe, Chateaubriand, *inter alia*) which decorate the exterior at first-floor height, looking out over the front door. Despite Dumas' strategic omission of Scott, the Chateau positions itself, like Abbotsford before it, as pertaining to an extremely successful writer specializing in historical subjects, appropriately enough for the founder of the Théâtre Historique in Paris and a best-selling exponent of historical fiction.

However, if you follow the winding path up the slope behind the Chateau through the *parc anglais*, threading through artificial rock arches and grottoes alive with the trickle of streams and pools, you will find a miniature Gothic castle set on a miniature island, surrounded by a spring-fed moat (Figure 7.2). Reached by a stone bridge, and guarded at its entrance by a stone dog chained in a kennel, this is Dumas' 'cabinet de travail'. It was commissioned as 'un pavillon gothique entouré d'eau' [a Gothic pavilion surrounded by

Figure 7.2. Alexandre Dumas' cabinet de travail, Chateau Monte Cristo. Shutterstock

water]. It is set with stones carved with the titles of eighty-eight of his works. Dumas called it the 'Chateau d'Îf', after the famous prison set on an island in the harbour of Marseilles. Like the Chateau Monte Cristo, the Chateau d'Îf was also a reference to one of Dumas' best-selling historical novels.

The Count of Monte Cristo (1845–6) has of recent years largely fallen out of the European literary canon. But I am old enough to have read many of the French popular classics serialized at length in graphic form in the children's weekly *Look and Learn*, and as a result the events of *The Count of Monte Cristo* are burnt indelibly into my memory—the unjust imprisonment of the hero Dantès as a supporter of Bonaparte during the Hundred Days, his fourteen years in solitary confinement in the high-security island prison of the ancient Chateau d'Îf in the bay of Marseilles, his ingenious and prolonged escape attempts culminating in success through substituting for the dead body of his fellow-prisoner, friend, and mentor the Abbé, his acquisition (following the instructions supplied by the arcane researches of the Abbé) of the fabulous treasure of Cardinal Spada hidden within the labyrinthine series of grottoes of the island of Monte Cristo between Corsica and Elba, and his subsequent ingenious acts of revenge upon those responsible for his years of imprisonment. Even read at full length (three fat

volumes), it is a compulsive page-turner. More to the point, it served as a
founding romance for post-Napoleonic France. It was wildly successful
both in France and in Britain, and the money it brought in funded the
building of this weekend pocket palace and its grounds. It was dubbed the
'Chateau Monte Cristo' by a friend (Dumas himself claimed, disingenu-
ously, that this was 'fatuous'), and with good reason, for the imagination of
the author of *The Count of Monte Cristo* is very clearly at work in the
building.[56]

Within Dumas' novel, the Chateau d'Îf is represented as indeed something of a 'cabinet de travail'; the imprisoned Abbé occupies himself reading
and studying and teaching Dantès, ingeniously contriving paper, pens, pen-
knife, and ink from two old shirts, fish-head cartilage, a broken candlestick,
and a mixture of soot, blood, and communion wine. Despite the privations
of his cell, he has an extensive library of memorized books: 'Thucydides,
Xenophon, Plutarch, Titus Livius, Tacitus, Strada, Tornandes, Dante,
Montaigne, Shakespeare, Spinoza, Machiavel, and Bossuet', and contrives
inter alia further writerly amenities in the shape of a clock, a lamp, and
matches, and finally the means of escape (in practice thwarted) in the shape
of a tunnel and a rope.[57] In referencing his own storying of the Chateau d'Îf
in *The Count of Monte Cristo*, Dumas mythologized his Gothic tower as
much more than the most sumptuous of writer's sheds. It describes the privations of the writer's life, and celebrates writerly ingenuity, which spins
treasure from mind, body, and basic materials. In point of fact, Dumas was
far more fastidious and ritualistic than the Abbé could afford to be: 'Je suis
trés maniaque sur ce point; je ne puis travailler que sur certain papier, je ne
puis écrire qu'avec certaines plumes...il me serait impossible de rien écrire
avec de l'encre bleue' [I am maniacal on this point; I cannot work without
a certain sort of paper, I cannot write without certain sorts of pens, it would
be impossible for me to write anything with blue ink].[58] And Dumas was
free, unlike the Abbé, to leave his prison when he chose, rather than being
released only by death.

This mythologization extends to the siting of the 'cabinet du travail' in
relation to the main house. The stream that flows downwards from the moat
forks: one rivulet feeds the 'pool of Haidée'. Symbolically, therefore, the
confinement of the writer within the Chateau d'Îf is the source of quasi-
Edenic domestic bliss; Haidée, derived from the girl who appears in Canto
I of Byron's *Don Juan* (1819), is the Greek child-bride rescued from slavery
whose love eventually consoles the Count. The other rivulet runs through

the grounds (in Dumas' time filled with exotic flora and fauna, including three monkeys, golden pheasants, peacocks, parrots, and a vulture) directly under the foundations of the Chateau Monte Cristo and into a 'bassin de dragon' which pours out below the terrace and falls down into what was once an extensive view across the river-plain of the Seine. The Chateau d'Îf thus sets itself up as the source of the Orientalist sensuality that Dumas staged within the main Chateau in his famous Moorish room, which bears a strong resemblance to the subterranean palace that the Count constructs within the grottoes of Monte Cristo:

> The entire chamber was lined with crimson brocade, worked with flowers of gold. In a recess was a kind of divan, surmounted by a stand of Arabian swords in silver scabbards, and handles resplendent with gems; from the ceiling hung a lamp of Venetian glass, of beautiful shape and colour, whilst his feet rested on a Turkey carpet, in which they sank to the instep; tapestry hung before the door...[59]

Here the Count serves banquets of the sort that Dumas, the celebrated author of the *Grand Dictionnaire de Cuisine* (published posthumously in 1873), produced for real at the Chateau ('roast pheasant, garnished with Corsican blackbirds' and 'a gigantic lobster'), topped off with coffee à la Turque, 'chibouques', and spoonfuls of hashish paste.[60] The whole extravaganza was financed by the real-life equivalent of Dantès' 'incalculable, unheard of and almost fabulous riches, which were his, with none to dispute his claim', riches produced by writing.[61] No wonder, then, that the façade of the Chateau d'Îf shows Dantès discovering his treasure. The Chateau d'Îf, as purpose-built writing-space, may describe writing as immurement; but the 'parc anglais' that surrounds it describes the pay-off, and relates how this made the author into the Count of Monte Cristo, a man who comes into possession of fabulous wealth as a direct result of his years of imprisonment.

While this estate was at one level a personal fantasy made for the pleasure of Dumas and his friends, it was also, like so much of Dumas' life, a myth made for and consumed by the public. The buildings were celebrated from the outset, extensively illustrated, for example, in the periodical *L'Illustration* of 26 February 1848. The enterprise was short-lived; the cost, combined with the crash of 1848 associated with the Revolution of that year, enforced the sale of the estate, although Dumas continued to live there until 1851 by permission of the new owner. The treasure, as Dantès feared, had turned out to be not just dreamlike, but indeed a dream:

Then he thought he tried to return to these wondrous grottoes, but the way leading into them had become a maze of twistings and turnings, and the entrance was no longer visible; he puzzled his wearied memory for the magical and mysterious word which opened Ali Baba's splendid caverns to the Arab fisherman; all was in vain—the vanished treasure had again become the property of the genii of the earth...[62]

Corelli's folly and Vita's tower

Immurement might actually have its advantages for a woman writer; it is possible to feel wistful at the idea that someone would push a plate of food through a door at set intervals and otherwise leave one severely alone.[63] Less skittishly, one might enquire how women writers have imagined themselves, and been imagined, as dreaming in an outhouse rather than sitting decorously in the house proper.

In 1899, the best-selling author Marie Corelli leased the house and garden of Mason Croft, in Stratford-upon-Avon, a property which she would eventually buy.[64] Corelli must have found Mason Croft's handsome mid-eighteenth-century frontage and garden, ornamented with a free-standing classical arch in stone, not only dispiritingly dilapidated but dispiritingly modern; for she set about energetically bringing it back 'to look something like it must have been in the fifteenth century', equipping the house with quantities of oak panelling and diamond panes of leaded glass. She gave full rein to this Elizabethanizing impulse in renovating the eighteenth-century folly in the garden as her summer study. She liked to think of this as originally an 'Elizabethan watch-tower', erected to look over an old farmhouse built by 'Rychard Mason'.[65] Now, thanks to Corelli's efforts, lavishly ornamented with leaded glass in the windows, dark oak panelling, and cabinet bookcases punctured with cut-outs of hearts, vine-covered and picturesque, the total effect is sweet, pretentious, aggressive, and sentimental. Even as it reinflects it, it is eloquent of a then century-old desire to retrieve, reconstruct, and evoke Stratford-upon-Avon's essential Elizabethan-ness, a desire which can be traced all the way back to Ireland's *Picturesque Views on the Upper or Warwickshire Avon* (1795).

Corelli's tower therefore is one among many instances of the long history of investing in Stratford-upon-Avon to make it more 'Shakespearean'. But it was also part of her private and public mythos. Contemporary publicity

"The small but intense pleasure of walking through dry leaves and kicking them up as you go ... they rustle, they brustle, they crackle..."

From *Walking Through Leaves*, Vita Sackville-West

Figure 7.3. Interior of top tower room in Vita Sackville-West's tower, Sissinghurst, National Trust. Author's own photograph

photos show Corelli leaning out of the window on the folly's first floor.[66] The 'watch-tower' thus envisioned Corelli as a heroine of romance charmingly immured in a tower, but it also furnished a pretty window from which to wave to a global public.

What is probably the most famous tower writing-space associated with a woman writer also invokes the romance trope of the maiden in the tower (Figure 7.3). In 1930 Vita Sackville-West and Harold Nicolson bought the mutilated remains of a moated Elizabethan courtyard house set within a small estate. Here Sackville-West, poet, novelist, journalist, and gardener, commandeered the most improbable-looking building in the motley collection, what might once have been a platform from which to view the hunt in the deer-park, and was now entirely isolated. Here she made a writing-space at the centre of what would become her famous garden, Sissinghurst. Unlike Corelli, Sackville-West chose to turn away from house, garden, and the wider landscape, folding in upon herself within the tower. Her study on the first floor is now set up by the National Trust as she used it, high-windowed, curtained, lamplit, and barred to all: as the interpretive caption notes, 'Vita allowed very few people into her sacrosanct space during her lifetime, including her two sons, this is why we do not allow access into this delicate room'. For Adam Nicolson, this room sits at the heart of the meaning of Sissinghurst Castle and its garden because the whole 'seems to enshrine a set of ever deeper privacies, gathering inwards in concentric rings':

> first the world of the farm and its woods, down and away from the road; then, the way in through the entrance arch into the garden itself; then the private enclosures of each of the smaller gardens contained within the garden; then, the Tower, the great fixed point at the centre of it all, visible from every part; and finally, in imagination anyway, into Vita's writing room within the Tower, a scarcely visited place in her lifetime, the heart of Sissinghurst and its nest of privacies.[67]

Visitors are obliged to peep through a barred gate to avoid disturbing this 'nest of privacies'; a flight of stairs further up, one finds a tower room echoing with the voice of Sackville-West reciting the lines she composed on the floor below, including her self-mythologizing poem 'Sissinghurst' (1931), dedicated to her ex-lover Virginia Woolf who had just celebrated her as the androgynous protagonist of her novel *Orlando* (1928). The lines painted on the walls describe the tower as 'Buried in time and sleep,/So drowsy, over-grown,/That here the moss is green upon the stone,/And lichen stains the keep'. The paralysis of time allows for the growth of dream: 'For here, where days and years have lost their number,/I let a plummet down in lieu of date,/And lose myself within a slumber...'. Sackville-West here characterizes herself as a counter-version of Tennyson's Mariana and the Lady of Shalott, a lady in a moated grange who is not waiting for a lover, and who is not seduced into looking out of the window. Instead, she remains devoted to the world of the imagination, living in the fragile illusions provided in reflection, mirror and trance: 'I've sunk into an image, water-drown'd.../ Illusive, fragile to a touch, remote/As no disturber of the mirrored trance/ I move...'. Both Corelli and Sackville-West abstract themselves from immediate domesticity into romance, whether conceived as Shakespearean or Tennysonian.

Although practicalities have clearly driven individual solutions to the problem of where to write undisturbed, this hardly explains the cultural power and longevity of the idea of the writer's outhouse. Whether the writer's escape from the ordinary is envisaged as vanishing from view or vanishing into the view, as wandering or immurement, these outhouses are first mythologized by their original owners and then preserved and celebrated by their admirers because they are taken to epitomize the mystery beyond the everyday and ordinary that is 'the dream of fancy'. It is not, however, coincidental that in most of the instances cited here, the writer's out-house has come to concentre a landscape conceived in some way as of national import. Thus, although Cowper's landscape is now decayed, it once described the English countryside, Rousseau's landscapes taken together once described a French revolutionary idyll, and Dumas' chateau once gave form in miniature to a post-Napoleonic France and its empire. Corelli's folly and Sackville-West's tower both deliberately rooted themselves in Elizabethanized 'English' places, although this effect has largely vaporized. But Thoreau's cabin still imagines the native wildness of the American woods, despite the crowds at Walden Pond, and, at need, the writer's out-house may still have such power to construct its native landscape as national that it can go wandering itself and yet remain at home. This surely accounts for the existence of a replica of Dylan Thomas' writing-shed made in 2014 in commemoration of the centenary of his birth. Created by the Arts Development Department of the Carmarthenshire County Council in association with Emily Hinshewood's 'Dictionary for Dylan' project, the idea was that the shed should tour Dylan Thomas's landscape, physical and linguistic, conceived as the entirety of Wales, inviting members of the public into the otherwise inaccessible interior to do a little writing of their own in tribute to the poet.[68] This project's ambition may be traced right back to the remarkable early nineteenth-century house and landscape constructed by a national writer as both outgrowth and celebration of his own creativity, Walter Scott's Abbotsford, arguably the model for all subsequent writer's house museums, and the subject of Chapter 8.

8

Enchanted ground

Scott's Abbotsford, Irving's Sunnyside, and Shakespeare's New Place

Some writers, especially those novelists such as Alexandre Dumas *père* who surfed the transition to a mass print culture in the mid-nineteenth century, achieved enough success, and with it, wealth and celebrity, to indulge the wildest self-mythologization in bricks and mortar, stucco and plaster, antiques and fabriques, gardens and grounds, instead of merely on paper. The houses they made argued for the inhabitant as unique, and it is this, paradoxically, that makes them akin. Thus what William Dean Howells said of his friend Mark Twain's enormous and enormously exuberant house in Hartford, Connecticut—'As Mark Twain was unlike any other man that ever lived, so his house was unlike any other house ever built'—might be the strapline (with suitable substitutions of names) for quite a number of nineteenth-century writer's houses.[1] Twain would come to think of the house he built from 1873 onwards as an exercise in autobiography, pertinent both to his private life as Samuel Clemens and his writerly alter-ego Mark Twain; in this, again, he was not singular. Equally, the house, built and decorated by the leading firms of the day, was not unlike other writer's follies in that its cost combined with business failure had half-ruined the family by 1891.

The subject of this chapter, then, is the house consciously made and shown by the writer as an expression of his 'genius', often immediately preserved in more or less the state in which he left it at his death. The nineteenth-century writers who made these houses were almost invariably male novelists, and, generally, historical novelists who had specialized in writing romances of nationhood.[2] This was not merely because it was possible to make large sums of money from the publication of such novels. As the writing-spaces discussed in Chapter 7 suggest, it is relatively easy to invent intriguingly freestanding spaces if you write in lyric, confessional mode about escape from domestic constraints. As Dumas' adoption of the counter-conceit of immurement in the Chateau d'Îf suggests, it is much harder to lay claim in interesting ways to a house as an historical novelist. A house 'owned' by such a writer must display both the material reality of the past and its romantic transformation and animation in the present. As a result, it begins to look very much less like a space of poetic self-expansion, and very much more like an antiquarian collection of 'curiosities'—things not necessarily valuable in themselves, but for their 'associations', things which therefore encode all sorts of stories in miniature, collectible form. Such houses look, in short, very like private museums, although the point of them is that they are museums that celebrate a coalescence of individual and national genius.[3]

These houses initiate and model the very concept of the writer's house as museum. They construct the house as a way of modelling how the writer's physical and imaginative life work in mysterious symbiosis and amalgamation. They argue that the house itself dramatizes the way the writer's imagination has saved and animated the hitherto mute detritus of the nation's past. The most influential of these self-museumized houses, Walter Scott's Abbotsford, was further conceived as set within an 'enchanted' locality, one that through the wizardry of the writer's imagination might at any moment swarm with fairies from the hill, or ghostly personages from the past. Thus Abbotsford is the first house to materialize what Joseph Addison called in 1710 the 'enchanted ground' of a writer's house.[4] It consciously models the idea that the genius of a writer is most fully encountered in his (or, much less often, her) 'homes and haunts'. It gave rise in due course to the idea that it would be possible and desirable to posthumously convert and even reconstruct writers' houses as national museums, and it invented the romantic ideology and the aesthetic of the writer's house museum as set within a haunted national landscape so successfully that the construct became exportable to America. This chapter, then, brings into focus something that has been flickering in the peripheral vision of the story so far—that making an author at home as owner of a house and a landscape is very frequently associated with the making of national locality, and by extension a national literature—as we have already seen in the cases of, for instance, William Cowper and Jane Austen.

The centrepiece of this chapter, then, is a discussion of Scott's Abbotsford, preceded by consideration of a number of fantasy houses made by historical novelists so as to lay claim to fathering national literatures. This is followed by a discussion of the copy-cat construction of national 'enchanted ground' in early nineteenth-century America by Washington Irving at Sunnyside in the Hudson Valley. The chapter concludes by meditating on the ideological continuities—and discontinuities—between these houses and the redevelopment of Shakespeare's New Place in 2016 to mark the 400th anniversary of his death.

Genius and enchantment

Twain's prodigy house in Connecticut sits within a long-standing tradition of writers making celebrity houses as expressions of authorial genius.[5] Horace Walpole's fantasia Strawberry Hill at Twickenham has some claim to being the first such house; in Walpole's words, it was 'built to please my own taste, and in some degree to realise my own visions'.[6] Developed from 1749 onwards, Strawberry Hill became famous in Walpole's lifetime as a vastly extended and egregiously improbable 'Gothick' folly, whitened and gilded, pinnacled and castellated, vaulted and turreted, looking-glassed and latticed, and incorporating within its fabric a vast and eclectic collection of art, valuables, and curiosities.[7] These curiosities came in due course to include the story of the origin of Walpole's Gothic novel, *The Castle of Otranto* (1764), said to be a vision on waking from a dream of the appearance of a giant armoured fist on the staircase.[8]

The formulation beginning to develop in Strawberry Hill, whereby the fantasy of the house is perceived as continuous with the fictions produced by its inhabitant, would find extended expression in Dumas' Chateau Monte Cristo and in even more extreme form in Victor Hugo's house, Hauteville, in St Peter Port on the island of Guernsey. Choosing exile here in 1855 following banishment after Louis Napoleon Bonaparte's coup d'état in 1851, Hugo bought this mansion in 1856 and would then spend some fourteen years refashioning it. On the outside a conventionally handsome five-floor Georgian house topped with the glass look-out characteristic of such houses, on the inside it developed 'a symbolic dimension' through referencing Hugo's writing, philosophy, and world-vision. In the words of his son, Charles Hugo, it became an 'autograph on three floors and a poem in several rooms' giving (in the words of the current website) 'this unique building an inner force and mystery'.[9] What the public made of it at the time is usefully summarized by an essay, 'Victor Hugo At Home' (1869), which drew on the publication of a guide in French by a M. Lecanu some years before:

> The peculiar interest of the house rests in the fact of its being the home of a master-mind, and that the apartments were arranged entirely after the idea, and from the designs, of Victor Hugo, who was employed for three years on this memorial of his fantastic taste... The interior of the house is a unique work of art... To describe the house is to make known the man.[10]

The lengthy description that follows details how 'most rare curiosities, oak carvings of the Middle Ages and Renaissance, ancient tapestries, enamels, porcelains, bric-à-brac, selected with fastidious choice... mixed with Venetian and Florentine elegances' were fashioned into 'masterpieces', elaborately dramatic built-in assemblages garnished with 'devices and inscriptions' 'which are so many unpublished lines of Victor Hugo', enlivened by curiosities pertaining to various celebrated historical figures including Madame Pompadour, Marie Antoinette, and Charles II, and punctuated by idiosyncratic conceits (such as the cathedral choir-stall chair reserved for dead Hugo ancestors).[11] What this mid-Victorian writer does not entirely convey is the way that individual artefacts are put together like freak-show fantasy monsters, matings enforced between the unrelated to produce new meanings, and the way that the integrity of any object or any space is comprehensively violated to produce an effect that might be described as something not unlike the gorgeously opportunistic carapace of a caddis-fly larva, albeit turned outside in.[12] The point of these grotesqueries is that they prove the animating power of genius; as the essayist is at pains to stress, while 'Hauteville House is worthy of more than a cursory examination as a mere museum of art, yet how lifeless and dissatisfying would it be without a living genius, as it were, to animate it'.[13] The conceit of the tour of the house he offers, as nowadays, is that the visitor moves from the shadowy entrance hall, through an inner porch 'frontispiece' citing Hugo's earliest work, up to the white light of Hugo's cabinet de travail in the glass look-out. Here, in 'the actual chambers occupied by the poet and author himself... his own particular sanctum', is discovered the source of the whole extravaganza:

> Let me approach nearer to the more private chamber of this genius, who lives almost entirely in the very attic, which forms an eyrie far above the petty

interruptions and noises of the lower world, and where nothing seems possible to arrest the soaring flight of the grandest genius.[14]

The imaginative geography of Hugo's house, and the possibility of reading it in this way, derives at a distance from the original such house, Walter Scott's Abbotsford, created half a century before.

Scott's Abbotsford

In 1811, Scott acquired the undistinguished farmhouse called Cartleyhole and its grounds on the banks of the Tweed, which he would transform into Abbotsford. Here he built, over the next twenty-one years, a fantasy house fit for a Romantic, complete with turrets, stepped gables, and architectural details modelled on Melrose Abbey and Rosslyn Chapel, which would eat up all the fairy gold generated by the astounding success of his poetry and fiction, and then some (Figure 8.1).[15] A monument to personal wealth, class ambition, and the Scottish past, at once in deadly earnest and a great joke, it was also a ground-breaking essay in the idea of the writer's house.

As well as providing a suitably castellated dwelling for an aspiring baronet, and space for a remarkable collection of old books and antiquarian objects of interest, this 'Conundrum Castle' showcased Scott's public identity

Figure 8.1. Walter Scott's Abbotsford. Author's own photograph

as 'The Minstrel of the North', that is to say, the poet of *The Lay of the Last Minstrel* (1805), and riddled his secret identity as 'The Great Unknown', that is to say, the 'Author of Waverley'. In particular, Abbotsford offered many clues to Scott's authorship of the best-selling third novel in the series, *The Antiquary* (1816). Clive Wainwright argues that *The Antiquary* was 'central to the understanding of Abbotsford and Scott's collecting activities', being written 'just when the interiors of Abbotsford were being planned'.[16] But even more pertinently, it reflected upon Scott's own persona as a historical novelist in his choice of central protagonist, the elderly Jonathan Oldbuck, the Antiquary of the title.

Oldbuck's antiquarianism is characterized by habits of acquisition—the habit of collecting material objects, and the habit of asserting personal intellectual property in local places. Neither objects nor places are of apparent value within modernity. When we are first introduced to Oldbuck, on the journey by carriage from Edinburgh to Queensferry, we discover him admiring his latest acquisition—a folio 'on which he gazed from time to time with the knowing look of an amateur, admiring its height and condition, and ascertaining, by a minute and individual inspection of each leaf, that the volume was uninjured and entire from title-page to colophon'.[17] This proves to be an edition of Alexander Gordon's *Itinerarium Septentrionale*, and it is plain that Oldbuck is already familiar with the text; it is the state of the copy that he has picked up that primarily preoccupies him. Besides books, Oldbuck seems to collect local, conjecturally ancient, historical sites; on the same journey, he beguiles a delay by showing his travelling companion, the mysterious young man Lovel, a 'specimen' of a Pict's camp.[18] Oldbuck's passion is retrieving and restoring the ruined, obsolete, and illegible, for in common 'with most of the virtuosi of his time' he 'measured decayed entrenchments, made plans of ruined castles, read illegible inscriptions, and wrote essays on medals in the proportion of twelve pages to each letter of the legend'.[19] Oldbuck is embodied in the inconveniences of the building of Monkbarns, 'an irregular old-fashioned building',[20] originally part of a monastic complex supposed founded by the Abbot of Trotcosey. It is approached through a garden distinguished by old-fashioned topiary and is characterized by dark, uneven, winding, and inconvenient passages. At its heart lies Oldbuck's '*sanctum sanctorum*', a study described at length:

> One end was entirely occupied by book-shelves, greatly too limited for the number of volumes placed upon them, which were, therefore, drawn up in

ranks of two or three files deep, while numberless others littered the floor and the tables, amid a chaos of maps, engravings, scraps of parchment, bundles of papers, pieces of old armour, swords, dirks, helmets, and Highland targets.[21]

The study evinces an interest in the various stages of Scottish history—artefacts from Scottish wars are mixed in with local Roman artefacts ('busts, and Roman lamps and paterae') and ancient British items, together with more recent history in the shape of 'two or three portraits in armour, being characters in Scottish history, favourites of Mr Oldbuck', and family history also embodied in portraits, 'many in tie-wigs and laced coats, staring representatives of his own ancestors'. However, it looks like eclecticism carried to the point of litter and chaos, a 'wreck of ancient books and utensils', unintelligible even to the intelligent eye, for they 'seemed to have little to recommend them, besides rust and the antiquity which it indicates'.[22] The space is overpowered by 'miscellaneous trumpery', a '*mare magnum*''in which it would have been as impossible to find any individual article wanted, as to put it to any use when discovered'. Considered as a description of Oldbuck's mind, heart, sensibility, and 'profession', then, the study argues industry and indolence, acquisitiveness and disorder, value in the unvalued, and property in the past rather than in the future.

One of the oddities of Oldbuck is his desire to figure as an author: as the narrator comments sardonically, 'like many other men who spend their lives in obscure literary research, he had a secret ambition to appear in print, which was checked by cold fits of diffidence, fear of criticism, and habits of indolence and procrastination'.[23] Oldbuck is a published author in the contemporary antiquarian periodical press but his ambitions far outstrip the scholarly controversy associated with the real-life antiquarian works of Joseph Ritson, Francis Grose, and William Stukeley.[24] He aims at epic poetry—or rather (since by his own admission he does not have the 'mechanical' facility for verse-making) he hopes to persuade Lovel to write an epic historical poem on a subject and plan of his choosing, to be entitled *The Caledoniad*, to which he proposes to provide an extensive apparatus of critical and historical notes together with a scholarly introduction.[25] These authorial ambitions, combined with Oldbuck's antiquarian bent, have long suggested some sort of identification of Scott with his character, and by extension, Abbotsford with Monkbarns.

Despite Scott's own insistence that his old friend George Constable was the original for Oldbuck, the identification of Scott with the figure of

Oldbuck is of long standing and remains current today. John Sutherland's biography points out the similarities between author and character: like Scott, Oldbuck is a younger brother, apprenticed to an attorney, who falls in love in youth with a noble young lady. Jilted for a better-connected and richer lover, both retreat for consolation into antiquarian pursuits on a modest competence provided on the death of father and older brother. On this reading, Oldbuck represents what Scott might have become, had he not become the Minstrel of the North and the Author of Waverley.[26] Such a fully fledged biographical parallel was, however, foreign to Scott's contemporaries and Victorian admirers. Rather, the parallel rested upon a sense of Oldbuck and Scott as brother antiquaries. Scott was undoubtedly a keen antiquarian and collector, elected to the Scottish Society of Antiquaries at the age of twenty-six, and becoming Vice-President of the Society for two years from 1827. The many adventures in Scott's collecting retailed in Scott's letters and those by others of his circle evince much of the passion and occasionally some of the discomfiture characteristic of Oldbuck's activities. Conversely, Oldbuck's antiquarian arguments are informed by controversies that engaged Scott. But much more powerful in developing the identification (because more available to the public) was the comparison between Monkbarns and Abbotsford solicited by that near-synonym.

This identification between Scott and Oldbuck and Abbotsford and Monkbarns usefully protected Scott's copyright in his own endeavours, changing them from being (rightly) viewed as related to, or even plagiarizing, Horace Walpole's fantasia Strawberry Hill to being peculiarly his own. In 1812 Joanna Baillie could write playfully to Scott that 'We shall see there [i.e. at Abbotsford] some years hence a collection like that at Strawberry Hill—the collection of a poetical, sentimental antiquarian'.[27] This joke had morphed into one possible commonplace by 1834:

> Sir Walter Scott, in the decorations and the pleasure he derived from his house at Abbotsford, seems, in a considerable degree, to have resembled the accomplished owner of Strawberry Hill. Like the residence of that fascinating writer...which became eventually the interesting memorial of its owner's taste; so Abbotsford arose, in similar mode: and the humble residence which was on the estate when it first came into the possession of its highly gifted owner, was converted into the remarkable monument it now remains of his genius and taste.[28]

In direct contrast to this, *The Antiquary* made it possible to reference the enterprise of Abbotsford primarily to Scott's own work. Recalling his visit to Abbotsford in 1816 as a young man in an essay of 1835, the American writer Washington Irving remembered amusing himself by auditing the detail of *The Antiquary*, just published, against Scott and his home. He comments that 'many of the antiquarian humours of Monkbarns were taken from [Scott's] own richly-compounded character', details at length Scott's remarks on antiquarianism ('It was a pity, he said, that antiquarians were generally so dry... They are always groping among the rarest materials for poetry, but they have no idea of turning them to poetic use'), remarks of their walk to the local Roman camp that it was evident that 'some of the scenes and personages of that admirable novel were furnished by his immediate neighbourhood', and notes further in the course of a boat trip on the Lake of Cauldsheil that a bench in the boat provided for the excursion was marked 'Search No. 1', which suggested either that it was the original of, or a joking allusion to, the treasure-chest in *The Antiquary* which was so labelled.[29]

As this might suggest, Scott himself would collude and play with this identification, deploying the pseudonym of Oldbuck occasionally in his later letters. Of particular interest in this respect is the fragmentary *Reliquiae Trotcosienses*, conceived in the summer of 1831. This, as David Hewitt remarks, 'describes Abbotsford and the artefacts which it contains, and simultaneously satirises the impulse of antiquarian collection'.[30] Subtitled variously 'the sweepings of the Study of the late Jonathan Oldbuck of Monkbarns', or 'The Gabions of Jonathan Oldbuck', it provides a semi-fictionalized account of a building and its collections that is *not* Monkbarns, but is not quite in the ordinary sense Abbotsford. Hewitt's sense that Scott is engaged in self-caricature perhaps derives from Scott's own private writing which verged on repudiating his much-loved pleasures in what he termed affectionately '*antiquarian old-womanries*',[31] and is congruent with John Gibson Lockhart's *Memoirs* (1837–8), which would further erode Scott's own editorial identification of the original for Oldbuck as George Constable (1719–1803) in the Magnum Opus. Lockhart's *Memoirs* construct the Laird of Abbotsford as the original for the Laird of Monkbarns: 'his own antiquarian propensities... had by degrees so developed themselves, that he could hardly, even when the Antiquary was published, have scrupled about recognizing a quaint caricature of the founder of the Abbotsford Museum, in the inimitable portraiture of the Laird of Monkbarns'.[32]

This sense that Scott is here satirizing himself should not betray us into ignoring Scott's surprising characterization of Abbotsford as also being like

Monkbarns in being haunted or bewitched. Monkbarns has a resident ancestral ghost who appears to the young protagonist Lovel during a disturbed night; and the Preface to *Reliquiae*, supposedly written by Oldbuck, describes Abbotsford by citing Coleridge's supernaturalist poem *Christabel* (1797–1801), suggesting it as Gothic, dream-like, and forbidden: 'for, in the words of Coleridge, the place is both its elevation and its interior, "a thing to dream of not to tell", and it is the opinion of many of the most respectable inhabitants of the neighbourhood that the halls themselves are haunted and the tenant bewitched'.[33] For Scott, then, Abbotsford embodied a creative tension between the witchery of romance and the antiquarian collection of 'miscellaneous trumpery' around which it had grown. It was at once a museum and a place enchanted. If it was dedicated to 'hobbi-horsical persons' such as antiquaries, it was also akin to fiction: 'my idea of such a villa as I have built is that it might be formed on such a plan as some of the novels which formed its principal foundation, where every style of composition is admitted save that which was decidedly tiresome'.[34] As both public and hidden, material and dream, it was central to Scott's persona as the Author of Waverley in death even more than in life.

For Irving, Abbotsford and its collections had certified the labour of the historical romancer; the source, the aides-memoire, and the debris of imaginative work. Abbotsford itself was seen as essentially novelistic in conception, a meta-narrative derived from, and referencing, material antiquities. Irving's technique of discussing Scott's collection of antiquities and curiosities at Abbotsford at length, relating them to the fiction of the still anonymous Author of Waverley, would become a conventional way of reading both Scott and Abbotsford. As William Howitt would write in 1847:

> No one could have seen Abbotsford itself without being at once convinced of [Scott's authorship of the Waverley Novels], if he had never been so before. Without, the very stones of the old gateway of the tollbooth of Edinburgh stated the fact in his face; within, it was a perfect collection of testimonies to the fact. The gun of Rob Roy; the pistols of Claverhouse; the thumbikins which had tortured the covenanters; nay, a whole host of things cried out—'We belong to the author of Waverley'.[35]

It was this sense of the house as a supplementary voice of or witness to the novels that in many ways produced the continuing celebrity of Abbotsford through the widespread circulation of representations of it after Scott's death: in 1838 Thomas Frognall Dibdin could remark that 'all the world has been there: though not stirring from their firesides'.[36]

This sensibility can be discerned powering the production of the Abbotsford Edition of the Waverley Novels, put out in the 1840s by Robert Cadell. This also effectively constituted 'Abbotsford' as a home to, and museum of, the Waverley Novels. As the frontispiece by William Harvey to the Abbotsford Edition suggests, entry to Abbotsford allowed readers to experience him not just as wizard, enchanter, and romancer, but as scholar, antiquarian, and editor. Volume 2, comprising *The Antiquary*, *The Black Dwarf*, and *Old Mortality*, published in 1843, may serve to illustrate this. Large in format, handsomely bound in cloth stamped with gilt, designed for the library of the well heeled, it is distinguished especially by lavish and varied illustration. In all, there are seventy-two illustrations to *The Antiquary* alone, ranging from whole-page plates to vignettes inserted within the text of chapters and at the head and tail of them. The Abbotsford Edition's mix of steel and wood, famous painters and journeymen illustrators, comic and heroic idiom is largely novel. It combines landscapes engraved from original oils by Royal Academicians with wood engravings of characters, generic figures, places, objects, and dramatic scenes. Thus, to give symptomatic examples of these categories, there is a view of 'Queensferry from the South-East', a portrait of 'Edie Ochiltree', a 'Fisherwoman of Newhaven, Midlothian', a representation of the Post Office in Fairport, a 'rude spear used in the Irish rebellion, 1798', and 'Dousterswivel tricked by the Gaberlunzie'. Most novel is the inclusion within the text of illustrative engravings of items—Roman urns, assorted spear-heads, 'thumbikins', an arrow-head, an ancient British sword, coins, seals, 'ancient trowels', a fifteenth-century spur, a Highland skull cap, a French eagle plundered from the field of Waterloo—drawn variously from the collections Scott made and displayed at Abbotsford. The illustration of the thumbscrews is one particular instance of remediation in which the antiquarian material of Abbotsford and the immaterial romance of *The Antiquary* were bound together.

Overall, the illustrations to *The Antiquary* are notable for the ways they work to bring Scott and Abbotsford into ever-closer identification with Oldbuck and Monkbarns. Most striking in this respect is the headpiece to chapter 3 in which the young hero Lovel pays his first visit to Monkbarns. The headpiece shows Scott's own study at Abbotsford as Oldbuck's, garnishing the floor with a pile of swords, a helmet, and various pieces of armour, including gauntlets, to make the likeness colourable.[37] This is part and parcel of the complex system of supplementation between fiction and Abbotsford, constructed by tourism and associated 'tie-in' publications whereby 'original' sites in Scott's novels and poetry would be supplemented by images or descriptions of Abbotsford as the site where the writing itself took place. Thus, echoing the practice of the Abbotsford Edition, *The Land of Scott: A Series of Landscape Illustrations, illustrative of real scenes, described in the novels and tales, of the author of Waverley* (1848) included a drawing of the study at Abbotsford alongside images of various sites that had figured in the fiction.[38]

The real-life, real-time experience of post-mortem Abbotsford was liable to be a bit more ambiguous than these publications suggested. Like Howitt, many nineteenth-century visitors experienced the antiquarianism of Abbotsford as enjoyable, characterizing it as a parlour-game or an immersive experience of historical romance. But others found its antiquarianism dismaying. Hawthorne wrote that 'the feeling of visiting Abbotsford is not that of awe; it is little more than going to a museum'.[39] They found it an assemblage of disparate dead objects, rather than living romance. As Theodore Fontane would write in 1858:

> Willy-nilly, the whole building proves that...the revival of the past, the embellishment of a modern creation with the rich poetic details from the Middle Ages, may bewitch and enchant us in one context while in another it can become something little better than an oddity and a joke. This romance in stone and mortar, if I am to maintain the metaphor on which the poet himself was so intent, affects one very much as though he had taken from a drawer of his desk a hundred pretty passages from all kinds of old ballads, in the firm hope that by patching such fragments together he would be able to achieve the perfect romance. There has been no flash of inspiration sufficiently strong to weld the hostile elements into a unity. While the writer was himself still alive for whom these things had real significance, for whom they were really a matter of the heart, they were endowed with life under the influence of the living word which proceeded from him...Now however, when these notes can no longer be heard, the stones are stone again, and even one who is familiar with Scottish history and song walks through these rooms as though they were a waxwork show.[40]

The unpleasantly dead-alive waxwork quality of Abbotsford is traced here to an overplus of 'things' and to a lack of an animating voice. But this effect was central to the (re)orientation of Abbotsford after Scott's death. In Scott's lifetime Abbotsford had been a living national romance referred primarily to Scott's antiquarian imagination; after his death, as Ann Rigney observes, its role of remembering Scottish history 'was overlaid by its role as a monument recalling the life and works of its maker'.[41] As W.S. Crockett wrote of Abbotsford in 1905, it was even more reminiscent of Scott than the custom-made memorial put up in Edinburgh in 1840: 'So far as monuments to Scott go, there is none to equal [Abbotsford], not even the most splendid and costly pile which is one of Edinburgh's proudest ornaments'.[42] Monument it may have been, but it also seems to have slowly become much more unequivocally a museum—a museum of the death of Scott or even the obsolescence of Scott's imagination. Thus although Abbotsford remained for some readers a space not so much of mourning the romancer as re-enabling the process of romancing within the individual reader, for others it insistently described melancholic failure and absence. Visitors might have echoed Scott's own remark in the *Reliquiae*, 'my treasures are useless to me because the spell is lost'.[43] The romantic interiors of Abbotsford always were meant to be personal to the collector; as Wainwright characterizes such collectors: 'his brain alone had the invisible yet vital cross-references that linked one object or group of objects with another. Their disappearance on the death of the collector frequently meant that what to him was a supremely logical assemblage of objects seemed to the next generation a chaotic jumble of curiosities'.[44] Abbotsford both lived and died because of this—lived and died because the only real point of Abbotsford was that it dramatized Scott's power of romancing of the past—and because part of its story was that Scott had lived, written, and then died. The point of Abbotsford as a museum after Scott's death was precisely that the study was emptied of its meaning-making imagination.

The successive making of Abbotsford as a material reality, as virtual museum disseminated in print, as tourist experience, and as museum eloquent of the (dead) writer's ability to imagine the nation was not entirely unique, or even entirely unprecedented. But it was uniquely influential within nineteenth-century European and Anglophone culture. The phenomenon of Abbotsford explains in very large measure how the generalized interest in literary places that had characterized eighteenth-century culture came to be transformed and elaborated into the notion of the writer's house *as museum*—and how that museum might be a place of nation-making.

Irving's Sunnyside

The young man who in 1816 had paid a fan visit to Abbotsford was to become a major writer himself, with a serious claim to being the founder of American literature. Washington Irving would set the agenda for American tourist response to the British literary landscape in his two-volume compilation of periodical essays, *The Sketchbook of Geoffrey Crayon, Gent.* (1819–20), together with the essays Irving published in 1835 detailing his visits to Abbotsford and Newstead Abbey, the homes of Sir Walter Scott and Lord Byron respectively. They would be enormously influential on both sides of the Atlantic. The two volumes of *The Sketchbook* proper present 'sketches' of 'English' life, counterposed with American scenes. Appropriately enough for a collection pointedly dedicated to Scott, the essays are preoccupied with a sense of heritage and its rootedness in physical place and physical object. In mapping British culture through literary tourism—the seeking-out and re-description of sites associated variously with authors' lives or with particular books—Irving helped develop a sense of the literary landscape of Britain. More to the point here, he helped define an American national literature at once dependent upon and antagonistic to the country that Nathaniel Hawthorne's book of travel essays would subsequently and rather patronizingly call 'Our Old Home'.[45] Intent upon redacting the experience of visiting the old country for their readers in the new, American travel writers of the early and mid-nineteenth century were especially alive to the implications, sentimental or ironic, of the act of trying to coalesce familiar texts with the ambiguously homely and yet intractably foreign landscape to which they were related. Their writings, using the leverage of an emerging common literary canon, sought to condense a usable version of Britain into a repository of, and prehistory to, an American cultural heritage and literary future. As Alison Booth has noted, the business of *The Sketchbook* was to claim that 'a new-world wanderer can possess the ghostly remains' of English heritage, to constitute Irving as himself in conversation with that heritage, and so to qualify him as a contender for inclusion in the canon.[46]

If *The Sketchbook* founded and modelled a whole genre of American travel and travel-writing, it also founded the whole idea of the American literary landscape. Washington Irving's home in upstate New York, Sunnyside, can best be described as the actualization of the argument of Irving's *Sketchbook* superimposed onto his long-standing interest in Scott and Abbotsford. In 1832, Scott had died at Abbotsford, exhausted by his efforts to pay off his debts and secure his estate; in 1835, by way of tribute, Irving had set down his reminiscences of visiting Abbotsford as a young man. In that same year Irving returned from seventeen years' residence in Europe and bought himself some land which he had been eyeing since 1832, a

Figure 8.2. Washington Irving's Sunnyside. Author's own photograph

property on the shores of the Hudson River which he intended to turn into
his own 'writer's house' (Figure 8.2).

Today the most striking affinity Sunnyside has with Abbotsford is a
slightly mournful air of being left high and dry by the receding waters of
nineteenth-century enthusiasm. (Put more bluntly, they are both in danger
of being monuments to forgotten national treasures.) But, although described
by American architectural historians as a 'cottage', Sunnyside clearly quotes
Abbotsford in its steeply pitched roofs, its clustering together of chimneys
in a consciously picturesque fashion, its romantic irregularity, and its high-
stepped gables. Most explicitly, it is still clothed in British ivy, grown from a
cutting brought from Melrose Abbey for the purpose. Sunnyside also quotes
Abbotsford in its antiquarian games: Irving installed two plaques menda-
ciously identifying the house as having been built in 1656, and in keeping
with his literary interest in the days of Peter Stuyvesant when New York was
'New Amsterdam', he imported a couple of antique Dutch weather vanes
from New York in much the same way as Scott incorporated the old door

from the Edinburgh prison depicted in several of his fictions, The Tolbooth. The house also reiterates Abbotsford in its sense of performing the author's identity—thus it too is consciously fantastical and autobiographical as, for example, in its later addition of a 'Moorish' turret in allusion to Irving's time spent as a diplomat in Spain. Sunnyside is also similar to Abbotsford in its claim to be a country retreat while actually standing on the highroad to the metropolis and serving as a centre for its literary gatherings; even before the coming of the railway, Sunnyside, sitting as it does on the banks of the river, was effectively built on the main escape-route out of the summer heat of New York.

However, it is in the matter of location that Irving most interestingly imitates Scott. Scott's choice of Cartleyhole depended upon strong personal and professional ties to the Borders: as a child he had lived at Smailholm, and much of the work for which he was celebrated was closely associated with the area, notably *Minstrelsy of the Scottish Border* (1802) and *The Lay of the Last Minstrel* (1805), which was partially set in nearby Melrose Abbey.[47] His enthusiasm for this 'storied' landscape extended beyond verifiable history to folk tradition. Abbotsford, after all, lies beneath the Eildon Hills, by tradition cleft by the very wizard Michael Scott who makes an appearance in *The Lay of the Last Minstrel*. Scott took especial pains to acquire otherwise entirely unproductive land in the vicinity of Huntley Bank where by tradition Thomas the Rhymer had met the Queen of the Fairies, had been spirited away by her as her lover to Fairyland for seven years, and had returned with the gift of accurately prophesying the future of the nation, a subject that Scott had tackled by extending the old ballad of 'Thomas the Rhymer' for his *Minstrelsy of the Scottish Border* (1802). He constructed a walk to the romantic cleft in the land which he called 'The Rhymer's Glen', building a bench by the waterfall; it was enough of a favourite to be a regular destination for walks with visitors, including the young Irving, and to be illustrated by J.M.W. Turner in 1834.[48] Scott's grounds were extended, that is, specifically to take in enchanted ground associated with a precursor as national minstrel and wizard. It expressed the same sentiment as the present-day plaque marking the (re-planted) Eildon Tree: 'This stone/marks the site of the Eildon Tree/Where legend says/Thomas the Rhymer/Met the/Queen of the Fairies/And where he was inspired to utter/the First Notes/of the Scottish Muse'.[49]

Whereas Scott set out to build a house that would match 'the charms of storied and poetical association' that he found in the local landscape, Irving, in addition to designing picturesque landscaping (vistas, winding walks, cascades, glens, and the like), had to build the storied and poetical association to go with the house. He must have been the more enabled and encouraged in this endeavour because, as the essay 'Abbotsford' (1832) reveals, he found to his surprise that the landscape of the Borders was disappointingly unromantic by comparison to the glamour that Scott's writing had shed upon it.[50] To cast his own Scott-like historical colouring over the Hudson valley, he fabricated a largely fictional and highly romantic history for the house and the landscape, and, by extension, laid the foundation for the 'home' of a new national literature.

One of the most celebrated tales in *The Sketchbook* was set in the area of Tarrytown and Sleepy Hollow, where Irving had spent some time as a boy, evacuated from New York during an outbreak of yellow fever. 'The Legend of Sleepy Hollow', 'found among the papers of the late Diedrich Knickerbocker', was a Scott-like exercise in inventing both an antiquarian writing persona and, as Booth has remarked, 'a gothic past' for the nation.[51] The tale concerns a country schoolmaster from Connecticut, Ichabod Crane, much possessed with the old tales of witchcraft and hauntings set down by Cotton Mather. He courts one Katrina van Tassel only to be eventually routed by his rival, a local Dutchman, who impersonates the local Headless Horseman one night in order to terrify him into fleeing the area. The story identifies Sleepy Hollow as a place bewitched, somewhere that channels the past into the present by enriching the real with the visionary and impalpable. It is a serio-comic exercise in describing locality as Romantic place:

> A drowsy, dreamy influence seems to hang over the land, and to pervade the very atmosphere. Some say that the place was bewitched by a high German doctor during the early days of settlement; others, that an old Indian chief, the prophet or wizard of his tribe, held his powwows there before the country was discovered by Master Hendrick Hudson. Certain it is, that the place still continues under the sway of some witching power, that holds a spell over the minds of the good people, causing them to walk in a continual reverie. They are given to all kinds of marvellous beliefs; are subject to trances and visions; and frequently see strange sights, and hear music and voices in the air. The whole neighbourhood abounds with local tales, haunted spots, and twilight superstitions...[52]

Although the subsequent apparently supernatural happenings are heavily ironized, Irving's agenda is fundamentally serious—this is a place where the national past is still present in all its multiplicity. Elsewhere in the text, the evocation of the Native Americans and of 'the early days of settlement' is supplemented by allusions to more recent history in the shape of the War of Independence, notably the fate of the British spy Major André, as well as the legend of the Headless Horseman of Hessian. The locality is described in considerable, and accurate, topographical detail, including the church and the bridge over the mill-dam, allowing for the 'associations' fabricated by the tale to be located and verified by illustration and subsequent tourism.

'The Legend of Sleepy Hollow' is sceptical about legends (in this instance almost entirely invented), but not to the point of debunking the need for them. As Duncan Faherty remarks, Irving's fiction may well have unveiled 'the mythic nature of...European domestic "histories"' but, even as Irving removed the veil, 'he concurrently imported that practice by "historicizing" his own home'.[53] The schoolmaster may be as absurdly superstitious as Scott's Dousterswivel, readily frightened by a local lad's hoax, but the sense of the desirability of recognizing the actuality of the past as a way of possessing and being possessed by the landscape is just as strongly registered here as it is in Scott's *The Antiquary*.[54] By 1839, just as Irving was building Sunnyside, his letters full of detailed plans and fizzing with ideas, he was also revisiting this early piece of myth-making. Thus he was building a house both in actuality and in fiction that might simultaneously be occupied by both his fictional personae—the antiquarian Diedrich Knickerbocker and the dilettante traveller Geoffrey Crayon. In a series of essays published in the *Knickerbocker Magazine* of March 1839–41, he fleshed out his early tale. In one, for example, Crayon boasts of his acquisition of 'one of the most ancient and historical mansions in the country' supposedly containing Diedrich Knickerbocker's possessions, most notably 'his elbow chair, and his identical old Dutch writing desk'.[55] In 'A Chronicle of Wolfert's Roost', 'Crayon' edits, extracts, and annotates a supposed history written by Knickerbocker of his house. This provided a detailed and largely fictional prehistory of his house in three main epochs: the occupation of the land by a native American 'wizard chieftain'; the original build by Jacob van Tassel (a relative of Katrina in the earlier story) which was sacked by the British and subsequently rebuilt after the War of Independence; and its final occupation by Knickerbocker himself as historian of the early settlers. As Faherty acutely notes, this makes the house a testimonial to the cultural and architectural heritage that preceded the birth of the nation, as well as to the young Republic's history, while positioning Crayon as inheriting, occupying, and renovating a house now conceived as a microcosm of American identity.[56] What Faherty does not register is the extent to which Irving conceives of the house and its environs as legendary and haunted. The frame-narrative at once ironizes and insulates the various assertions that the place is occupied by 'spell-bound [Indian] warriors', that one of the occupant's wives was a witch, that there is sometimes heard the sound of ghostly British oars upon the river, that there is the ghost of 'a young lady who died of love and green apples', that there is an enchanted fountain. The jokey mock-heroic does not so much undo but protect the agenda of the piece which is expressed at the outset: to evoke 'A little old-fashioned mansion, all made up of gable-ends, and as full of angles and corners as an old cocked hat. Though but of small dimensions...it is of mighty spirit, and values itself greatly on its antiquity...It claims to be an ancient seat of empire...'.[57]

Sunnyside would subsequently become celebrated as an influential model of American architecture, but it should be more greatly celebrated for having invented the American writer's house and its surrounding 'haunts'. When Irving held court here in his later years, he seems to have constructed an experience for his guests not unlike that provided for him as a young man by Scott, and this was recognized by visitors. N.P. Willis would remark that 'in later years of Irving at Sunnyside, there was much to remind the privileged visitor of the pilgrimages to Abbotsford'.[58] Visitors were typically admitted to the 'workshop of genius' for a little chat about Irving's working practices, and, before or after, a drive round the environs would be enlivened with Irving's set-piece sentimental musings. Willis's account highlights the ambiguously fraudulent pleasures of literary tourism: as he drives with Irving around the vicinity of Sleepy Hollow he looks around whimsically for the figure of Katrina van Tassel and other characters from Irving's story, he picks up on topographical features described by Irving, and he takes especial pleasure in the moment that Irving tells him of a childhood memory of shooting squirrels in the wood, a memory that also features in 'The Legend': 'this little point was wonderfully charming to me—being such a literal verification, as it were, of one of the passages of his description of the spot, and one of those, too, of which the music lingers longest in the ear!'[59] This account catches both men in the act of laying down Scott-like 'associations' within the landscape, a potent compound of authorial memory, fiction, and topography. It was not accidental that a version of Thomas Faed's celebrated conversation-piece 'Scott and his contemporaries' hung in Irving's study, or that it is paired with a very similar exercise, Christian Shussele's 'Washington Irving and His Literary Friends at Sunnyside' (1863).[60]

Like Scott, Irving would choose to be buried in one of the settings he had made his own through his writing; Scott chose Dryburgh Abbey, Irving the cemetery of the church at Sleepy Hollow.

If Irving's tourist gaze upon literary Britain was characteristically both sentimental and ironic in *The Sketchbook*, it remained so when it came to inventing romantic ground for himself. This 'home' of American literature was not only fundamentally plagiaristic, it was also self-admittedly a hoax. Romantic locale, exported and translocated to New England, is occupied only by the fraudulent Gothic. Put another way, the Romantic under-standing of literary genius as expressed and best encountered in the writer's house and its associated landscape does not, apparently, survive the Atlantic crossing entirely intact. However, the final twist in Irving's 'Legend of Sleepy Hollow', whereby Ichabod Crane rises to be a major political figure gov-erning New York, and is buried on Staten Island (where to this day you can visit his real grave), was prophetic in its comic literalism. In 1856, three years before Irving's death, *Harper's New Monthly Magazine* ran a long article which celebrated Sunnyside as a now unproblematically Romantic location, a place of 'magic by which it has bewitched the public heart', a place of memory and fantasy unlike anywhere except a long-past England. Fully Romantic now, according to the journalist, it will only become more so in the future, as it settles into a Romantic ruin marking the origins of American literature as a world literature: 'Long after its modest walls shall have crum-bled away will the charm cling to its memory, for its associations with one, who . . . has reared to himself a perpetual and fragrant altar in the pantheon of the world's literature'.[61] In practice, its fate has been quite the opposite; the walls remain sturdy but the 'charm' is wavering; in 2007 we spent a long hot July day there undisturbed by anyone except volunteer guides as enthu-siastic about the house's specimens of once-state-of-the-art nineteenth-century plumbing as about the writings of its builder.

Irving was not the only American writer to attempt to import what Abbotsford had modelled—a house redolent of national history set in envir-ons 'enchanted' by the imagination of the author. James Fenimore Cooper, whose 'Leatherstocking' novels attempted to do for America what Scott had done for the history of Scotland and then Britain as a whole, would also build a house in emulation of Abbotsford. Returning in 1834 from seven years spent in Europe to his home in Cooperstown, he bought back the family home, Otsego Hall, resolved to remodel it in the Gothic Revival style. The house did not survive a devastating fire, but there is evidence that suggests that Cooper's makeover picked up on the styling of Abbotsford both exterior and interior. Hugh MacDougall asserts that 'By the time Cooper was ready to move in permanently, in 1836, the building stood eight feet taller than before, was painted stone-gray, and its roof was edged with battlements like a medieval castle...The windows were narrower, with pointed Gothic arches, and in place of the stone stoop a small battlemented tower enclosed a stairway to an oaken front door. At the west end of the building rose a small new wing with a circular tower', and this description is borne out by contemporary engravings.[62] 'Cooper's Castle' sat at the epi-centre of the landscape described in great detail in *The Pioneers: or, The Sources of the Susquehanna* (1823), a national landscape to rival that of Sunnyside.[63] But in the event historical accident dictated that it would be Irving's imagined history that would survive and provide the model for the American literary landscape. When Hawthorne meditates on his experi-ence in the storied landscapes of England, he imagines himself as Irving's Rip Van Winkle:

> Almost always, in visiting such scenes as I have been attempting to describe, I had a singular sense of having been there before...This was a bewildering, yet very delightful emotion, fluttering around me like a faint summer-wind, and filling my imagination with a thousand half-remembrances, which looked as vivid as sunshine at a half-glance, but faded quite away whenever I attempted to grasp and define them. Of course the explanation of the mystery was, that history, poetry, and fiction, books of travel, and the talk of tourists, had given me pretty accurate preconceptions of the common objects of English scenery, and these being long ago vivified by a youthful fancy, had insensibly taken their place among the images of things actually seen. Yet the illusion was so powerful, that I almost doubted whether such airy remembrances might not be a sort of innate idea, the print of some recollection in some ancestral mind, transmitted, with fainter and fainter impress through several descents, to my own. I felt, indeed, like the stalwart progenitor in person, returning to the her-editary haunts after more than two hundred years, and finding the church, the hall, the farm-house, the cottage, hardly changed during his long absence...while his own affinities for these things, a little obscured by disuse, were reviving at every step.[64]

Hawthorne's imaging of himself as 'the stalwart progenitor' revisiting his haunts 200 years later makes him as much the ancestor as the heir to British literary landscapes.

Shakespeare's New Place

Neither Abbotsford nor Sunnyside are the powerful locales for imagining the nation that they once were, but the idea of locating a writer of national and international importance in a historic house and set within 'enchanted grounds' does remain potent, and it informed the redevelopment in 2016 of Shakespeare's New Place in Stratford-upon-Avon to commemorate the 400th anniversary of the National Poet's death.[65] On the face of it, relating New Place to Abbotsford might seem altogether quixotic. If Abbotsford may be regarded as the most perfect model of a Romantic-Victorian writer's house and grounds—designed by the writer himself to exemplify and reference his aesthetic and his individual works, and consumed as such by readers in Scott's own lifetime and long after—in Stratford-upon-Avon there is very little trace left above ground of any house on the site. Shakespeare's original house, bought in 1597 when he had become a wealthy writer, was first of all rebuilt from scratch in 1702, and then entirely demolished by the then owner the Reverend Francis Gastrell in 1759, an act said to have been inspired equally by his annoyance at the growing number of tourists on the doorstep demanding to see Shakespeare's mulberry tree, and at the growth in demand for local taxes.[66] The loss both to the local tourist trade and to the national project of making Shakespeare head up a literary canon was keenly felt, and there have been many attempts to make good the deficit, starting with Samuel Ireland's fanciful engraving of what he thought New Place must have looked like in the early 1790s.[67] Making New Place measure up to the sort of authentic comprehensiveness of the conventional writer's house museum as an appropriate home for a national author has thus long been a problem.[68] The solution found for 2016 would be a new variant on the old idea of 'enchanted ground'.

Having conducted an archaeological survey between 2010 and 2012 to determine the shape and size of the original courtyard house, the Shakespeare Birthplace Trust embarked on a lengthy process of consultation. Early discussions focused on ways of evoking the original building; they were discarded in the light of focus-group work which suggested that any structure above ground, however tentatively skeletal, would not be perceived as 'authentic'. The SBT then engaged a distinguished stage designer, Tim O'Brien, who had worked for the Royal Shakespeare Company in the 1960s, 70s, and 80s, and had designed part of The Shakespeare Exhibition for the 400th anniversary of Shakespeare's birth in 1964. O'Brien's initial intervention in 2014 began by criticizing the materialism of the Birthplace as deadening ('Visit Shakespeare's place of birth and you will find that it is here and he is not. The survival of the building renders it untouchable and prosaic')[69] and celebrating New Place as a place where, by contrast, the imagination could operate as enlivening: 'What tremendous fortune to find that the house, in which he died, is represented to you by a mute scar on a neighbouring wall, triggering your imagination to dwell on Shakespeare's end, until he is there, but the house is not'. The problem as O'Brien saw it was not how to bring to life the subject (and subject of) Shakespeare through 'resurrected architecture, conjectural at best' but how 'to approach and bring to life our subject, Genius (Shakespeare) and [its relation to] the human spirit (us)'. In a subsequent presentation directly to the SBT Project Committee, he argued for exploiting 'the scanty evidence for the house and Shakespeare's life in it' as 'an invitation to the imagination' and 'a source of wonder' through 'the evasion of the literal'.

O'Brien, then, comprehensively junked the idea of a biographical house museum. In place of a house, he proposed a garden.[70] In place of verisimilitude, he offered allegory. In place of information, he suggested the interrogative. And he overwrote the material evidence of the past with a series of Romantic tropes concerning poetic genius—notably the sense of the writer affiliated to his native earth and, more generally, to Nature. If Abbotsford had conceived itself as a museum of authentic fragments of history preserved within an architectural romance set in a magic landscape, a place in which to encounter the phenomenon that was compounded of the Minstrel of the North and the Author of Waverley, New Place would conceive itself as altogether less invested in the material, the authentic, and the biographical:

> To the scar, add a totem fragment. To that, add a hologram that comes and goes. At its heart, in a shelter fashioned from smoke, set a tantalisingly unapproachable man, oblivious of us.

New Place would offer a vision of a ghostly and inaccessible Shakespeare through building a garden set with fragmentary objects. In O'Brien's triumphant summation of his vision:

> In a flourishing garden, open to the sky, we do not offer a recreation of New Place, but a celebration of Shakespeare's genius. The welcoming Gate, the long golden garden, the precious objects, the ring of pleached hornbeams, and—at the heart of the house—the windblown bronze tree and the massive shining and shadowed orb beneath it; all these illuminate and express Shakespeare's

power…At the fulcrum of the project, Shakespeare is represented by his empty chair and forsaken writing desk. In our mind's eye, in one direction, Shakespeare looks back down the Long Garden, depicting the golden fruits of his life; and, in another, towards his materials. These are Humanity, represented by us, the visitors, and Nature, by the tree that bends before the gale of his creative power. Above all, we harness the power of the earth of Warwickshire and that particular inch of it and we are glad of the throngs of all comers that pass over it.[71]

Perhaps what strikes the student of writer's house museums most forcefully here (besides the absence of a house, that is) are the insistent assertions of Shakespeare's ownership. The visitor enters by the bronze gate, marking the site of the original gatehouse, which is prominently surmounted by Shakespeare's crest. Jinking to the right round a screen-wall, one comes across a globe on a plinth, incised with an Elizabethan map of the world. This sites Shakespeare as 'owning' the globe and is balanced by an object that sites him as equally a local property-owner, an open deed-box made in bronze and captioned 'Shakespeare has the/True title to his house'. Crossing into the space of the original courtyard, the visitor is confronted with a bed of brightly coloured pennants that swivel with the wind among tall flowering grasses, inscribed with the titles of the earliest plays through to the latest. These describe Shakespeare's work as living and elemental, air as much as text. Stepping towards the steel ribbon set into the paving inscribed 'The Heart of the House', one passes a stainless-steel model of an Elizabethan ship floating above a pit of sand. The caption cites Prospero's order to Ariel to bring back into being a ship thought to be irretrievably lost: 'To the King's ship, invisible as thou art!/There shalt thou find the Mariners asleep/Under the hatches'.[72] The ship, salvaged and transformed to silver, perfect, pristine, spectral, evidences Shakespeare as Prospero in absolute command of his magic, and this construction is reiterated in the circular space enclosed by pleached hornbeams at the centre of the site of the house proper, which is thus conceived as at once Shakespeare's study and Prospero's cell.

This climactic space contains two related installations (Figure 8.3). The first is a deliberately over-large bronze replica of a period wood and leather chair, drawn a little apart from a cast of a deliberately small period writing-desk, apparently locked, and without a key.[73] Although they are faithful enough to be mistaken for real wood and leather, the disparity of scale between them sabotages the relatively simple claims to realism and/or authenticity usually made by the central display of a writer's desk and chair. Moreover, the second installation deliberately undoes these conventional

Figure 8.3. Shakespeare's New Place, 2016. Author's own photograph

suggestions of the time-bound and domestic labour of the act of writing. It is a bronze cast of a hawthorn tree, bent over by the wind towards a metal sphere. This installation, conceived by O'Brien and executed by Jill Berlowitz, is entitled 'The Mind's Eye'. In conversation, O'Brien cited Puck's lines from Rudyard Kipling's *Rewards and Fairies* (1910) celebrating the Englishness of 'oak and ash and thorn' as his inspiration here, and Berlowitz's commentary notes in addition that the leafless hawthorn, cast from a real tree embellished with casts of branches and twigs from others, was chosen as 'typically English'. The aim, however, was not verisimilitude but metaphor: 'Although drawn from the life, [the tree] is not counterfeiting its natural source, but dignifying its gesture by representing it as a brazen monument, the metaphorical force of his writing that bends before the gale of his creative power'.[74] The wind imagined here drives the poet's dead thoughts across the universe, scouring the silver globe to brilliance. The tortured tree also suggests sympathetic resonances with the storm in *The Tempest*, rising and falling at Prospero's behest, and the place of Ariel's captivity prior to the opening of the play.[75] The whole effectively represents the island of Britain as the origin of a genius that is no longer merely national but global in its reach and effects.

O'Brien's re-presentation of New Place thus comprehensively re-represents the idea of the writer's house museum. 'Shakespeare' as man is accorded the biographical basics of life and form by deed-box, desk, and chair, but the emphasis falls much more heavily upon Shakespearean inspiration, well beyond the confines of any single text, locality, or nation. Still, the continuities with the ways that the ownership of Abbotsford realized Scott are clear, even if Abbotsford was 'a romance in stone' conceived by the writer himself, while New Place is an after-thought. Shakespeare's ownership of New Place is crucially important to O'Brien because he reads this (unlike the Birthplace) as the act of an artist choosing a place in which to live and work. From that flows O'Brien's sense of Shakespeare's dwelling as a deliberate expression of Shakespearean creativity, and this can be traced directly back to the ways that Scott and his admirers have thought of Abbotsford as an expression of creativity congruent with Scott's more literary works. Abbotsford and New Place both display the writer's desk and chair at the heart of a house studded with objects conceived as conundrums of authorship. Abbotsford describes Scott's wizardry through displaying antique objects as his raw material, whereas New Place describes Shakespeare's genius through transforming historically bound real objects into allegory. Both sites are heavily invested in the idea that they are enchanted and indeed have the power to enchant.

This last point may be illustrated by considering the Christmas entertainment that ran at New Place between 15 and 17 December 2016 as part of the anniversary celebrations. This was a masque-like joke upon the idea of a literary museum of global significance. The invitation was to 'Become a Muse Catcher with the United Nations Board Of Significant Inspiration'. Visitors were to help capture what was described as 'a harmless, odorless, invisible substance which emanates from geological fissures at a number of locations on the earth's surface. This substance which UNBOSI scientists have named MUSE (Micro-molecular Unseen Sensory Emanations) is most prevalent at sites where there is a strong relationship with literary genius'. UNIBOSI's research project, the visitor brochure further explained, was trialling in Stratford, commencing with 'a period of muse collection to try to locate the possible source of literary inspiration which they believe is located somewhere at the site':

> This will be followed by a period of detailed analysis to discover the nature and effect of Muse emanating in Stratford Upon Avon. Finally the results of this research will be tested on the general public who will be invited to attend a night-time immersive experience, the UNBOSI A' MUSE ment Park™. This public experiment will be designed to search for moments of significant inspiration in members of the public while they are exposed to Muse.[76]

Members of the public were therefore invited to visit 'The Garden of Curious A-MUSE-ments' at New Place after dark. This, the write-up continued, had been identified as the 'ultimate site of creativity' and therefore 'the perfect place to catch your muse':

> Enter the gardens of Shakespeare's New Place to embark on your muse catching mission. Investigate reports of unusual activities and embrace the elements as you complete tasks set by the muses of earth, fire, air and water. Dig deep to unearth a special muse-storing marble, ready to be charged full of the inspiration that still leaks from the site where Shakespeare found his. Then visit each of our muse stations and be dazzled by interactive shows of colour, light and sound that will ignite your senses and imagination…[77]

A 'muse-catcher' marble (now sitting by my computer), charged up through passing through Shakespeare's earth, air, fire, and water, was capable of making thin air speak, root-vegetables sing, and coloured lights flicker at command through the trees. Coming into personal possession of such Prospero-like power made it very easy to forget Shakespeare altogether. The proposition was that it is, as it were, accidental that Shakespeare happened to possess a house on a site favoured by the Muses. This is not a matter of catching Shakespeare's inspiration by example or even contagion, but of going personally to the very source of it emanating from beneath the earth's crust.

As an immersive experience wholly removed from the business of imparting historical or biographical information, the 'Garden of Curious A-MUSE-ments' is highly suggestive about how writer's house museums might be developing. Clearly, it has energetically forgotten some Victorian fantasies: we are not in the realm of Charles Cattermole's efforts to imagine Shakespeare conversing with his friends in the same way that Scott and Irving were depicted at home with their friends, and in fact 'Shakespeare's chair' on the night in question was occupied by a skeleton, a neat joke on the fetishization of the authorial body. It privileged effect over object, experience over information, encounter with enchantment rather than encounter with the enchanter. Simultaneously sardonic and exploitative, it half laughed at, half exploited the necessity of marketing immediate, pleasurable, and quantifiable transference of 'significant inspiration' to museum-visitors. The extent to which this promise to visitors of access to 'significant inspiration' on the site of the writer's house is in fact new is the subject of Chapter 9.

9

Exit through the gift shop

To sum up my argument so far, every writer is different, and every writer's house museum is different, but the desire to represent the mystery of writing, and the ambition to house the moment and state of authorial being *before* writing, endure and remain fundamental to the genre. The power of the writer's house museum, to invoke Gaston Bachelard, is to conjure a waking dream associated with the idea that we call 'the Author'.[1] Over the last two centuries, efforts have been made to invoke and locate the source of this power appropriately within the writer's body—in physical traces of brain, 'bosom', or hand. Or perhaps, as house museums characteristically hypothesize, it might be more suitably located within the equipment and detritus of writing—the pen, inkstand, chair, desk, or waste-paper basket—or in those fetishized objects that mark the inception and cessation of writing, unfinished manuscripts. It might still fizz in the flirtations between the prosthetic oddities and curiosities that writers often collect at the level of the desk, such as those amassed by Rudyard Kipling or Roald Dahl, or at larger scale in cabinets of curiosities such as that in Walter Scott's library at Abbotsford.[2] There again, it might be detectable in the spaces, times, routines, and relationships indicated by everyday objects from coffee-pot to sewing-box. It might still be possible to look through the writer's eyes by borrowing his or her spectacles, or adopting his or her viewpoint. The mystery might be written at large in outhouses or larger still in fantasy buildings, or even upon an entire, generative landscape. So powerfully conventionalized are these ideas nowadays that they can appear overlaid one on another in a single frame from the biopic of Enid Blyton, *Enid* (dir. James Hawes, 2009). This is the shot of Blyton's window as anatomized by Judith Buchanan: 'The final shot of the sequence anthologizes the component elements of the writing-process...the writer (her image reflected in the window); the typewriter (its carriage arm visually remembered in the window latch); the page (its text superimposed on the scenery); and the natural space viewed through the window collectively prompting... the evocation of the fictional narrative [and characters] of the Famous Five'.[3] The mystery of writerly inspiration is certainly there, however located, because it is all too evident when it is not. At that point, a house formerly inhabited by a writer ceases to be a writer's house, even if it claims to be a writer's house museum. There are plenty of such houses, rapidly decaying into beautifully preserved heritage properties with the general project of evoking 'the old'.[4] Decay overtakes museums such as the George Borrow museum in Norwich (established in 1913, closed because of lack of public interest in 1994) as authors' works are forgotten. Conversely, and more rarely, it occurs, as in the case of the closure of the recently opened museum at Derek Walcott's boyhood home on St Lucia, because there is not enough desire—or at any rate not yet enough desire—to remember.[5]

Although the writer's house museum invariably imagines itself in this way as remembering the author's acts of writing, it may actually memorialize and materialize acts of reading. To put it another way, when a poetic travel-writer describes himself as 'seeking lost autographs', what is telling is not his focus on the always already lost autograph itself, but the desire to seek it out.[6] The mystery sought is nothing less than the trace of the production of an extra-ordinary, perpetually self-renewing subjectivity that outlives the writer, a subjectivity that we call 'The Author' and in extreme cases 'genius'. The house, as a sort of 'lost autograph', describes the place and time of this making of subjectivity. But the subjectivity in question is conjecturally that of the reader. Without the reader's desire to make their subjectivity on-site in this way, author and house fade into 'nothing'. This conundrum is thrown into sharp relief by the exchange between Mr and Mrs Wititterly on the subject of Shakespeare's Birthplace in a book written by one of the future founders of the Shakespeare Birthplace Trust, Charles Dickens, namely *The Life and Adventures of Nicholas Nickleby* (1838–9). Mrs Wititterly effectively puts the case for literary tourism as a mode of understanding the works: she enthuses that 'Shakespeare is such a delicious creature... I find I take so much more interest in his plays, after having been to that dear little dull house he was born in!... I don't know how it is, but after you've seen the place and written your name in the little book, somehow or other you seem to be inspired; it kindles up quite a fire within one'. Her husband, however, ascribes this reaction not to the author or the place itself, but to the fair tourist's own 'poetical temperament': 'It is your poetical temperament, my dear—your ethereal soul—your fervid imagination, which throws you into a glow of genius and excitement. There is nothing in the place, my dear—nothing, nothing'.[7] This final chapter, accordingly, and perhaps not before time, turns to focus squarely upon the ways in which readers have engaged with such houses as tourists, with special reference to those associated with Petrarch, Rousseau, and Shakespeare, as sites that founded these practices and which have long enjoyed international fame. It shifts from thinking about the author's body to thinking about that of the reader, speculating that the writer's house museum may be seen not so much as staging the scene of writing, but as staging scenes of reading. The first part of this chapter concentrates on what tourists have typically brought with them on their visits, the second on what they have left behind, and the third on what they have taken away. These scenes of reading tend to disavow the medium of the book, erasing it in favour of a fantasy of immediate intimacy with the author. But as the stories that follow show, when that fantasy, as it is liable to, falters, readers expand into other forms of exasperated or empathetic sociability—with guides, with companions, with strangers, or with visitors long-gone and yet to come. The chapter concludes with a summing-up of the argument of the book in its entirety on a pseudo-postcard.

Bringing things

In 2009, I flew to New York City, hired a car, and drove up-state to Elmira, New York. My purpose was to visit Quarry Farm, the place where Mark Twain had spent his summers writing as the guest of his sister's family. The draw was his wooden summerhouse, once perched up on the stony ridge overlooking the river at the furthest extent of the farm property, now preserved and displayed at the centre of Elmira College campus along with an extensive Twain archive. I put up for the night at Quarry Farm, where after a long and solitary day in the archive looking at photos of Twain and his friends, it was hardly surprising that a long and solitary night spent in Twain's bed should produce something unnervingly like Twain's ghost over my shoulder in the bedroom mirror.[8]

Momentarily shocked as I was by this fleeting impression, perhaps I should not have been. The principal driver for going to a place where the author once lived is, after all, precisely to achieve this sort of personal, if posthumous, encounter by entering the author's space and place. 'What recollections, sad yet sweet, are mine/As slow I pace thy solitary round!'[9] The Romantic poet and dramatist Vittorio Alfieri's inscription at Petrarch's house in Arquà, composed in 1783, neatly skewers a tension at the heart of literary tourism. On the one hand, the solitude of Petrarch is being mimicked and emulated here by the contemporary poet-tourist's romantic pose of solitariness. On the other hand, there was likely to be quite a crowd trying to adopt this pose. By the late eighteenth century, visitors arrived with expectations set by an often-quoted letter of Petrarch's:

> I read; I write; I think; thus, my life and pleasures are like those of youth. I take pains to hide myself, but I cannot escape visits: it is an honour which displeases and wearies me. In my little house … I hope to pass my few remaining days in tranquillity, and to have before my eyes my dead, or my absent friends.[10]

This letter hardly suggests that Petrarch would be enthusiastic about the possibility of a swarm of tourists invading his study. There is some pressure to be, at best, an 'absent' friend.[11] A private visit, as of one living poet to another, seems to have been the ideal, and this is supported by William Beckford's account of his visit in 1778 which he introduces as something of a social obligation between equals: 'At Padua, I was too near the last and one of the most celebrated abodes of Petrarch, to make the omission of a visit excusable'. He sets off, with 'the poems of Petrarch in my pocket', which he reads at intervals along the way 'to indulge my pensive humour over some ejaculatory sonnet'.[12]

Encountering the author is made possible, as my own experience suggests, through superimposing recollected reading experience upon place, a complicated process of memory and re-mediation. As Beckford's account suggests, sometime around the 1780s a new reading practice emerged, that of bringing books to re-read on the spot where they were set, or had been composed, and sometimes both. At its inception it was the province of the elite; by the 1830s it had become codified for a wider public. The evidence for this practice may be found in private papers, in published accounts which represent the practice, and in the shape of publications designed to facilitate it, such as, in due course, John Murray's guidebook series of the 1830s. *A Handbook for Travellers in Switzerland, and the Alps of Savoy and Piedmont* (1838), for instance, contained Rousseau, Byron, Voltaire, Gibbon, and Staël helpfully excerpted to fit a pocket, a compendium of 'deathless associations' efficiently indexed to 'immortalised localities'.[13]

Fifty years before Murray's publishing coup, Rousseau's novel *La Nouvelle Héloïse* was already functioning as a proto-guidebook; by the 1780s tourists carried its volumes and were familiar enough with it to read the appropriate sections out to their travelling companions.[14] His *Rêveries d'un Promeneur Solitaire* (1782) elicited a similar response; as Friedrich von Matthissen would remark: 'How deeply were we affected with reading this most interesting writer's description of St Peter's Island on the very spot'. Von Matthissen develops an early version of what would become cliché:

> What a melancholy delight did we feel in following his footsteps from the room he inhabited.[15]

Matthissen's account of his visit makes plain the ways that reading on the spot could map and narrate place for the tourist, and the way that it allowed for simultaneous stalking and simulation of 'Rousseau' with a view to virtual encounter. Here, for example, is the young German Friedrich Stolberg also engaging in this thought experiment:

> Here, said we, did the pensive Jean Jacques ruminate. On this steep height … he contemplated the clear waters of the lake. Here he did calm his ardent sensibility, by viewing the dewy plants … Under this rock, reclining in a boat, he touched the soft flute … As we left the island, we were awakened by the recollection of what must have been the sensation of Rousseau, when he was obliged to leave this place of refuge …[16]

As this last remark makes plain, imagined encounter slips readily into the substitution of the tourist's body for the writer's.

Other literary travellers might bring their library in memorized form, but to the same purpose. The American Grace Greenwood, touring Britain in 1854, visited Alloway in pursuit of Burns. Conjuring the rustic poet leaning over the picturesque ' "auld brig", following with his great, dark, dreamy eyes, the windings of the stream below', she begins to quote from a memory activated by the power of place:

> As I lingered there, countless snatches of the poet's songs, and stanza after stanza of long-forgotten poems, sprang to my lips; rare thoughts, the sweet flowers of his genius, seemed suddenly to blossom out from all the hidden nooks and still, shaded places of memory …[17]

Again, this account describes the substitution of the tourist's body and memory for those of the dead writer.[18]

Leaving things

Despite these performances of solitary musing, the imagined encounter with the author was essentially communal, undertaken in company, or in the imagined company of tourists that had come before or were yet to come. This goes a long way to explaining the desire to leave a mark on the writer's house.[19]

The habit of leaving pious graffiti at writer's houses has a long and distinguished history. Carved into one of the mantelpieces of Petrarch's house at Arquà in the Eugean Hills, for instance, is a date, 13 October 1564, together with the names of a group of Austrian students who had travelled right across the Alps to see the room in which the poet worked for some four years and died in July 1374. This inscription speaks of the historical longevity of Petrarch's fame, of the geographical reach of it beyond France and Italy, of the multi-lingual educational culture of the Renaissance that made it possible, and of the extension of the poet's cult from the poet's tomb (just down the road) to his house, probably the earliest instance of this contagion of pilgrimage. It suggests that the owners must have given permission; it takes a long time to chip an inscription of this length into stone. Its survival tells us that visitor origin, number, and response were valued as certifying the site's significance within the poet's mythos; the fact that this is one of the features of the house that is pointed out even nowadays shows that this is still of import. This habit held for centuries: when Beckford arrives to make his imagined call upon Petrarch in the spirit of one gentleman to another, the intended personal visit proves something of an entrance into an exclusive literary salon held in Petrarch's study:

> The walls of it, from top to bottom, are scribbled over with sonnets, and poetical eulogies on Petrarch, ancient and modern: many of which are subscribed by persons of distinguished name and talents...[20]

Whether visitors actually 'carved' their names on the walls is questionable; the evidence from the history of pious inscription generally is that it was a good deal easier to write at elegantly effusive length in pencil once more than rough initials and a date were requisite.[21] The surviving evidence in Cowper's summerhouse and Rousseau's bedroom in the Ile St Pierre suggests that slate pencil was very often used on plaster and interior wood as faster, and more convenient both to use and to carry.[22]

Much of the on-site evidence of this culture of inscription has vanished, but where a mass of inscription does occasionally survive intact, as on a much-shown windowpane at Shakespeare's birthplace, it suggests not merely the desire to inscribe one's name in such a place and the wealth of many such tourists (given that they would have been using a specially cut diamond ring or even a purpose-made diamond stylus), but also the time tourists expected to spend in such rooms looking at other tourists' inscriptions. That is to say, an important part of the experience of literary pilgrimage was an exercise in cultural and social imagined community, to borrow Benedict Anderson's resonant phrase.[23] As the author of *An Account of the Principal Pleasure Tours of England and Wales* (1822) put it, the underwhelming experience of visiting Shakespeare's Birthplace ('a small mean-looking house of wood and plaster') was only redeemed by looking at the inscriptions:

> The walls of its squalid chambers are covered with names and inscriptions, in every language, by pilgrims of all ranks and conditions, from the prince to the peasant and present a simple but striking instance of the spontaneous and universal homage of mankind to the great poet of nature.

This production of readerly community across time was also evidenced in the phenomenon of the site-specific visitors' book (Figure 9.1).[24] In 1812 Shakespeare's Birthplace opened a visitors' book; by 1817 a visitors' book had appeared in the farmhouse on the Ile St Pierre;[25] and in 1818, John Chetwode Eustace, describing the interior of Petrarch's house at Arquà, noted a visitors' book, known then more often as an 'album': 'On the table is a large book, an album, containing the names and sometimes the sentiments of various visitants'.[26] While recording your name, the date, and where you come from is already in some sort an expression of 'sentiment', and capable of interesting those who follow, this album solicited more; Eustace recorded 'the...verses...inscribed in the first page...addressed to the traveller'. Thomas Roscoe thought these important enough to accord them a careful and elaborate verse translation into English:

> Thou who with pious footsteps lovest to trace
> The honour'd precincts of this sacred place,
> Where still th'immortal spirit hovers near,
> Of him who left his fleshly burden here,
> Inscribe thy name, thy country, and impart
> The new emotions that expand thy heart.[27]

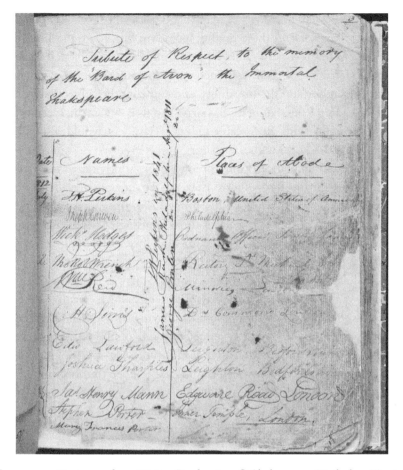

Figure 9.1. First page from Visitor Book, 1812. © Shakespeare Birthplace Trust

Travellers often recorded and translated inscriptions that especially appealed to them whether they found them on the walls or in visitors' books, and this practice was highly conventionalized. This is evident in Wagner's guidebook to the Ile St Pierre, which not only makes it plain that tourism to this location from the 1790s onwards entailed becoming a writer yourself (through inscribing your own effusion on the walls of Rousseau's bedroom and the pavilion perched on the heights above the farmhouse), but that part of the tourist experience was reading the effusions of others. Wagner dwells upon the proliferation of multi-lingual inscription in the pavilion and the bedchamber as evidence of the sheer amount of Rousseauistic experience supplied by the island to readers of many nationalities. He even lists a number of eminent names left in these graffiti, including Pitt, Kant, the Empresses Josephine and Marie-Louise, and Napoleon, and he transcribes a number of inscriptions, striking in their insistence upon tourism as visionary encounter with the author and the possibility of occupying the subjectivity of the author.[28] Reading Rousseau in his favourite haunts is, for instance, elaborated into conversation with Rousseau's ghost.[29] Travellers would also leaf, if sometimes fruitlessly, through the visitors' books in search of similar models of encounter and reiteration. Louis Simond rather sourly noted in 1817 that the farmhouse on the Ile St Pierre now put up 'curious travellers, whose names are recorded in a book, with sentimental effusions about Rousseau': 'We copied a few of them…some of them amusing enough, but it would scarcely be fair to swell this book with quotations of young ladies' and gentlemen's poetry'.[30]

Personal inscription by individual admirers may be seen as the most minimal, but also the foundational way, of reading and (re-)writing a literary site. From the practice flows the house-visit lyric poem, extended accounts in travel-writings both privately circulated and published, the genre of 'homes and haunts', and that most modern form of site-specific inscription, the instagrammed selfie.[31] Personal reading experience thus becomes communal and sociable through the public representation of the tourist-reader's experience. The academic version of this is The Postcard Project, which in 2015 invited contributions to a blog associated with the 'Placing the Author' conference: 'all you need to do is send us a photo, telling us when and where the photo was taken, why you went (max 100 words) and what you got out of the experience (max 150 words)'.[32] The photo was to be of the writer at a literary site. It constructed therefore a quasi-postcard, a picture of the site, and a message to 'friends' elsewhere about the visit, but with these novel features: that it visually inserted the writer of the postcard into a celebrated literary site or landscape, and effectively offered the opportunity of writing a virtual prose inscription. Here, for example, was 'Sarah's' self-inscription on Newstead Abbey, home of Byron, in March 2016: 'Its beauty and unending grace has the ability to inspire current and future generations of literary minds like me, just as it had inspired one of Britain's greatest romantic poets'.[33] This inscription, like so many others, makes the tourist-reader and author into colleagues, fellow-vehicles for the MUSE-like 'inspiration' supposedly exerted by place.

Taking things

If Romantic and Victorian tourists typically left inscriptions at the site of the writer's house, as typically they brought away mementoes by which to remember their visit.[34]

For early tourists there was always the possibility, however faint, of a real find: one cannot but feel for Samuel Ireland's horrible disappointment on being told by a local that the last of a bundle of Shakespeare's manuscripts had just been used to light a domestic fire. Scholarship has concluded that this was a mischievous prank played on the enthusiast, but it is all the same an instructive joke, because it plays on what was in the 1790s a locally recognizable tourist lust for material traces of Shakespeare.[35] However, even Romantic tourists were generally obliged to content themselves with shards and scraps filched, often semi-officially, from the literary site. As already noted, 'Shakespeare's chair' was progressively sold off to tourists by Mary Hornby from the 1790s.[36] The custodian of Voltaire's house at Ferney winked at tourists snipping away scraps of Voltaire's silk bed-hangings.[37] The doors of Tasso's cell and Ariosto's study seem to have gone much the same way: the English tourist Marianne Colston, visiting Ferrara in 1820, noticed apropos of Ariosto's house that 'some of our countrymen have carried their veneration for the poet's residence so far, that they have actually taken away a considerable part of the wooden door of the apartment in which he used to pass his days'.[38] There is a largish chunk missing from what was known as 'Juliet's tomb' in Verona (in fact a Roman sarcophagus) because so much was chipped away in the early nineteenth century to be made into jewellery for sentimental ladies.[39] Occasionally, new opportunities would arise as a result of building or restoration works—this was how bits of Shakespeare's demolished family home New Place came to be recycled into a box, and how wood from his birthplace came to be refashioned as the 'Shakespeare walking-stick' in 1877 and used by the local Masonic Lodge Grand Master at the ceremony of laying the foundation stone of the Shakespeare Memorial Theatre in 1879.[40] This was also how I myself came to be the possessor of a piece of a rafter from Dr Johnson's garret.

Once it occurred forcibly to custodians that the materiality of the place that was making them a good living was in danger of disappearing altogether and was not readily replaceable, they became more protective.

Tourists were obliged to fall back on picking flowers and leaves, and as a result systematically destroyed trees celebrated for their association with authors in their desire for evidence of organic continuity. This seems to have started at least as early as the mid-eighteenth century. Little remains of 'Tasso's oak' in Rome, under which the author is supposed to have sat, and even less of the crab-apple tree under which Shakespeare was supposed to have slept off a drinking binge. The hawthorn under which Robert Burns was said to have taken his last leave of 'Highland Mary' has long been chipped away. The oak near Yardley Lodge about which Cowper wrote his poem 'Yardley Oak', which became celebrated as a result of being depicted in the frontispiece to William Hayley's *Supplementary Pages to the Life of Cowper* (1806), also suffered considerable depredations.

William Howitt's account of the fate of Cowper's oak makes plain that more is going on here than tourists merely chipping a little bark off to put in their pocket-book. The wood was going towards the preparation of 'different articles', presumably carved by locals for the tourist trade.[41] One of the most extensively documented trades in such items is that developed from the remains of Shakespeare's mulberry tree. Said to have been planted by the poet himself at New Place, felled by the Reverend Francis Gastrell in an effort to discourage tourists, the tree made the fortune of a local craftsman, William Sharp. Sharp had bought up much of the timber and proceeded to turn out an implausibly large number of expensive knick-knacks which he sold for good prices from 1756 onwards to all comers, including David Garrick himself, who commissioned a medallion and goblet for his role as organizer and star-turn at the Jubilee in 1769. Such objects operated within the Shakespeare cult with something of the power of the shards of the True Cross, although the wood itself, carved, polished, and often inlaid, would serve as its own reliquary.[42] The Shakespeare Birthplace Trust alone holds some sixty-six mulberry-wood items of different sorts, clearly aimed at both men and women of different levels of wealth. They include a writing stand-ish, various boxes, a tankard, snuff-boxes, tobacco stoppers, a card-case, a goblet, a jug, a tea chest, sugar-tongs, rosary beads, a vial of mulberry juice, and most incongruous of all, a pastry cutter. These souvenir items incarnate Shakespeare variously as writer, drinker, smoker, alleged Catholic, and gentleman visitor for other, more genteel, domestic settings.[43] Each argues for the possibility of encounter with Shakespeare through the organic continuity of the tree that he supposedly planted with his own hand, and each

argues for the ability of possessors to incorporate the Shakespearean within
the domestic routines of their own embodied lives. The effect extended to
items made of the famous crab-apple tree at Bidford, already mentioned,
under which Shakespeare was supposed to have passed out for the night.
Said to have been slowly demolished by 'American curio-hunters',[44] the
crab-apple, refashioned into bibelots, could certify metonymically not just
Shakespeare's bodily reality but a sort of merrie masculinity at one with the
Warwickshire countryside through this vignette of Shakespeare dreaming
on the sward like Bottom, as in the crab-apple tree box that opens to reveal
a depiction of Shakespeare doing just that. So important was this idea of an
organic continuity between land and poet mediated by flora that it gave rise
to the replanting of mulberry trees around the site of New Place (in 1862
and 1946) and of a crab-apple tree in Bidford (some time towards the very
end of the nineteenth century).[45] Modern variants of this sentiment are
represented by the replanting at Sigrid Undset's home in Lillehammer of
a birch tree to replace the one she had planted herself, or the planting of a
flower-garden specifically to recreate the displays of cut flowers Karen
Blixen created in her home at Rungsted.

It was, of course, altogether more economical as a tourist to pluck a few
leaves or flowers from the site, press them, and incorporate them as extra-
illustration within narrative frames, whether letter, diary, embellished
engraving, or full-blown album.[46] This habit held at grave-sites, leading to
the preservation of flowers and leaves from authors' funeral flowers and later,
their graves—both the Ibsenmuseet in Oslo and the Andersen museum at
Odense include among their collections sprigs preserved from grave-bou-
quets. The habit also extended to writer's houses. Julia Thomas describes
one letter sent back to America from Stratford-upon-Avon on 6 September
1858 which 'still shows the stitching where [the sender] attached an ivy leaf
from the wall of the church'.[47] As already noted elsewhere, the Keats-Shelley
House in Rome displays an engraving picturing the site of the tombs of
Shelley and Keats in the Cimiterio Acattolici (or the so-called Protestant
Cemetery) in Rome embellished with pressed flowers and handwritten
inscriptions identifying the date they were picked.[48] Americans, indeed, got
a particular reputation for such enterprising depredation. Harriet Beecher
Stowe was teased by her English companion for insisting on visiting
'Shakspeare's house, when it wasn't his house' and for being 'so earnest to get
sprigs from his mulberry, when it wasn't his mulberry'.[49] Elbert Hubbard's

account of his frustrated visit to Wordsworth's home at Rydal Mount in the early 1900s records his conversation with the man barring his inquisitive and acquisitive way:

> Mostly 'mer'cans, they don't know no better, sir. They picks all the ivy orf the outside of the wall, and you sees yourself there's no leaves on the lower branches of that tree. Then they carries away so many pebbles from out there that I 'ave to dump in a fresh weel-barrel full o' gravel every week, sir...
>
> I pressed [his] hand firmly, pocketed a handful of gravel as a memento, then turned and went my way.[50]

Until very recently, there was still a sign outside Dove Cottage, begging tourists not to pick the daffodils from the window-box, doubtless in vain.

Although the vast majority of this material is now lost, a very large cache is still extant in the albums of Mrs Emma Shay, a redoubtable sixty-four-year-old retired college English teacher from Wessington Springs, North Dakota, who on attaining release from her long years of inculcating literary taste in the young conceived the desire to tour the literary landscapes of Britain.[51] As her manuscript diary relates, over the course of three months in the summer of 1926 she sailed to Britain, and visited, *inter alia*, George Eliot's birthplace on the Floss, Burns' birthplace at Alloway and the bank of the 'bonny Doon', Gladstone's house at 62 Rodney Street, Liverpool, Shakespeare's birthplace and grave and his 'country' around Stratford-upon-Avon, Tintern Abbey on the Wye in homage to Wordsworth, Tennyson's house Faringford on the Isle of Wight, Gray's grave at Stoke Poges, Milton's house in Chalfont St Giles, Poets' Corner in Westminster Abbey, Pope's house at Twickenham, Walpole's Strawberry Hill, Bunyan's birthplace, Cowper's home in Olney, Keats' home in Hampstead, Dickens' home at Gad's Hill, Byron's home at Newstead Abbey, Wordsworth's houses at Dove Cottage and Rydal Mount, Felicia Hemans' house close by, Robert Southey's home in Keswick, Ruskin's home at Coniston, Burns Country in Ayrshire and Dumfries, and several sites associated with Sir Walter Scott, including Kenilworth, Abbotsford, Melrose Abbey, and Loch Katrine.

Shay funded this punishing itinerary by subscription through the college; it was possible to participate vicariously in her adventure for $5. Her letter announcing the project makes clear what she thought would sell the idea: subscribers were promised a 'mountain daisy' from Burns' birthplace, 'a yellow primrose from the Lake Region', or 'a snapshot of some spot dear to lovers of literature'. This, along with the diary and the albums themselves, suggests the importance of choosing the most sentimentally or poetically appropriate

Fern from driveway of Byron's home Newstead Abbey.

Figure 9.2. Page from Mrs Shay's album (Fern from Newstead Abbey). Author's own photograph

flowers available for the setting. In response, some forty friends and well-wishers provided money up front in exchange for a promise that she would make up forty identical albums of photographs plus associated pressed plant-material collected from the sites she planned to visit.

The surviving albums devote a page to each literary location (Figure 9.2). Each page is variably made up of a photograph of the location, a plant specimen, and a caption detailing the provenance of the plant and, more importantly, its biographical and often poetically allusive import. Included are a leaf from the tree under which Keats wrote 'To a Nightingale', 'privet from the hedge of Tennyson's lane where he loved to walk', 'flower from a 'crannied wall', Tennyson's Lane', 'Bark from old yew tree under which Gray sat when writing his elegy', and a leaf from a syringa bush at Dove Cottage 'planted by [Wordsworth]'. The sheer scale and enterprise of Mrs Shay's activities in Stratford-upon-Avon alone—forty daisies from Holy Trinity churchyard, forty leaves from the garden at New Place, forty specimens of flowers from the inspirational banks of 'Shakespeare's river', forty assorted pansies and rosemary springs from the environs of Anne Hathaway's cottage, and forty clover leaves from Mary Arden's house—gives some sense of the exhausting travelling, the predatory botany, and the quantity of the required in-transit flower-pressing that on occasion nearly defeated and often exhausted even the intrepid Shay.[52]

The albums were eventually handsomely bound as 'Floral Souvenirs of English Authors' and duly distributed. Those that survive are now kept, under the aegis of the local Shakespeare Club in Wessington Springs, in the house Mrs Shay and her husband built for their retirement on her return. This is a would-be replica of Anne Hathaway's cottage, copied by local workmen from a postcard brought back by Mrs Shay. (Since the postcard shows the original from only one angle, the replica, it has to be conceded, only really resembles it at all when viewed from one side.) Around it, there spreads one of America's many 'Shakespeare gardens'. The whole, then, is an exercise in bringing the materiality of Shakespeare 'home'.

Shay's replica cottage is perhaps the souvenir of souvenirs. As I glance up from the kitchen table where I am presently writing, my own eye snags on the modern commercial mass-produced equivalent, a collection of souvenir fridge magnets, each of which memorializes a trip to a writer's house museum, and indeed, to the museum gift shop. Here in jumbled microcosm assembled within my own home are a myriad of other writerly domesticities: Edgar Allan Poe's Cottage at Fordham, Nathaniel Hawthorne's Birthplace in Salem, Mark Twain's Boyhood Home in Hannibal, Dylan Thomas' boathouse at Laugharne, Edith Wharton's house in Lenox, Walt Whitman's Birthplace on Long Island, Longfellow's house in Cambridge MA, Hawthorne's in Concord, the Mark Twain house in Hartford, Longfellow's Birthplace in Portland, Washington Irving's Sunnyside, Melville's Arrowhead, Alcott's Orchard House, and Wordsworth's Dove Cottage, amongst others.

The literary tourist souvenir describes in miniature the writer's house as a compound of materiality and memory, actuality and representation, location and super-location, writer and reader. It is itself a sort of portable museum. It is in some sort an exception to Susan Stewart's melancholic take on the souvenir—that it exists as evidence of the inadequacy of the body to adequately inhabit or remember its experience.[53] Rather, it speaks of an extension of the body across time (that is, connecting back to the author's lifetime) and space (connecting the space of the author's home with that of the tourist). Taken home, the souvenir extends the writer's homes and haunts to places that sometimes did not exist when the writer was alive. This history of removal, which allows for nostalgic return in imagination, comments on (and is commented upon by) Susan Stewart's remark that the souvenir is a sort of 'scandal' in 'its removal from its "natural" location. Yet it is only by means of its material relation to that location that it acquires its value'.[54]

Stewart's edgy vocabulary refuses legitimate power to the souvenir—she counterposes the Romantic values of origin, lived experience, the natural, and location, against the consumption, the secondhand, and the denaturalization associated with the souvenir. But she does concede its 'romance of contraband', a phrase which might well describe my own desk, scattered as it is with memories smuggled from other locations: a Virginia Woolf souvenir mug, a resin replica of 'Tolly's mouse' from the Manor at Hemingford Grey, a replica of Dylan Thomas' blue stripy coffee mug, a Victorian ceramic model of Scott's chair, a tiny model of The House of Seven Gables, and a scrimshaw whale from Melville's house at Arrowhead.

A postcard

A few final thoughts despatched from yet another desk, this time in Milford-on-Sea (I have been driven out from my own home entirely by that wretched dog, and am now peripatetic, living out of suitcases). Throughout working on *The Author's Effects*, I have been conscious of keeping a precarious poise between acknowledging and celebrating the unique charms and idiosyncrasies of individual writer's house museums dotted across the map and my growing conviction, bound to appear to some of my readers as wantonly de-glamourizing, that although all writer's house museums may appear to be very different, they are all designed to pull off much the same trick.

That trick is to put the reader into the imagined presence of the author, to bring about an illusion of intimacy. Writer's house museums stereotypically begin by making the statement 'I was here' on behalf of the writer. In the phraseology of popular cliché, entering the writer's house is supposed to bring on a feeling that it is 'as if the writer has just this moment stepped out', and might at any point return. The 'I-ness' of any dead writer is generated in the first place most successfully by that writer, through 'talking' in the first person, ideally to an imagined or implied audience of one or at any rate one-at-a-time.[55] 'I was here', however, is a strangely disembodied and displaced statement, one that tells you that the writer 'was' but no longer 'is', one that tells you that they were 'here' but are no longer 'here'. This statement is crucial—it's the excess to showing an empty room which proves to be just that, an empty room, plus a straightforwardly historical statement, thus: 'So-and-so once lived in this house'. This statement may be classed as mere information. It does not produce the frisson of encounter.

Writer's house museums generate this encounter through collecting, co-locating, and narrating certain categories of objects associated with the author within places associated with the author. They activate a particular and surprisingly stable set of conventions: access to the writer's bodily remains, encounter with surrogates for the author's body in the shape of animal-bodies or clothing, partial entry into spaces dedicated to writerly creativity, occupation of framed writerly viewpoints, exploration of spaces designed as immersive versions of the authorial aesthetic. In so doing, they meditate upon authorial embodiment—birth, death, or the moment when the mortal body, projecting itself through the medium of writing, achieves immortality. In doing this, they conceive of themselves as sites of genesis and, as such, as generative and regenerative places. They erase the secondariness of literary text, disassemble, unwrite, hybridize, and remediate it. They aim to offer a site-specific fiction of the originating authorial body and the moment before writing.

My original intention was to look at the writer's house museum conceived as a form of biography or autobiography as a way of looking at the history and continuity of the popular idea, indeed, the cult of the Author. But though I began by asking, 'what is a writer's house museum?', I soon found myself asking instead, 'what does a writer's house museum do?' and eventually, 'what does a writer's house museum cause the reader to do?' If writers' houses give measure to the imagination, they actually measure the *reader's* imagination. The body in the writer's house is actually that of the reader, who impersonates the author. Writer's house museums are in fact all about readers, about the act of reading as bringing the author into existence. Thus, although the body that the book is being 'rewound' into may claim to be that of the author, it is in fact that of the reader-tourist. The 'hereness' of the author is more accurately and verifiably the 'hereness' of the literary tourist. This 'hereness' is registered in the popular cliché of 'I'm standing on the very spot where …'.

Thus, while I began with trying to account for the fetishization of the scene of writing, I end with understanding it as actually the mystification of the scene of reading. Ultimately, the most important of the author's effects turns out to be you, dear readers. The scene of reading turns out however, to be an impersonation of the author. Hence the curious case of the recent appearance of 'Wordsworth's typewriter' at Allan Bank, once home to the Wordsworths and now run by the National Trust. Visitors are invited to express themselves through an obsolete technology (albeit not one used by Wordsworth); according to the curator, so popular is emulating Wordsworth upon a typewriter that the machine continually breaks down under heavy use and has to be replaced.[56] But this scene of writing also turns out to be a scene of sociable, affectionate, even jokey reading; because such imper-sonation of the author, whether by guide, companion, or previous visitor, is always impertinent. A hundred years after Beckford recorded his pleasure at sitting in Petrarch's chair, a traveller from Ohio wryly commented that

> The walls of the chamber…were thickly over-scribbled with names…This passion for allying oneself to the great, by inscribing one's name on places hal-lowed by them, is certainly very odd; and (I reflected as I added my name to the rest) it is, without doubt, the most impertinent and idiotic custom in the world. People have thus written themselves down, to the contempt of sensible futurity, all over Petrarch's house.[57]

This desire to encounter and to impersonate the author has remained remarkably stable over time. But it has served to various effects and ends across the history of the writer's house as idea and actuality. The idea of the writer's house museum was generated from new conceptions of subjectivity, was given shape by anxieties produced by mass print culture, and demon-strably took a good deal of impetus from Romantic nationalisms. One might add that in an era of great and rapid social and economic change, there came to be a need for strong models of the experimental creative life. Thus the writer's house museum came into being as a way of bringing the reader into immediate intimacy with the imagined body of the author within a mythic national landscape, and is at once a mechanism and an effect of Romantic nationalism. This popular form, founded on a fiction of the outpouring of the author's unmediated genius and the possibility of unmediated access to its flow, has continued to flourish pretty much regardless of changing fashions in academic literary scholarship and even in museology.

This has in the main been a historicist study, focused on how and why nineteenth-century culture evolved a new pleasure, a new way of reading and relating to books, conceived and enacted as a personal encounter with the author at home. But that said, there are to my mind strong and clearly traceable continuities between what the writer's house museum has done in the past, what it does nowadays, and what it might do in the future. And there are strong and traceable continuities between *how* it has done it in the past and the present, too, despite the many new technological tools at curators' disposal these days. The versions of the author and the reader that the writer's house museum came to realize by the second half of the nineteenth century prove to be still very much alive today. Those interested in the history and future of this genre of specialist museums, such as Linda Young, one-time historic house curator, tend to note that their reputation in popular culture verges on the 'deathly, dubious, or quaint', and tend to express pessimism about their survival as a genre unless they are reinvented for a 'more culturally diverse, differently educated, and visually oriented public, for whom the pilgrimage to the writer's house will become a journey of discovery, rather than the fulfilment of a long-held desire'.[58] This is quite likely so. But it is worth remarking that all the same there seems to be no lack of appetite for an immersive experience within the materiality of celebrated lives. There has been a boom in a new type of literary biography with a marked tendency to think its subjects' lives through in terms of the material objects preserved in writer's house museums, in exercises such as Paula Byrne's *The Real Jane Austen: A Life in Small Things* (2013) or Deborah Lutz's *The Brontë Cabinet: Three Lives in Nine Objects* (2015).[59] Works of fiction are experimenting with other ways of reading, and some are being reconstructed in whole or part as museums; one might cite here the chapter designed as an auctioneer's catalogue listing the heroine's belongings, complete with photographs, featured in Maggie O'Farrell's experimental novel *This Must Be the Place* (2016), or more spectacularly Orhan Pamuk's project *The Museum of Innocence* (2008) which was 'to write a novel in the form of a museum catalogue, while simultaneously building the museum to which it referred'.[60] The entirety of the work (now a triptych consisting of novel, museum, and museum catalogue) is still at the time of writing on world tour. Meanwhile, the internet revolution continues to produce a proliferation of new forms of subjectivity and celebrity. The virtualization of culture produces as an equal and opposite effect a desire for 'liveness' and personal, lived experience; we live in an era where the local faces off against the global with ever-increasing intensity; the pressure for self-expressive yet commercially viable 'creativity' shows little sign of abating. And finally, although in Britain and the USA the nation-making function of the writer's house museum has become so thoroughly naturalized and/or discredited that individual museums are often struggling, there has been a boom in the making of state-funded writer's house museums across the world which began around the millennium. This is at its most intense in countries engaged in contemporary projects of nation-making upon the global stage—in eastern Europe, South Africa, Scandinavia, China, and Taiwan—however noticeably tricky it has been to invent Ibsen as satisfactorily at home in Norway, Bulgakov as adequately at home in an independent Ukraine, or Camões as perfectly at home in Portugal. However transnational such figures may in actuality have been, it seems likely in the current state of geopolitics that many new writer's house museums will put at their core a sense of national identity.

My guess is that reader-tourists will continue to seek to construct themselves as imaginative individuals in relation to common cultural memory. They will accordingly continue to make themselves at home in iconic literary places, take selfies of themselves to share the statement 'I was there' with a community of like-minded fans, and buy souvenir tea-towels and mugs to give to others and to enrich their own domestic spaces. Even as they take advantage of new technology to invent new immersive experiences, the future makers of writer's house museums might do well to take account of the long history of tourist encounter with the writer's house and the deep and abiding sentiments that I have been excavating and describing here: the erasure of print through immediate personal encounter with the author, the impersonation by the tourist of the author, the ambiguously solitary quality of the experience, made communal through visitor book, blog, Instagram, or Facebook, and of course the judicious purchase of postcard, souvenir, or gift as, finally, you exit the enchanted space via the gift shop.

Notes

INTRODUCTION

1. For an account of the establishment of Shakespeare as National Poet in the eighteenth century, see Michael Dobson, *The Making of the National Poet* (Oxford: Oxford University Press, 1993). For a comprehensive account of the history of Shakespeare's Birthplace and the inception of the Shakespeare Birthplace Trust, see Julia Thomas, *Shakespeare's Shrine: The Bard's Birthplace and the Invention of Stratford-upon-Avon* (Philadelphia, PA: University of Pennsylvania Press, 2012).
2. On these paintings and their history, see Sylvia Morris, http://theshakespeareblog. com/2015/05/henry-wallis-a-pre-raphaelites-views-of-shakespeares-stratford, last accessed 04/05/2017.
3. For full-length studies of literary tourism as a cultural formation which also deal in part with writer's houses, see Nicola J. Watson, *The Literary Tourist: Readers and Places in Romantic and Victorian Britain* (Basingstoke: Palgrave, 2006); Andrea Zemgulys, *Modernism and the Locations of Literary Heritage* (Cambridge: Cambridge University Press, 2008); Paul Westover, *Necroromanticism: Traveling to Meet the Dead, 1750–1860* (Basingstoke: Palgrave Macmillan, 2012); and Alison Booth, *Homes and Haunts: Touring Writers' Shrines and Countries* (Oxford: Oxford University Press, 2016).
4. On Ireland's *Picturesque Views* in relation to the development of the Shakespeare tourist trade, see Nicola J. Watson, 'Shakespeare on the Tourist Trail' in Robert Shaughnessy ed., *The Cambridge Companion to Shakespeare in Popular Culture* (Cambridge: Cambridge University Press, 2007), pp. 208–11. For authoritative coverage and discussion of the genre of 'homes and haunts' writing, see Alison Booth, *Homes and Haunts: Touring Writers' Shrines and Countries* (Oxford: Oxford University Press, 2016).
5. http://www.tate.org.uk/art/artworks/wallis-the-room-in-which-shakespeare-was-born-t00042, last accessed 06/12/2017.
6. For a succinct and helpful discussion of this commonplace, see Peter Davidházi, *The Romantic Cult of Shakespeare: Literary Reception in Anthropological Perspective* (Basingstoke: Palgrave, 1998). For a more recent and wide-ranging take on this, see Marijan Dović and Jón Karl Helgason, *National Poets, Cultural Saints: Canonization and Commemorative Cults of Writers in Europe* (Leiden: Brill, 2017).
7. Morris remarks additionally of this fascinating transaction that 'Landseer's additions apart, the painting is interesting as it shows a quiet corner of the building in the

period between its purchase for the nation in 1847 and its restoration about 10 years later'. Sylvia Morris, http://theshakespeareblog.com/2015/05/henry-wallis-a-pre-raphaelites-views-of-shakespeares-stratford, last accessed 04/05/2017.

8. Landseer is reading 'handsaw' as a corruption of 'hernshaw', a dialect term for a heron, in line with contemporary editorial commentary.

9. In so doing, he reimagines Shakespeare's Birthplace as rather like the most important writer's house of his day. Abbotsford, where he had himself spent time as a guest, was at the time a carefully preserved shrine to the memory of a writer whom contemporaries regarded as a genius fully equal to, and of the same type as, Shakespeare: Sir Walter Scott. See Chapter 8.

10. Julian Barnes, *Flaubert's Parrot* (London: Jonathan Cape, 1984), p. 12; Simon Goldhill, *Prospect*, October 2011, p. 72.

11. Michel Foucault argues that the figure of the Author emerges around 1800 and that the 'Author' (or rather, 'the author-function') is produced by reading practices; thus, studying 'the modes of circulation, valorization, attribution, and appropriation of discourse' can reveal how this fiction is produced, and to what ends. Michel Foucault, *Aesthetics, Method, and Epistemology*, ed. James D. Faubin, trans. Robert Hurley et al., *Essential Works of Foucault 1964–1984*, vol. 2 (New York: The New Press, 1998), pp. 205–22, p. 211.

12. See Polly Atkin, 'Ghosting Grasmere: the Musealization of Dove Cottage', in Nicola J. Watson ed., *Literary Tourism and Nineteenth-century Culture* (Basingstoke: Palgrave Macmillan, 2009), pp. 84–94.

13. For an important collection of essays on individual writer's houses, see Harald Hendrix ed., *Writers' Houses and the Making of Memory* (New York, London: Routledge, 2008). For a representative selection of further studies of individual houses, see Stephen Bann, *The Clothing of Clio: a Study of the Representation of History in Nineteenth-Century Britain and France* (Cambridge, New York: Cambridge University Press, 1984), pp. 93–111; Douglas Pocock, 'Haworth: The Experience of a Literary Place', in W.E. Mallory and P. Simpson-Housley eds., *Geography and Literature: A Meeting of the Disciplines* (Syracuse, NY: Syracuse University Press, 1987); S. Squire, 'The Cultural Values of Literary Tourism', *Annals of Tourism Research*, 21 (1994), pp. 103–20; Charles Lemon ed., *Early Visitors to Haworth* (Haworth: Brontë Society, 1996); David Herbert, 'Literary Places, Tourism, and the Heritage Experience', *Annals of Tourism Research*, 28:2 (2001), pp. 312–33 ; Aaron Santesso, 'The Birth of the Birthplace: Bread St and Literary Tourism Before Stratford', *English Literary History*, 71:2 (Summer 2004), pp. 377–403 Diana Fuss, *The Sense of an Interior: Four Writers and the Rooms That Shaped Them* (London: Routledge, 2004); Alexis Easley, *Literary Celebrity, Gender, and Victorian Authorship, 1850–1914* (Newark, DE: University of Delaware Press, 2011); Nuala Hancock, *Charleston and Monk's House: The Intimate House Museums of Virginia Woolf and Vanessa Bell* (Edinburgh: Edinburgh University Press, 2012); Thomas (2012). For studies of literary tourism which deal in part with writer's houses, see Watson (2006), Zemgulys (2008), Westover (2012), Booth (2016).

14. Hendrix (2008), p. 1.

15. See Mike Robinson and Hans Christian Andersen eds., *Literature and Tourism: Essays in the Reading and Writing of Tourism* (London: Thomson, 2003).

16. This definition depends in turn upon detailed thinking about the terms 'cultural heritage', 'literature', 'museum', and 'institution'. http://network.icom.museum/iclm/what-we-do/what-is-a-literary-museum, last accessed 05/12/2017.

17. Linda Young, 'Writers' House Museums: English Literature in the Heart and on the Ground' in LuAnn McCracken Fletcher ed., *Literary Tourism and the British Isles: History, Imagination, and the Politics of Place* (Lanham, MD, Boulder, CO, New York, London: Lexington Books, 2019), pp. 165–90, p. 180.

18. By the term 'genre', I mean the shared sense on the part of producer and consumer that there is inherited form which relies for ideological legibility on a set of stable conventions, recognizable even if or when they are flouted deliberately or accidentally; and that this form is conventionally associated with a certain content or subject-matter in such a way as to produce a recognizable emotional experience. This does not preclude thinking about the genre of the writer's house museum as comprising various subgenres, distinguished by their dominant stories and emotional mode, and which may further be variously hybridized. Nor does it preclude the recognition that cognate forms may also exhibit the same features in lesser prominence, combination, or function. See Stephen Neale, *Genre* (London: British Film Institute, 1980), pp. 22–3, cited Daniel Chandler, 'An Introduction to Genre Theory' (1997), http://www.aber.ac.uk/media/Documents/intgenre/intgenre.html, last accessed 11/08/2017, p. 2. Here the formulation of genre proposed by Robert Hodge and Gunther Kress remains useful: genres are 'typical forms of texts which link kinds of producer, consumer, topic, medium, manner and occasion', and 'control the behaviour of the producers of such texts and the expectations of potential consumers'. Robert Ian Vere Hodge and Gunther R. Kress, *Social Semiotics* (Ithaca, NY: Cornell University Press, 1988), p. 7, cited Daniel Chandler (1997) p. 6.

I have frequently been asked why I make a distinction between the writer's house museum and museums devoted to artists and composers. Writer's houses are far more numerous, and historically anterior—arguably the practice of making artists' and composers' homes into museums is modelled upon the writer's house museum. My view is that writer's house museums are brought into being earlier and with more urgency by the rise of mass print culture. The full mechanical reproduction of paintings and music comes much later; furthermore, when in the presence of a painting, one is in the presence of the original space of production and therefore has no need to locate it elsewhere; the same is in part true of music in the space of the concert-hall. Notwithstanding, the celebrity of the author's sketch and the composer's holograph manuscript arises in the late nineteenth century from the same impulse to return the work of art to its moment of origin.

19. Tom Mole, *Romanticism and Celebrity Culture* (Cambridge: Cambridge University Press, 2009); see also 'Celebrity and Anonymity in Romantic Britain'. Paper given at the Celebrity Studies Seminar, Centre for Life Writing, Oxford University, November 2014. On literary celebrity, see David Minden Higgins, *Romantic Genius and the Literary Imagination: Biography, Celebrity, and Politics* (London: Routledge, 2005), Mole (2009), Eric Eisner, *Nineteenth-Century Poetry and Literary Celebrity* (New York: Palgrave, 2009); Easley (2011); and two unpublished papers, Andrew Piper's 'The Werther Effect: Topologies of Literary Fame' (September 2014) and Mole (2014). See also the project 'The Author and the World' led by Rebecca Braun out of Lancaster University; see http://www.authorsandtheworld.com.

20. Andrew Bennett, *Romantic Poets and the Culture of Posterity* (Cambridge: Cambridge University Press, 1999).

21. Watson (2006); Westover (2012).

22. Jayne Lewis, '"A Lock of Thy Bright Hair": The Enlightenment's Milton and Our Auratic Material', *Humanities*, 4 (2015), pp. 797–817, p. 801.

23. Deidre Shauna Lynch, *Loving Literature: A Cultural History* (Chicago, IL: Oxford University Press, 2015), p. 17.

24. On literary biography in the period, see Julian North, *The Domestication of Genius: Biography and the Romantic Poet* (Oxford: Oxford University Press, 2009). On investment in authorial graves in relation to the cult of genius, see Samantha Matthews, *Poetical Remains: Poets' Graves, Bodies, and Books in the Nineteenth Century* (Oxford: Oxford University Press, 2004). On the development of literary tourism and forms of literary biography/travel-writing or 'prosopography' see Booth (2016). On cultures of literary commemoration relating to Shakespeare see esp. Clara Calvo and Coppélia Kahn eds., *Celebrating Shakespeare: Commemoration and Cultural Memory* (Cambridge: Cambridge University Press, 2015) and as relating to Walter Scott see esp. Ann Rigney, *The Afterlives of Water Scott: Memory on the Move* (Oxford: Oxford University Press, 2012). See more generally Joep Leerssen and Ann Rigney eds., *Commemorating Writers in Nineteenth-Century Europe: Nation-Building and Centenary Fever* (Basingstoke: Palgrave, 2014).

25. On 'author-love' and its modes see Helen Deutsch, *Loving Dr Johnson* (Chicago, IL: University of Chicago Press, 2005), and Paul Westover and Ann Wierda Rowland, eds. *Transatlantic Literature and Author Love in the Nineteenth Century* (Basingstoke: Palgrave Macmillan, 2016).

26. In pursuing this secret history of print, literary scholarship has been increasingly enticed into the histories of collecting and displaying manuscripts, books, and personalia found in archives and museums, as evidenced by edited collections such as Ina Ferris' and Paul Keen's *Bookish Histories: Books, Literature, and Commercial Modernity 1700–1900* (Basingstoke: Palgrave Macmillan, 2009) and Rowland and Westover's collection (2016). See also Lynch (2015) and Lynch (2019).

27. Hendrix (2008).

28. Visited c. 2004. Leaflet, Dept. of Recreation, Museums and Galleries Division, City of Edinburgh District Council.

29. 1 June to 28 October 2018. https://tolkien.bodleian.ox.ac.uk, last accessed 18/12/2018.

30. First visited c. 2004. Since the bicentenary of 2009 the display has been expanded to a full museum. See https://www.theguardian.com/artanddesign/2009/aug/06/tennyson-museum-bicentenary-poet, last accessed 05/12/2017.

31. 'Objects' are, as Bill Brown has neatly put it, the sum of 'the values, functions and social meanings contained in, or attributed to, objects over the duration of their life-span'. Bill Brown, 'Introduction: "Things"', *Critical Inquiry*, 28.1 (Autumn 2001), p. 7.

32. Jean Baudrillard, 'Subjective Discourse or the Non-Functional System of Objects' in Fiona Candlin and Raiford Guins, eds. *The Object-Reader* (London and New York: Routledge, 2009), p. 41.

33. Baudrillard, p. 41.

34. Baudrillard, p. 45.

35. See Hicks on the possibility of understanding 'things, and also the knowledge that is generated by them, as *events* and *effects*' and therefore the notion that the object is produced through a conjunction of materiality and witness, *Oxford Handbook to Material Culture Studies*, Mary Carolyn Beaudry and Dan Hicks, eds. (Oxford: Oxford University Press, 2010). Such observations might suggest affinities with theorization of the 'agency' of objects on the back of Hegel's insight in *Phenomenology of the Spirit* (1807) that subject and object exist in a mutual feedback loop.

36. *The London Scene* (first pub. 1931) (London: Snowbooks, 1975), pp. 37–47, pp. 37–8.

37. Greenway, Devon. Visited August 2015.

38. Anne Trubek, *A Skeptic's Guide to Writers' Houses* (Philadelphia, PA, Oxford: University of Pennsylvania Press, 2011), p. 3.

39. Ibsen Museum, Oslo. Visited October 2015. See Anne-Sofie Hjemdahl ed., *A Thing or Two About Ibsen: His Possessions, Dramatic Poetry and Life* (Oslo: Andrimne, 2006), p. 127.

40. See, for example, Suzanne Macleod, *Reshaping Museum Space: Architecture, Design, Exhibitions* (London: Routledge, 2005); Kali Tzortli, *Museum Space: Where Architecture Meets Museology* (London: Routledge, 2015).

41. Adrian Searle, Exhibition Review: 'Rachel Whiteread at Tate Britain', 11 September 2017, https://www.theguardian.com/artanddesign/2017/sep/11/rachel-whiteread-exhibition-review-tate-britain, last accessed 06/12/2017.

42. One might also cite Virginia Woolf in this respect. See Woolf, 'The Mark on the Wall' (1917) in David Bradshaw ed., *The Mark on the Wall, and Other Short Fiction* (Oxford: Oxford World's Classics, 2008).

43. *Memoirs of Thomas Jones*, https://www.llgc.org.uk/pencerrig/thjones_s_003.htm, last accessed 15/08/2017.

44. See, for example, 'On the annual meeting of some Gentlemen to celebrate SHAKESPEARE'S BIRTHDAY', *London Magazine*, 24 (1755), p. 244.

45. http://www.miltonscottage.org, last accessed 05/12/2017.

46. Flyleaf, William Howitt, *Homes and Haunts of the Most Eminent British Poets* (London: George Routledge and Sons, 1847).

47. Hendrix, 'Epilogue: The Appeal of Writers' Houses', in Hendrix (2008), p. 239.

48. 'The sentimental poet ... *reflects* on the impression, which the objects make in him, and only on this reflection is the emotion grounded, in which he himself is moved and moves us. The object is here connected with an idea, and only in this connection does his poetical force rest. The sentimental poet is therefore always concerned with two conflicting conceptions and feelings, with reality as limit and with his idea as the infinite, and the mixed feeling, which he arouses, will always testify to this two-fold source ... For now arises the question, whether he dwells more on the reality, or more on the ideal, or whether he wants to achieve the former as an object of aversion, or the latter as an object of inclination. His representation will therefore be either *satirical* or it will (in a broader sense of this word, which will be explained afterward) be *elegiac*'. Friedrich Schiller, 'On Naïve and Sentimental Poetry', 1795. https://archive.schillerinstitute. com/transl/Schiller_essays/naive_sentimental-1.html, last accessed 18/12/2018.

49. As an instance, see Susannah Walker, *The Life of Stuff: Possessions, obsessions and the mess we leave behind* (London: Doubleday, 2018).

50. For work on this, see for example Max Saunders, http://www.ego-media.org/ projects/imagining-the-future, last accessed 18/12/2018.

51. Harald Hendrix, 'Literary Heritage Sites Across Europe: A Tour d'Horizon' in 'Ce que le musée fait à la littérature', *Interferences Litteraires*, 16 (June 2015). http://www.interferenceslitteraires.be/en/node/481, last accessed 13/12/2017.

52. A 2016 survey conducted for VisitEngland found that 55 per cent of those surveyed would be interested in visiting a literary location on holiday, and 24 per cent had done so over the last twelve months; the most popular locations listed were associated with J.K. Rowling, Charles Dickens, Shakespeare, Roald Dahl, Beatrix Potter, and J.R.R. Tolkien. 'VisitEngland: Year of Literary Heroes', *Survey Report 2017*, p. 1, p. 3.

53. For a project devoted in part to exploring the national and transnational affordances of the literary museum and the writer's house museum in particular, see TRAUM (Transforming Author Museums in Norway), https://traum.hisf.no, last accessed 06/12/2017.

54. See the latest Chinese project in Fuzhou devoted to building replicas of houses associated with near-contemporaries Miguel Cervantes, Shakespeare, and Tang Xianzu.

55. Simon Goldhill, *Freud's Couch, Scott's Buttocks, Brontë's Grave* (Chicago, IL, London: University of Chicago Press, 2011); Brock Clarke, *An Arsonist's Guide to Writer's Homes in New England* (Chapel Hill, NC: Algonquin Books, 2007); Trubek (2011), p. 13; Liz Workman, *Dr Johnson's Doorknob—And Other Significant Parts of Great Men's Houses* (New York: Rizzoli International Publications, 2007).

56. Seamus Heaney, *District and Circle* (London: Faber and Faber, 2006).

57. My use of the term 'functions' here intentionally if silently recalls Vladimir Propp's identification of the characteristic 'functions' of the folk-tale; I argue that the story of any writer's house museum is similarly built up of a sufficient number of conventional objects. Vladimir Propp, *Morphology of the Folktale* (1928; trans. 2nd edn. 1968).

58. Walter Benjamin, 'The Work of Art in the Age of Mechanical Reproduction', *Illuminations* (1955), ed. with introd., Hannah Arendt, trans. Harry Zorn (London: Penguin, 1969), p. 215.

59. Rigney, Ann, 'Portable Monuments: Literature, Cultural Memory, and the Case of Jeanie Deans', *Poetics Today*, 25:2 (Summer 2004).

60. In this respect, my practice takes its cue from recent insistence amongst archaeologists that such object biographies can and should be more about relationality than materiality: 'The biography of an object should not be restricted to an historical reconstruction of its birth, life and death. Biography is relational and an object biography is comprised of the sum of the relationships that constitute it'. See, for instance, Jody Joy, 'Reinvigorating Object Biography: Reproducing the Drama of Object Lives', *World Archaeology*, 41:4 (2009), pp. 540–56, p. 552. For how this plays out in one museum's online exhibition see http://web.prm. ox.ac.uk/rpr/index.php/objectbiographies/index.html, last accessed 05/12/2017.

61. Fuss (2004), p. 2.

CHAPTER I

1. In 2019 this ceremony was rescheduled to the Shakespeare service on the Sunday; but the import of the gesture remains the same.

2. Malcolm Bradbury, *To the Hermitage* (London: Picador, 2000), p. 153.

3. Indeed, it is possible for the place of death not just to become more celebrated than the grave itself, but to serve as a microcosmic writer's house museum in itself. This is true, for example, of the case of the chair in which Molière is said to have died in 1673 while on stage at the Comédie Française in the title role of *Le Malade Imaginaire*. See 'Why Do We Care about Molière's Armchair?' http://hannahwill.blogspot.com/2021/01/why-do-we-care-about-molieres-chair.html, last accessed 15/06/2019.

4. Michael Kammen, *Digging Up the Dead*: *A History of Notable American Reburials* (Chicago, IL, London: University of Chicago Press, 2009), p. 17.

5. See, most pertinently. Thomas Laqueur, *The Work of the Dead: A Cultural History of Mortal Remains* (Princeton, NJ: Princeton University Press, 2015).

6. On the development of Poets' Corner see Watson (2006), chapter 1. Also Thomas A. Prendergast, *Poetical Dust: Poets' Corner and the Making of Britain* (Philadelphia, PA: University of Pennsylvania Press, 2015).

7. See Laqueur (2015).

8. See Samantha Matthews, *Poetical Remains: Poets' Graves, Bodies, and Books in the Nineteenth Century* (Oxford: Oxford University Press, 2004). Bodies relocated

included (for example), those of René Descartes, Jean-Jacques Rousseau, Voltaire, Raphael, Thomas Browne, Thomas Paine, Emanuel Swedenborg, Joseph Haydn, Alexander Pope, Jonathan Swift, Friedrich Schiller, George Gordon Lord Byron, Percy Bysshe Shelley, Edgar Allan Poe, and later, Thomas Hardy and William Butler Yeats—each of which suffered its own rather grotesque adventures. For more on this see, variously, Bess Lovejoy, *Rest in Pieces: The Curious Fates of Famous Corpses* (London: Duckworth Overlook, 2014); Kammen (2009); Christine Quigley, *The Corpse: A History* (Jefferson, NC, London: McFarland, 1996); and Teresa Barnett, *Sacred Relics: Pieces of the Past in Nineteenth-Century America* (Chicago, IL: University of Chicago Press, 2013).

9. 'Good friend, for Jesus' sake forebeare/To digg the dust enclosed heare/Bleste be the man that spares thes stones/And curst be he that moves my bones'.

10. For the tomb opening in December 1873 see *The Athenaeum*, 2441 (8 August 1874), p. 177. For a full account of the exhumation of Petrarch's body in 2003 and the results of DNA analysis see Elena Pilli et al., 'Ancient DNA and the Forensics of Genetics: The Case of Francesco Petrarca', *Forensic Science International: Genetics Supplement Series*, 1:1 (August 2008), pp. 469–70. For discussion of the cultural impact of the discovery that the skull supposed to be Petrarch's was actually a woman's, see Patricia Clare Ingram, 'Amorous Dispossessions: Knowledge, Desire, and the Poet's Dead Body' in Elizabeth Scala and Sylvia Federico eds., *The Post-Historical Middle Ages* (New York: Palgrave Macmillan, 2009), pp. 13–36, esp. p. 13.

11. On the letter of 26 February 1806 in which Napoleon angles for the return of Rousseau's remains to Ermenonville, see F.G. Healey, *The Literary Culture of Napoleon* (1959), p. 66; for more detail of how this was seen in the nineteenth century see Joseph Marie Quérard, *La France Littérraire, ou Dictionnaire bibliographique des savants* …(Paris: Chez Firmin Didot Frères, Libraires, 1836), vol. 8, pp. 229–30.

12. Visited September 2018. For Napoleon's removal of Ariosto's body see the information boards at the museum; for nineteenth-century comment see Octavian Blewitt, *A Handbook for Travellers in Central Italy* (2nd edn. London: John Murray, 1850), p. 21.

13. For discussion of the conception that genius manifested within the exceptional body of the writer, see Helen Deutsch, *Resemblance and Disgrace; Alexander Pope and the Deformation of Culture* (Cambridge, MA; London: Harvard University Press, 1996).

14. See Clement Ingleby, *Shakespeare's Bones: The Proposal to Disinter Them, considered in relation to their possible bearing on his portraiture: illustrated by instances of visits of the living to the dead* [1879] (London: Trubner & Co, 1883), pp. 11–12. Ingleby seems to have derived this account from Andrew Hamilton, 'The Story of Schiller's Remains', *Macmillan's Magazine*, VIII (May 1863), pp. 302–10.

15. Ingleby (1883), p. 12.

16. DNA analysis carried out in 2008 has determined that the reconstructed skeleton was composed of multiple bodies, and that none of the DNA corresponds with Schiller's known relatives, with the result that the monument now presides over

an empty grave. https://en.wikipedia.org/wiki/Friedrich_Schiller%27s_skull, last accessed 19/12/2018.

17. For a survey of these arguments see James Rigney, 'Worse than Malone or Sacrilege: The Exhumation of Shakespeare's Remains', *Critical Survey*, 9:3 (1997), pp. 78–90. For a brief discussion of the latest suggestions made in the *Stratford Herald, BBC America*, and *Fox News*, see Sylvia Morris, 'Unearthing Shakespeare: Good Friend for Jesus sake forbear', *The Shakespeare Blog*, 26 June 2011, http:// theshakespeareblog.com/2011/06/unearthing-shakespeare-good-friend-for-jesus-sake-forbear, last accessed 13/11/2015. For discussion of the exhumation controversy, see Samuel Schoenbaum, *Shakespeare's Lives* (Oxford: Clarendon Press, 1970), pp. 471–3 and Alan R. Young, *Punch and Shakespeare in the Victorian Era* (Bern, New York: Peter Lang, 2007), pp. 126–8.

18. Phrenological collections in the early years were made by private collectors and specialists, including the founder of phrenology, Franz Joseph Gall (1758–1828), and consisted of a mix of real skulls and casts made either from life, post-mortem, or from exhumed skulls. With the formation of Phrenological Societies in Britain and America (the first being the Edinburgh Phrenological Society founded by George Combe and his brother in 1820), collections were made within these societies; subsequently, as the movement was popularized, cabinets of miniature phrenological specimens were manufactured, and popular museums were opened such as the Phrenological Museum at 367 The Strand, London, which advertised in *The Times* on 11 September 1851 a display of some 4,000 casts and ceramics, and offered 'readings' of visitors' heads. Visitors included George Eliot and Charlotte Brontë. See Roger Cooter, *Phrenology in the British Isles: An Annotated Historical Bibliography and Index* (Methuen, NJ; London: Scarecrow, 1989), p. vii.

19. On exhumation fever see Stanley Wells, 'Digging Up Shakespeare', *The Shakespeare Blog*, http://bloggingshakespeare.com/digging-up-shakespeare-by-stanley-wells, 30 June 2011, last accessed 13/11/2015. For American enthusiasm see Nathaniel Hawthorne's account of Delia Bacon's attempt in 1856, who hoped to find evidence that Shakespeare of Stratford was not the author of the works attributed to him but lost her nerve at the last moment at the dead of night, 'Recollections of a Gifted Woman', *Atlantic Monthly*, XI (January 1863), pp. 43–58. For satire on the American desire to exhume Shakespeare and turn him into Bacon figuratively or actually, see *Harper's Weekly*, 3 October 1874, 'Bohemians at the Grave of Shakespeare', which shows a number of American journalists, writers, and academics preparing to dig Shakespeare up: see Robert E. Kennedy, https://www.nytimes.com/learning/general/onthisday/harp/10003.html, last accessed 13/11/2015.

20. For the outcry see Thomas D. King, 'Shall We Open Shakespeare's Grave? No. A Reply…to the Question Put by Mr Parker Norris in the July number for the *Manhattan Montreal*', 1884, pp. 6–8. See also *The Saturday Review*, 8 September 1883 and *London Daily News*, 1 September 1883. Discussed at more length by Rigney (1997), pp. 82–3.

21. Ingleby (1883), p. 33.

22. Ingleby (1883), p. 2.
23. See Graham Holderness and Bryan Loughrey, 'Shakespearean Features', Jean Marsden ed., *The Appropriation of Shakespeare: Post-Renaissance Reconstructions of the Work and the Myth* (New York; London: Harvester Wheatsheaf, 1991), pp. 183–201.
24. Ingleby (1883), p. 2.
25. Ingleby (1883), p. 2. For the romantic desire to converse with the dead see Paul Westover, *Necromanticism: Traveling to Meet the Dead, 1750–1860* (Basingstoke,; New York: Palgrave Macmillan, 2012), pp. 28–9.
26. [C.L. Langstone], *How Shakespeare's Skull was Stolen* (London: Elliot Stock, Paternoster Row, 1884), p. 10.
27. Langstone, p. 18.
28. Langstone, p. 32.
29. Langstone, p. 33.
30. Langstone, p. 37.
31. Langstone, p. 46.
32. What lust that ending must have triggered in readers! Indeed, I suspect the writer both suffered from that lust and inspired it in others, as he was the then incumbent of Beoley Vicarage. See Schoenbaum (1970), pp. 271–383. In 2015 an application was made by the University of Worcester to open the Sheldon vault at Beoley in search of this skull and at the same time to open the tomb in Holy Trinity; it was refused in part on the grounds that the Beoley skull 'had been informally removed on previous occasions', doubtless by late Victorian enthusiasts, and conceivably after a good dinner at the vicarage. Shiranikha Herbert, 'Shakespeare's Skull to Stay in Vault', *Church Times* (November 2015), https://www.churchtimes.co.uk/articles/2015/6-november/news/uk/shakespeare-s-skull-to-stay-in-vault, last accessed 09/07/2017.
33. Rigney (1997).
34. 'Secret History: Shakespeare's Tomb', broadcast on Channel 4 in March 2016. There are still regular applications to exhume Shakespeare's body; as interesting is the persistence of this within scholarly discourse, as Robert Hampson's lines reflecting upon a life of scholarship, 'caught in the toils of this strange compulsion/ to finger the bone of the master's skull', suggest.'Blood, moon' sonnet sequence, *The Wolf.* Personal email correspondence 21/12/2018.
35. Kammen (2009), p. 30, n.147; derived from Russell Shorto, *Descartes' Bones: A Skeletal History of the Conflict between Faith and Reason* (London: Abacus, 2008).
36. Hamish Mathison, 'Robert Burns and Tradition', *The Association for Scottish Literary Studies* (2007), http://asls.arts.gla.ac.uk/Hamish_Mathison.html, last accessed 21/06/2017.
37. Anonymous, *Scots Magazine and Edinburgh Literary Miscellany*, 79 (May 1817), pp. 323–4.
38. http://www.robertburns.plus.com/MonumentsDumfries.htm, last accessed 14/01/2016. See also Murray Pittock and Christopher A. Whatley, 'Poems and

Festivals, Art and Artefact and the Commemoration of Robert Burns c. 1844-c. 1896', *Scottish Historical Review*, XCIII:1, 236 (April 2014), pp. 56–79. For John McDiarmid's account of this event, see 'St Michael's Church-Yard—Disinterment of Burns' in *Sketches from Nature* (Edinburgh: Oliver and Boyd; London: Simpkin and Marshall, 1830), pp. 367–80. Cited by Megan Coyer, 'The Literary Empiricism of the Phrenologists: Reading the Burnsian Bumps', *The Drouth*, 30 (Winter 2008), pp. 69–77, p. 5; accessed via http://www.electricscotland.com/familytree/frank/burns_lives53.htm, last accessed 11/11/2015, pages 1–13.

39. Quoted Matthews (2004), p. 70.

40. An account of the exhumation was published in *The Dumfries Courier* and abridged in *The Caledonian Mercury*, but we owe the lengthiest account of both the exhumation and the analysis of the skull to a pamphlet by a leading phrenologist George Combe (1788–1858), *Four Views of the skull of Robert Burns: taken from a cast moulded at Dumfries, the 31st day of March 1834*. See the catalogue entry for the copy of this rare volume held in the National Library of Scotland, http://www.nls.uk/collections/rarebooks/acquisitions/singlebook.cfm/idfind/866, last accessed 11/11/2015. I consulted the copy on Project Gutenberg. See also the appendix to Allan Cunningham, *The Life and Land of Burns* (New York, J. & H.G. Langley, 1841) with an account of an examination of the tomb in 1834. It is said that there were only three casts made initially from the original; there were subsequent secondary castings. Cast, Robert Burns Centre, Dumfries and Galloway, http://www.burnsscotland.com/items/c/cast-of-robert-burns-skull.aspx, last accessed 11/11/2015; Cast, Writers' Museum in Edinburgh, http://www.burnsscotland.com/items/p/plaster-cast-of-the-skull-of-robert-burns.aspx, last accessed 11/11/2015; Cast, Irvine Burns Club, http://www.cobbler.plus.com/wbc/news;etter/0003/0300_burns_skull.htm, last accessed 11/11/2015; Cast in the collection of G. Ross Roy in the University of South Carolina, formerly in the collection of Colin Hunter McQueen. Elizabeth A. Saddeth, Clayton Carlyle Tarr and George Ross Roy eds., *The G. Ross Roy Collection of Robert Burns: An Illustrated Catalogue* (Columbia, SC: University of South Carolina Press, 2009), p. 375; Cast, Princeton University, http://library.princeton.edu, last accessed 11/11/2015; Cast in the collection of Perth Burns Club.

41. See http://www.burnsscotland.com/items/p/plaster-cast-of-the-skull-of-robert-burns.aspx, last accessed 11/11/2015.

42. According to Coyer, McDiarmid had at least four requests for casts. Two were sent to Combe, one for personal use and the other for the Edinburgh Phrenological Society. Coyer (2008), pp. 1–13. The story goes that three casts in all were subsequently made, but as there are certainly more in existence now, Coyer's contention that the cast 'made its way into the mass produced phrenological lecture sets sold by Anthony O'Neil' seems to be borne out. Coyer (2008), p. 10, and Mark Fraser, 'The Phrenologists and Robert Burns', *Burns Chronicle* (1996), pp. 215–21.

43. George Combe, *The Phrenological Development of Robert Burns From a Cast of His Skull Moulded at Dumfries, the 31st Day of March 1834* (Edinburgh: W. & A.K. Johnson, 1859), pp. 5–6.

44. Gary Nisbet, 'John Steell's Sculpture', *Glasgow City of Culture*, http://www.glasgowsculpture.com/pg_biography.php?sub=steell_j, last accessed 09/07/2017.

45. *Daily Record*, 18 January 2013. The fashion for such reconstructions extends beyond Burns; in 2007 a reconstruction of Dante's face was undertaken as a joint project between Pisa University and the University of Bologna. See Stefano Benazzi et al., 'The Face of the Poet Dante Alighieri, Reconstructed by Virtual Modelling and Forensic Anthropology Techniques', *Journal of Archaeological Science*, 36:2 (February 2009), pp. 278–83. The remodelling was based on morphological and metric data collected during the formal identification of Dante's remains by the anthropologist Fabio Frassetto in 1921.

46. Anonymous, 'The Real Face of Robert Burns Revealed', *The Scotsman* (January 2013), http://www.Scotsman.com/heritage/people-places/th, last accessed 09/07/2017.

47. Burns Scotland, Cast, http://burnsscotland.com/items/c/cast-of-robert-burns-skull-(1).aspx, last accessed 09/07/2017.

48. Richard Howitt, *The Gipsy King: And Other Poems* (London, 1840), p. 85.

49. The death mask has been displayed since 2002; the period-correct bed was acquired and installed in 2003.

50. A death mask was taken in much the same fashion as a life mask except that a life mask entailed the insertion of quills into the nostrils to make it possible for the subject to just about continue to breathe as the face was covered with plaster. The hair was drawn back, the jaw bound up and the skin oiled, a muslin placed over the face, a thread laid down the centre of the face, plaster poured over and allowed to harden, the two halves separated by the thread removed and put back together again, and plaster then poured into the resulting mould or matrix to give a positive 3D cast of the face. On the production of death masks, see Marcia Pointon, 'Casts, Imprints, and the Deathliness of Things: Artifacts at the Edge', *The Art Bulletin*, 96:2 (July 2014), pp. 170–95.

51. It is said that Ludwig van Beethoven's famously furrowed brow was the result of his anxiety and discomfort at the process of having a life mask taken. See Rita Steblin, 'Beethoven's Life Mask of 1812 Reconsidered', *The Beethoven Newsletter*, 8/9:3/1 (Winter/Spring 1993), pp. 66–70.

52. In Wentworth Place there is a history of displaying the life and death masks alongside one another: according to the curator, when they were last so displayed in 'Keats' Parlour', 'visitors generally enjoyed it when you asked them to guess which was which'. Because the difference between the two is so slight, the two taken together describe the slip between the generation of poetry as dream and the generation of the poet as post-mortem icon. Personal conversation with the then Senior Curator, Frankie Kubicki, winter 2015.

53. See David Bindman, *The Shadow of the Guillotine: Britain and the French Revolution* (London: British Museum Press, 1989), p. 147.

54. They might also be, more practically, forensic: masks were routinely taken of unidentified corpses in the Paris morgue, allowing identification long after the face and body had decayed; this was the origin of the famous mask of a drowned young woman, 'L'inconnue de la Seine'.

55. See Martin Heidegger, 'Image and Schema'; *Kant and the Problem of Metaphysics* (1929); Susan Sontag, *On Photography* (1977); Jean-Luc Nancy, 'Masked Imagination'; *The Ground of the Image*, trans. Jeff Fort (2005); Emily Wright, *Casting Presence: Death Masks and Portraiture in the Eighteenth to Nineteenth Centuries* (MSt, History of Art and Visual Culture), University of Oxford (2012), and Pointon (2014). Pointon's argument is of especial relevance here in that she acknowledges the ideological suggestion made by death masks of their own uniqueness and faithfulness to the moment of death, while challenging it through pointing out that it is the fragile and rarely surviving matrix that is unique, rather than the casts subsequently taken from it. Moreover, casts taken from the original matrix are of variable quality depending on when the matrix began to erode and degrade; casts are also made subsequently from new matrices made from casts. Thus a death mask, especially where the subject was famous and whose fame has continued, is not unique and is much less closely related to the original than it might initially appear. Pointon therefore argues that the death mask is not (as it implicitly claims to be) a contact-relic but a work of portraiture, pointing additionally to evidence that dead features were often quite extensively rearranged so as to appear more lifelike through artistic intervention. My interest is additionally in the contexts/collections within which masks are displayed. Although nowadays collections of death masks are typically exercises in post-modern domestic chic, until the early twentieth century they were a mode of pantheonization or indeed anti-pantheonization. See Ernst Benkard's famous photographic essay on his own collection of death masks published in the 1930s; or Madame Tussaud's exhibition in Edinburgh in May 1803 mostly of the executed (see Philippe Guillaume Mathé Curtius, *Sketches of the Characters Composing the Cabinet of Compositions, executed by the celebrated Curtius of Paris, and his successor [Madame Tussaud]* (Edinburgh: for the proprietors, printed by Donovan and Co., 1803), exhibition catalogue. For Tussaud's career, see Anita Leslie and Pauline Chapman, *Madame Tussaud: Waxworker Extraordinary* (London: Hutchinson & Co., 1978).

56. Now displayed in Birmingham Library's 'Shakespeare room', and another in the King Edward VII Schoolroom, Stratford-upon-Avon. For earlier siting in the Birthplace, see photograph of Shakespeare's House, The Library 17101, Shakespeare Birthplace Trust Archive, Ref. No. SC4/18/32 (1885), http://collections.shakespeare.org.uk/search/archive/sc41832-henley-street-shake-speares-birthplace-library-c-1885-item/search/everywhere:library-69719/page/1/view_as/grid, last accessed 09/07/2017.

57. Making the argument that the dead were still living, such masks were typically displayed vertically as quasi-live faces. The mask might be simply hung as a mask, framed as something approximating a bas-relief, or converted into a bust

through the provision of a plinth. Enlivening the death mask often entailed modifying the cast so it had the open eyelids and blank eyeballs associated with conventional statues.

58. Personal conversation at Wentworth House, winter 2015.

59. Consider, for example, http://www.open.ac.uk/blogs/literarytourist/?p=47, last accessed 21/06/2017.

60. *John Keats at Wentworth Place: Poems Written December 1818 to September 1820* (London: London Borough of Camden, 1971); also Peter Malone, 'Keats's Posthumous Existence in Plaster', *The Keats-Shelley Review*, 26:2 (September 2012), pp. 125–31.

61. Email correspondence with Frankie Kubicki, Senior Curator, 16/03/2016.

62. Life mask: by Benjamin Haydon, one of the original batch of casts. This one belonged to Charles Dilke; Keats House possesses another cast; as do the Keats-Shelley House in Rome, and the National Portrait Gallery, which holds the cast that belonged to Keats' friend John Hamilton Reynolds. We know additionally that Fanny Brawne possessed a cast. Death mask: one of two held by Keats House; the one on display is the older of the two. The original was said to be by Gherardi of Rome; the copy by Charles Smith of Stanhope St, London; the bronzed version was mentioned by Robert Gittings in his essay collection *The Mask of Keats: A Study of Problems* (London, Melbourne, Toronto: Heinemann, 1956) and belonged to the curator of Keats House, Jeff Preston. Brooch: of Joseph Severn's design, originally meant as a gift to Fanny Brawne as a mourning jewel, eventually given by Severn to his daughter on her wedding in 1861, and afterwards given to Keats House in 1932 as part of a bequest from Joseph Severn's family. Email correspondence with Kenneth Page, Interpretation Officer, Keats House, 01/07/2017.

63. Personal conversation, winter 2015. The recent re-interpretation moved the life mask from the bedroom and put on display for the first time the bronzed death mask. Email correspondence with Frankie Kubicki 09/03/2016.

64. Gittings (1956), pp. 1–4.

65. Louis A. Godey, *Godey's Lady's Book and Magazine*, 50 (May 1855), p. 435.

66. Pointon (2014), p. 185.

67. Leigh Hunt, 'The Wishing Cap', No. 1, *Tait's Edinburgh Magazine*, X (January 1883), pp. 435–42 (p. 439). Cited in Jane Stabler, 'Leigh Hunt's Aesthetics of Intimacy', Nicholas Roe ed., *Leigh Hunt: Life, Poetics, Politics* (London: Routledge, 2003), pp. 95–118, p. 104.

68. http://collections.shakespeare.org.uk/search/museum/strst-sbt-1971-121-various-locks-of-human-hair/search/everywhere:locks-of-human-hair/page/1/view_as/grid, last accessed 29/06/2017. Rogers was eventually offered the position of Poet Laureate in 1850 but turned it down on the score of age and failing health.

69. See Catherine Payling, *Keats and Italy: A History of the Keats-Shelley House in Rome* (London: The Museum Collection, 2005), pp. 91–2.

70. It is unclear who combined the locks of hair. According to Harvey Rachlin, 'there is no evidence that Robert Browning placed the locks of either Milton or Elizabeth...in the reliquary when he was alive. More likely, the locks were placed there after the poet died in 1889, either by his son, Robert Wiedeman Barrett Browning, or by his daughter-in-law, Fannie Browning'. See Harvey Rachlin, *Lucy's Bones, Sacred Stones, and Einstein's Brain* (New York: Henry Holt and Co., 1996), pp. 272–3. It subsequently came up for auction in New York in 1933 and was bought by the American collector Dallas Pratt, who would eventually gift it to the Keats-Shelley House along with other items in 1971. See Keats-Shelley House, 'Scallop-Shell Reliquary', *Treasure of the Month*, February 2015, http://www.keats-shelley-house.org/en/events/treasure-of-the-month-100.htm, last accessed 09/07/2017.

71. Beverley Nichols, *Twenty-Five: An Autobiography* [1926] (London: Penguin Books, 1935), chapter 3, pp. 33–4.

72. Sally Brown, 'An Echo and a Light unto Eternity: The Founding of the Keats-Shelley House', *Keats and Italy: A History of the Keats-Shelley House in Rome* (Rome: Edizioni Il Labirinto, 2005), pp. 51–67, p. 64.

73. Payling (2005), p. 92.

74. Pointon (2014), *passim*.

CHAPTER 2

1. Charlotte Cory, 'Capturing the Brontës', exhibition 4 October to 31 December 2013. See also the complete catalogue of the exhibition.

2. Rachel Poliquin's study of taxidermy is bookended by other systems of whole-body preservation that preceded it (including mummification) and have succeeded it (including freeze-drying). I take this as warrant for considering the case of Petrarch's cat, clearly meant to be displayed 'as if still alive', as continuous with the practice of whole-specimen taxidermy as it reached a cultural zenith in nineteenth-century Britain and America. See Poliquin, *The Breathless Zoo: Taxidermy and the Cultures of Longing* (Philadelphia, PA: Penn State University Press, 2012), pp. 22–3. Although Poliquin is not interested in the very specialized sub-set of taxidermic specimens as they are staged within writer's house museums, her emphasis on the 'intense desire' of taxidermy 'to keep particular creatures from disappearing' (p. 6) and to construct them as 'objects of remembrance' (p. 7) together with her remark that 'taxidermy offers the unsettling presence of liveliness in the face of death' suggest affinities with the project of the writer's house museum (p. 108). Her remarks on the power of the specimen to produce 'encounter' (p. 39, p. 194) are equally suggestive, as is her thinking about the variable nature of these encounters—pleasurable, unsettling, sometimes both at the same time.

3. See Poliquin (2012), p. 205.

4. Lorraine Daston, *Things That Talk: Object Lessons from Art and Science* (New York: Zone Books, 2004), p. 15. Quoted in Poliquin (2012), p. 20.

5. It was allegedly Francesco da Carrara (1325–93) who let the house to Petrarch. Peter Houses, 'Francesco Petrarca', *Sociology of Italian Lifestyle* (2017), http://www.peterhouses.com/italian-great-people-of-the-past/francesco-petrarca, last accessed 09/07/2017.

6. For a discussion of tourism to this house and other places associated with Petrarch see Harald Hendrix, 'From Early Modern to Romantic Literary Tourism: A Diachronical Perspective' in Nicola J. Watson ed., *Literary Tourism and Nineteenth-Century Culture* (Basingstoke: Palgrave Macmillan, 2009), pp. 13–20.

7. Or, more lightheartedly, set as a Petrarchan sonnet thus: 'The Etruscan poet burned with double love;/I was his greatest flame, Laura came after;/And now, I wonder, what provokes your laughter?/If she was granted beauty from above,/ She makes me, by compare, the faithful one;/If little books her beauty once inspired;/For my part I ate mice just as required;/And kept them from the sacred bounds beyond/So my great master never was distracted;/Or startled by those squeaking bold incursions;/And, although dead, I still perform my duty./ Thus runs the epitaph we love redacted/On Petrarch's cat—and do not cast aspersions./For thus we see, mouse-catching excels mere beauty'. Trans. Elizabeth Dobson.

8. On cats from the medieval period onwards as anti-pets, associated with female sexuality and marginality, and with unconventional intellectual bohemianism and individualism see Kathleen Kete, *The Beast in the Boudoir: Petkeeping in 19C Paris* (Berkeley, CA: University of California Press, 1994), pp. 123–7.

9. See Jennifer Rushworth, *Petrarch and the Literary Culture of Nineteenth-Century France: Translation, Appropriation, Transformation* (Woodbridge: The Boydell Press, 2017).

10. See Teresa Guiccioli, *Lord Byron's Life in Italy (Vie de Lord Byron en Italie)* trans. Michael Reese, ed. Peter Cochran (Newark, DE: University of Delaware Press, 2005), pp. 173–83; especially p. 175. This was Byron's third and most well-documented visit to the house; he had paid two previous visits in 1817.

11. To Lady Hesketh, 12 October 1785, *The Letters and Prose Writings of William Cowper*, 5 vols ed. James King and Charles Ryskamp (Oxford: Clarendon Press, 1981–6), II, p. 383. Henceforth referred to as *Letters* (1981).

12. To William Bull, 7 March 1783, *Letters* (1981) II, pp. 115–17; to William Unwin, 30 March 1783, *Letters* (1981) II, pp. 119–20.

13. To Lady Hesketh, 23 January 1786, *Letters* (1981) II, p. 465, and 31 January 1786, *Letters* (1981) II, p. 469.

14. To Lady Hesketh, 9 February 1787, *Letters* (1981) II, p. 477.

15. Nicola Durbridge, *Cowper's Tame Hares* (Olney: Cowper and Newton Museum, 2011), p. 14. Online access to the booklet is available at http://www.cowperandnewtonmuseum.org.uk/wp-content/uploads/2012/02/mw_tame_hares.pdf, last accessed 09/07/2017.

16. Durbridge (2011), p. 15.

17. Durbridge (2011), p. 17.

18. Cowper, 'To Mr Urban', 28 May 1784, *Letters* (1981) V, p. 40.

19. 'To Mr Urban', 28 May 1784, *Letters* (1981) V, pp. 41, 42.

20. 'To Mr Urban', 28 May 1784, *Letters* (1981) V, p. 44.

21. Keith Thomas, *Man and the Natural World: Changing Attitudes in England 1500–1800* (London: Allen Lane, 1983), p. 182, p. 240. See also Harriet Ritvo, *The Animal Estate: The English and Other Creatures in the Victorian Age* (Cambridge, MA: Harvard University Press, 1987) and Hannah Velten, *Beastly London: A History of Animals in the City* (London: Reaktion Books, 2013), p. 196. Velten deals generally with the keeping of wild animals and birds in London on pp. 192–4, 197–9.

22. Velten (2013), p. 196.

23. *The Collected Works of John Stuart Mill*, ed. John M. Robson (Toronto: University of Toronto Press, London: Routledge and Kegan Paul, 1963–91) 33 vols, I, *Autobiography and Literary Essays*, p. 21.

24. Cowper, *Letters* (1981) II, p. 117. The published version slightly reduces the claim here made of the hare as part of the extended family, rewriting 'service' as 'humour', *The Poems of William Cowper*, ed. John D. Baird and Charles Ryskamp (Oxford Clarendon Press, 1995) 3 vols. II, 19–20, lines 33–6.

25. Cowper, *Letters* (1981) II, p. 117.

26. *Poems of William Cowper* II (1995), pp. xiii–iv.

27. *Poems* (1995) III, l. 386.

28. *Poems* (1995) II, lines 351ff.

29. *Poems* (1995) II, lines 20–1.

30. William Hayley, *The Life, and Posthumous Writings of William Cowper esq…*3 vols, 2nd edn (Chichester: Printed by J Seagrave for J. Johnson, 1802) I, unpaginated.

31. Hayley (1802) I, p. 90.

32. Hayley (1802) III, pp. 425–6.

33. [J.S.S. i.e. John Storey], *The Rural Walks of Cowper; displayed in a series of views near Olney, Bucks; with descriptive sketches, and a memoir of the poet's life* (London: Sherwood, Gilbert and Piper, c. 1825), frontispiece. This frontispiece does not appear in all editions/copies of this work.

34. Conversation with house manager Amanda Molcher, September 2018.

35. Charles Dickens Museum, Nursery, January 2017.

36. Bransby Williams acted Barnaby Rudge first in 1922, and, as Barnaby is invariably accompanied by his pet raven, Grip, it is possible that this pet raven was kept by Williams in reference to his triumph in that role. Either way, the photograph held in the museum archive showing him with his pet suggests that it was part of his personal publicity.

37. Derek Ratcliffe, *The Raven: A Natural History in Britain and Ireland* (London: Poyser, 1997), p. 25; Anonymous, *The Youth's Companion*, Vol. 28 (1854), p. 199; Josephine (pseud.), *Our Children's Pets* (London: S.W. Partridge, 1865), p. 22;

'Boy with Raven by H.C.' Dutch, 1879; *Children's Friend: A Magazine for Boys and Girls at Home and School*, Vol. 36 (London: S.W. Partridge & Co, 1896), p. 26.

38. In the biography of Dickens written by his daughter Mamie, she writes of the raven and how her father remarked that 'He bit their ankles, but that was in play'. See Mamie Dickens, *My Father as I Recall Him* (London: The Roxburghe Press, 1897), p. 78.

39. *The Letters of Charles Dickens*, ed. Madeline House and Graham Storey, assoc. editor Kathleen Tillotson (Oxford: Clarendon Press, 1969) 2 Vols. II, pp. 266–7, p. 412.

40. See *Letters* (1969) II, p. 202.

41. *Letters* (1969) II, p. 231.

42. *Letters* (1969) II, p. 232n.

43. *Letters* (1969) II, pp. 266–7.

44. *Letters* (1969) II, pp. 266–7, 304.

45. *Letters* (1969) II, p. 412.

46. *Letters* (1969) II, p. 438, p. 449.

47. *Letters* (1969) II, p. 304. There is some evidence that he conflated first and third raven together for the purposes of entertaining correspondents; on his return from America in July 1842 he wrote to his new American acquaintance Charles Sumner: 'The Raven, I am sorry to say, has become a Maniac. He falls into fits periodically; throws himself wildly on his back; and plucks his own feathers up, by the roots. To hurt anybody else would have been quite in character, but to hurt himself—Insanity in its most hopeless aspect' (31 July 1842). Dickens then rehearses in short form part of the account of the death of Grip, but attributing it to this raven.

48. John Forster, *The Life of Charles Dickens*, ed. and introduction by J.W.T. Ley (London: Cecil Palmer, 1928). See pp. 164–5.

49. *Barnaby Rudge: A Tale of the Riots of 'Eighty* by Charles Dickens, incl. seventy-six illustrations by George Cattermole and Hablot K. Browne ('Phiz') and an introduction by Kathleen Tillotson (London, New York, Toronto: Oxford University Press, 1954). On 28 January 1841, Dickens wrote to his friend George Cattermole that 'my notion is to have [Barnaby] always in company with a pet raven, who is immeasurably more knowing than himself. To this end I have been studying my bird, and think I could make a very queer character of him'. *Letters*, II, p. 197.

50. *Barnaby Rudge*, p. 42.

51. *Barnaby Rudge*, pp. 51–2.

52. Of the second Dickens writes: 'after some three years he too was taken ill, and died before the kitchen fire. He kept his eye to the last upon the meat as it roasted, and suddenly turned over on his back with a sepulchral cry of "Cuckoo!" Since then I have been ravenless', *Barnaby Rudge,* pp. xxiii–iv.

53. 'Chigwell Church, surrounded by its quiet churchyard. This locality will be remembered as having afforded a resting-place to Barnaby and his mother after their visit to Mr Haredale (chapter 25). 'In the churchyard they sat down to take their frugal dinner'—Grip, the raven, being one of the party—'walking up and down when he had dined with an air of elderly complacency, which was strongly suggestive of his having his hands under his coat tails, and appearing to read the tombstones with a very critical taste", Robert Allbut, *Rambles in Dickens' Land* (New York: Truslove, Hanson & Comba, 1899) Ramble IX, p. 129. The suggested outing replicates that taken by Dickens and Forster: 'Name your day for going. Such a delicious old inn opposite the churchyard—such a lovely ride—such beautiful forest scenery—such an out of the way, rural place—such a sexton! I say again, name your day'. See also Frank Foulsham, 'In the Footsteps of Barnaby Rudge', *The Royal Magazine* (December 1900). Such literary tourism was facilitated by F.G. Kitton's extensive topographical notes to his three-volume edition of *Barnaby Rudge* (London: Methuen & Co, 1901). Bransby Williams would take his first rendition of dramatized extracts from *Barnaby Rudge* to the inn itself in 1900; a subsequent production at the Tivoli used the 'old chairs'. *Bransby Williams by Himself* (London: Hutchinson, 1954), pp. 103–4.

54. See 'Dickens' relief', *London Remembers*, http://www.londonremembers.com/memorials/charles-dickens-relief (2017), last accessed 09/07/2017.

55. John F. Dexter, *Dickens Memento, with an intro by F. Phillimore, and Hints to Dickens Collectors: Catalogue with Purchaser's Names and Prices Realised of the Pictures, Drawings, and Objects of Art of the Late Charles Dickens, sold by auction on July 9th, 1870. With introduction by Francis Phillimore, and Hints to Collectors, by John F. Dexter* (London: Field & Tuer, 1884), p. 9.

56. R.T. Jupp, *The Dickens Collection of Books, Manuscripts and Relics Formed by the late Dr R.T. Jupp of London* (London: Anderson Galleries, 1922), p. 5.

57. On Gimbel, see his obituary, *New York Times,* 28 May 1970, *New York Times*, http://www.nytimes.com/1970/05/28/archives/col-richard-gimbel-dies-at-71-flier-was-yale-library-curator-donor.html, last accessed 09/07/2017. See also Donald C. Dickinson, *Dictionary of American Book Collectors* (New York: Greenwood Press, 1986), p. 138.

58. The associative identification of Dickens' raven with that of Poe has had a long genealogy. A Mr Brigden's recollections of his visit to England in old age were recorded thus: 'When Dickens walked about his house or place he was followed by a black raven, as black and as ghostly as the one that squawked "Nevermore" in Poe's masterpiece'. Robin Sterling ed., *People and Things from the Walker County; Alabama Jasper Mountain Eagle 1910–1913* (Morrisville, NC: Lulu, 2016), p. 89.

59. Thomas Ollive Mabbott, *Collected Works of Edgar Allan Poe* (Cambridge, MA: Belknap Press of Harvard University Press, 1969) 3 vols. I, 'Poems', pp. 550–2.

60. *Grahams' Magazine*, February 1842. Quoted in Mabbott (1969), p. 355.

61. James Russell Lowell, 'A Fable for Critics' [1848], *The Poetical Works of James Russell Lowell* (London: Macmillan and Co., 1873), pp. 123–65, p. 153.

62. *Barnaby Rudge*, p. 42.

63. The nature of the raven as a carrion bird is buried but still at work here; that Dickens was not imaginatively unaware of the raven's associations with death is suggested by his short piece 'The Raven in the Happy Family', *Household Words*, Vol. 1, no. 7 (1850) on the trade of the undertaker and the expensive folly of funeral customs at the time. Bertram Waldrom Matz, ed. *Miscellaneous Papers of Charles Dickens* (London: Chapman and Hall, 1908), pp. 192–6.

64. *The Poetical Works of Edgar Allan Poe. Together with his Essays on the Poetic Principle and The Philosophy of Composition and a Critical Memoir. With illustrations…* (London: Ward, Lock & Co, 1882), p. 230.

65. Mabbott (1969) I, p. 354.

66. Mabbott (1969) I, pp. 534–5 and p. 550. For other notions of the raven's precursors see Mabbott (1969) I, p. 372, n. 48.

67. George W. Peck (*The American Review* March 1850) commented on how realistic the raven was: 'The "tapping", the appearance of the Raven, and all his doings and sayings are…perfectly in character (we were once the "unhappy master" of one of these birds)…Poe…considered what motions a bird of that species would…make, and concluded to choose the most natural, as the most fantastic' (quoted Mabbott, I, p. 355).

68. *Poetical Works*, p. 243.

69. *Poetical Works*, p. 248.

70. Philip Bruce Alexander, *History of the University of Virginia 1819–1919: The lengthened shadow of one man* (London: The Macmillan Company, 1922), pp. 357–8. See also *New York Times* (19 January 1909), Travis Robertson, The Raven Society, https://aig.alumni.virginia.edu/raven, last accessed 09/07/2017. Disconcertingly, Poe's old rooms are now described for visitors by an undead sound recording: a wonderfully Poe-ish label to a doorbell-like fixture beside their door reads 'Push Button for Narrative'.

71. Equally, the 2011 redisplay of the Poe Cottage in the Bronx New York included a raven perched on a set of shelves. Report by Kiran Alvi in *The Bronx Times* 17/10/2011, http://www.bronx.com/news/local/1799.html, last accessed 24/01/2017.

72. See J. W. Ocker, *Poe-land: The Hallowed Haunts of Edgar Allan Poe* (Woodstock, VT: The Countryman Press, 2014), chapter 4.

73. The ubiquity of the raven as a signifier mediating between authorial body and poetic imagination holds for other monuments to Poe that lie beyond the scope of this investigation. A raven appears on the stone marking Poe's original burial-place in Baltimore, in general reference both to Poe's most famous poem and to the raven as an emblem within that poem of grief at bereavement. The statue erected to Poe in Philadelphia in 1876 shows the raven perched upon his

shoulder as a version of his poetic subjectivity. The statue of a raven in flight outside Poe's house in Philadelphia describes the poem as an impending flight of otherworldly inspiration; and the statue installed on Boston Common in 2014, 'Poe Returns to Boston', shows an enormous raven flapping around the poet as he strides at ground-level and life-size towards the house in which he was born in Carver St. This raven is sized as something beyond plausibility and certainly beyond the merely lifelike or life-sized, embodying the grandeur and immortality of poetic creation.

74. Laurence Sterne, *A Sentimental Journey through France and Italy ...*, in *The Florida Edition of the Works of Laurence Sterne*, ed. Melvyn New and W.G. Day (Gainesville, Tallahassee, FL: University Press of Florida, 2002) 8 vols, VI, pp. 94–5.

75. This excursus was possibly prompted by a request in a letter of 1766 from the ex-slave Ignatius Sancho (1729–80) that Sterne write something on the subject in support of contemporary abolitionism. See Markman Ellis, *The Politics of Sensibility: Race, Gender and Commerce in the Sentimental Novel* (Cambridge: Cambridge University Press, 1996), pp. 55–79; Elizabeth Kowaleski-Wallace, *The British Slave-Trade and Public Memory* (New York: Columbia University Press, 2013), p. 168; Ignatius Sancho, *The Letters of the late Ignatius Sancho, an African* (London: J. Nichols et al., 1782) Also see the notes to the standard edition.

76. *The Florida Edition of the Works of Laurence Sterne* (2002) VI, p. 96.

77. See *The Florida Edition of the Works of Laurence Sterne* (2002) VI, pp. 332–3 on Sterne's heraldry; on the pun, see p. 324.

78. William Howitt, *Ruined Abbeys and Castles of Great Britain and Ireland*, 2nd series (London: Alfred W. Bennett, 1862, 1864), p. 155.

79. Howitt (1862, 1864), p. 157.

80. See *The Florida Edition of the Works of Laurence Sterne* (2002) VI, pp. 159, 158.

81. See *The Florida Edition of the Works of Laurence Sterne* (2002) VI, p. 100.

82. See *The Florida Edition of the Works of Laurence Sterne* (2002) VI, p. 100. As with a book, what once belonged to him now belongs to others. Sterne sets this under the sign of illegitimacy. This is the point of his joke about the question of which way the starling on his coat of arms should face: 'let the herald's officers twist his neck about if they dare' (p. 100).

83. Annie Leibovitz, *Pilgrimage* (London: Jonathan Cape, 2011), pp. 24–5.

84. Daston (2004) quoted in Poliquin (2012), p. 20.

85. See Judith Pascoe, *The Hummingbird Cabinet: A Rare and Curious History of Romantic Collectors* (Ithaca, NY and London: Cornell University Press, 2006). For a discussion of Bullock's collection of hummingbirds, conventions of display and cataloguing, and nomenclature, see pp. 28–9; on hummingbirds conceived and displayed as 'bijouterie' see p. 34. On Victorian views of hummingbirds see Poliquin (2012), p. 43, and on display practices see p. 48.

86. For discussion of Victorian texts on taxidermy see Pascoe (2006), p. 39.

87. Pascoe (2006), p. 40.

88. William Bullock, *Six Months Residence and Travels in Mexico* (1824; reprint, Port Washington, NY: Kennikat Press, 1971), pp. 267–8, cited in Pascoe (2006), p. 42.

89. Pascoe (2006), p. 33.

90. Pascoe (2006), pp. 43–4.

91. See *The Letters of Emily Dickinson* ed. Thomas H. Johnson, assoc. editor Theodora Ward (Cambridge, MA: Belknap Press of Harvard University Press, 1958) 3 vols, II, p. 639, Letter to Helen Hunt Jackson (1879); in early 1880, possibly as a New Year's greeting, to Mrs Edward Tuckerman (no. 627; III, p. 655); to T.W. Higginson in November 1880 (no. 675, III, p. 681) where she refers to it as 'A Humming-bird'; to Mabel Loomis Todd in October 1882 (no. 770, III, p. 740–1); to Thomas Niles in April 1883 (no. 814, III, p. 769). On the poem as 'calling-card' see Christopher Benfey, *A Summer of Hummingbirds: Love, Art, and Scandal in the Intersecting Worlds of Emily Dickinson, Mark Twain, Harriet Beecher Stowe & Martin Johnson Heade* (London: Penguin, 2008), pp. 208–9.

92. '…your transfusions/mere wings to me, the push of numerous/hummingbirds, souvenirs of Evanescence/seen disappearing down a route of veins/in an electric rush of cochineal'. Agha Shahid Ali, 'A Nostalgist's Map of America', *Language and Object: Emily Dickinson and Contemporary Art* ed. Susan Danly (Mead Art Museum: Amherst College in assoc with University of Massachusetts Press, 1997). Jonathan Safran Foer, 'Behold, Thoreau Sings for Owls, Dickinson Hummingbirds', *A Convergence of Birds: Original Fiction and Poetry Inspired by the Work of Joseph Cornell* (New York: Distributed Art Publishers, 2001).

93. See *The Letters of Emily Dickinson* (1958), to Charles H. Clark, mid-May 1883 (no. 825, III, p. 777).

94. *The Letters of Emily Dickinson* (1958) to Eudocia Flynt, c. July 1862, no. 270, II, p. 414.

95. *The Letters of Emily Dickinson* (1958) August 1861, no. 235, I, p. 377.

96. Benfey (2008), pp. 208–9.

97. *The Tempest*, Act 2, Scene 1, lines 213–16.

98. 'Within my Garden, rides a Bird', *The Poems of Emily Dickinson*, edited by Thomas H. Johnson (Cambridge, MA: Belknap Press of Harvard University Press, 1955) 3 vols. II, no. 500, p. 384.

99. Helen Fields, 'Museum Tourist: Charles Dickens Museum', Blogosphere (6 February 2014), http://heyhelen.com/2014/02/museum-tourist-charles-dickens-museum, last accessed 04/07/2017.

100. A passing reference to the animal is found in chapter 43 of *Bleak House*, in which Mr Skimpole describes Mr Jarndyce as a 'rough kind of fellow—a sort of human hedgehog rolled up'. Charles Dickens, *Bleak House* (London: Bradbury and Evans, 1853) 3 Vols, I, p. 475.

101. Dickens' hedgehog has no power to embody author or works, but it does still have a function within the museum. It embodies, very exceptionally, the

child-reader. Small, within the home but not fully acculturated, down in the basement, the child-visitor finds its own, semi-wild guide into the house-museum. Flickering within that hedgehog is a cultural memory of Mrs Tiggywinkle introducing Lucy to her cosy Edwardian kitchen-world. It is hardly accidental that the gift shop on occasion sells miniature hedgehogs as Christmas tree ornaments. But it is worth remarking that if that very same stuffed hedgehog had been installed in the Beatrix Potter house in the Lake District, it most certainly would have become at one and the same time 'Beatrix Potter's hedgehog' and 'Mrs Tiggywinkle'.

102. The best that the postcard of the Small Parlour, The Old Manse, Concord, MA can do is thus: 'The great horned owl dates to the time of Nathaniel Hawthorne'.

103. Poliquin (2012), pp. 203–4.

104. See http://philiplarkin.com/larkin-with-toads, last accessed 20/12/2018; https://www.bbc.co.uk/news/uk-england-humber-33833813, last accessed 20/12/2018.

105. See William Shakespeare, *A Midsummer Night's Dream* 5: 1, ll. 12–15.

CHAPTER 3

1. Visited summer 2015.

2. For remarks on portraiture and dress see Marcia Pointon, 'Accessories as Portraits and Portraits as Accessories' (2016), https://www.researchgate.net/profile/Marcia_Pointon/publication/311705617_Accessories_as_Portraits_and_Portraits_as_Accessories/links/5856990108ae8f695558a0d8/Accessories-as-Portraits-and-Portraits-as-Accessories.pdf?origin=publication_detail, last accessed 20/12/2018; for relevant theory of fashion see Roland Barthes, *The Fashion System* trans. Matthew Ward and Richard Howard (New York: Hill and Wang, 1983); for theory of cross-dressing see, for example, Marjorie Garber, *Vested Interests: Cross-Dressing and Cultural Anxiety* (New York and London: Routledge, 1992).

3. Pointon (2016), p. 57.

4. My thanks to Emese Asztalos of the Petöfi Museum, Budapest, for drawing my attention to this unusual instance and supplying me with images.

5. For a discussion of this shawl, 'reputedly embroidered by Jane Austen', and, less explicitly, the decision to include it within the project 'Jane Austen in 41 Objects', see https://www.jane-austens-house-museum.org.uk/6-muslin-shawl, last accessed 31/01/2018.

6. *The Unabridged Journals of Sylvia Plath* (2000), pp. 588–9.

7. Visited May 2015.

8. Rydal Mount was much visited informally both within and after Wordsworth's lifetime. The Wordsworth Trust has kept Dove Cottage open to the public since July 1891; Rydal Mount was acquired in 1969 by Mary Henderson, and was formally opened to the public in 1970. For an in-depth study of how the Victorians shaped Wordsworth's afterlife, see Stephen Gill, *Wordsworth and the*

Victorians (Oxford: Clarendon Press, 1998), esp. chapter 8, 'The Last Decade: From Wordsworth Society to National Trust'.

9. See Dorothy Wordsworth, *Grasmere Journals*, ed. Pamela Woof (Oxford: Clarendon Press, 1991) p. 83.

10. For a discussion of the import of Thomas Carlyle's hat, see Aileen Ribieiro, 'In Search of Carlyle's Hat', *Costume*, April 2017, Vol. 30, No. 1, pp. 85–9. The walking-stick is so powerful a metonym for the author that in Ruskin's home at Brantwood, a walking-stick whittled halfway down its length almost to breaking point was shown lying on Ruskin's bed as an artistic evocation of his nervous breakdown.

11. I am indebted to Johan Schimanski and Ulrike Spring for this information, based on their visit in c. 2017.

12. Visited spring 2016.

13. Visited autumn 2015, autumn 2017.

14. Anne-Sofie Hjemdahl ed., with contributions from Thomas Hylland Eriksen, Henry Notaker, Finn Skåderud, Marit Ingeborg Lange et al., *A Thing or Two About Ibsen: His Possessions, Dramatic Poetry, and Life* (Oslo: Andrimne, 2006), p. 143.

15. Hjemdahl (2006), p. 144.

16. Hjemdahl (2006), p. 144.

17. On this, see an as yet unpublished paper by Narve Fulsås, 'Housing World Literature: Norwegian Ibsen Museums', Reading-group, TRAUM, October 2018.

18. Louisa M. Alcott, *Little Women; or, Meg, Jo, Beth, and Amy* (London: Sampson Low, Marston, Low and Searle, 1871), 6th edn, p. 250.

19. Oliver Goldsmith, *Letters from a Citizen of the World to His Friends in the East* (Bungay: J. and R. Childs, 1820), 2 vols. II, p. 159.

20. See Emma Barker, unpublished conference paper, 'Figuring the Sibyl: pictorial models for women writers and readers', 'Jane Austen and Germaine de Staël, 1817–2017', Chawton House, July 2017.

21. Augustine Birrell, *The Collected Essays and Addresses of the Rt Hon Augustine Birrell, 1880–1920* (New York: Charles Scribner's Sons, 1923), I, p. 271.

22. Charles Dickens, *The Old Curiosity Shop* (London: Chapman and Hall, 1871), p. 207.

23. See Browning's imagined museum display of nightcaps: 'dare I doubt/Some future enterprise shall give the world/Quite as remarkable a Night-cap-show?/ Methinks we, arm-in-arm, that festal day,/Pace the long range of relics shrined aright,/Framed, glazed, each cushioned curiosity,/And so begin to smile and to inspect:/Pope's sickly head-sustainment…Voltaire's imperial velvet! Hogarth eyed/The thumb-nail record of some alley-phiz,/Then chucklingly clapped yonder cosiness/On pate …!' Robert Browning, *Red Cotton Night-cap Country: or, Turf and Towers* (London: Smith, Elder and Co., 1873), pp. 19–20.

24. G.K. Chesterton, 'The Mystery of the Pageant' reprinted in *Tremendous Trifles* (Cosimo, 2007), p. 123.

25. The practice of costuming a dummy to represent the author at home in a place is fairly rare, and nearly always risible. In Cowper's case, the effect is complicated

by the use of a cast-off female shop dummy. More plausible if slightly grotesque and merely occasional was the use of a similar dummy costumed as Jane Austen working at her writing-table sited over her grave in Winchester Cathedral for the Flower Festival of 2013 (see Chapter 4). More expensive efforts in this direction have included bespoke waxwork versions of Robert Burns in Dumfries, marked by a replica of his trademark striped silk waistcoat, and that of Virginia Woolf, commissioned by and on display at King's College, London.

26. See Garber (1992) esp. pp. 49, 249, 374.

27. Rosemary Hill, 'What does she think she looks like?' *London Review of Books*, 5 April 2018, p. 5.

28. Hill (2018), p. 7.

29. Visited 2014.

30. Last visited 2016. The case has been on public display in this form since the museum was re-opened on 5 October 2014. Email correspondence with curator Adam Daber, 29/06/2017. Items shown in this cabinet rotate for conservation reasons, but the general structure and narrative remains the same.

31. Email correspondence with curator Sarah Laycock, 21/06/2017. After all the sisters had died, their father Patrick Brontë gave away their remaining clothes to the servant Martha Brown, who altered them to fit her niece. She subsequently left them to her sisters, who eventually passed them on to the museum.

32. Elizabeth Gaskell, *A Life of Charlotte Brontë* (London: Smith Elder, 1857), 2 vols, Vol. II, p. 170.

33. Email correspondence with curator Sarah Laycock, 21/06/2017.

34. See Mrs Ellis Chadwick, *In the Footsteps of the Brontës* (London, 1914), p. 459. Also Deborah Lutz, *The Brontë Cabinet: Three Lives in Nine Objects* (New York, London: W.W. Norton and Co., 2015), p. 247. Auctions of the relevant Brontëana were held at Sotheby's 1907, 1916; see Ann Dinsdale, Sarah Laycock, and Julie Akhurst, *Brontë Relics: A Collection History* (Haworth, Yorkshire: Brontë Society Publications, 2012).

35. Dinsdale, Laycock, and Akhurst (2012), pp. 4–5.

36. Charlotte Brontë to Elizabeth Gaskell (?), early June 1854: 'Of the third—the wedding-dress—I wholly decline the responsibility. It must be charged upon a sort of friendly compulsion or over-persuasion. Nothing would satisfy some of my friends but white which I told you I would <u>not</u> wear. Accordingly they dressed me in white by way of trial—vowed away their consciences that nothing had ever suited me so well—and white I had to buy and <u>did</u> buy to my own amazement—but I took care to get it in cheap material—there were some insinuations about silk, tulle and I don't know what—but I stuck convulsively to muslin—plain book muslin with a tuck or two. Also the white veil—I took care should be a matter of 5s being simply of tulle with little tucks. If I must make a fool of myself—it shall be on an economical plan'. *Selected Letters of Charlotte Brontë*, ed. Margaret Smith (Oxford: Oxford University Press, 2010), pp. 231–2.

37. Virginia Woolf, 'Haworth, November 1904', published in *The Guardian* on 21 December 1904.

38. Email correspondence with curator Sarah Laycock, 16/06/2017.

39. Woolf (1904).

40. Tanya Gold, 'Reader, I shagged him: Why Charlotte Brontë was a filthy minx', *The Guardian*, 25 March 2005.

41. Martha Kearney, Helen Oyeyemi, and Lucy Mangan, 'Being the Brontës' (2016), http://www.bbc.co.uk/programmes/p03n0wsy/p03n0r4n, last accessed 09/07/2017.

42. http://www.katrinanaomi.co.uk/poetry, last accessed 31/01/2018.

43. Richard Moss, 'Brontë Society and National Portrait Gallery Combine for Brontë200 celebrations', *Culture 24* (January 2016), http://www.culture24.org.uk/history-and-heritage/literary-history/art543485-bronte-society-and-national-portrait-gallery-combine-for-bronte200-, last accessed 09/07/2017.

44. For a much more detailed reading of the installation 'Accessories', see 'Fabricating Uncertainty: Virginia Woolf, Serena Partridge, and the Interpretive Possibilities of Brontë Pseudo-Relics', *Journal of Victorian Culture*, forthcoming. The author and I are in broad agreement that these pseudo-relics in blurring fact and fiction at once critique ongoing cultural investment in the Brontës' personal possessions and endeavour to exploit it to suture together Charlotte Brontë's biography and fiction in new ways. The author notes that Partridge was 'inspired by Brontë's ink-stained glove in the Parsonage Museum's archives' (p. 1), as good a description of the intimacy of clothing with both body and the scene of writing as can be found. Where we differ is the degree to which we regard this exercise as subversive; for the author it has the power 'to disrupt entrenched readings of Brontë's material remains' (p. 15) whereas I would place more emphasis on the continuity of presuming that clothing can speak of the author as an ambiguous construct of biography and fiction.

45. The detail of Dickinson's death has attracted significant scholarly attention. See, for example, Norbert Hirschhorn and Polly Longsworth, '"Medicine posthumous": A new look at Emily Dickinson's medical conditions', *The New England Quarterly* (June 1996), pp. 299–316 and Jay Leyda (ed.), *The Years and Hours of Emily Dickinson* (New Haven, CT: Yale University Press, 1960).

46. See Trustees of Amherst College, 'Emily Dickinson's white dress', *Emily Dickinson Museum* (2009), https://www.emilydickinsonmuseum.org/white_dress, last accessed 09/07/2017.

47. See J.D. McClatchy and Erica Lennard, *American Writers at Home* (New York: The Vendome Press, 2004), p. 44.

48. See Trustees of Amherst College (2009), https://www.emilydickinsonmuseum.org/white_dress, last accessed 09/07/2017.

49. Visited summer 2008.

50. Brock Clarke, *An Arsonist's Guide to Writers' Homes in New England: A Novel* (London: William Heinemann, 2008).

51. Clarke (2008), p. 68.

52. Clarke (2008), p. 70.

53. Annie Leibovitz, *Pilgrimage* (London: Jonathan Cape, 2011), p. 42.

54. Penny Colman, 'A poet's pocket: Emily Dickinson's dress' (April 2013), http://pennycolman.com/a-poets-pocket-emily-dickinsons-dress, last accessed 09/07/2017.

55. Billy Collins, 'Taking Off Emily Dickinson's Clothes' in *Taking Off Emily Dickinson's Clothes* (London: Picador, Pan Macmillan, 2000).

56. Collins (2000).

57. Visited October 2018. My thanks to the Director, Fru Bente Forberg, for kindly opening the house outside the season, providing a guided tour, and patiently answering many and varied questions.

CHAPTER 4

1. Author's own collection. Photo Twinkle Fitzgerald 2/2602. See also Jamaica Inn, 'Daphne DuMaurier', http://www.jamaicainn.co.uk/daphne-du-maurier' (2014), last accessed 22/06/2017.

2. Visited c. 2005.

3. Jane Dunn, *Du Maurier and Her Sisters: The Hidden Lives of Piffy, Bird and Bing* (London: Harper Press, 2013), pp. 199–200.

4. For an important study of photojournalism in the French context, see Elizabeth Emery, *Photojournalism and the Origins of the French Writer's House Museum (1881–1914): Privacy, Publicity and Personality* (Surrey, UK: Ashgate, 2013).

5. See tourist leaflet 'Self-Guided Tour: The Mount' (n.d.) 'Edith Wharton's bedroom': 'Wharton did most of her writing here; she would awaken early and write in bed, dropping the finished pages to the floor to be collected later for typing by her secretary'. Photographic image of Wharton seated at her desk in the library at The Mount c. 1905 sold as souvenir postcard at The Mount, 2007: the caption reads: 'Although she did most of her writing in private in bed...Edith Wharton...sometimes posed at her desk to give the impression that she wrote there'. See also Susan Goodman, 'Portraits of Wharton', *Edith Wharton in Context*, ed. Laura Rattray (Cambridge: Cambridge University Press, 2012), pp. 61–73. For the state of the house in 2016 see articles and images in *Miladysboudoir* (October 2016), https://miladysboudoir.net/tag/edith-wharton, last accessed 07/01/2019.

6. Fisher's paintings of writers' rooms include: Arthur Ransome's desk, P.G. Wodehouse's study, Daphne du Maurier's desk, 'Charles Dickens' writing desk at Bleak House', Dylan Thomas' writing desk at Laugharne [the Boat House], Thomas Hardy's desk at Max Gate, Rudyard Kipling's desk at Bateman's, and Beatrix Potter's desk at Hill Top in Cumbria. http://www.franciskylegallery.com/sites/Fshr.htm, last accessed 22/06/2017.

7. See Lynne Mashhadi, 'Visiting Greenway: Agatha Christie's House', *In Plymouth* (2004–17), http://inplymouth.com/visiting-greenway-agatha-christies-house, last accessed 26/06/2017. For depictions of the writer's desk in film that depend on these conventions, see Judith Buchanan ed., *The Writer on Film: Screening Literary Authorship* (Basingstoke: Palgrave Macmillan, 2013), esp. Megan Murray-Pepper, 'The "Tables of Memory": Shakespeare, Cinema and the Writing-Desk',

pp. 92–105. For an example of the worldwide convention of the writer's desk, see *inter alia* the display of the desk and writing-tools of Kawatake Mokuami (1816–93), reputed the greatest of Kabuki play writers, on display at the National Theatre of Japan, Tokyo. I am indebted to Michael Dobson for this information and accompanying image, sourced November 2018.

8. Alison Booth, *Homes and Haunts: Touring Writers' Shrines and Countries* (Oxford: Oxford University Press, 2016), p. 57.

9. BBC Radio 4 interview with A.L. Kennedy, 'Rachel Johnson meets A.L. Kennedy', broadcast Monday 24 April 2017, 1.45pm.

10. Marcel Proust's brass bed is displayed as part of an installation in the Musée Carnavalet in Paris. Entitled 'Marcel's Proust's bedroom', it is a fiction composed from furniture taken from the three Parisian apartments in which he lived after the death of his parents.

11. For a depiction of Goethe dictating while standing, see Johann Joseph Schmeler (1794–1841), 'Goethe seinem Schreiber John diktierend' (1831). For a depiction of Wordsworth working with his wife Mary as amanuensis see Margaret Gillies, 'William and Mary Wordsworth' (1839), currently displayed in the upstairs sitting-room of Dove Cottage.

12. Dean MacCannell, *The Tourist: A New Theory of the Leisure Class* (London: Macmillan, 1976), pp. 43–5.

13. William Beckford, *Dreams, Waking Thoughts and Incidents; In a series of letters from various parts of Europe* (London: J. Johnson and P. Elmsley, 1783), p. 129.

14. *The Works of the Right Honourable Lord Byron* (London: John Murray, 1819), 8 vols., VII, p. 207.

15. I should like to thank Paul Taylor of the Shakespeare Birthplace Trust collections for much help in tracking these chairs through the archive in 2014.

16. It is sometimes suggested that this chair might be it but this is thought by the Shakespeare Birthplace Trust to be very unlikely. See Shakespeare Birthplace Trust, 'David Garrick's Chair', *Shakespeare Birthplace Trust Archive*, Ref. No. STRST1868-31392 (1769), http://collections.shakespeare.org.uk/search/museum/strst-sbt-1868-3392-david-garricks-chair/search/everywhere:david-garrick/page/1/view_as/grid, last accessed 09/07/2017.

17. Horace Walpole, *Anecdotes of Painting in England…*(London: for J. Dodsley, 1782), 4 vols, IV, p. 180. John Nichols and George Steevens add in 1810 that the chair was still in the Pavilion at Hampton and provide an illustration derived from Samuel Ireland's *Graphic Illustrations*. See *The Genuine Works of William Hogarth: Illustrated with Biographical Anecdotes* (London: Longman, Hurst, Rees and Orme, 1810), 2 vols, II, p. 285. This chair is presently on display as part of the collections in the Folger Library, Washington. Mrs Delany records seeing a number of other Shakespeare relics in the Temple in 1770, presumably displayed alongside this chair. See Mary Granville, *The Autobiography and Correspondence of Mary Granville, Mrs Delany: with interesting reminiscences of King George the Third and Queen Charlotte* (London: Bentley, 1861), 3 vols, I, p. 284. On the 'Temple', see also Alan Kendall, *David Garrick* (London: Harrap, 1985), pp. 130–42.

18. On this, and the accompanying letter, see Julia Thomas, *Shakespeare's Shrine: The Bard's Birthplace and the Invention of Stratford-upon-Avon* (Philadelphia, PA: University of Pennsylvania Press, 2012), p. 69.

19. Nicholas Fogg, *Stratford-upon-Avon: The Biography* (Stroud: Amberley, 2014), p. 104.

20. Mary Hornby was a tenant of the Hart Family until 1806, when the Harts sold the property to the Courts. In 1820 Mary Hornby was deliberately forced out by rent rises, and removed the Shakespeare relics she had previously shown to a property across the street. The result was a notorious rivalry between the two attractions of the Birthplace on the one hand and the relics on the other.

21. See Samuel Ireland, *Picturesque Views on the Upper or Warwickshire Avon* (London: R. Faulder and T. Egerton, 1795), p. 207. For a lively account of the acquisition of this chair by the Shakespeare Birthplace Trust in 2010, together with an account of Ireland's correspondence surrounding his acquisition of the chair, speculation as to whether William Henry Ireland forged the initials to fool his father Samuel, and further images, see https://www.shakespeare.org.uk/explore-shakespeare/blogs/shakespeares-courting-chair, last accessed 07/01/2019.

22. Shakespeare Birthplace Trust, 'Falcon Chair', *Shakespeare Birthplace Trust Archive*, Ref. STRST186831392 (1630), http://collections.shakespeare.org.uk/search/museum/strst-sbt-1865-5-the-falcon-inn-chair/page/1, last accessed 26/06/2017.

23. See Ireland (1795), frontispiece. The only material example of 'Shakespeare's desk' is the school-desk now located in Shakespeare's School Room, which was opened to the public in April 2013. http://www.shakespearesschoolroom.org/shakespeares-schoolroom, last accessed 30/06/2017.

24. Originals now held in the Royal Shakespeare Company collection; date uncertain but pre-1900. The work was originally commissioned by William Ryland to accompany a lecture on Shakespeare's life. Ryland bequeathed the works to the Shakespeare Memorial Theatre in 1901.

25. See Thomas (2012), chapter 3, 'Bringing down the House: Restoring the Birthplace', pp. 60–91.

26. Compare Scott's possession of a small writing-desk made from pieces of wood from the ships of the Spanish Armada and the 'Wallace chair', made from wood taken from the house of Robroyston, the scene of Wallace's betrayal, and presented to Scott by his friend and correspondent Joseph Train. See also the armchair made for Longfellow out of the wood of 'the spreading chestnut tree' that he had celebrated in his poem 'The Village Blacksmith'. 'The chair has been ebonized, and is carved with forms of horse-chestnut leaves and with lines from the poem inscribed around the base' presented by the children of Cambridge in 1879 to commemorate his seventy-second birthday. See Henry Wadsworth Longfellow Dana, *The Longfellow House: History and Guide* [1948] Eastern National Park and Monument Organisation, 2003), p. 8, first published *Old-time New England* (April 1948).

27. John Ferrar, *A Tour from Dublin to London in 1795: through the Isle of Anglesea, Bangor, Conway … and Kensington* (Dublin, 1796), p. 38.

28. Washington Irving, *'Stratford-upon-Avon', from 'The Sketchbook' of Washington Irving, with Notes and Original Illustrations*, eds. Richard Savage and William Salt Brassington (Stratford-upon-Avon: Shakespeare Quiney Press, 1920), pp. 34–5. Originally published as part of *The Sketchbook of Geoffrey Crayon* (1820).

29. Simon Goldhill, *Freud's Couch, Scott's Buttocks, Brontë's Grave* (Chicago, IL: University of Chicago Press, 2011); Sir Samuel Luke Fildes, 'The Empty Chair' (1870), see http://www.victorianweb.org/painting/fildes/drawings/7.html, last accessed 07/01/2019.

30. The website for the museum at 48 Doughty Street provides a key to identifying the characters in the painting. See Allan Clack, https://cdn.shopify.com/s/files/1/0925/3888/files/Dickenss-Dream-Key1.pdf?11895023243879211879, last accessed 09/07/2017.

31. The image was produced by Penguin publishers, and was initially used as the front cover to Michael Rosen's 2012 work, *Fantastic Mr Dahl*. The photograph of Roald Dahl that forms the basis of the image was taken by Michael Dyer.

32. Indeed, to represent something as a writer's chair, it is not necessary for it to be a chair at all: William Wordsworth's 'chair' in the grounds of Lancrigg House in Easedale, where he once recited the lines he was composing to his sister Dorothy, is a large stone. Celebrated by the Victorians, if neglected now, it still bears an inscription in Latin which roughly translated reads: 'On this perch/ Dorothy Wordsworth sat/while her brother,/walking about nearby,/declaimed poetry'. Again, walk up along the path out of the village of Haworth towards Top Withens, and by a little stream crossed by a stone bridge you will come across the stone on which it is sometimes said that Charlotte Brontë sat while writing *Jane Eyre* and sometimes that this is where Emily Brontë 'rested…to gather her thoughts and to gain inspiration' (walking brochure). It is marked on the map as 'Brontë's chair'. Brontë Country, 'Brontë Chair', Eagle Intermedia Publishing (1997–2015). http://www.bronte-country.com/bronte-chair.html, last accessed 07/01/2019.

33. Washington Irving, *'Stratford-upon-Avon', from 'The Sketchbook' of Washington Irving, with Notes and Original Illustrations*, eds. Richard Savage and William Salt Brassington (Stratford-upon-Avon: Shakespeare Quiney Press, 1920), p. 25.

34. See Sylvia Morris, 'Early American Visitors to Stratford-upon-Avon', The Shakespeare Blog (April 2014), http://theshakespeareblog.com/2014/08/shakespeare-and-americans-early-visitors-to-stratford, last accessed 26/06/2017.

35. According to William Hayley, in July 1783 Lady Austen said to Cowper, 'O…you can never be in want of a subject:—you can write upon this Sofa!' William Hayley, *The Life and Posthumous Writings of William Cowper, Esqr.* (Chichester: Seagrave, 1803–4), 3 vols, I, p. 135.

36. Madelaine Smith, 'Jane Austen's Writing Table', *Jane Austen in 41 Objects* (2014), https://www.jane-austens-house-museum.org.uk/1-jane-austens-writing-table, last accessed 04/07/2017.

37. See James Edward Austen-Leigh, *A Memoir of Jane Austen* (London: Richard Bentley, 1870), pp. 43–5.

38. T.E. Kebbel, 'Jane Austen at Home', *Fortnightly Review*, 4 (Feb. 1885), pp. 262–70, p. 265. For a detailed reading of Kebbel's article, see Felicity James, 'At Home with Jane: Placing Austen in Contemporary Culture', in Gillian Dow and Clare Hanson eds., *Uses of Austen: Jane's Afterlives* (Basingstoke: Palgrave Macmillan, 2012), pp. 132–53, pp. 135–6.

39. Kebbel (1885), p. 266.

40. Cindy Jones, 'I Met Jane Austen's Writing Table', *First Draft* (August 2010), cindysjones.wordpress.com/2010/08/24/i-met-jane-austens-writing-table, last accessed 09/07/2017.

41. Claire Tomalin, *The Guardian*, Saturday 12 July 2008, 'Writer's Rooms: Jane Austen'.

42. Freydis Jane Welland, 'The History of Jane Austen's Writing-Desk', *Persuasions*, 30 (2008), pp. 125–8.

43. Elsa A. Solender, 'News, Views & Titbits', Antique Boxes at the Sign of the *Hygra*, http://www.hygra.com/uk/wb2/WB469/Jane%20Austens%20Writing%20Box.htm, republished from http://www.jasa.net.au/newsdc99.htm, last accessed 09/07/2017.

44. See, for instance, Burns' 'travelling writing companion' which holstered quills, a knife, and an inkbottle, written up by the guidebook to the Robert Burns Birthplace Museum as evidence of his persistence: 'It is hard to imagine today, looking at the hundreds of elegantly written manuscripts and letters produced by Burns, that most of his writing would have been done, after a hard day's work or travel, using rudimentary quill pens, by the dim light of a candle or a primitive oil lamp'. Nat Edwards, *Burns National Heritage Park* (Ayr: Jarrold Publishing, 2003), p. 5. Hans Christian Andersen's miniature writing-set is presently displayed at Odense as evidence of his lifelong love of travel. William Cowper's portable writing box or slope, dating from c. 1790, achieves more importance through having appeared in the portrait of Cowper by Lemuel Frances Abbott in 1792, now owned by the National Portrait Gallery, although a copy hangs in the hall of the Cowper and Newton Museum. In his right hand resting on his knee he holds a quill (to the peril, one would think, of his yellow silk breeches); his left rests on a large book, itself supported on the writing-slope. For further details and a full description of the writing-desk, see Nicola Durbridge, *Cowper's Writing Slope: A Material World* (for Cowper-Newton Museum, 2012).

45. Lynne Cunliffe, 'The Hidden Charlotte Brontë', *The Hathaways of Haworth* (April 2013), https://hathawaysofhaworth.wordpress.com/2013/04/14/the-hidden-charlotte-bronte, last accessed 09/07/2017. See also Durbridge on Cowper's figuration in c. 1779 of his own secretiveness about his writing as a 'mahogany box' (2012), p. 6.

46. Again, for gifts to Cowper of writing-desks, see Durbridge (2012).

47. For a listing of what might be held in such desks see the catalogue entry for Emily's: 'Emily Brontë's fold-up writing desk and contents; desk is rose-wood inlaid with mother-of-pearl round the key-hole in a simple design and has a purple velvet lining; pen compartment; two ink bottle compartments; incomplete;

fair condition; 453mm l x 303mm [desk laid open] desk contents: three pieces white/cream sealing wax, metal writing pen with broken handle, small piece pink/white card, metal pen handle, metal pen nib with embossed letter T, green sealing wax, cracked, fragment dirty woven material, triangular fragment white/cream plaster, piece of cream waxed paper, piece folded black paper, faded, white/blue round box containing blue, green and yellow circular and rectangular wafers, card-box contains lumps of sealing wax; quill pen nib, multi-colour card box containing 4 sealing wax circles and a sticker; metal seal with criss-cross pattern & ivory handle, two red wax seals on cream paper, metal pen nib, piece red sealing wax, newspaper review *Wuthering Heights*, newspaper review *Wuthering Heights* from Britannia, card box contains wax circles, puzzle wafers, sealing wax, two small pieces crochet lace'. See Blackriverrosi (pseud.), 'Emily in Her Belongings', *Brontë Family Blog*, http://brontefamilyblog.blogspot.co.uk/2010/03/emily-seen-in-her-belongings.html, last accessed 09/07/2017.

48. 'The desk on which Charlotte Brontë wrote her classic novels will go on display at her former home in West Yorkshire, having been hidden for over a century. The desk is to be shown at the Brontë Parsonage in Haworth after being given to the museum by an anonymous donor. Charlotte Brontë, author of Jane Eyre, wrote at the desk in the now world-famous parsonage in the 19th Century. The mahogany desk has been held in private collections for over 100 years. It was once part of a collection owned by William Law, an avid collector of rare Brontë-related material. After Mr Law's death in 1901 the collection passed to his nephew, Sir Alfred Law. Sir Alfred died in 1939 and the whereabouts of his collection of Bronte rarities has remained a mystery ever since...However, a number of items from the Law collection did go up for auction in December 2009, including Charlotte Brontë's desk which was bought anonymously for £20,000. Other items from the Law collection which have been donated to the Brontë Parsonage Museum include a pen holder, sugar tongs and copies of Brontë books. Museum director Andrew McCarthy said it was "always exciting" when new Brontë items came to light. "But a donation on this scale, with an item as significant as the writing desk used by Charlotte Brontë, is very rare", he said. "We are delighted that these items are now where they belong, here in Haworth, where they can be enjoyed by generations of visitors to the museum"'. 'Charlotte Brontë's Desk Will Go on Show at the Parsonage Museum from Tuesday 31 May', BBC News, May 2011, http://www.bbc.co.uk/news/uk-england-leeds-13524136, last accessed 26/06/2017.

49. Claire Tomalin, *The Guardian*, Saturday 12 July 2008, 'Writer's Rooms: Jane Austen'.

50. Visited with the members of Project TRAUM in September 2017.

51. See Michael McCluskey, 'Afterlives of Dickens Objects' (May 2012), http://www.autopsiesgroup.com/dickenss-desks.html, last accessed 22/06/2017.

52. Luke Fildes' sense of the importance of the desk, exemplified in his 'portrait' of it, was ratified in Georgina Dickens' gift to him of some of the furnishings of the desk—a memorandum slate, a quill pen, and a piece of Dickens' favourite

blue paper—by way of memento. Jane R. Cohen, *Charles Dickens and His Original Illustrators* (Columbus, OH: Ohio State University Press, 1980), p. 226. The power of the idea of the writer's desk has continued to drive the subsequent history and value of this desk. In 2012, it was displayed in Gad's Hill as part of the Cultural Olympiad; and in 2015 it was 'saved for the nation' through a grant of upwards of £780,000 from the National Heritage Memorial and is now on display at 48 Doughty St, London. See *The Telegraph*, 29 March 2015.

53. For Charlotte Brontë's desk displayed at New York Public Library see Elissa Lerner, 'What's on View at the New York Public Library Centennial Exhibit?' (May 2011), http://www.newyorker.com/books/page-turner/whats-on-view-at-the-n-y-p-l-s-centennial-exhibit-slide-show, last accessed 09/07/2017.

54. For Edgeworth's possession of Petrarch's inkwell, see William Hone ed., *The Everyday Book and Table-book*, 3 vols, vol. III (London: for Thomas Tegg, 1827), frontispiece and opening article. Henry Wadsworth Longfellow Dana, *The Longfellow House: History and Guide* [1948] (2003), p. 7.

55. My thanks to Anita Israel of the Longfellow National Historic Site for opening the house to me on a summer day of 2008 when it was not open for tours, and to her and Jim Shea for patiently answering all sorts of questions.

56. The Houghton holds in addition her spinet, chair, cabinet, and the chest of drawers which held her poetry, only discovered after her death. My thanks to Lesley Morris for arranging that I might see them, and discussing with me the amassing, acquisition, and display of collections pertaining to Johnson, Keats, Amy Lowell, and Dickinson.

57. 38 rue Hauteville, St Peter Port, Guernsey. Hugo lived here between the years 1856 and 1870.

58. 6 Place des Vosges, Paris 75004. Hugo lived here between the years 1832 and 1848.

59. See 'Victor Hugo At Home', *Every Saturday: A Journal of Choice Reading*, 7:162 (Boston, MA: Ticknor and Fields, 1869), 6 February 1869, p. 165.

60. For an authoritative account of this table, see Jean-Marc Hovasse, 'La Table aux Quatre Encriers', http://euromanticism.org.

61. http://www.birmingham.ac.uk/schools/edacs/departments/shakespeare/about/mason-croft-history.aspx, last accessed 03/07/2017.

62. The 1972 reconstruction conducted by Dr Göran Söderström was produced after an inventory made not long after Strindberg's death in 1912 which included a meticulous sketch of the desk. The museum opened to the public in 1973. Email correspondence with senior curator, Camilla Larrsson, 29/06/2017. I am also indebted to the previous curator, Stefan Blomberg, for discussing the history of the display with me in October 2018.

63. 'Other items on the table will include a manuscript of Anne's long poem Self-Communion and one of the imaginary histories the four children produced together which features a map by Branwell—as well as the handwritten manuscript of Charlotte's Jane Eyre, open to show Rochester's proposal. Each night after their father retired to bed, the sisters would walk around the table and discuss their writing. After the early deaths of her brother and sisters, Charlotte

was unable to break the habit and sadly continued the nightly routine on her own. The table is in private ownership; it was purchased at the sale of the household effects of the parsonage after the death of Reverend Brontë in 1861 and was sold soon afterwards to the family in whose possession it has since remained. It has only once been seen outside the family when it was lent to the Brontë museum at Haworth for a short period. It has been lent anonymously to the British Library for the purposes of this special Millennium exhibition. Chris Fletcher, curator of Chapter & Verse, who arranged the loan of the table, said, "This table played an important and moving part in the extraordinary imaginative world of the Brontës. It clearly became a focus for their creative efforts, whether individual or collaborative. To be able to reunite the manuscripts with the table upon which they were created—and which seemed to play such an essential part in their creation—is a remarkable and powerful thing." The table will be one of the three hundred or so exhibits that form Chapter & Verse in the Pearson Gallery at the British Library, which opens on March 10'. Chris Fletcher, 'Charlotte Brontë's writing desk' (2010), http://www.bl.uk/onlinegallery/features/chpverse/news.html, last accessed 10/01/2015.

64. Blackriverrosi (pseud.), 'Emily Seen in Her Belongings', *Brontë Family Blog*, http://brontefamilyblog.blogspot.co.uk/2010/03/emily-seen-in-her-belongings.html, last accessed 09/07/2017.

65. In using the term 'trace' I do not mean to invoke Jacques Derrida's construction of the notion as that which is contained within the sign as its non-meaning; nor, in adopting the idea of writing and reading surface, do I much want to evoke Stephen Best and Sharon Marcus' influential discussion of the possibilities of 'surface reading'. The writer's house museum is embarrassingly unavailable to avant-garde criticism and theorization in this respect: the trace scored upon the material surface is used to point precisely to what it is not—to its native spectrality, the invisible, immaterial, and absent author-text—and upon this hangs the entire affective experience. See Jacques Derrida, *Writing and Difference* [1967], trans. Alan Bass (Chicago, IL: University of Chicago Press, 1978) and Stephen Best and Sharon Marcus, 'Surface Reading: An Introduction', *Representations*, 108:1 (Fall 2009), pp. 1–21.

66. Annie Leibovitz, *Pilgrimage* (London: Jonathan Cape, 2011).

67. Rudyard Kipling, *Something of Myself, for my friends known and unknown* (London: Macmillan and Co. Limited, 1937), pp. 229–31.

68. Laura Knight, 'Mystery Guest. We Send a Writer Under the Covers…This Week the Balmoral Hotel, Princes Street, Edinburgh', *The Times* (cutting) n.d. c. 2007.

69. Pottermore, 'It's Been 10 Years Since J.K. Rowling Finished Writing Deathly Hallows', *Pottermore News* (January 2017), https://www.pottermore.com/news/10-years-since-jk-rowling-finished-writing-deathly-hallows, last accessed 10/06/2017.

70. 47 rue Raynouard, Paris 75016. Visited in 2013. Originally a 'summerhouse' in the grounds of the old Passy village, the Maison de Balzac is where Balzac

produced between 1840 and 1847 much of his novel cycle, the *Comédie Humaine,* financed by the patronage of Madame Laure de Berny. Balzac's huge labour of novelistic creation is dramatized within the Maison de Balzac through the display, with his chair and desk as centrepiece, of his extraordinarily extensive corrections to his first proofs, which show sheet after sheet of print elaborately amended and extended by lengthy handwritten notation in the margins. For further details, http://www.literarytraveler.com/articles/honore-de-balzac-paris, last accessed 30/06/2017.

71. Antique postcard c. 1904, author's own collection.

72. Pane from the Cross Keys Inn in Falkirk displayed in the Burns Birthplace Museum. Tumbler displayed in Abbotsford collection.

73. 'Self Portrait in Masks—János Arany (1817–1882) Memorial Exhibition', Petőfi Irodalmi Múzeum, Budapest, 15 May 2017 to 2 June 2018. For my account of this exhibition I am indebted to Emese Asztalos' unpublished paper given at the TRAUM conference, Sogndal, September 2018.

CHAPTER 5

1. T.E. Carpenter, correspondence, unpaginated, Chawton Cottage archive. Consulted 2006.

2. See Constance Hill, *Jane Austen: Her Homes and Her Friends* (London: J. Lane, 1902). For more detailed discussions of the history of imagining Chawton Cottage before and after it became a museum to Austen see Nicola J. Watson, 'Austen Exhibited', *Kafkas Gabel: Überlegungen zum Ausstellen von Literatur* ed. Katerina Kroucheva and Barbara Schaff (Bielefeld: transcript Verlag), pp. 227–50; also Felicity James, 'At Home with Jane: Placing Austen in Contemporary Culture', *Uses of Austen: Jane's Afterlives*, ed. Gillian Dow and Clare Hanson (Basingstoke: Palgrave Macmillan, 2012), pp. 132–53.

3. Much scholarly effort has been expended on discussing the idea of 'authenticity' around the tourist experience; see, for example, Britta Tim Knudsen and Anne Marit Waade eds., *Re-Investing Authenticity: Tourism, Place and Emotions* (Bristol: Channel View, 2010) and Charles Taylor, *The Ethics of Authenticity* (London: Harvard University Press, 1992).

4. Casa Ariosto, Ferrara. Visited September 2018.

5. Julian Barnes, *Flaubert's Parrot* (London: Jonathan Cape, 1984), p. 12.

6. *Hans Christian Andersen's Odense Museum guidebook*, 2017, n.p.

7. Online exhibit: 'A Monument More Durable Than Brass: The Donald and Mary Hyde Collection of Samuel Johnson', 2009, Houghton Library, Harvard University. Bequest of Mary, Viscountess Eccles 1912–2003. Exhibition catalogue (Boston, MA: Harvard University Press, 2010).

8. 6 December 1784. Houghton Library, Harvard University. MS Hyde 50 (17). Online image (2003) JM-63.

9. For more detail on the autopsy, see Helen Deutsch, *Loving Dr Johnson* (Chicago, IL and London: University of Chicago Press, 2005). Deutsch's development of

the theoretical work of Joel Fineman and Jane Gallop in her characterization of anecdote as an 'eternally present-tense … extra-textual, and semi-corporeal supplement' (pp. 23–4) suggested and informs my reading of literary relics as the materialization of anecdote.

10. 'My wife had Tea ready for him, which it is well known he delighted to drink at all hours, particularly when sitting up late … He showed much complacency upon finding that the mistress of the house was so attentive to his singular habit; and as no man could be more polite when he chose to be so, his address to her was most courteous and engaging, and his conversation soon charmed her into a forgetfulness of his external appearance'. Frederick A. Pottle and Charles H. Bennett eds., *Boswell's Journal of A Tour to the Hebrides with Samuel Johnson LL.D,* (New York: The Viking Press; London: William Heinemann, Ltd, 1936), p. 12.

11. Ann Rigney, 'Portable Monuments: Literature, Cultural Memory, and the Case of Jeanie Deans', *Poetics Today*, 25:2 (Summer 2004), pp. 361–96.

12. Quoted in Deutsch (2005), p. 19.

13. Deutsch (2005), p. 20.

14. The word 'caption' itself in this sense is of very recent origin, appearing in the 1920s in relation to the titling of silent films, which seems appropriate enough. The second instance the OED lists as appearing in 1924 picks up on two important qualities of the caption, viz. that it is always added as an afterthought, and that it is never fully expressive: 'It is true that the expression on a film actor's face may occasionally suggest that he, or she, is saying something worth hearing, but the audience cannot supply it from their imaginations; neither can the caption writer'. Caption specifically provides 'voice' to the silently vocal actors.

15. James Boswell, *Life of Johnson, Together with Boswell's Journal of a Tour of the Hebrides and Johnson's Diary of a Journey into North Wales*, ed. George Birkbeck Hill, rev. L.F. Powell, 6 vols (Oxford: Clarendon Press, 1934–50), vol. I, pp. 520–1. The teapot was manufactured at around the same time that Johnson was resident in Gough Square (July 1749 to March 1759).

16. This wording derives from a remark made in the memoir entitled *The Life of Samuel Johnson* (1787) authored by the very John Hawkins who sold off the coffee-pot about Johnson's relationship with the Thrales and his personal habits while visiting their country house, Streatham Park: 'That this celebrated friendship subsisted so long as it did, was a subject of wonder to most of Johnson's intimates, for such were his habits of living, that he was by no means a desirable inmate. His unmanly thirst for tea made him very troublesome. At Streatham, he would suffer the mistress of the house to sit up and make it for him, till two or three hours after midnight'. Johnson's 'unmanly thirst for tea' was certainly regarded by others, as we have seen in Boswell's own account, as singular, and it was by his own account prodigious: he confessed to being 'a hardened and shameless tea-drinker, who has, for twenty years, diluted his meals with only the infusion of this fascinating plant … who with tea amuses the evening, with tea solaces the midnight, and, with tea, welcomes the morning'; elsewhere he wrote that he had been 'known to drink up to fourteen cups at one sitting', and

there are other corroborative anecdotes. Hawkins further remarked severely that 'he was a lover of tea to an excess hardly credible…by his impatience to be served, his incessant calls for those ingredients which make that liquor palatable, and the haste with which he swallowed it down, he seldom failed to make that a fatigue to everyone else, which was intended as a general refreshment'. See O.M. Brack ed., *The Life of Samuel Johnson, LL.D by Sir John Hawkins* (Athens, GA and London: University of Georgia Press, 2009), pp. 214, 338; James Boswell, *Life of Johnson, Together with Boswell's Journal of a Tour of the Hebrides and Johnson's Diary of a Journey into North Wales,* ed. George Birkbeck Hill, rev. L.F. Powell, 6 vols (Oxford: Clarendon Press, 1934–50), vol. I, pp. 103, 313; vol. III, p. 264.

17. 'A mug, tea towel, fridge magnet and a free set of postcards featuring the great man's thoughts on the matter as well as the Dr Johnson's House publication', 'Tea and Coffee in the Age of Dr Johnson', http://www.drjohnsonshouse.org/gifts/html, last accessed 22/03/2016. The tea towel quotes remarks on tea by Boswell, Northcote, and Johnson.

18. This violates the dramatic unities of time, as the *Guardian* reviewer of *A Dish of Tea with Dr Johnson* complained: 'most disruptive of the device … is the fact that this is no one particular evening at which we are all companionably drinking tea'. *The Guardian*, 10 September 2011. http://www.theguardian.com/stage/2011/sep/11/dr-johnson-boswell-arts-theatre, last accessed 23/03/2016.

19. The house into which the Gaskells moved in spring 1850, 84 Plymouth Grove, came into ownership by Manchester University in 1968 when it was first displayed as 'The Gaskell House/Home of the Writer Elizabeth Gaskell and her Family'. In 2004 it was acquired by the Manchester Historic Buildings Trust with a view to 'helping to re-create a middle-class house of 1857' and has been open to the public in the form now extant since October 2014. https://www.elizabethgaskellhouse.co.uk/house, last accessed 09/07/2017.

20. *The Poems of Samuel Taylor Coleridge* ed. Ernest Hartley Coleridge (London, Oxford: Oxford University Press, 1935), pp. 240–2, lines 13–15.

21. Cf. Roland Barthes, 'The Reality Effect' (1968) in *The Rustle of Language*, trans. Richard Howard (Berkeley, CA: University of California Press, 1989).

22. See Watson, 'Rambles in Literary London' in Watson ed., *Literary Tourism and Nineteenth-Century Culture* (Basingstoke: Palgrave Macmillan, 2009), pp. 139–49, esp. 141–4.

23. See Oliver St John Gogarty, *It Isn't This Time of Year at All: An Unpremeditated Autobiography* (Garden City, NY: Doubleday, 1954), p. 25. See also Richard Ellmann, *Ulysses on the Liffey* (New York: Oxford University Press, 1972), pp. xiv–xv.

24. It provides a still-recognizable description of the view from the rooftop: 'Stephen stood up and went over to the parapet. Leaning on it he looked down on the water and on the mailboat clearing the harbourmouth of Kingstown. He mounted to the parapet again and gazed out over Dublin bay, his fair oakpale hair stirring slightly.—God! he said quietly. Isn't the sea what Algy calls it: a great sweet mother? The snotgreen sea. The scrotumtightening sea. EPI OINOPA

PONTON. Ah, Dedalus, the Greeks! I must teach you. You must read them in the original. THALATTA! THALATTA! She is our great sweet mother. Come and look'. James Joyce, *Ulysses* (Paris: Sylvia Beach, 1922), p. 5.

25. Joyce, *Ulysses* (1922), p. 11.

26. Joyce, *Ulysses* (1922), p. 4.

27. Joyce, *Ulysses* (1922), p. 12.

28. Accession numbers JJM 79/53; JJM 82/62; JJM 00/268; JJM 90/112; and JJM 82/57.

29. Exhibition leaflet, acquired May 2018.

30. This may be exemplified by the huge Dutch-style tiled stove blanked out in white because it appears within the novel personified thus:

'How many years before their mother's death, at No. 13 St Alexei's Hill, had little Yelena, the elder son Alexei and tiny Nikolka been warmed and nurtured by the tiled stove in the dining-room! How often had they sat by its glowing tiles, reading "The Shipwright of Saardam", with the clock playing its gavotte! At the end of every December the air had been filled with the scent of pine-needles... The black clock on the dining room wall had chimed in response to the gavotte played by the bronze clock standing in their mother's bedroom—now Elena's... These clocks had become so familiar that if, by some strange chance, they had vanished from the walls, everybody would have been affected as much as if a familiar voice had died, creating a gap that nothing could fill. But clocks, fortunately, live for ever, just as...like some wide, ancient rock, the tiled Dutch stove continued, even in the most difficult times, to radiate warmth and life'. Mikhail Bulgakov, *The White Guard*, trans. Roger Cockrell (Richmond, VA: Alma Classics, 2016), p. 8.

31. https://discover-ukraine.info/places/kyiv/kyiv/875, last accessed 17/10/2018.

32. Hans Christian Andersen, *The Fairytale of My Life*, trans. with an introduction by Naomi Lewis (Lanham, MD: Cooper Square Press, 2000).

33. The inscription by Ariosto reads: 'Sis lautus licet et beatus hospes/Et quicovid cupis affluens referto/Cornucopia subministret ultro/Ne suspende humilem casa brevemove/Mensam nauribus hanc tamen recursis:/Sic ne, bauci, tuam, tuam, molorche,/Tua move, Icare, pauperem tabernam/Et viles modica cibos patella/Sprevit Juppiter, Hercules, Lyaeus'. For an early nineteenth-century account of viewing the house and garden which dwells on various earlier inscriptions, see M. Valéry, *Historical, Literary and Artistical Travels in Italy*, 2nd edn. trans. C.E. Clifton (Paris: Baudry's European Library, 1839), pp. 229–30.

34. Casa Magni, Lerici, visited February 2011.

35. Important use of dummies of the author is made in the Cowper and Newton Museum at Olney, the Charles Kingsley Museum in Clovelly (visited 2016), and in the rooms dedicated to Casanova in Duchcov Castle, Czechoslovakia.

36. Visited 2008. The Mark Twain Boyhood Home and Museum comprises a number of attractions including an interpretive centre, the Huckleberry Finn House, the Mark Twain Boyhood Home, the Boyhood Home Gift Shop, the Becky Thatcher House, the J.M. Clemens Justice of the Peace Office, Grant's Drug Store, and a Museum Gallery; other Twain-related offerings

include an excursion on the Mark Twain Riverboat (my thanks to the captain for pressing me to take the wheel), the Mark Twain Cave, and a continuous promenade performance by local children of scenes from *The Adventures of Tom Sawyer* along the restored Main Street. My focus here is on the display of the Boyhood Home proper. My thanks go to the proprietors of the Painted Lady guest-house for their hospitality. Although this section was written before I came across the account of the redisplay of the boyhood home in 2005 as 'haunted' provided by Hilary Iris Lowe, it is congruent with the curatorial thinking there described. See Lowe, *Mark Twain's Homes and Literary Tourism* (Columbia, MO and London: University of Missouri Press, 2012), pp. 90–7.

37. Visited August 2007.

38. To William Dean Howells, 22 August 1887; 'Old Times on the Mississippi' (1874–5), repr. within *Life on the Mississippi*, chapter IV (1883); *Life on the Mississippi*, chapter LIII (1883).

39. Mark Twain, *The Adventures of Tom Sawyer*, eds. John C. Gerber, Paul Baender, and Terry Firkins (Berkeley, Los Angeles, CA; London: University of California Press, 1980), chapter IX, p. 92.

40. See George Noszlopy and Fiona Waterhouse, *Public Sculpture of Staffordshire and the Black Country* (Liverpool: Liverpool University Press, 2005), pp. 86, 274; Jacqueline Bannerjee, http://www.victorianweb.org/sculpture/lucas/3f.jpg, last accessed 08/04/2015.

41. Samuel D. Gross, *Autobiography of Samuel D. Gross: with sketches of his contemporaries* (1887) (Philadelphia, PA: W.B. Saunders, 1893) I, p. 349.

42. Nathaniel Hawthorne, 'Lichfield and Uttoxeter', *Our Old Home* (London: Walter Scott Ltd, 1863), p. 110.

43. *Our Old Home* (1863), p. 112.

44. *Our Old Home* (1863), p. 113.

45. *Our Old Home* (1863), p. 115.

46. Both the Lichfield statue and the statue outside St Clement Danes by Percy Fitzgerald erected in 1910 exemplify a trend towards the naturalistic, biographical, and located. The Fitzgerald statue shows Johnson reading, with two more books and an inkpot by his feet. *The New York Times* mentions a quill as well, but that has long gone, probably acquired as a souvenir. The plinth is ornamented with a medallion of Boswell and two bas-reliefs, one depicting Johnson and Boswell walking in the Highlands, and one depicting Johnson and Mrs Thrale. See Jacqueline Bannerjee, http://www.victorianweb.org/sculpture/fitzgeralQ72.html, last accessed 08/04/2015; Margaret Baker, *London Statues and Monuments* (London: Shire, 1995); Claire Bullus and Ronald Asprey, *The Statues of London* (London and New York: Merrell, 2009); 'London's Newest Statue' *New York Times*, 14 August 1910.

47. For discussion of Janeism in inter-war England, see Deidre Shauna Lynch, 'At Home with Jane Austen' in Deidre Shauna Lynch and William B. Warner eds., *Cultural Institutions of the Novel* (Durham, NC and London: Duke University

Press, 1996), pp. 159–92. On wartime Austen, see Claudia L. Johnson, *Jane Austen's Cults and Cultures* (Chicago, IL: Chicago University Press, 2012), pp. 99–152.

48. Chawton scrapbook, p. 13.

49. Such plaques, along with accounts of the ceremonies that accompanied their unveiling, provide invaluable evidence of when and how the house began to be written and rewritten as a 'writer's house', who by and who for; to put it another way, who or what was being remembered, and why.

CHAPTER 6

1. The word 'vitrine', derived via Old French from the Latin for glass, appears in English usage from about 1875. For a brief history of the use of the vitrine in religion, scientific specimen cabinet, department store, natural history museum, and art gallery, see Cornell University (2017), 'Vitrine', *Intypes*, https://intypes. cornell.edu/expanded.cfm?erID=204, last accessed 10/05/2017.

2. 'When a group of objects is exhibited together in a vitrine, a kind of visual construction or statement is involved, suggesting that they have some formal relationship or cultural relationship one with another'. Claire Walsh, 'Shop Design and the Display of Goods in Eighteenth-century London', *Journal of Design History*, 8:3 (1995), pp. 157–76 (pp. 162–3), quoted 'Intypes', https://intypes. cornell.edu/expanded.cfm?erID=204, last accessed 10/05/2017.

3. The writing desk was stolen from Nuneaton Museum on 15 November 2012. See BBC News, 'George Eliot Writing Desk Stolen from Nuneaton Museum' (November2012),http://www.bbc.co.uk/news/uk-england-coventry-warwickshire-20339748, last accessed 09/07/2017.

4. Anna Woodhouse 'Windows to the Soul', *Four Thought*, BBC Radio 4 (2013), http://www.bbc.co.uk/programmes/b01snbm0, last accessed 09/05/2017. A podcast derived from and condensing Woodhouse's doctoral thesis 'Looking through Glass: Windows, Lenses and Spectacles in American Literature and Culture, 1900–1960', PhD thesis (2011), University of Leeds. For Walter Benjamin on glass see *The Arcades Project* [1927–40] (London: Harvard University Press, 2002), p. 734. Benjamin's interest in glass as the framer and producer of desire is important enough to govern the form of the memorial created to him by Dani Karavanhe in Portbou, Spain. Benjamin committed suicide there on 25 September 1940 having failed to secure passage to escape deportation to the Nazi concentration camps. The memorial is 'named "Passages" in remembrance of Benjamin's final passage from France to Spain', and the unfinished *Arcades Project* (in German, *Passagenwerk*). 'The name also refers to the several passages visitors make during their time at the memorial, from the journey down the steps to the glassed-off view of the ocean whirlpool', to Benjamin's words etched on the glass panel, 'and back up to the rectangle of sunlight in the dark'. Atlas Obscura, 'Walter Benjamin's Memorial' (2017), http://www.atlasobscura. com/places/walter-benjamin-memorial, last accessed 09/05/2017.

NOTES TO PAGES 142–146

5. James Putnam, *Art and Artifact: The Museum as Medium* (London: Thames and Hudson, 2001), p. 36.

6. Dylan Thomas, *Collected Poems 1934–1952* (London: J.M. Dent & Sons Ltd, 1952), lines 4–5, and 15, pp. 170–3.

7. See Min Lewis, *Laugharne and Dylan Thomas* (London: Dobson, 1967), 'Postmortem' pp. 118–27.

8. At the extreme end of the scale there is the fascinating case of the birthplace of Samuel Clemens, later known as Mark Twain outside Hannibal, Missouri, the log-cabin entirely enclosed within a glass and steel building, a walk-in vitrine.

9. Jeannette Winterson, 'Virginia Woolf', in *Writers and their Houses: A Guide to the Writers' Houses of England, Scotland, Wales and Ireland*, ed. Kate Marsh (London: Hamish Hamilton, 1993), p. 466.

10. Along with this go all sorts of ideas—replacing viewing hierarchy with a sense of equality, amplifying 'knowledge' of the object through 'experiencing' it, allowing the object to 'perform', thinking of the museum as a theatre, and so forth. Academics have not been immune to this; they are very inclined to boast about having been allowed, because they are *not* tourists, actually to get into the case or the archive, and to touch and handle the real things, albeit usually in white protective gloves.

11. E.T.A. Hoffman, *Tales of Hoffman,* translated by R.J. Hollingdale (London: Penguin, 2004), pp. 85–125 (pp. 109–10).

12. Marina Warner 'Preface', *20 Maresfield Gardens: A Guide to the Freud Museum London* (London: Serpent's Tail, 1998), p. vii.

13. J.D. McClatchy, with photographs by Erica Lennard, *American Writers at Home* (New York: Library of America and Vendome Press, 2004), p. 8.

14. Elizabeth Gaskell, *A Life of Charlotte Brontë* (London: Smith Elder, 1857), 2 vols, II, p. 298.

15. Richard Ellmann, *James Joyce* (New York: Oxford University Press, 1982 [1959]), pp. 566–74. See also Francisco J. Ascaso and Jan L. van Velze, 'Was James Joyce Myopic or Hyperopic?', *British Medical Journal*, 343:7837 (2011), p. 1295.

16. Richard Ellmann's long-standing contention that Joyce was near-sighted was challenged in 2011 by researchers for the *British Medical Journal* on the basis of the prescription for glasses written in 1932 by Joyce's then ophthalmologist Alfred Vogt which revealed that at any rate that prescription was actually for far-sightedness, a conclusion supported by examination of photographs which suggest that the lenses are convex rather than concave. See Eilish O'Regan, 'Portrait of the Artist in a New Light', *Irish Independent* (16 December 2011), http://www.independent.ie/lifestyle/health/portrait-of-the-artist-in-a-new-light-james-joyce-was-farsighted-26802665.html, last accessed 09/05/2017. There are various pairs of spectacles supposedly owned by Joyce extant. 'Joyce's famous walking-sticks, glasses, and passport' were part of the gift of Margaretta F. Wickser to the University of Buffalo in 1950. Michael Basinski, 'The James Joyce Collection: Its History and Future', University of Buffalo (November 2008), http://library.buffalo.edu/pl/collections/jamesjoyce/collection/history-future.

php, last accessed 09/07/2017. The glasses are in Folder 28 described as 'Joyce's glasses, including the lenses, the ear pieces, and a case'; the collection also holds the relevant Vogt prescription. http://library.buffalo.edu/pl/collections/jamesjoyce/catalog/xix.htm, last accessed 09/05/2017. According to the curator of the Dublin Writers' Museum, Robert Nicholson, a pair of Joyce's spectacles were put on auction in 2004 and were bought by Michael Flatley of Riverdance fame for his private collection. Personal correspondence 14 June 2017. In 2005 the James Joyce Centre acquired a pair of spectacles and a case similar to those that Joyce had possessed, but these spectacles have not been displayed because of their lack of authentication.

17. Anne-Sofie Hjemdahl ed., *A Thing or Two about Ibsen: His Possessions, Dramatic Poetry and Life* (Oslo: Andrimne, 2006), p. 61.

18. 'Virginia Woolf', two photographs by Ottoline Morrell (1926), National Portrait Gallery Ax142604 and Ax142598.

19. Nuala Hancock, 'Virginia Woolf's Glasses', Sandra Dudley ed., *Museum Materialities: Objects, Engagements, Interpretations* (London and New York: Routledge, 2010), p. 116.

20. Hancock (2010), pp. 116–17.

21. Hancock (2010), p. 118.

22. For the National Trust image, see Richard Shone, *Virginia Woolf and Monk's House* (National Trust, January 1970), p. 16. See also Annie Leibovitz, *Pilgrimage* (London: Jonathan Cape, 2011).

23. Alison Booth, *Homes and Haunts: Touring Writers' Shrines and Countries* (Oxford: Oxford University Press, 2016), p. 254.

24. Frontispiece, *Writers and Their Houses: A Guide to the Writers' Houses of England, Scotland, Wales and Ireland*, ed. Kate Marsh (London: Hamish Hamilton, 1993).

25. 'Freud once suggested that a house, when summoned in a dream, represents the soul of a dreamer. This is certainly true of writers, who make a profession of dreaming, and whose houses often reflect their spirit long after they have departed the premises. I've always been fascinated by houses where writers have lived and worked, and have made far-flung pilgrimages to many of these sites of significant dreaming. One longs to sit in these houses, to wander their dark corridors and look out of their windows, to observe their peculiar angle of vision on the outside world'. http://www.franciskylegallery.com/sites/Fshr. htm, last accessed 22/06/2017.

26. Mead Art Museum, Amherst College, MA, USA.

27. Anna Groves, *Hardy's Cottage* (National Trust, 2002), p. 9.

28. Tour conducted in August 2007 by Kurt Masdea.

29. See the tourist brochure to Arrowhead (2007), which copes with this problem by quoting a letter to Evert Duyckink (December 1850) from Arrowhead: 'I have a sort of sea-feeling here in the country…'.

30. Charles Hale, letter to his mother, 11 November 1861. Charles Lemon ed., *Early Visitors to Haworth* (Haworth: Brontë Society, 1996), p. 80. For a discussion of the emergence of the cult of Haworth Parsonage, see Watson (2006), pp. 106–27.

31. *Writers and Their Houses* (1993), p. 13.

32. Visited most recently November 2016.

33. See, for instance, the courting inscription in English at the manor of Frogner, Oslo, 1797: '1797—/the only one/the single one/the particular one/the happy one'.

34. Nathaniel Hawthorne, *Our Old Home: A Series of English Sketches* (Boston, MA: Houghton, Mifflin and Co., 1883), chapter 9, 'Near Oxford'.

35. My thanks to Frances Benjamin, our guide for the day in summer 2007, and to Tom Beardsley who showed us the attic.

36. Nathaniel Hawthorne, *Mosses from an Old Manse* (Boston, MA: Houghton, Mifflin and Co., 1882 [1854]), p. 13.

37. George William Curtis, 'Nathaniel Hawthorne' (1853) in ed. Elbert Hubbard, *Little Journeys to the Homes of American Authors* (New York: G.P. Putnam's Sons, 1896), pp. 199–200.

38. Hawthorne (1882), p. 14.

39. For a representation of this desk in relation to the window, see J.D. Maclatchy, *American Writers at Home* with photographs by Erica Lennard (New York: Library of America in association with the Vendome Press, 2004), p. 98.

40. Published originally as a series in *The Atlantic Monthly* of 1871. Excerpted in Ronald A. Bosco and Jillmarie Murphy eds., *Hawthorne in His Own Time: A Biographical Chronicle of His Life, Drawn from Recollections, Interviews, and Memoirs by Family, Friends and Associates* (Iowa City, IA: University of Iowa Press, 2007), p. 140.

41. Helen Archibald Clarke, *Hawthorne's Country* (Garden City, NY: Doubleday, Page & Co., 1913), facsimile reprint (New Delhi: Isha Books, 2013), p. 178.

42. Renée L. Bergland reads this inscription as a critique of Emersonian assertions of transparency in his essay 'Nature' and therefore as a reassertion of history, plus a struggle for significant authorship between husband and wife. Bergland also notes, more to my purpose, that 'the glass must be read in its particular locational context'. See 'The Puritan Eyeball, or Sexing the Transcendent', in Tracy Fessenden, Nicholas F. Radel, and Magdalena J. Zaborowska eds., *The Puritan Origins of American Sex: Religion, Sexuality, and National Identity in American Literature* (New York, London: Routledge, 2001), pp. 93–108.

43. Theodore F. Wolfe, *Literary Shrines: The Haunts of Some Famous American Authors* (Philadelphia, PA: Lippincott, 1897), p. 35. Shirley Hoover Biggers, *American Author Houses, Museums, Memorials, and Libraries: A State-by-State Guide* (Jefferson, NC and London: McFarland and Co., 2000), p. 86.

44. Robert Graves notes in *The Spiritual Quixote: or, the summer's ramble of Mr Geoffrey Wildgoose. A comic romance* (London: Printed for J. Dodsley, 1773) that his hero Wildgoose had come across a pane supposedly inscribed by the author Jonathan Swift, but 'did not take out the pane, as he probably might have done for three half pence, as was done soon after by some more curious traveller', p. 514; such panes, as this suggests, became collectable as curiosities very early. The culture of writing on glass produced its shadow or reflection in print culture in the

shape of verse that referenced or masqueraded as such inscription, as evidenced by John Donne's 'A Valediction: Of my Name in the Window' through to Victor Hugo's poem 'Écrit sur la vitre d'une fenêtre flamande'. It also gave rise to the habit of transcribing and collecting such inscriptions in print form specifically in order to preserve them, whether within travel-writing and guidebooks or in popular essays such as the little piece entitled 'Rhymes in Panes' that *Chambers' Journal* published in 1887, widely reprinted. Some of Robert Burns' window verse, indeed, only exists in print, such as 'Verses written on a window of the Inn at Carron'. There seems to have been a sense that this type of inscription could give added value to the place; this idea may have lain behind the Earl of Glencairn's gift to Robert Burns of a diamond stylus specifically designed to write on glass. The upshot was that Burns became a prolific writer of window verse, writing a number of pithy and not always good-tempered verses on a variety of inn windows or on summerhouses (presumably by invitation), some of which still survive, and which retain their own form of celebrity. There were instances at The Black Bull Inn, Moffat; the Cross Keys Inn, Falkirk; the Globe Inn, Dumfries; and the Queensbury Arms, Sanquhar. Many have had a long and interesting history of being collected, reproduced, and replicated, including the two panes from the Globe Inn at Dumfries carefully replicated from those in the collections of the Birthplace at Alloway and reinstalled in the very bedroom where Burns amused himself by impregnating the chambermaid. Burns' ability to add value with his verses was not, however, sufficient to excuse spoiling a set of expensive lead crystal wine-glasses. The Earl chucked the damaged glass away in a fury; an admirer collared it as a literary relic. By the 1880s, however, inscribing glass seems to have become much less socially acceptable, as this rhyme (one of many such) suggests: 'Should you ever chance to see/ A man's name writ on a glass,/ Be sure he owns an diamond,/ And his parent owns an ass'. *Chambers' Journal of Popular Literature, Science, and Art*, 5th series, February 1887, 'Rhymes on Panes', p. 117. For a discussion of eighteenth-century graffiti, see Christina Lupton, *Knowing Books: The Consciousness of Mediation in Eighteenth-Century Britain* (Philadelphia, PA: University of Pennsylvania Press 2012), esp. chapter 5, 'Gray and Mackenzie Printing on the Wall'. Window verses were sometimes associated with the idea of signing off on a major literary project: Pope's Tower, the remains of Stanton Harcourt Manor Chapel in Oxfordshire, is said to have a 'piece of red glass' which Pope inscribed in 1718 marking the completion of his translation of *The Iliad*; this was celebrated and shown as late as 1993—see Gavin Ewart's essay and accompanying photograph, 'Alexander Pope: Stanton Harcourt, Oxfordshire, Chiswick House, London W4, Pope's Grotto, Twickenham, Middlesex', *Writers and Their Houses* (1993), pp. 305–19 (pp. 315–16). This cultural commonplace also accounts for a number of forgeries that exist, including the sonnet supposedly scratched by Milton in a window at the cottage in Chalfont St Giles where he finished *Paradise Lost*.

45. Hawthorne would make something of a habit of signing the view; he would in later life return to the 'remote little window' in the so-called 'House of Seven Gables' in Salem where he 'engraved his name on the ancient glass. With a prophetic diamond'. See 'Chamber under the eaves' in Virginia Grilley, *Hawthorne: Great Scribe of Salem with Homes and Houses He Knew* (Amherst, MA: University of Massachusetts Press, 1981) n.p. House of Seven Gables visited summer 2007.

46. Hawthorne (1882), p. 29.

47. N.B. Ripley, 'A Visit to the Old Manse', *The Book News Monthly*, 28 (1909), p. 593. Sophia also inscribed another pane downstairs in the dining-room with the words 'Endymion painted in this room/finished January 20th 1844' and below it a mention of their infant daughter: 'Una Hawthorne stood on this window sill/Jan 22 1845 while the trees were/all glass chandelier. A goodly show/which she liked much tho' only/10 months old'. For a modern reaction to this inscription see Viva la Violette, 'Weeping at a House Museum', My History Fix (August 2015), http://myhistoryfix.com/inaroundnewengland/weeping-at-a-house-museum, last accessed 09/07/2017.

48. Hawthorne (1882), p. 29.

49. *The Prose Works of William Wordsworth*, ed. W.J.B. Owen and Jane Worthington Smyser (Oxford: Clarendon Press, 1974), 3 vols: vol. 2 'Essay on Epitaphs, III', p. 60.

50. It requires not just 'slow writing', but what Mary Favret has described with respect to inscription in stone, 'slow reading'. Mary Favret, unpublished paper for the panel 'Slow Romanticism', NASSR 2011.

51. Wolfe (1897), p. 32.

52. *Hamlet*, 3.2.20–3.

53. Guide to The Church of Sant'Onofrio Al Gianicolo in Rome, c. 2007. Veterans of museum-visiting in Italy will be unsurprised that applying to the Knights of the Holy Sepulchre as required did not in the event gain admittance, so this is the extent of my information. Given the tourist celebrity of this spot in the eighteenth and early nineteenth centuries (Leopardi, Goethe, and Chateaubriand all visited amongst many others), it is conceivable that the mirror emerged in response to the fame of the scenes in *Gerusalemme Liberata* set in the garden of the enchantress Armida. The knight Rinaldo carried a mirror in which Armida admired herself: 'Dependent from his side (unusual sight,)/Appear'd a polish'd mirror, beamy bright,/This in his hand th' enamour'd champion rais'd,/On this, with smiles, the fair Armida gaz'd./She in the glass her form reflected spies,/And he consults the mirror of her eyes'. (Bishop Hoole's translation of Canto XVI.20, cited in John Black's *Life of Torquato Tasso* (London: John Murray, 1810), 2 vols, vol. I, p. 382.).

54. See *Virginia Woolf and Monk's House* (1970), p. 13.

55. Mirror originally from Gad's Hill, now displayed in 48 Doughty St. 10 January 2017.

56. *The Letters of Charles Dickens*, ed. Graham Storey (Oxford: Clarendon Press, 2002), 12 vols, vol. 12 (1868–70), p. 119; see also John Forster, *The Life of Charles Dickens*, ed. J.W.T. Ley (London: Cecil Palmer, 1928 [1892]), pp. 654–5 and J.T. Fields, *Yesterdays with Authors* (James R. Osgood, late Ticknor & Fields, and Fields, Osgood, & Company, 1874 [1871]), p. 189.

57. To Charles Nosotti, 13 May 1868, *The Letters of Charles Dickens* (2002), vol. 12 1868–70, p. 107.

58. For this as a commonplace, see Theodore F. Wolfe, *A Literary Pilgrimage Among the Haunts of Famous British Authors* (Philadelphia, PA: J.B. Lippincott, 1895), pp. 52–3. 'Of the work produced at Gad's Hill ... much was written in that leaf-environed nook; here the master wrought through the golden days of his last day of conscious life, here he wrote his last paragraph and at the close of that June day let fall his pen, never to take it up again. From the place of the chalet we behold the view which delighted the heart of Dickens,—his desk was so placed that his eyes would rest upon this view whenever he raised them from his work,—the fields of waving corn, the green expanse of meadows, the sail-dotted river', p. 55. See also William R. Hughes, *A Week's Tramp in Dickens-Land* (London: Chapman and Hall, 1891), p. 187 and Christian Tearle, *Rambles with an American* (London: Mills and Boon, c. 1910), p. 319.

59. Charles Collins, commentary glossing Samuel Luke Fildes' painting 'The Empty Chair', quoted by Forster (1928), pp. 654–5 n.

60. 'Dickens erected the chalet sent to him in pieces ... the upper room of which—up among the quivering boughs, where "birds and butterflies fly in and out, and green branches shoot in at the windows"—Dickens lined with mirrors and used as his study in summer'. Forster (1928), p. 655n. On the removal of the chalet, see William R. Hughes, *A Week's Tramp in Dickens-Land* (London: Chapman and Hall, 1891), p. 186. See also Alison Booth, 'Time-Travel in Dickens' World', *Literary Tourism and Nineteenth-Century Culture*, ed. Nicola J. Watson (Basingstoke: Palgrave Macmillan, 2009), pp. 150–63.

61. Hawthorne (1882), p. 30.

62. See Diana Fuss, *The Sense of an Interior: Four Writers and the Rooms That Shaped Them* (London and New York: Routledge, 2004), pp. 80–7.

63. Freud discusses the 'uncanny' feeling one experiences when looking at one's reflection in a mirror in his essay of 1919, 'The Uncanny', *The Standard Edition of the Complete Psychological Works of Sigmund Freud* (New York: International Universities Press, 1984), 6 vols. *Volume XVII (1917–1919): An Infantile Neurosis and Other Works*, pp. 217–56. See also Sabine Melchior-Bonnet, *The Mirror: A History*, trans. Katbarme H. Jewett (London: Routledge, 2001), p. 223.

64. Now a writer's house museum, open to the public since 1986.

65. The importance of mirrors for Freud has been further emphasized by artistic endeavours in recent years. In 2016 the Turner Prize-winning artist Mark Wallinger mounted a mirror onto the ceiling of Freud's study in the Freud Museum as part of an installation entitled 'Self Reflection'. This installation marked the thirtieth anniversary of the museum and ran 28 July to 25 September 2016.

66. Michel Foucault, 'Of Other Spaces', *Diacritics*, 16:1 (Spring 1986), pp. 22–7 (p. 24).
67. *Writers' Houses* (London: Cassell, 1995), p. 170, pp. 178–9.
68. *Writers and Their Houses* (1993), pp. 466–7.

CHAPTER 7

1. Thanks are due here to The Writer's Retreat in Sheepwash, Devon which provided me with one temporary refuge—https://www.retreatsforyou.co.uk—and to Dame Hermione Lee, who provided another at Wolfson College.
2. William Cowper, *The Task*, Book I, ll. 234–6.
3. In an article on the reopening of the museum, the journalist Kate Youde repeats the characteristic account of the volunteer guides: 'Without a room of her own, she used to pen wonderfully gossipy letters, and parts of her novels, sitting at a small table in the dining-room window overlooking the garden she so loved'. 'Victorian Novelist Elizabeth Gaskell's Home to Re-Open to the Public', *The Independent* (27 September 2014), http://www.independent.co.uk/arts-entertainment/books/news/victorian-novelist-elizabeth-gaskells-home-to-re-open-to-the-public-9759694.html, last accessed 09/07/2017.
4. J.E. Austen-Leigh, *A Memoir of Jane Austen*, 2nd edition (London: Bentley, 1871), p. 96.
5. Virginia Woolf, *The Common Reader* (London: Hogarth Press, 1925), p. 172.
6. I am indebted to Harald Hendrix for drawing my attention to this heritage site; see 'Literary Heritage Sites Across Europe; A Tour d'Horizon', *Interférences littéraires/Literaire interferenties*, 16, 'Literature at the Museum: The Muzealisation and Exposition of Literature', Marie-Clémence Régnier ed., June 2015, pp. 23–38.
7. Tour guide (Liz Cohen) information, August 2007. See Linda (mouseski58), 'A Virtual Visit to Salem's House of the Seven Gables', *The Distracted Wanderer* (December 2011), http://www.thedistractedwanderer.com/2011/12/virtual-visit-to-salems-house-of-seven.html, last accessed 09/07/2017. My thanks to Diana Boston for showing us the Manor at Hemingford Grey in 2005.

    Both of the staircases in these last houses explicitly memorialize access to the writer's imagination. The House of Seven Gables has been progressively developed to correspond more nearly to Hawthorne's novel which it was thought to have inspired. This development included building a staircase sometime between 1908 and 1910 leading up out of the false back of a closet to an attic beneath one of the gables, in allusion to Hawthorne's character Holgrave, artist, writer, and descendant of wizards, who may be read as in some sort a double for the young Hawthorne himself. The Manor has been preserved not merely as the home of Lucy M. Boston but also as the setting of her series of children's books, *The Children of Green Knowe* (1954–76). The attic is conceived as filled with the magical potential of child-imagination (as in The Manor at Hemingford Grey) which shows the fictive Tolly's attic bedroom just as it appears in the first book of the series, a place of dreams, ghosts, and magic.

8. In Gaston Bachelard's psychological anatomy of the house, the attic is identified as the place of the imagination. *La Poétique de l'espace* (Paris: Presses Universitaires de France, 1958) translated as *The Poetics of Space* (New York: Orion Press, 1964), p. 170.

9. Richard Shone, *Virginia Woolf and Monk's House* (National Trust, 1970), p. 13.

10. On the motivations for purpose-building the retreats of Bazán and others as driven by the desire for 'intense physical relationship with remote locations', see Jesus Angel Sanchez-Garcia, 'Ivory Towers as Creative Refuges for Writers', https://www.researchgate.net/publication/326368597_Ivory_Towers_as_Creative_Refuges_for_Writers_EAHN_Conference_Tallinn_2018, last accessed 08/01/2019.

11. To Hill, 25 June 1785, *The Letters and Prose Writings of William Cowper*, eds. James King and Charles Ryskamp (Oxford: Clarendon Press, 1981), 3 vols, II, pp. 359–60.

12. To Newton, 22 June 1786, *The Letters and Prose Writings of William Cowper* (1981) II, p. 569.

13. To Lady Hesketh, 29 May 1786, *The Letters and Prose Writings of William Cowper* (1981) II, p. 559.

14. *The Task*, Book III, ll. 352–78.

15. *The Task*, Book I, ll. 266–8.

16. William Hayley, *The Works of William Cowper: His Life and Letters* (London: Saunders and Otley, 1835), 8 vols, III, pp. 37–8.

17. *The Task*, Book I ll. 278–325; Book I, ll. 220ff.; William Hayley, *The Life and Posthumous Writings of William Cowper* (Chichester: Johnson, 1803–6), 4 vols.

18. Edward Wedlake Bradley and James Sargant Storer, *Cowper, illustrated by a series of views in, or near, the park of Weston-Underwood, Bucks. Accompanied by copious descriptions and a brief sketch of the poet's life* (London, 1803), pp. 278, 279.

19. William Howitt, *Homes and Haunts of the Most Eminent British Poets* (1847) I, p. 269.

20. Howitt (1847) I, p. 272.

21. Howitt (1847) I, pp. 278, p. 279. In due course the landscape itself would break out into corroboratory inscription, as in the Alcove itself, which nowadays carries a plaque with a quotation from the poem describing the view:

> The summit gain'd, behold the proud alcove,
> That crowns it! yet not all it's pride secures
> The grand retreat from injuries impress'd
> By rural carvers, who with knives deface
> The pannels, leaving an obscure, rude name,
> In characters uncouth, and spelt amiss.
> So strong the zeal t'immortalize himself
> Beats in the breast of man…Now roves the eye;
> And posted on this speculative height,
> Exults in its command. The sheepfold here
> Pours out it's fleecy tenants o'er the glebe.

At first, progressive as a stream, they seek
The middle field; but scatter'd by degrees,
Each to his choice, soon whiten all the land.
There from the sunburnt hayfield homeward creeps
The loaded wain; while, lighten'd of it's charge,
The wain that meets it passes swiftly by;
The boorish driver leaning o'er his team
Vocif'rous, and impatient of delay...
O'er these, but far beyond (a spacious map
Of hill and valley interpos'd between),
The Ouse, dividing the well water'd land,
Now glitters in the sun, and now retires,
As bashful, yet impatient to be seen. *The Task*, Book II, ll. 278–325 *passim.*

22. In *The Confessions*, Rousseau writes, 'Montmollin [the pastor] procured from the Classe (the ministers) a commission to summon me to the Consistory, there to give an account of the articles of my faith, and to excommunicate me should I refuse to comply'. Rousseau then writes of '[a] shower of stones thrown against the window' on 6 September 1765, which, along with several other bouts of abuse, caused Rousseau to leave Môtiers-Travers two days later. *The Confessions of Jean Jacques Rousseau* [1782] (Blackbird: Virginia Tech, 2001), p. 402, p. 408.

23. Sigismond Wagner [Sigmund von Wagner], *L'Île Saint-Pierre ou L'Île de Rousseau* (Berne: G. Lory et C. Rheiner, 1815), p. 51.

24. Louis Simond, *Switzerland; or, A Journal of a Tour and Residence in that Country, in the years 1817, 1818, and 1819: followed by An Historical Sketch on the manners of Ancient and Modern Helvetia in which the events of our own time are fully detailed, together with the causes to which they may be referred* (London: John Murray, 1822), 2 vols, I, pp. 62–3.

25. Richard Boyle Bernard, *A Tour through some parts of France, Switzerland, Savoy, Germany and Belgium, during the Summer and Autumn of 1814* (London: Longman, Hurst, Rees, Orme, and Brown, 1814), p. 215. This was the third of Rousseau's bedrooms to achieve celebrity: the others were the room which adjoined that of his mistress Madame de Warens at Les Charmettes, and the room at Môtiers-Travers ('where Rousseau's house is shown, and the desk against the wall, where he wrote standing, and the two peep-holes in a sort of wooden gallery upstairs, through which he could, unperceived, watch people out of doors'). Simond (1822) I, p. 30.

26. For an illustration and further information see https://www.euromanticism. org/rousseaus-trapdoor, last accessed 09/01/2019.

27. Sigismond Wagner [Sigmund von Wagner], *L'Île Saint-Pierre ou L'Île de Rousseau*, with an introduction by Pierre Kohler [1815] (Lausanne: Éditions SPESS, 1926), p. 74.

28. Samuel Rogers, *Italy* in *Poems by Samuel Rogers* (London: for T. Cadell and W. Davies, 1816), p. 144.

29. Marianne Colston, *Journal of a Tour in France, Switzerland, and Italy, during the years 1819, 20, and 21 illustrated by fifty lithographic prints, from original drawings taken in Italy, the Alps, and the Pyrenees* (Paris: A. and W. Galignani, 1822), 2 vols, II, p. 23.

30. To design and execute such a garden was a politically progressive statement, for it referenced not just English landscape gardening, with its elevation of the natural and its celebration of the picturesque, but also an associated liberal politics, exemplified by the great landscape garden of Stowe and by William Shenstone's ferme ornée of Leasowes, which last Girardin had visited. The English garden's interest in the wild and the natural, the sinuous line and the kinetic prospect, stood in strong contrast to the formal styles of gardening associated with absolutism and the aristocracy as exemplified by the gardens of Marley-le-Roi, Versailles, Chantilly, or Vaux-le-Vicomte.

31. Nowadays, only about a quarter of the original garden remains open to the public on a regular basis, and many of the original features have vanished. Enough remains, however, to give a strong sense of the experience it was meant to offer, and this can be fleshed out further by reference to two books: Girardin's own essay on his philosophy of gardening, *De la composition des paysages* (1777), and a guide to the garden published in 1788, *Promenade ou Itineraraire des Jardins d'Ermenonville*, which was offered for sale both in Paris and at Ermenonville itself. This includes not merely lengthy descriptions of the features and their inscriptions, with twenty-five engravings of the most important, but also offers clues as to how the gardens were and should be encountered and what they conveyed to contemporaries on the brink of revolution.

32. These included exercises in sensory extremes and allegorical narrative, such as the grotto entrance to the garden proper which amplified the roar of a waterfall, and conducted the visitor from dripping darkness up stone steps into a flood of light. It also included reworkings of the classical as modern exemplar: most particularly in the intentionally unfinished Temple of Modern Philosophy which reworked the Temple of Vesta at Tivoli with columns inscribed to seven modern philosophers, including Rousseau. Dominique Césari, 'Ermenonville', *The most famous Anglo-Chinese gardens of France* (July 2000), http://parcsafabriques.org/erm/dErm1e.htm, last accessed 19/06/2017.

33. S.W. Orson 'Introduction', *The Confessions of Jean Jacques Rousseau*, trans. S.W. Orson (London: Privately printed for members of the Aldus Society, 1903), p. 6. For a discussion of this phenomenon in full see Watson (2006), pp. 133–49.

34. *The Traveller's Guide to Switzerland*, 3rd edn (London: M.A. Leigh & Son, 1835), p. 258.

35. J. Mérigot, *Promenade ou Itineraire des Jardins d'Ermenonville* (Paris: Gattey, Goyot, Mérigot, 1788), p. 48. Illustrated in 1860 as 'La cabane du philosophe fabrique du Désert où Jean-Jacques Rousseau passait de longues heures lors de son séjour en 1778' in Joanne Adolphe, *Les environs de Paris, illustrés*, 2nd edn (Paris: Hachette, 1868).

36. *Promenade* (1788), p. 49.

37. *Promenade* (1788), p. 58.

38. *Promenade* (1788), p. 24.

39. Henry David Thoreau, *Walden; or, Life in the Woods* [1854] (London: Macmillan Collector's Library, 2016), p. 54.

40. *Walden* (2016), pp. 51–52.

41. *Walden* (2016), p. 7.

42. Ellery Channing, *Thoreau, the Poet-Naturalist* (London: Roberts Bros, 1873), pp. 7–8. See Walter Harding, *The Days of Henry Thoreau: A Biography* (New York: Dover Publications, 1962),pp. 179–99. See also William Howarth,'Introduction' to *Walden and Other Writings by Henry David Thoreau*, ed. Howarth (New York: The Modern Library, 1981), p. xvii.

43. *Walden* (2016), p. 138.

44. See Michael Frederick (2015),www.thoreausociety.org,last accessed 09/07/2017.

45. Guide, Walden Pond State Reservation, http://www.mass.gov/eea/docs/dcr/ parks/pdf/walden-pond.pdf, last accessed 19/06/2017.

46. Wilson Flagg, *A Year Among the Trees: Or, The Woods and By-ways of New England* [1872] (Boston, MA: Estes & Lauriat, 1881).

47. Onsite information, 2007.

48. Caption, Concord Museum, 2007.

49. Theodore F. Wolfe, *Literary Shrines: The Haunts of Some Famous American Authors* (Philadelphia, PA: Lippincott Company, 1895), pp. 17–83 (pp. 68–74). For more details on the 'Thoreauvian Pilgrimage' see Lawrence Buell,'The Thoreauvian Pilgrimage: The Structure of an American Cult', *American Literature*, 61:2 (1989), pp. 175–99.

50. Scott Hess argues that the emptiness is a necessary component of the 'landscape of genius' in 'Wordsworthshire and Thoreau Country: Transatlantic Landscapes of Genius', Paul Westover and Ann Wierda Rowland eds., *Transatlantic Literature and Author-Love in the Nineteenth Century* (New York: Springer International Publishing, 2016), pp. 175–201 (p. 190).

51. See postcard images copyright Bonnie McGrath, Lightdance Photography Acton MA, in association with The Thoreau Society.

52. Brochure quoted in Donald Linebaugh, 'Walden Pond and Beyond' in ed. John H. Jameson, *The Reconstructed Past: Reconstruction and the Public Interpretation of Archaeology and History* (Walnut Creek, CA: Altamira Press, 2004), pp. 21–46 (p. 23).

53. Gifted by Thoreau's sister Sophia to the Museum c. 1873. See Concord Museum, 'The Henry David Thoreau collection', http://www.concordmuseum.org/ henry-david-thoreau-collection.php, last accessed 09/07/2017. There is yet another replica in the Tyler Arboretum, Philadelphia, built by Pine Street Carpenters for an exhibition called *Totally Terrific Treehouses*, which was open between 16 April and 27 November 2011. See Tyler Arboretum, www.tylerarboretum.org, last accessed 09/07/2017 and Pine Street Carpenters (October 2011), http://www.pinestreetcarpenters.com/news.aspx?prid=3, last accessed 09/07/2017.

54. Although my A-level French is perfectly adequate for reading and translating eighteenth- and nineteenth-century texts, it's not up to French bureaucratic niceties, and so my thanks to my friend Martine Penwarden for helping me get admittance and permission to take photographs at the Chateau Monte Cristo which she did by puffing off my academic status in a manner entirely foreign to English modesty. My thanks also to Sophie Kerrouche of the Chateau Monte Cristo for facilitating my visit there, on 6 March 2016.

55. All translations are my own unless otherwise stated.

56. For Dumas' account, see Alexandre Dumas, *Histoires de mes bêtes* [1867], 2nd edn (Paris: Librairie Nouvelle, 1868), p. 9.

57. Alexandre Dumas, *The Château d'If: A Romance* (vol. 1) and *The Count of Monte Cristo* (vols 1 and 2), trans. Emma Hardy (Belfast: Simms and M'Intyre, 1846) I, pp. 198–200.

58. Alexandre Dumas, 'Ah vous voilà Dumas!?', *Mon Odyssée à la Comédie Française, Paris et les Parisiens au XIX siècle: mœurs, arts et monuments* (Paris: Morizot, 1856), pp. 317–403 (p. 400).

59. *The Count of Monte Cristo* (1846) I, p. 308.

60. *The Count of Monte Cristo* (1846) II, p. 17, p. 19, pp. 19–25.

61. *The Count of Monte Cristo* (1846) I, p. 308.

62. *The Count of Monte Cristo* (1846) I, p. 287.

63. Very occasionally, the writer's escape from the domestic appears to be less about accessing solitude than disappearing into the crowd and s/he is celebrated not as vanishing into the undergrowth but into the urban jungle. The plaque in Edinburgh marking the café in which J.K. Rowling wrote at any rate part of *Harry Potter and the Philosopher's Stone* (1997) and the celebrity of the hotel room in Princes St Edinburgh where she completed *Harry Potter and the Deathly Hallows* (2007) nonetheless conjecturally connote desperation over the encroachments of the domestic.

64. My thanks to The Shakespeare Institute, which has occupied Corelli's former home since its foundation in 1951, for allowing me to write some part of this chapter within Corelli's folly.

65. Thomas F.G. Coates and Warren R.S. Bell, *Marie Corelli: The Writer and the Woman* (London: Hutchinson, 1903), p. 319. On the history of the folly itself, see Maureen Bell, 'A Brief History of Mason Croft', Shakespeare Institute, Birmingham University (2011), http://www.birmingham.ac.uk/schools/edacs/departments/shakespeare/about/mason-croft-history.aspx, last accessed 09/07/2017.

66. For a contemporaneous photograph, see Coates and Bell (1903), plate facing p. 312.

67. Adam Nicolson, *Sissinghurst Castle Garden*, (National Trust, 1979), p. 4. Also see Nicolson's *Sissinghurst: An Unfinished History* (London: Harper Press, 2008).

68. 'A Postcard to Dylan Thomas' (2014), http://doozie.org.uk/projects/a-postcard-to-dylan-thomas-emily-hinshelwood, last accessed 09/07/2017.

CHAPTER 8

1. William Dean Howells, *My Mark Twain: Reminiscences and Criticisms* (1910), chapter XXXVI, repr. in *The Life and Times of Mark Twain*, ed. and intro. Marilyn Austin Baldwin (Baton Rouge, LA: Louisiana State University, 1999, 2014).

2. In the Romantic period, the exception that proves the rule is the house of Sir John Soane. For an extended discussion of Soane's house as part of a more generalized Romantic culture of self-monumentalization that includes Bentham and Haydon, see Chris Haffenden, *Every Man His Own Monument: Self-Monumentalizing in Romantic Britain* (Uppsala: Uppsala Universetet, 2018), chapter 3. There are also very occasionally women writers who have occupied this position of nation-making, and had it ratified in the preservation of their house as a museum after death; such a one was the first woman Nobel Laureate, Selma Lagerlöf (1858–1940). Her prize money made it possible to buy back and renovate her family home, Mårbacka, which she then worked tirelessly to have preserved after her death.

3. For a discussion of the emergence of the idea of the museum in the period, see Emma Peacocke, *Romanticism and the Museum* (Basingstoke: Palgrave Macmillan, 2015), 'Introduction', pp. 1–15, esp. pp. 1–8, 'Romantic Writing and the Institution of the Public Museum'.

4. Joseph Addison, *Tatler*, no. 254 (1710).

5. Where there was no such residence of genius, it was sometimes possible to commandeer something appropriate. By tradition the medieval ruined castle that that commands the village of Vaucluse, one of Petrarch's retreats, was known as 'Petrarch's Castle': 'Not far from the source of the river, on the summit of an almost inaccessible rock, stands a ruin of the wall of Petrarch's castle. The story which assigned to the poet this fabric as a residence, with a subterranean passage from hence to the house of his far-famed mistress, has been long considered as a fable'. *Monthly Magazine, or British Register* (1822), vol. 53, p. 16. See also 'Fountain of Vaucluse, and Petrarch's Castle' steel engraving, from George R. Wright, *France Illustrated*, drawn by T. Allom, engraved by J.C. Bentley (London: Fisher, Son & Co. 1845–7), 4 vols in 2, I, p. 36.

6. Horace Walpole, *A Description of the Villa of Horace Walpole at Strawberry Hill* (Twickenham: Printed by Thomas Kirkgate, 1774), preface. For a recent extended discussion of the ambitions and aesthetic of Strawberry Hill, see Marion Harney, *Place-Making for the Imagination: Horace Walpole and Strawberry Hill* (London: Routledge, 2016).

7. For a full listing see Horace Walpole, *A Description of the Villa of Horace Walpole* (1774, revised and enlarged 1784).

8. http://www.telegraph.co.uk/culture/art/art-features/7376172/Horace-Walpole-and-Strawberry-Hill-stairway-to-a-thousand-horrors.html, last accessed 2/07/2017.

9. http://museums.gov.gg/hauteville, last accessed 24/05/2017.

10. *Every Saturday: A Journal of Choice Reading* (London: Ticknor and Fields, 6 February 1869), p. 166.

11. *Every Saturday* (6 February 1869), p. 166.

12. Visit made summer 1984.

13. *Every Saturday* (6 February 1869), p. 169.

14. *Every Saturday* (6 February 1869), p. 169.

15. Abbotsford was first opened to the public in 1833, a year after Scott's death.

16. Clive Wainwright, *The Romantic Interior: The British collector at home*, 2nd ed. (London: Palgrave, 1989), p. 160.

17. Walter Scott, *The Antiquary* (Edinburgh: Printed by James Ballantyne and Co. for Archibald Constable and Co. Edinburgh; and Longman, Hurst, Rees, Orme, and Brown, London, 1816), 3 vols, vol. I, p. 16.

18. *The Antiquary* (1816) I, p. 19.

19. *The Antiquary* (1816) I, pp. 32–3.

20. *The Antiquary* (1816) I, p. 43.

21. *The Antiquary* (1816) I, p. 51.

22. *The Antiquary* (1816) I, pp. 51–2.

23. *The Antiquary* (1816) I, p. 307.

24. 'I have myself published two essays in The Antiquarian Repository—and therefore am an author of experience. There was my remarks on Hearne's edition of Robert of Gloucester, signed *Scrutator*; and the other signed *Indagator*, upon a passage in Tacitus—I might add, what attracted considerable notice at the time, and that is my paper in the Gentleman's Magazine, upon the inscription of OElia Lelia, which I subscribed Oedipus—So you see I am not an apprentice in the mysteries of author-craft, and must necessarily understand the taste and temper of the times', *The Antiquary* (1816) I, p. 303.

25. *The Antiquary* (1816) I, pp. 308–9.

26. John Sutherland, *The Life of Sir Walter Scott: A Critical Biography* (Oxford: Blackwell, 1995), pp. 190–1.

27. To Walter Scott, 4 March 1812. *The Collected Letters of Joanna Baillie*, ed. Judith Bailey Slagle (Charlottesville, VA: InteLex Corporation, 2004), 2 vols, I, p. 296.

28. John Martin, *Illustrations; Landscape, Historical, and Antiquarian to the Poetical Works of Sir Walter Scott Bart* (London: Charles Tilt, 1834), 2 vols, I, facing page 'Hall at Abbotsford'.

29. Washington Irving, *Abbotsford and Newstead Abbey* (Philadelphia, PA: Carey, Lea & Blanchard, 1835), p. 42.

30. *Reliquiae Trotcosienses, or The Gabions of The Late Jonathan Oldbuck, Esq. of Monkbarns* [1831], edited by Gerard Carruthers and Alison Lumsden, with an introduction by David Hewitt (Cambridge: Edinburgh University Press in association with the Abbotsford Library Project Trust, 2004), p. xv.

31. Walter Scott, 9 March 1828, *The Journal of Walter Scott*, edited and introduced by W.E.K. Anderson (Edinburgh: Canongate, 1998), p. 495.

32. J.G. Lockhart, *Memoirs of the Life of Sir Walter Scott, Bart.* (1837–8), 7 vols, IV, p. 12.

33. *Reliquiae*, pp. 24–5.

34. *Reliquiae*, p. 29.

35. William Howitt, *Homes and Haunts of the Most Eminent British Poets*, 4th ed. 2 vols (London: George Routledge, 1847) II, p. 154.

36. James Bohn, *A Biographical, Antiquarian and Picturesque Tour in the Northern Counties of England and in Scotland* (London: for the author, 1838), 2 vols, vol. II, p. 1008.

37. Something of the same insistence on the disorderly antiquarian study as the origin for the fiction began to make itself felt in later and post-mortem portraits of the author; Francis Russell's catalogue of portraits includes no fewer than five of Scott depicted in his study painted from 1828 through to the 1840s, in which antiquities seem to take an ever larger role. See Francis Russell, *Portraits of Sir Walter Scott: A Study of Romantic Portraiture* (London: Russell, 1987), pp. 121–3.

38. Cited in Ann Rigney, *The Afterlives of Walter Scott: Memory on the Move* (Oxford: Oxford University Press, 2012), p. 146.

39. Nathaniel Hawthorne, *Passages from the English Notebooks* (Boston, MA: Fields, Osgood, 1870), 2 vols, I, pp. 339–40.

40. Theodore Fontane, *Across the Tweed: A Tour of Mid-Victorian Scotland*, trans. Sir James Ferguson (London: Phoenix House, 1965), p. 195.

41. Rigney (2012), p. 146.

42. W.S. Crockett, *Abbotsford* (London: Adam and Charles Black, 1905), p. 44. Cited Rigney (2012), p. 146.

43. *Reliquiae*, pp. 45–6.

44. Wainwright (1989), p. 8.

45. Much of the work done to date on nineteenth-century American travel-writing has focused upon American reactions to Italy and Europe more generally: see especially Mary Suzanne Schrieber, *Writing Home: American Women Abroad 1830–1920*; Sara Mills, *Discourses of Difference: An Analysis of Women's Travel Writing and Colonialism* (London: Routledge, 1991); William W. Stowe, *Going Abroad: European Travel in Nineteenth-Century American Culture* (Princeton, NJ: Princeton University Press, 1994). However, see the essays by Shirley Foster and Paul Westover in Nicola J. Watson ed., *Literary Tourism and Nineteenth-Century Culture* (Basingstoke: Palgrave, 2009), both of which deal with American writers' responses to British literary sites. Foster considers tourist strategies of enhancement and self-ironization; Westover is interested in the rhetoric by which writers variously claim English heritage. Considering some of the same material, I develop a rather different view of the project of American literary tourists. See also Allison Lockwood, *Passionate Pilgrims: The American Traveller in Great Britain 1800–1914* (New York, London: Associated University Presses, 1981); Paul Giles, *Transatlantic Insurrections: British Culture and the Formation of American Literature* (Philadelphia, PA: University of Pennsylvania Press, 2001); Booth (2016).

46. Alison Booth, 'The Real Right Place of Henry James: Homes and Haunts', *The Henry James Review*, 25:3 (Fall 2004), pp. 216–27 (p. 217).

47. For an account of the transformations that the celebrity of Scott's verse wrought on Melrose Abbey see Nicola J. Watson, 'Melrose Abbey', Michael Carter,

Peter N. Lindfield, and Dale Townshend eds., *Writing Britain's Ruins* (London: British Library, 2018), chapter 4.

48. Irving's account is misleading, conflating as it does the Rhymer's Glen, Huntley Bank, and the Eildon Tree together in ways that have confounded generations of literary tourists ever since. See Irving (1825) I, p. 42. See Tearle: "'We must find the Eildon Stone" said my friend that afternoon. "It's on the road to St. Boswells". We must have passed it two or three times. The tree that once stood by it has vanished. That's not wonderful, if Thomas used to stand under it when he had a bit of prophecy to let loose upon the neighbourhood. And the Bogle Burn's quite near. That was where Thomas was lying when he was carried off by the Faery Queen. Till I came into these parts I always supposed the stone and the burn were both in the Rhymer's Glen. I'm afraid Washington Irving was to blame for that". "Washington Irving was at least consistent in his mendacity… He put the stone and the burn and the glen all together. Here's another child; I'll ask her."' Christian Tearle, *Rambles with an American* (London: Mills and Boon, 1910), p. 244.

49. Visited April 2017.

50. For a more extensive discussion of Irving's essay, see Watson (2006), pp. 93–9.

51. Booth (2004), p. 217.

52. Irving (1825) II, pp. 322–3.

53. Duncan Faherty, *Remodelling the Nation: The Architecture of American Identity 1776–1858* (Durham, NH: University of New Hampshire Press, 2007), p. 10.

54. See Judith Richardson, *Possessions: The History and Uses of Hauntings in the Hudson Valley* (Cambridge, MA: Harvard University Press, 2003).

55. Faherty (2007), p. 106.

56. Faherty (2007), pp. 103–6.

57. Washington Irving, 'A Chronicle of Wolfert's Roost', *Knickerbocker*, 13 (April 1839).

58. Evert Augustus Duycksinck ed., *Irvingiana: A Memorial of Washington Irving* (New York: Charles B. Richardson, 1860), p. viii.

59. Duycksinck (1860), pp. xlvii–viii.

60. See also Thomas Oldham Barlow, 'Washington Irving and His Literary Friends at Sunnyside' (London: Moore, McQueen & Co., 1864).

61. *Harper's Monthly Magazine*, 14:79 (December 1856), pp. 1–21 (p. 20).

62. Hugh Cooke MacDougall, *A Bicentennial Guide of Sites in Otsego County Associated with the Life and Fiction of James Fenimore Cooper 1789–1851* (Cooperstown, NY: Historical Association, 1989), p. 33.

63. Longfellow pulled off something analogous when he acquired a house in Cambridge, MA in 1837. This house had been built in 1759, and was notable for having served as George Washington's headquarters during the American Civil War between 1775 and 1776. Longfellow immediately set about mythologizing the house as a national historic site, and himself as national poet within it. The room he used as his study was not coincidentally the room used by Washington for various meetings and councils: to this day the guidebook claims that 'it is possible to say that the idea of the United States as a separate country was born

in this very room'. Henry Dana Longfellow, *The Longfellow House: History and Guide* (Eastern National, 2003).

64. Nathaniel Hawthorne, *Our Old Home: A Series of English Sketches* (Boston, MA: Houghton, Mifflin and Co., 1883), pp. 52–3.

65. In 2013 Abbotsford was redisplayed, provided with a handsome annex exhibition which works hard to construct Scott, in the spirit of contemporary Scottish nationalism, as a national author. Sunnyside's claims to house the national author have been overtaken by the rival claims of Concord's pantheon of Emerson, Thoreau, Hawthorne, and Alcott. What follows is based on my participation from 2014 in the discussions at the Shakespeare Birthplace Trust over the past, present, and future affective meanings of the Birthplace and the other Shakespeare properties as part and parcel of the conversation leading up to redevelopment.

66. On eighteenth-century tourist interest in New Place, see Richard Schoch, 'The Birth of Shakespeare's Birthplace', *Theatre Survey*, 53:2 (2012), pp. 181–201.

67. Samuel Ireland, *Picturesque Views on the Upper or Warwickshire Avon* (London: R. Faulder and T. Egerton, 1795).

68. On the original development of interest in Shakespeare's birthplace as a substitute for the lost New Place, see Schoch (2012).

69. Email exchange Watson/O'Brien; statement transcribed from O'Brien's working notebooks. Recorded interview conducted spring 2017.

70. For a discussion of the long history of Shakespeare gardens as instructive precursors to O'Brien's see Nicola J. Watson, 'Gardening with Shakespeare', Clara Calvo and Coppélia Kahn eds., *Commemorating Shakespeare* (Cambridge: Cambridge University Press, 2015) and Roy Strong, *The Quest for Shakespeare's Garden* (London: Thames and Hudson, 2016).

71. O'Brien's 'Note of Intention', manuscript notebook in O'Brien's collection.

72. *William Shakespeare: The Complete Works*, ed. Stanley Wells and Gary Taylor, 2nd edn. Oxford: Clarendon Press, 2005): *The Tempest* 5:1, ll. 99–101.

73. Perhaps surprisingly, given the proliferation of Shakespeare's chairs, there is only a single Shakespeare desk extant. This is the school desk and bench at King Edward School where he is said to have carved his initials in the wood in an idle moment. Known as 'The Desk of the Bard of Avon', it was shown during the nineteenth and early twentieth centuries in the Birthplace in close proximity to the Shakespeare chair. Now that the Victorian and Edwardian cult of Shakespeare's boyhood has long waned (see Michael Dobson, 'A Boy from Stratford', paper first given Shakespeare Institute, Stratford, 2012), it is newly located in Shakespeare's School Room, opened to the public in April 2013. The desk at New Place does not reference this precursor.

74. Berlowitz commentary. See http://www.jillberelowitz.com/press/minds-eye-tree-sculpture-unveiled-at-shakespeares-new-place, last accessed 02/07/2017.

75. *The Tempest* governed the project from its inception, in accordance with the long tradition of regarding *The Tempest* as Shakespeare's last play, Prospero as Shakespeare's avatar, and his farewell to the island and his magic as Shakespeare's autobiographical renunciation of the stage and his art. This choice was inflected

by W.H. Auden's sense of the author's predicament, strung between Life and Art in *The Sea and the Mirror* (1942–4); this determined O'Brien to present the tension between a life bound to time and space, and works that reach across time and space.

76. 'Return to Stratford Upon Avon England for UNBOSI', United Nations Board Of Significant Inspiration (April 2016), http://www.unbosi.org/unbosi-announce-return-to-stratford-upon-avon-england, last accessed 21/06/2017.

77. Shakespeare Birthplace Trust, 'A Garden of Curious A-Muse-ments', https://www.shakespeare.org.uk/about-us/news-media/press-releases/garden-curious-amusements, last accessed 09/07/2017.

CHAPTER 9

1. As such, it is a special case of Bachelard's insight regarding the house more generally, viz. that 'the house shelters day-dreaming, the house protects the dreamer, the house allows one to dream in peace'. Gaston Bachelard, *The Poetics of Space* [1957] translated from the French by Maria Jolas (Boston, MA: Beacon Press, 1994), p. 6.

2. See Kipling's desk at Bateman's; Dahl's shed at Great Missenden.

3. Judith Buchanan, 'Image, Story, Desire' in Judith Buchanan ed., *The Writer on Film: Screening Literary Authorship* (Basingstoke: Palgrave Macmillan, 2013), p. 11.

4. *Vide* the homesteads of William Cullen Bryant and John Whittier. Bryant's homestead, located at 205 Bryant Road in Cunningham, Massachusetts, boasts of its 'pastoral landscape …largely unchanged for more than 150 years'. See 'About William Cullen Bryant Homestead', http://www.thetrustees.org/places-to-visit/pioneer-valley/bryant-homestead.html, last accessed 27/06/2017.

   Similarly, the website for Whittier's homestead, located at 305 Whittier Road, Haverhill, Massachusetts, describes the house as 'substantially the same as when the poet lived there'. See Whitter Birthplace, http://www.johngreenleafwhittier.com, last accessed 27/06/2017.

5. On the closure of this museum in 2017, see https://www.theguardian.com/books/2017/jun/21/derek-walcott-museum-st-lucia-caribbean-tourism, last accessed 08/01/2019; on the fate of the Borrow museum in brief see http://www.literarynorfolk.co.uk/Norwich/george_borrow.htm, last accessed 08/01/2019.

6. Richard J. Hutchings, *Isle of Wight Literary Haunts* (enlarged edition) (Newport: Isle of Wight County Press, 1989), p. iii.

7. Charles Dickens, *The Life and Adventures of Nicholas Nickleby* (1838–9), chapter 27.

8. My thanks to Elmira College for generously accommodating me in Quarry Farm during my research trip in the autumn of 2009.

9. Quoted in Thomas Roscoe, *The Tourist in Switzerland and Italy* (London: Robert Jennings, 1830), p. 181.

10. This version is cited in William Beckford, *Dreams, Waking Thoughts and Incidents in a series of letters from Various Parts of Europe* (London: Printed for J. Johnson and P. Elmsley, 1783), Letter XII (6 September 1778), p. 127.

11. Perhaps this accounts for the uncertain tone of Samuel Rogers' verses on the subject, which hover uneasily between reiterating what must have been the standard guide's account and describing his own personal experience walking the site:

    This was his chamber. 'Tis as when he left it;
    As if he now were busy in his garden.
    And this his closet. Here he sate and read.
    This was his chair; and in it, unobserved,
    Reading, or thinking of his absent friends,
    He passed away, as in a quiet slumber.

    Samuel Rogers, *Italy: a poem* (London: printed for Longman, Hurst, Rees, Orme, and Brown, 1822) 'Arquà', pp. 117–21 (p. 120).

12. Beckford (1783), p. 127.

13. John Murray, *A Handbook for Travellers in Switzerland, and the Alps of Savoy and Piedmont* (London: John Murray, 1838), p. 144.

14. See, for instance, Helen Maria Williams, *Letters written in France* (London: printed for T. Cadell, 1790), 2 vols, II, pp. 179–80. For a more extended discussion see Watson (2006), pp. 133–50.

15. Friedrich von Matthisson, *Letters written from various parts of the Continent, between the years 1785 and 1794*, trans. Anne Plumptre (London: T.N. Longman and O. Rees, 1799), p. 522.

16. Friedrich Leopold Stolberg, *Travels through Germany, Switzerland, Italy and Sicily*, trans. Thomas Holcroft, (London, 1796–7), 2 vols, I, pp. 142–3.

17. Grace Greenwood, *Haps and Mishaps of a Tour in Europe* (London: Richard Bentley, 1854), pp. 129–30.

18. Being Burns and Rousseau in this way perhaps should have been solitary, meditative, a matter of 'ardent sensibility' and acute attunement to the beauties of nature, but such tourist experiences were very often shared with friends and like-minded strangers. This sometimes seems to have verged on public performance of their shared re-embodiment of the author, if Nikolai Karamzin's account of his encounter with a young Englishman is anything to go by: 'As I sat meditating, I suddenly saw a young man ... approaching me with unhurried steps. In his right hand he was carrying a book. He stopped, looked at me, and said, "Vous pensez à lui". Then he walked away ...'. Nikolai Karamzin, *Letters of a Russian Traveller 1789–90: The Account of a Young Russian Gentleman's Tour through Germany, Switzerland, France and England*, trans. F. James (New York: Columbia University Press, 1957), p. 163.

19. Compare the habit of leaving offerings on authors' tombs, a practice that was certainly in place in the last half of the nineteenth century and probably before,

and which continues to this day. See Susan Coolidge, *What Katy Did Next* (1886; Hertfordshire: Wordsworth Classics, 1995), pp. 76–7, for a fictional account of visiting Jane Austen's tomb in Winchester and laying 'a few rain-washed flowers upon the tomb'. J.R.R. Tolkien's grave in Oxford regularly attracts a remarkable array of offerings referencing 'the one ring'; Oscar Wilde's tomb in Père Lachaise has had to be protected by an acrylic sheet from the damage caused by the lipstick used by admirers to leave the imprint of their kisses on the white stone. And so forth.

20. Beckford (1783), p. 129. Harald Hendrix notes apropos of the house at Arquà that as of the late 1780s 'the owners of the house got impatient with the visitors' habit of carving their names on the walls and furniture, and decided to invite them to sign a visitors' book instead'. Harald Hendrix, 'From Early Modern to Romantic Literary Tourism' in Nicola J. Watson, ed. *Literary Tourism and Nineteenth-century Culture* (Basingstoke: Palgrave Macmillan, 2009), pp. 13–25 (p. 19).

21. The titles of Wordsworth's early inscription poems specify the use of slate pencil, as in 'Lines written with a pencil, upon a Stone in the Wall of the House (an out-house), on the island at Grasmere' (1800), 'Written with a slate pencil on a stone, the largest of a heap lying near a deserted quarry, upon one of the Islands at Rydal' (1800) or 'Written with a slate pencil on a stone, on the side of the Mountain of Black Comb' (1813). See on Wordsworthian inscription Peter Simonsen, *Wordsworth and Word-Preserving Acts: Typographic Inscription, Ekphrasis and Posterity in the Later Work* (Basingstoke: Palgrave Macmillan, 2007), p. 43.

22. Equally, the poetic inscription on the wall of Petrarch's study by Alfieri, quoted above, is described in 1834 as having been written in pencil with 'a sort of frame ... placed before it, to preserve it from being effaced'; it is only by the second half of the nineteenth century that a traveller describes it as 'written in ink on the wall', so it seems possible that the inscription had been inked in afterwards as a prize exhibit. William Dean Howells, 'A Pilgrimage to Petrarch's House at Arquà', *Italian Journeys: from Venice to Naples and beyond* (Edinburgh: David Douglas, 1887), p. 22.

23. Benedict Anderson, *Imagined Communities: Reflections on the Origin and Spread of Nationalism* (1983; London: Verso, 2006).

24. For a discussion of the visitors' book as housing micro-forms of travel writing, that also includes a useful survey of extant scholarship, see Rita Singer, 'Leisure, Refuge, and Solidarity: Messages in Visitors' Books as Microforms of Travel Writing', *Studies in Travel Writing*, 20:4 (March 2017), pp. 392–408.

25. Louis Simond, *Switzerland; or, A Journal of a Tour and Residence in that Country, in the years 1817, 1818, and 1819: followed by An Historical Sketch on the manners of Ancient and Modern Helvetia in which the events of our own time are fully detailed, together with the causes to which they may be referred* (London: John Murray, 1822), 2 vols, I, pp. 62–3.

26. John Chetwode Eustace, *A Classical Tour Through Italy* ([1802] 1818), 2 vols, I, p. 217. Quoted at length in Thomas Roscoe, *The Tourist in Switzerland and Italy*

(London: Robert Jennings, 1830). Roscoe provides the translation of the album verse, p. 177.

27. Quoted Roscoe (1830), p. 177. Eustace notes that in spite of this amenity 'the walls are covered in names, compliments, and verses'. Eustace (1818) I, p. 217.

28. Sigismond Wagner [Sigmund von Wagner], *L'Île Saint-Pierre ou L'Île de Rousseau* (A Berne: G. Lory et C. Rheiner, 1815), p. 15.

29. Wagner (1815), p. 16. 'One evening, in moonlight, wandering in this wood/ I found the wild and mournful shade of Rousseau/'What do you want?' he said, turning his eyes on me/'The same as you, master, to admire these beautiful places'./'You are right, all is beautiful', said he, 'in nature/Except man, who disfigures it'.

30. Simond (1822) I, pp. 62–3.

31. See as instances Seamus Heaney, 'A Scuttle for Dorothy Wordsworth', *District and Circle: Poems* (New York: Farrar, Straus and Giroux, 2006), Paul Edmondson, *Destination Shakespeare* (Vancouver: Misfit Press, 2016).

32. https://placingtheauthor.wordpress.com/postcards, last accessed 29/05/2017.

33. Jo Taylor, 'Postcards from Newstead Abbey', Placing the Author (August 2016), https://placingtheauthor.wordpress.com/2016/08/31/breathtaking-sarahs-postcard-from-newstead-abbey, last accessed 29/05/2015.

34. The very first paying visitors to a dead writer's house were, after all, those who arrived at the house-auction of the author's effects. Catalogues for such auctions are importantly informative about the variable cultural value of the contents of writer's houses, partly through how they are puffed, and partly through how much they fetched. In 1824, for example, the poet Robert Bloomfield's effects were auctioned off to meet his funeral costs. Potential buyers were offered his books, his literary manuscripts, his inkstand, and Lot 72, 'the celebrated OAK TABLE, which Mr Bloomfield may be said to have rendered immortal by the beautiful and pathetic poem inscribed to it in his *Wild Flowers*'. The copies of the catalogue are partially annotated with buyers and prices, and one such note reveals the astonishing price—£14—paid for Lot 57, 'The ORIGINAL MANUSCRIPT of *Mr Bloomfield's* popular poem of "The Farmer's Boy" *in the Author's Handwriting,* elegantly bound'. It was unlikely that a tourist would find much left on site after this sort of clear-out.

35. On the prank, see Doug Stewart, 'To Be ... Or Not: The Greatest Shakespeare Forgery' (June 2010), *The Smithsonian Magazine*, http://www.smithsonianmag. com/history/to-beor-not-the-greatest-shakespeare-forgery-136201, last accessed 09/07/2017. The lust for relics is well illustrated by the recognition in March 1810 of a gold signet ring unearthed in a field next to Holy Trinity Churchyard and bearing the initials WS as that of William Shakespeare himself. The provenance is doubtful, complicated by the fact that Garrick had displayed a similar ring in his Temple in the 1750s. See Peter Hewitt, https://www.shakespeare.org.uk/ explore-shakespeare/blogs/shakespeare-100-objects-shakespearessignetring, last accessed 07/01/2019.

36. See Maddie Cox, 'On the Trail of Mary Hornby', Finding Shakespeare (October 2015), http://findingshakespeare.co.uk/trail-mary-hornby, last accessed 09/07/2017.

37. Simond remarked in 1822 that 'Time and travellers have much impaired the furniture of light-blue silk ... the bed-curtains especially, which for the last forty years have supplied each traveller with a precious little bit, hastily torn off, are of course in tatters; the house-keeper indeed is so well aware of this, that she purposely turns away, to afford you an opportunity for the poetical theft, expecting her fees to be the more liberal on that account'. Simond (1822) I, pp. 552–3. Charles Tennant also remarked on the shreds of curtains 'so snipped and twitched by visitors'. *A Tour through parts of The Netherlands, Holland, Germany, Switzerland, Savoy, and France, in the year 1821–2. Including a description of the Rhine Voyage in the Middle of Autumn, and the Stupendous Scenery of the Alps in the depth of Winter...*, (London: Longman, Hurst, Rees, Orme, Brown and Green, 1824), 2 vols, vol. 2, p. 260. In 1833, Lewis Agassiz recorded seeing the bed curtains mostly cut away, but that they were now protected from further depredations. *A Journey to Switzerland, and Pedestrian Tours in that Country; including A Sketch of its History, and of the Manners and Customs of its Inhabitants* (London: Smith, Elder and Co, 1833), pp. 129–34. According to Lise Emilie Fosmo Talleraas <lise.talleraas@vestfoldmuseene.no>, there is a piece of Voltaire's bed-hangings extant in the Naval Museum in Horten. It was part of the collection of one of the museum founders, Kommandørkaptein Christen Frederik Klinck, and was given to him by the landowner Løwenskiold in 1825. Museum number 521. I am indebted to Johan Schimanski for tracking this reference down for me.

38. Marianne Colston, *Journal of a Tour in France, Switzerland, and Italy, during the years 1819, 20, and 21 illustrated by fifty lithographic prints, from original drawings taken in Italy, the Alps, and the Pyrenees* (Paris: A. and W. Galignani, 1822), 2 vols, I, pp. 246–51, 274–8. See also Nathaniel Hazeltine Carter, *Letters from Europe, the journal of a tour through Ireland, England, Scotland, France, Italy, and Switzerland, in 1825, '26, and '27* (New York, 1827). For the mass of inscription at Ariosto's house see John Murray's *Handbook for Travellers in Northern Italy: Comprising Turin, Milan, Pavia, Cremona, the Italian Lakes, Bergamo, Brescia, Verona, Mantua, Vicenza, Padua, Venice, Ferrara, Bologna, Ravenna, Rimini, Modena, Parma, Piacenza, Genoa, the Riviera, and the Intermediate Towns and Routes* (London: John Murray, 1877) which records pencilled inscriptions by Byron, Casimir Delavigne, and Lamartine (p. 432). For an account of visiting Tasso's cell, see Percy Bysshe Shelley's letter to Thomas Peacock, 8 November 1818: 'I enclose you a piece of the wood of the very door which for seven years and three months divided this glorious being from the air and light...'. Percy Bysshe Shelley, *Essays, Letters from Abroad, Translations and Fragments*, ed. Mrs Shelley (London: Edward Moxon, 1852), 2 vols, I, p. 151.

39. For more on this, see Watson, 'At Juliet's Tomb: Anglophone Travel-Writing and Shakespeare's Verona, 1814–1914' in ed. Silvia Bigliazzi and Lisanna

Calvi, *Shakespeare, Romeo and Juliet and Civic Life* (London: Routledge, 2016), pp. 224–37.

40. Both held by the Shakespeare Birthplace Trust. Thus, this was not even, really, a walking-stick in anything but a ceremonial sense. Its purpose was to bring the roof that witnessed the birth of genius to sponsor the birth of the theatre. Shakespeare Birthplace Collection, acquired 2015.

41. By 1847 William Howitt recorded the effects of readerly enthusiasm: 'The fame which [Cowper] has conferred on this tree has nearly proved its destruction. Whole arms and great pieces of its trunk have been cut away with knife, and axe, and saw, to prepare different articles from. The marquis of Northampton, to whom the chase belongs, has had multitudes of nails driven in to stop the progress of this destruction, but, finding that not sufficient, has affixed a board bearing this inscription:—"Out of respect to the memory of the poet Cowper, the Marquis of Northampton is particularly desirous of preserving this oak. Notice is hereby give, that any person defacing or otherwise injuring it will be prosecuted...".'. William Howitt, *Homes and Haunts of the Most Eminent British Poets* (London: Richard Bentley, 1847), 2 vols, I, p. 407.

42. As Cowper's (fanciful) lines on the Jubilee's deployment of the mulberry tree make plain:

> Ah! pleasant proof
> That piety has still in human hearts
> Some place, a spark or two not yet extinct.
> The mulberry tree was hung with blowing wreaths,
> The mulberry tree stood centre of the dance,
> The mulberry tree was hymned with dulcet airs,
> And from his touchwood trunk the mulberry tree
> Supplied such relics as devotion holds
> Still sacred, and preserves with pious care...
> *The Task*, Book VI, ll. 682–90.

43. Tara Hamling and Cathryn Enis have argued that these souvenir items speak of an anxiety about lost Shakespearean domesticity and the desire to reproduce it, and note the way that they imagine genteel idylls, so creating an implicit if problematic connection to Shakespearean domesticity. Unpublished paper, 'Material Loss' conference, Birmingham, 2017.

44. F.G. Savage, *The Flora and Folk Lore of Shakespeare* (London: E.J. Burrow, 1923), p. 202.

45. See *Illustrated London News*, 12 April 1862; Savage (1923), p. 202.

46. This sentimental structure was related to the curious sub-genre of books about 'Shakespeare's flowers'. See Watson, 'Gardening with Shakespeare' in Clara Calvo and Coppélia Kahn eds., *Commemorating Shakespeare* (Cambridge: Cambridge University Press, 2015), pp. 301–29.

47. Julia Thomas, *Shakespeare's Shrine: The Bard's Birthplace and the Invention of Stratford-Upon-Avon* (Philadelphia, PA: University of Pennsylvania Press, 2012), p. 154.

48. Emma Novello, 'The Tomb of Percy Bysshe Shelley in the Protestant Cemetery at Rome' (1851), mixed media. See Samantha Matthews, *Poetical Remains: Poets' Graves, Bodies, and Books in the Nineteenth Century* (Oxford: Oxford University Press, 2004), pp. 113–54. See also Jessica Roberson, 'Shelley's Grave, Botanical Souvenirs, and Handling Literary Afterlives', *Victoriographies*, 6:3 (October 2016), pp. 276–94.

49. Harriet Beecher Stowe, *Sunny Memories of Foreign Lands* (London; Sampson Low, Son and Co., 1854), 2 vols, I, p. 214.

50. Elbert Hubbard, *Little Journeys to the Homes of the Great* (New York: East Aurora, 1895–1910), 14 vols, I, pp. 221–2.

51. Visit paid in 2008. My heartfelt thanks to my hostess who put me up in her home, organized a delightful tea with the local Shakespeare Ladies' Club, gave me access to the manuscript diary and the albums, told me of Mrs Shay's ghost, and rescued me from a tornado into the bargain.

52. G. Abrahamson, *Mrs Shay Did It!* (Wessington Springs, SD: A.L. Webb, 1976), pp. 28–31.

53. 'Through narrative, the souvenir substitutes a context of perpetual consumption for its context of origin. It represents not the lived experience of its maker but the 'secondhand' experience of its possessor/owner'.. Susan Stewart, *On Longing: Narratives of the Miniature, the Gigantic, the Souvenir, the Collection* (Durham, NC and London: Duke University Press, 1993), p. 135.

54. Stewart (1993), p. 135.

55. Diarists, letter-writers, essayists, autobiographers, and poets have proven most successful at this; playwrights are the least successful, as they characteristically 'talk' through many masks, and to large theatre audiences. Novelists, even realist novelists, unless they are particularly given to writing in a first-person mode which can be conveniently conflated with the author's persona, or unless they are especially intrusive and chatty, tend to require a fair amount of work to render them visible and seductive as an 'I' to the reader-tourist.

56. Allan Bank. Visited c. 2014.

57. Anonymous, *An Account of the Principal Pleasure Tours of England and Wales* (London: for Baldwin, Cradock and Joy, 1822), p. 365.

58. Linda Young, 'Writers' House Museums: English Literature in the Heart and on the Ground' in LuAnn McCracken Fletcher ed., *Literary Tourism and the British Isles: History, Imagination, and the Politics of Place* (Lexington, KY: Lexington Press, 2019), chapter 7.

59. Paula Byrne, *The Real Jane Austen: A Life in Small Things* (London: HarperPress, 2013); Deborah Lutz, *The Brontë Cabinet: Three Lives in Nine Objects* (New York, London: W.W. Norton & Co., 2015).

60. Having bought 'Füsun's house', Pamuk proceeded to furnish it with objects and to write the novel: according to Elif Batuman, reporting on Pamuk's remarks at the press launch, 'writing and shopping proceeded in a dialectical relationship. Pamuk would buy objects that caught his eye, and wait for the novel

to "swallow" them, demanding, in the process, the purchase of further objects'. In its entirety, the museum finally consisted of eighty-three vitrines corresponding to the novel's eighty-three chapters. The museum mimics in every detail museum practice: exhibits are carefully captioned, and replicas, including of one of the more sentimentally important exhibits, the heroine's lost butterfly earring, are sold as souvenirs in the museum shop. Elif Batuman, 'Diary', *London Review of Books*, 7 June 2012, p. 38. Exhibition visited in part in Oslo, September 2017.

Bibliography

Abrahamson, G., *Mrs Shay Did It!* (Wessington Springs, SD: A.L. Webb, 1976)

Addison, Joseph, *Spectator*, no. 417 (1710)

Addison, Joseph, *Tatler*, no. 254 (1710)

Adolphe, Joanne, *Les environs de Paris, illustrés*, 2nd edn (Paris: Hachette, 1868)

Agassiz, Lewis, *A Journey to Switzerland, and Pedestrian Tours in that Country; including A Sketch of its History, and of the Manners and Customs of its Inhabitant* (London: Smith, Elder and Co, 1833)

Alcott, Louisa M., *Little Women; or, Meg, Jo, Beth, and Amy*, 6th edn (London: Sampson Low, Marston, Low and Searle, 1871)

Alexander, Philip Bruce, *History of the University of Virginia 1819–1919: The Lengthened Shadow of One Man* (London: The Macmillan Company, 1922)

Ali, Agha Shahid, 'A Nostalgist's Map of America', in Susan Danley ed., *Language and Object: Emily Dickinson and Contemporary Art* (Mead Art Museum: Amherst College in association with University of Massachusetts Press, 1997)

Allbut, Robert, *Rambles in Dickens' Land* (New York: Truslove, Hanson & Comba, 1899)

An Account of the Principal Pleasure Tours of England and Wales (London: for Baldwin, Cradock and Joy, 1822)

Andersen, Hans Christian, *The Fairytale of My Life*, trans. and introd. by Naomi Lewis (New York: Cooper Square Press, 2000)

Anderson, Benedict, *Imagined Communities: Reflections on the Origin and Spread of Nationalism* (London: Verso, 2006)

Ascaso, Francisco J. and Jvan Velze, 'Was James Joyce Myopic or Hyperopic?', *British Medical Journal*, 343:7837 (2011), p. 1295

Atkin, Polly, 'Ghosting Grasmere: The Musealization of Dove Cottage', in Nicola J. Watson ed., *Literary Tourism and Nineteenth-Century Culture* (Basingstoke: Palgrave Macmillan, 2009), pp. 84–94

Austen-Leigh, James Edward, *A Memoir of Jane Austen* (London: Richard Bentley, 1870)

Austen-Leigh, J.E., *A Memoir of Jane Austen*, 2nd edition (London: Bentley, 1871)

Bachelard, Gaston, *La Poétique de l'Espace* (Paris: Presses Universitaires de France, 1957) trans. as *The Poetics of Space* (New York: Orion Press, 1964)

Bachelard, Gaston, *The Poetics of Space* trans. by Maria Jolas (Boston, MA: Beacon Press, 1994)

Baker, Margaret, *London Statues and Monuments* (London: Shire, 1995)

Baillie, Joanna, *The Collected Letters of Joanna Baillie*, ed. Judith Bailey Slagle (Charlottesville, VA: InteLex Corporation, 2004) 2 vols

Bann, Stephen, *The Clothing of Clio: A Study of the Representation of History in Nineteenth-Century Britain And France* (Cambridge, New York: Cambridge University Press, 1984), pp. 93–111

Barker, Emma, unpublished conference paper, 'Figuring the Sibyl: pictorial models for women writers and readers', 'Jane Austen and Germaine de Staël, 1817–2017', Chawton House, July 2017

Barlow, Thomas Oldham, 'Washington Irving and His Literary Friends at Sunnyside' (London: Moore, McQueen & Co., 1864)

Barnes, Julian, *Flaubert's Parrot* (London: Jonathan Cape, 1984)

Barnett, Teresa, *Sacred Relics: Pieces of the Past in Nineteenth-Century America* (Chicago, IL: The University of Chicago Press, 2013)

Barthes, Roland, *The Fashion System*, trans. Matthew Ward and Richard Howard (New York: Hill and Wang, 1983)

Batuman, Elif, 'Diary', *London Review of Books*, 34:11 (7 June 2012), p. 38.

Baudrillard, Jean, 'Subjective Discourse or the Non-Functional System of Objects', in Fiona Candlin and Raiford Guins eds., *The Object-Reader* (London and New York: Routledge, 2009), pp. 41–63

Beckford, William, *Dreams, Waking Thoughts and Incidents; In a series of Letters from Various Parts of Europe* (London: J. Johnson and P. Elmsley, 1783)

Benazzi, Stefano, et al., 'The Face of the Poet Dante Alighieri, Reconstructed by Virtual Modelling and Forensic Anthropology Techniques', *Journal of Archaeological Science*, 36:2 (February 2009), pp. 278–83

Benfey, Christopher, *A Summer of Hummingbirds: Love, Art, and Scandal in the Intersecting Worlds of Emily Dickinson, Mark Twain, Harriet Beecher Stowe & Martin Johnson Heade* (London: Penguin, 2008)

Benjamin, Walter, *The Arcades Project* (London: Harvard University Press, 2002)

Benjamin, Walter, 'The Work of Art in the Age of Mechanical Reproduction, *Illuminations*' (1955) ed. with introd., Hannah Arendt, trans. Harry Zorn (London: Penguin, 1969)

Bennett, Andrew, *Romantic Poets and the Culture of Posterity* (Cambridge: Cambridge University Press, 1999)

Bergland, Renée L., 'The Puritan Eyeball, or Sexing the Transcendent', in Tracy Fessenden, Nicholas F. Radel, and Magdalena J. Zaborowska eds., *The Puritan Origins of American Sex: Religion, Sexuality, and National Identity in American Literature* (New York, London: Routledge, 2001), pp. 93–108.

Bernard, Richard Boyle, *A Tour through some parts of France, Switzerland, Savoy, Germany and Belgium, during the Summer and Autumn of 1814* (London: Longman, Hurst, Rees, Orme, and Brown, 1814)

Best, Stephen and Sharon Marcus, 'Surface Reading: An Introduction', *Representations*, 108:1 (Fall 2009), pp. 1–21

Betts, W., *A Catalogue of the Valuable Books, Household Furniture, etc To be sold at Auction by W. Betts on Friday and Saturday the 28th and 29th May 1824 ...the Property of the late Mr R. Bloomfield, the Poet, on the Premises, at Shefford, Beds* (Biggleswade: Jackson, 1824)

Biggers, Shirley Hoover, *American Author Houses, Museums, Memorials, and Libraries: A State-by-State Guide* (Jefferson, NC and London: McFarland and Co., 2000)

Bindman, David, *The Shadow of the Guillotine: Britain and the French Revolution* (London: British Museum Press, 1989)

Birrell, Augustine, *The Collected Essays and Addresses of the Rt Hon Augustine Birrell, 1880–1920* (New York: Charles Scribner's Sons, 1923)

Black, John, *Life of Torquato Tasso* (London: John Murray, 1810)

Blewitt, Octavian, *A Handbook for Travellers in Central Italy*, 2nd edn (London: John Murray, 1850)

Bloomfield, Robert, *Wild Flowers: or, Pastoral and Local Poetry* (London: for Vernor, Hood and Sharpe, and Longman, Hurst, Rees and Orme, 1806)

Bohn, James A., *Biographical, Antiquarian and Picturesque Tour in the Northern Counties of England and in Scotland* (London: for the author, 1838), 2 vols

Booth, Alison, 'The Real Right Place of Henry James: Homes and Haunts', *The Henry James Review*, 25:3 (Fall 2004), pp. 216–27

Booth, Alison, 'Time-Travel in Dickens' World', in Nicola J. Watson ed., *Literary Tourism and Nineteenth-Century Culture* (Basingstoke: Palgrave Macmillan, 2009), pp. 150–163

Booth, Alison, *Homes and Haunts: Touring Writers' Shrines and Countries* (Oxford: Oxford University Press, 2016)

Bosco, Ronald A. and Jillmarie Murphy, eds., *Hawthorne in His Own Time: A Biographical Chronicle of his Life, Drawn From Recollections, Interviews, and Memoirs by Family, Friends and Associates* (Iowa City, IA: University of Iowa Press, 2007)

Boswell, James, *Life of Johnson, Together with Boswell's Journal of a Tour of the Hebrides and Johnson's Diary of a Journey into North Wales*, ed. George Birkbeck Hill, rev. L.F. Powell, (Oxford: Clarendon Press, 1934–50), 6 vols

Brack, O.M. ed., *The Life of Samuel Johnson, LL.D by Sir John Hawkins* (Athens, GA and London: University of Georgia Press, 2009)

Bradbury, Malcolm, *To the Hermitage* (London: Picador, 2000)

Bradley, Edward Wedlake and James Sargant Storer, *Cowper, illustrated by a series of views in, or near, the park of Weston-Underwood, Bucks. Accompanied by copious descriptions and a brief sketch of the poet's life* (London, 1803)

Brown, Bill, 'Introduction: "Things"', *Critical Inquiry* 28:1 (Autumn 2001), pp. 1–22

Brown, Sally, 'An Echo and a Light unto Eternity: The Founding of the Keats-Shelley House', in *Keats and Italy: A History of the Keats-Shelley House in Rome* (Rome: Edizioni Il Labirinto, 2005), pp. 51–67

Browning, Robert, *Red Cotton Night-cap Country: or, Turf and Towers* (London: Smith, Elder and Co., 1873)

Buchanan, Judith, 'Image, Story, Desire', in Judith Buchanan ed., *The Writer on Film: Screening Literary Authorship* (Basingstoke: Palgrave Macmillan, 2013)

Buchanan, Judith ed., *The Writer on Film: Screening Literary Authorship* (Basingstoke: Palgrave Macmillan, 2013)

Buell, Lawrence, 'The Thoreauvian Pilgrimage: The Structure of an American Cult', *American Literature*, 61.2 (1989), pp. 175–99

Bulgakov, Mikhail, *The White Guard*, trans. Roger Cockrell (Richmond, VA: Alma Classics, 2016)

Bullock, William, *Six Months Residence and Travels in Mexico* (Port Washington, NY: Kennikat Press, 1971)

Bullus, Claire and Ronald Asprey, *The Statues of London* (London and New York: Merrell, 2009)

Byrne, Paula, *The Real Jane Austen: A Life in Small Things* (London: Harper Press, 2013)

Byrne, Paula, *The Genius of Jane Austen: Her Love of Theatre and Why She Is a Hit in Hollywood* (London: Harper Collins, 2017)

Byron, George Gordon, *The Works of the Right Honourable Lord Byron* (London: John Murray, 1819), 8 vols

Calvo, Clara and Kahn, Coppélia, eds., *Commemorating Shakespeare* (Cambridge: Cambridge University Press, 2015)

Carter, Nathaniel Hazeltine, *Letters from Europe, the Journal of a tour through Ireland, England, Scotland, France, Italy, and Switzerland, in 1825, '26, and '27*

Chadwick, Mrs Ellis, *In the Footsteps of the Brontës* (London, 1914; Cambridge: Cambridge University Press, 2011)

Channing, Ellery, *Thoreau, the Poet-Naturalist* (London: Roberts Bros, 1873)

Chesterton, G.K., 'The Mystery of the Pageant' reprinted in *Tremendous Trifles* (New York: Cosimo, 2007)

Children's Friend: A Magazine for Boys and Girls at Home and School, vol. 36 (London: S.W. Partridge & Co, 1896)

Clarke, Brock, *An Arsonist's Guide to Writers' Homes in New England: A Novel* (London: William Heinemann, 2008)

Clarke, Helen Archibald, *Hawthorne's Country* (Garden City, NY: Doubleday, Page & Co., 1913), facsimile reprint (New Delhi: Isha Books, 2013)

Coates, Thomas F.G. and Warren R.S. Bell, *Marie Corelli: The Writer and the Woman* (London: Hutchinson, 1903)

Cohen, Jane R., *Charles Dickens and His Original Illustrators* (Columbus, OH: Ohio State University Press, 1980)

Coleridge, Samuel Taylor, *The Poems of Samuel Taylor Coleridge* ed. Ernest Hartley Coleridge (London, Oxford: Oxford University Press, 1935)

Collins, Billy, *Taking Off Emily Dickinson's Clothes* (London: Picador, Pan Macmillan, 2000)

Colston, Marianne, *Journal of a Tour in France, Switzerland, and Italy, during the years 1819, 20, and 21 illustrated by fifty lithographic prints, from original drawings taken in Italy, the Alps, and the Pyrenees* (Paris: A. and W. Galignani, 1822), 2 vols

Combe, George, *Four Views of the skull of Robert Burns: taken from a cast moulded at Dumfries, the 31st day of March 1834* (Edinburgh: W. & A.K. Johnson, 1834)

Combe, George, *The Phrenological Development of Robert Burns From a Cast of His Skull Moulded at Dumfries, the 31st Day of March 1834* (Edinburgh: W. & A.K. Johnson, 1859)

Coolidge, Susan, *What Katy Did Next* (Hertfordshire: Wordsworth Classics, 1995)

Cooter, Roger, *Phrenology in the British Isles: an annotated historical bibliography and index* (Metuchen, NJ and London: Scarecrow, 1989)

Cory, Charlotte, 'Capturing the Brontës', exhibition at Haworth Parsonage, 4 October to 31 December 2013

Cowper, William, *The Letters and Prose Writings of William Cowper*, ed. James King and Charles Ryskamp (Oxford: Clarendon Press, 1981), 5 vols

Cowper, William, *The Poems of William Cowper*, ed. John D. Baird and Charles Ryskamp (Oxford Clarendon Press, 1995), 3 vols

Coyer, Megan, 'The Literary Empiricism of the Phrenologists: Reading the Burnsian Bumps', *The Drouth*, 30 Winter (2008), pp. 69–77

Crockett, W.S., *Abbotsford* (London: Adam and Charles Black, 1905)

Cunningham, Allan, *The Life and Land of Burns* (New York, J. & H.G. Langley, 1841)

Curtis, George William, 'Nathaniel Hawthorne' (1853), in Elbert Hubbard ed., *Little Journeys to the Homes of American Authors* (New York: G.P. Putnam's Sons, 1896)

Curtius, Philippe Guillaume Mathé, *Sketches of the Characters Composing the Cabinet of Composition Figures, executed by the celebrated Curtius of Paris, and his successor [Madame Tussaud]* (Edinburgh: for the proprietors, printed by Donovan and Co., 1803)

Dana, Henry Wadsworth Longfellow, *The Longfellow House: History and Guide* (Eastern National Park and Monument Organisation, 2003)

Daston, Lorraine, *Things That Talk: Object Lessons from Art and Science* (New York: Zone Books, 2004)

Davidházi, Peter, *The Romantic Cult of Shakespeare: Literary Reception in Anthropological Perspective* (Basingstoke: Palgrave, 1998)

Derrida, Jacques, *Writing and Difference* trans. Alan Bass (Chicago, IL: University of Chicago Press, 1978)

Deutsch, Helen, *Resemblance and Disgrace; Alexander Pope and the Deformation of Culture* (Cambridge, MA and London: Harvard University Press, 1996)

Deutsch, Helen, *Loving Dr Johnson* (Chicago, IL: University of Chicago Press, 2006)

Dexter, John F., *Dickens Memento, with an intro by F. Phillimore, and 'Hints to Dickens Collectors: Catalogue with Purchaser's Names and Prices Realised of the Pictures, Drawings, and Objects of Art of the Late Charles Dickens, sold by auction on July 9th, 1870. With introduction by Francis Phillimore, and Hints to Collectors, by John F. Dexter* (London: Field & Tuer, 1884)

Dickens, Charles, *The Life and Adventures of Nicholas Nickleby* (Oxford: Oxford University Press, 2008)

Dickens, Charles, *The Old Curiosity Shop* (London: Chapman and Hall, 1871)

Dickens, Charles, *Bleak House* (London: Bradbury and Evans, 1853), 3 vols

Dickens, Charles, *The Letters of Charles Dickens, 1833–1870*, ed. Georgina Hogarth and Mamie Dickens, 2nd edn (Piccadilly: Chapman and Hall, 1880), 2 vols

Dickens, Charles, *Barnaby Rudge*, ed. F.G. Kitton (London: Methuen & Co, 1901), 3 vols

Dickens, Charles, *Barnaby Rudge: A Tale of the Riots of 'Eighty*, incl. 76 illustrations by George Cattermole and Hablot K. Browne ('Phiz') and an Introduction by Kathleen Tillotson (London, New York, Toronto: Oxford University Press, 1954)

Dickens, Charles, *The Letters of Charles Dickens*, ed. Madeline House and Graham Storey, associate editor Kathleen Tillotson (Oxford: Clarendon Press, 1969), 12 vols

Dickens, Mamie, *My Father as I Recall Him* (London: The Roxburghe Press, 1897)

Dickinson, Donald C., *Dictionary of American Book Collectors* (New York: Greenwood Press, 1986)

Dickinson, Emily, *The Letters of Emily Dickinson*, ed. Thomas H. Johnson, associate editor Theodora Ward (Cambridge, MA: Belknap Press of Harvard University Press, 1958), 3 vols

Dickinson, Emily, *The Poems of Emily Dickinson*, ed. Thomas H. Johnson (Cambridge: Belknap Press of Harvard University Press, 1955)

Dinsdale, Ann, 'The Brontë Parsonage Museum, the Brontë Society, and the Preservation of Brontëana', in Diane Hoeveler and Deborah Denenholz eds., *A Companion to the Brontës*, (Chichester: Wiley & Blackwell, 2016)

Dinsdale, Ann, Sarah Laycock, and Julie Akhurst, *Brontë Relics: A Collection History* (Keighley: Brontë Society Publications, 2012)

Dobson, Michael, *The Making of the National Poet: Shakespeare, Adaptation, and Authorship, 1660–1769* (Oxford: Oxford University Press, 1992)

Dobson, Michael, 'A Boy from Stratford, 1769–1916: Shakespearean Biography and Romantic Nationalism', in Zachary Leader ed., *On Life Writing* (Oxford: Oxford University Press, 2015), pp. 25–47

Dovíc, Marijan and Jón Karl Helgason, *National Poets, Cultural Saints: Canonization and Commemorative Cults of Writers in Europe* (Leiden: Brill, 2017)

Dumas, Alexandre, *The Château d'If: A Romance* (vol 1) and *The Count of Monte Cristo,* (vols 1 and 2), trans. Emma Hardy (Belfast: Simms and M'Intyre, 1846)

Dumas, Alexandre, 'Ah vous voilà Dumas!?', *Mon Odyssée à la Comédie Française, Paris et les Parisiens au XIX siècle: mœurs, arts et monuments* (Paris: Morizot, 1856)

Dumas, Alexandre, *Histoires de mes bêtes*, 2nd edn (Paris: Librairie Nouvelle, 1868)

Dunn, Jane, Du Maurier *and her sisters: The Hidden Lives of Piffy, Bird and Bing* (New York: Harper Press, 2013), pp. 199–200.

Durbridge, Nicola, *Cowper's Tame Hares* (Olney: Cowper-Newton Museum, 2011)

Durbridge, Nicola, *Cowper's Writing Slope: A Material World* (Olney: Cowper-Newton Museum, 2012)

Duyckinck, Evert A., *Irvingiana: A Memorial of Washington Irving* (New York: Charles B. Richardson, 1860)

Easley, Alexis, *Literary Celebrity, Gender, and Victorian Authorship, 1850–1914* (Newark, DE: University of Delaware Press, 2011)

Edmondson, Paul, *Destination Shakespeare* (Vancouver: Misfit Press, 2016)

Edwards, Nat, *Burns National Heritage Park* (Ayr: Jarrold Publishing, 2003)

Eisner, Eric, *Nineteenth-Century Poetry and Literary Celebrity* (New York: Palgrave, 2009)

Ellis, Markman, *The Politics of Sensibility: Race, Gender and Commerce in the Sentimental Novel* (Cambridge: Cambridge University Press, 1996)

Ellmann, Richard, *James Joyce* (New York: Oxford University Press, 1982)

Ellmann, Richard, 'Portrait of the Artist in a New Light' *Irish Independent*, 16 December 2011

Emery, Elizabeth, *Photojournalism and the Origins of the French Writer's House Museum (1881–1914): Privacy, Publicity and Personality* (Surrey, UK: Ashgate, 2013)

Eustace, John Chetwode, *A Classical Tour Through Italy* ([1802] 1818)

Every Saturday: A Journal of Choice Reading (London: Ticknor and Fields, 6 February 1869)

'Fabricating Uncertainty: Virginia Woolf, Serena Partridge, and the Interpretive Possibilities of Brontë Pseudo-Relics', *Journal of Victorian Culture*, forthcoming

Faherty, Duncan, *Remodelling the Nation: The Architecture of American Identity 1776–1858* (Durham, NH: University of New Hampshire Press, 2007)

Ferrar, John, *A Tour from Dublin to London in 1795: through the Isle of Anglesea, Bangor, Conway…and Kensington* (Dublin, 1796)

Ferris, Ina and Paul Keen eds., *Bookish Histories: Books, Literature, and Commercial Modernity 1700–1900* (Basingstoke: Palgrave Macmillan, 2009)

Fields, James T., *Yesterdays with Authors* (James R. Osgood, late Ticknor & Fields, and Fields, Osgood, & Company, 1874)

Flagg, Wilson, *A Year Among the Trees: Or, The Woods and By-ways of New England* (Boston, MA: Estes & Lauriat, 1881)

Fletcher, LuAnn McCracken ed., *Literary Tourism and the British Isles: History, Imagination, and the Politics of Place* (Lanham, MD, Boulder, CO, New York, London: Lexington Books, 2019)

Foer, Jonathan Safran, *A Convergence of Birds: Original Fiction and Poetry Inspired by the Work of Joseph Cornell* (New York: Distributed Art Publishers, 2001)

Fogg, Nicholas, *Stratford-upon-Avon: The Biography* (Stroud: Amberley, 2014)

Fontane, Theodore, *Across the Tweed: A Tour of Mid-Victorian Scotland*, trans. Sir James Ferguson (London: Phoenix House, 1965)

Forster, John, *The Life of Charles Dickens*, ed. and introd. J. W. T. Ley (1872: London: Cecil Palmer, 1928)

Foster, Shirley, 'Americans and Anti-Tourism', in Nicola J. Watson ed., *Literary Tourism and Nineteenth-Century Culture* (Basingstoke: Palgrave Macmillan, 2009), pp. 175–83

Foucault, Michel, 'Of Other Spaces', *Diacritics*, 16:1 (Spring 1986), pp. 22–7

Foucault, Michel, *Aesthetics, Method, and Epistemology*, ed. James D. Faubin, trans. Robert Hurley et al., *Essential Works of Foucault 1964–1984* vol. 2 (New York: The New Press, 1998), pp. 205–22

Foulsham, Frank, 'In the Footsteps of Barnaby Rudge', *The Royal Magazine* (December 1900)

'Four Walks from Haworth Village' (Bradford: Bradford District Council, 2003)

Fraser, Mark, 'The Phrenologists and Robert Burns', *Burns Chronicle*, 6 (December 1996), pp. 215–21

Freud, Sigmund, *The Standard Edition of the Complete Psychological Works of Sigmund Freud* (New York: International Universities Press, 1984), 6 vols

Frey, Bruno S., and Pommerehne, Werner R., 'Art Investment: An Empirical Inquiry', *Southern Economic Journal*, 56:2 (October 1989), pp. 396–409

Fulsås, Narve, 'Housing World Literature: Norwegian Ibsen Museums', unpublished paper, reading-group, TRAUM, October 2018

Fuss, Diana, *The Sense of an Interior: Four Writers and the Rooms That Shaped Them* (London and New York: Routledge, 2004)

Garber, Marjorie, *Vested Interests: Cross-Dressing and Cultural Anxiety* (New York and London: Routledge, 1992)

Gaskell, Elizabeth, *A Life of Charlotte Brontë* (London: Smith Elder, 1857), 2 vols

Gauthier, Madame de, *Voyage d'une Française en Suisse et en Franche-Comté depuis la révolution* (Neuchâtel[?]: chez les libraires associés, 1790), 2 vols

Gibbs, Alderman, *Stratford upon Avon Herald*, 5 October 1883

Giles, Paul, *Transatlantic Insurrections: British Culture and the Formation of American Literature* (Philadelphia, PA: University of Pennsylvania Press, 2001)

Gill, Stephen, *Wordsworth and the Victorians* (Oxford: Clarendon Press, 1998)

Gittings, Robert, *The Mask of Keats: A Study of Problems* (London, Melbourne, Toronto: William Heinemann, 1956)

Godey, Louis A., *Godey's Lady's Book and Magazine*, 50 (May 1855)

Gogarty, Oliver St John, *It Isn't This Time of Year at All: An Unpremeditated Autobiography* (Garden City, NY: Doubleday, 1954)

Gold, Tanya, 'Reader, I Shagged Him: Why Charlotte Brontë Was a Filthy Minx', *The Guardian*, 25 March 2005

Goldhill, Simon, *Freud's Couch, Scott's Buttocks, Brontë's Grave* (Chicago, IL; London: University of Chicago Press, 2011)

Goldhill, Simon, *Prospect*, October 2011, p. 72

Goldsmith, Oliver, *Letters from a Citizen of the World to his Friends in the East* (Bungay: J. and R. Childs, 1820), 2 vols

Goodman, Susan, 'Portraits of Wharton', in Laura Rattray ed., *Edith Wharton in context*, (Cambridge: Cambridge University Press, 2012), pp. 61–73

Grahams' Magazine, February 1842

Grant, S.H., *Collecting Shakespeare: The Story of Henry and Emily Folger* (Baltimore, MD: Johns Hopkins University Press, 2014)

Granville, Mary, *The Autobiography and Correspondence of Mary Granville, Mrs. Delany: with interesting reminiscences of King George the Third and Queen Charlotte* (London: Bentley, 1861), 3 vols

Graves, Robert, *The Spiritual Quixote: or, the summer's ramble of Mr. Geoffrey Wildgoose. A comic romance* (London: Printed for J. Dodsley, 1773)

Greenwood, Grace, *Haps and Mishaps of a Tour in Europe* (London: Richard Bentley, 1854)

Grilley, Virginia, *Hawthorne: Great Scribe of Salem with Homes and Houses He Knew* (Amherst, MA: University of Massachusetts Press, 1981)

Gross, Samuel D., *Autobiography of Samuel D. Gross: with sketches of his contemporaries*, (1887: Philadelphia, PA: W.B. Saunders, 1893)

Groves, Anna, *Hardy's Cottage* (National Trust, 2002)

Guiccioli, Teresa, *Lord Byron's Life in Italy (Vie de Lord Byron en Italie)*, trans. Michael Reese, ed. Peter Cochran (Newark, DE: University of Delaware Press, 2005)

Haffenden, Chris, *Every Man His Own Monument: Self-Monumentalizing in Romantic Britain* (Uppsala: Uppsala Universetet, 2018)

Hamilton, Andrew, 'The Story of Schiller's Remains', *Macmillan's Magazine*, 8 (May 1863), pp. 302–10

Hamling, Tara and Cathryn Enis, unpublished paper for 'Material Loss' conference, Birmingham, 2017

Hancock, Nuala, 'Virginia Woolf's Glasses', in Sandra Dudley ed., *Museum Materialities: Objects, Engagements, Interpretations* (London and New York: Routledge, 2010)

Hancock, Nuala, *Charleston and Monk's House: The Intimate House Museums of Virginia Woolf and Vanessa Bell* (Edinburgh: Edinburgh University Press, 2012)

Harding, Walter, *The Days of Henry Thoreau: A Biography* (New York: Dover Publications, 1962)

Harney, Marion, *Place-Making for the Imagination: Horace Walpole and Strawberry Hill* (London: Routledge, 2016)

Harper's Monthly Magazine, Volume 14, Issue 79 (December 1856)

Harper's Weekly, 'Bohemians at the Grave of Shakespeare' 3 October 1874

Hawthorne, Nathaniel, *Mosses from an Old Manse* (1854: Boston, MA: Houghton, Mifflin and Co, 1882)

Hawthorne, Nathaniel, *Our Old Home: A Series of English Sketches* (1863: Boston, MA: Houghton, Mifflin and Co, 1883)

Hawthorne, Nathaniel, 'Recollections of a Gifted Woman', *Atlantic Monthly*, XI (January 1863), pp. 43–58

Hawthorne, Nathaniel, *Passages from the English Notebooks* (Boston, MA: Fields, Osgood, 1870), 2 vols

Hayley, William, *Memoirs of the Life and Writings of William Cowper, Esq.* (London: T. Williams, 1803)

Hayley, William, *The Life, and Posthumous Writings of William Cowper Esq ...* 2nd edn (Chichester: Printed by J Seagrave for J. Johnson, 1803), 3 vols

Hayley, William, *The Life and Posthumous Writings of William Cowper, Esqr.* (Chichester: Seagrave, 1803–4), 3 vols

Hayley, William, *The Life and Posthumous Writings of William Cowper* (Chichester: Johnson, 1803–6), 4 vols

Hayley, William, *The Works of William Cowper: His Life and Letters* (London: Saunders and Otley, 1835), 8 vols

Healey, Frank George, *The Literary Culture of Napoleon* (Geneva, Paris: Libraries E. Droz and Minard, 1959)

Heaney, Seamus, *District and Circle: Poems* (New York: Farrar, Straus and Giroux, 2006)

Heath, Shannon Raclene, *"Paper Bullets of the Brain": Satire, Duelling and the Rise of the Gentleman Author*, MA Thesis, Virginia Polytechnic Institute (2007)

Hendrix, Harald, *Writers' Houses and the Making of Memory* (New York, London: Routledge, 2008)

Hendrix, Harald, 'From Early Modern to Romantic Literary Tourism', in Nicola J. Watson ed., *Literary Tourism and Nineteenth-Century Culture* (Basingstoke: Palgrave Macmillan, 2009), pp. 13–25

Herbert, David, 'Literary Places, Tourism, and the Heritage Experience', *Annals of Tourism Research*, 28:2 (2001), pp. 312–33

Hess, Scott, 'Wordsworthshire and Thoreau Country: Transatlantic Landscapes of Genius', in Paul Westover and Ann Wierda Rowland eds., *Transatlantic Literature and Author-Love in the Nineteenth Century* (New York: Springer International Publishing, 2016), pp. 175–201

Higgins, David Minden, *Romantic Genius and the Literary Imagination: Biography, Celebrity, and Politics* (London: Routledge, 2005)

Hill, Constance, *Jane Austen: Her Homes and Her Friends* (London: J. Lane, 1902)

Hill, Rosemary, 'What Does She Think She Looks Like?' *London Review of Books*, 40:7 (5 April 2018)

Hirschhorn, Norbert and Polly Longsworth, '"Medicine Posthumous": A New Look at Emily Dickinson's Medical Conditions', *The New England Quarterly* (June 1996), pp. 299–316

Hjemdahl, Anne-Sofie ed., *A Thing or Two About Ibsen: His Possessions, Dramatic Poetry and Life* (Oslo: Andrimne, 2006)

Hodge, Robert Ian Vere and Gunther R. Kress, *Social Semiotics* (Ithaca, NY: Cornell University Press, 1988)

Hoeveler, Diane and Denenholz, Deborah, *A Companion to the Brontës* (Chichester: Wiley & Blackwell, 2016)

Hoffman, E.T.A., *Tales of Hoffman,* trans. R.J. Hollingdale (London: Penguin, 2004)

Holderness, Graham and Byran Loughrey, 'Shakespearean Features', in Jean Marsden ed., *The Appropriation of Shakespeare: Post-Renaissance Reconstructions of the Work and the Myth* (New York; London: Harvester Wheatsheaf, 1991), pp. 183–201.

Hone, William ed., *The Everyday Book and Table-book,* (London: for Thomas Tegg, 1827), 3 vols

Howells, William Dean, *Italian Journeys: from Venice to Naples and beyond* (Edinburgh: David Douglas, 1887)

Howells, William Dean, *My Mark Twain: Reminiscences and Criticisms* (1910), chapter XXXVI, repr. in *The Life and Times of Mark Twain*, ed. and intro. Marilyn Austin Baldwin (Baton Rouge, LA: Louisiana State University, 1999, 2014)

Howitt, Richard, *The Gipsy King: and other poems* (London, 1840)

Howitt, William, *Homes and Haunts of the Most Eminent British Poets*, 4th edn (London: George Routledge, 1847), 2 vols

Howitt, William, *Ruined Abbeys and Castles of Great Britain and Ireland*, 2nd series (London: Alfred W. Bennett, 1862, 1864)

Hubbard, Elbert, *Little Journeys to the Homes of the Great* (New York: East Aurora, 1895–1910), 14 vols

Hughes, William R., *A Week's Tramp in Dickens-land* (London: Chapman and Hall, 1891)

Hunt, Leigh, 'The Wishing Cap', No. 1, *Tait's Edinburgh Magazine*, vol. X (January 1883)

Hutchings, Richard J, *Isle of Wight Literary Haunts* (enlarged edition) (Newport: Isle of Wight County Press, 1989)

Illustrated London News, 12 April 1862

Ingleby, Clement M., *Shakespeare's Bones: The Proposal to Disinter Them, considered in relation to their possible bearing on his portraiture: illustrated by instances of visits of the living to the dead* (1879: London: Trubner & Co, 1883)

Ingram, Patricia Clare, 'Amorous Dispossessions: Knowledge, Desire, and the Poet's Dead Body', in Elizabeth Scala and Sylvia Federico eds., *The Post-Historical Middle Ages* (New York: Palgrave Macmillan, 2009), pp. 13–36

Ireland, Samuel, *Picturesque Views on the Upper or Warwickshire Avon* (London: R. Faulder and T. Egerton, 1795)

Irmscher, Christoph, *Public Poet, Private Man: Henry Wadsworth Longfellow at 200* (Amherst and Boston, MA: University of Massachusetts Press, 2009)

Irving, Washington, *"The Sketchbook" of Washington Irving, with Notes and Original Illustrations*, Richard Savage and William Salt Brassington eds. (1819: Stratford-upon-Avon: Shakespeare Quiney Press, 1920)

Irving, Washington, *Abbotsford and Newstead Abbey* (Philadelphia, PA: Carey, Lea & Blanchard, 1835)

Irving, Washington, 'A Chronicle of Wolfert's Roost', *Knickerbocker*, vol. XIII (April 1839)

James, Felicity, 'At Home with Jane: Placing Austen in Contemporary Culture', in Gillian Dow and Clare Hanson eds., *Uses of Austen: Jane's Afterlives* (Basingstoke: Palgrave Macmillan, 2012), pp. 132–53

Johnson, Claudia L., *Jane Austen's Cults ad Cultures* (Chicago, IL: Chicago University Press, 2012)

Josephine (pseud.), *Our Children's Pets* (London: S.W. Partridge, 1865)

Joy, Jody, 'Reinvigorating Object Biography: Reproducing the Drama of Object Lives', *World Archaeology*, 41:4 (2009), pp. 540–56

Joyce, James, *Ulysses* (Paris: Sylvia Beach, 1922)

Jupp, R.T., *The Dickens Collection of Books, Manuscripts and Relics Formed by the late Dr R.T. Jupp of London* (London: Anderson Galleries, 1922)

Kammen, Michael, *Digging Up the Dead: A History of Notable American Reburials* (Chicago, IL and London: University of Chicago Press, 2010)

Karamzin, Nikolai, *Letters of a Russian Traveller 1789–90: The Account of a Young Russian Gentleman's Tour through Germany, Switzerland, France and England*, trans. F. James (New York: Columbia University Press, 1957)

Keats, John, *John Keats at Wentworth Place: Poems Written December 1818 to September 1820* (London: London Borough of Camden, 1971)

Kebbel, T.E., 'Jane Austen at Home', *Fortnightly Review*, 4 (February 1885), pp. 262–70

Kendall, Alan, *David Garrick* (London: Harrap, 1985)

Kete, Kathleen, *The Beast in the Boudoir: Petkeeping in 19C Paris* (Berkeley, CA: University of California Press, 1994)

King, Thomas D., 'Shall We Open Shakespeare's Grave? No. A Reply...to the Question Put by Mr Parker Norris in the July number for the *Manhattan Montreal*' (Montreal: Robinson, 1884), pp. 6–8

Kipling, Rudyard, *Something of Myself, for my friends known and unknown* (London: Macmillan and Co. Ltd, 1937)

Knight, Laura, 'Mystery Guest: We Send a Writer Under the Covers... This Week the Balmoral Hotel, Princes Street, Edinburgh', *The Times*, cutting, n.d. c. 2007, p. 26

Knudsen, Britta Tim and Anne Marit Waade eds., *Re-Investing Authenticity: Tourism, Place and Emotions* (Bristol: Channel View, 2010)

Kowaleski–Wallace, Elizabeth, *The British Slave-Trade and Public Memory* (New York: Columbia University Press, 2013)

Laqueur, Thomas, *The Work of the Dead: A Cultural History of Mortal Remains* (Princeton, NJ: Princeton University Press, 2015)

Leerssen, Joep and Ann Rigney eds., *Commemorating Writers in Nineteenth-Century Europe: Nation-Building and Centenary Fever* (Basingstoke: Palgrave, 2014)

Leibovitz, Annie, *Pilgrimage* (London: Jonathan Cape, 2011)

Lemon, Charles ed., *Early Visitors to Haworth* (Haworth: Brontë Society, 1996)

Lennard, Erica and Premoli-Droulers, Francesca, *Writers' Houses* (London: Cassell, 1995)

Leslie, Anita and Pauline Chapman, *Madame Tussaud: Waxworker Extraordinary* (London: Hutchinson & Co, 1978)

Lewis, Jayne, '"A Lock of Thy Bright Hair": The Enlightenment's Milton and Our Auratic Material', *Humanities*, 4 (2015), pp. 797–817

Lewis, Min, *Laugharne and Dylan Thomas* (London: Dobson, 1967)

Leyda, Jay ed., *The Years and Hours of Emily Dickinson* (New Haven, CT: Yale University Press, 1960)

Linebaugh, Donald, 'Walden Pond and Beyond', in John H. Jameson ed., *The Reconstructed Past: Reconstruction and the Public Interpretation of Archaeology and History* (Walnut Creek, CA: Altamira Press, 2004), pp. 21–46

Lockhart, John Gibson, 'The Cockney School of Poetry', *Blackwood's Edinburgh Magazine*, vol. VI (October 1820)

Lockhart, John Gibson, *Memoirs of the Life of Sir Walter Scott, Bart.* (1837–8), 7 vols

Lockwood, Allison, *Passionate Pilgrims: the American traveller in Great Britain 1800–1914* (New York, London: Associated University Presses, 1981)

The London Scene (first pub. 1931) (London: Snowbooks, 1975)

'London's Newest Statue', *New York Times*, 14 August 1910.

Longfellow Remembrance Books: A Memorial for the Poet's Reader-friends (Boston, MA: D. Lothrop, 1888)

Lovejoy, Bess, *Rest in Pieces: The Curious Fates of Famous Corpses* (London: Duckworth Overlook, 2014)

Lowe, Hilary Iris, *Mark Twain's Homes and Literary Tourism* (Columbia, MO and London: University of Missouri Press, 2012)

Lowell, James Russell, *The Poetical Works of James Russell Howell* (London: Macmillan and Co., 1873)

Lupton, Christina, *Knowing Books: The Consciousness of Mediation in Eighteenth-Century Britain* (Philadelphia, PA: University of Pennsylvania Press, 2012)

Lutz, Deborah, *The Brontë Cabinet: Three Lives in Nine Objects* (New York, London: W.W. Norton and Co., 2015)

Lynch, Deidre Shauna, *Loving Literature: A Cultural History* (Chicago, IL: Oxford University Press, 2015)

Lynch, Deidre Shauna and William B. Warner eds., *Cultural Institutions of the Novel* (Durham, NC and London: Duke University Press, 1996)

McClatchy J.D. and Erica Lennard, *American Writers at Home* (New York: Library of America in association with The Vendome Press, 2004)

McDiarmid, John, 'St Michael's Church-Yard—Disinterment of Burns', in *Sketches from Nature* (Edinburgh: Oliver and Boyd; London: Simpkin and Marshall, 1830), pp. 367–80

McFarland, Thomas, *The Masks of Keats: The Endeavour of a Poet* (Oxford: Oxford University Press, 2000)

MacDougall, Hugh Cooke, *A Bicentennial Guide of Sites in Otsego County Associated with the Life and Fiction of James Fenimore Cooper 1789–1851* (Cooperstown, NY: Historical Association, 1989)

Mackenzie, George Stewart, *Illustrations of Phrenology. With engravings* (Edinburgh: Archibald Constable and Co and Hurst, Robinson and Co London, 1820)

Macleod, Suzanne, *Reshaping Museum Space: Architecture, Design, Exhibitions* (London: Routledge, 2005)

Malone, Peter, 'Keats's Posthumous Existence in Plaster', in *The Keats-Shelley Review*, 26:2 (September 2012), pp. 125–13

Marsh, Kate ed., *Writers and their Houses: A Guide to the Writers' Houses of England, Scotland, Wales and Ireland* (London: Hamish Hamilton, 1993)

Martin, John, *Illustrations; Landscape, Historical, and Antiquarian to the Poetical Works of Sir Walter Scott Bart* (London: Charles Tilt, 1834), 2 vols

Matthews, Samantha, *Poetical Remains: Poets' Graves, Bodies, and Books in the Nineteenth Century* (Oxford: Oxford University Press, 2004)

Matthisson, Friedrich von, *Letters written from various parts of the Continent, between the years 1785 and 1794*, trans. Anne Plumptre (London: T.N. Longman and O. Rees, 1799)

Matz, Bertram Waldrom ed., *Miscellaneous Papers of Charles Dickens* (London: Chapman and Hall, 1908)

Melchior-Bonnet, Sabine, *The Mirror: A History*, trans. Katbarme Jewett (London: Routledge, 2001)

Mérigot, J., *Promenade ou Itineraire des Jardins d'Ermenonville* (Paris: Gattey, Goyot, Mérigot, 1788)

Mill, John Stuart, *The Collected Works of John Stuart Mill*, ed. John M. Robson (Toronto: University of Toronto Press, 1963), 33 vols

Mills, Sara, *Discourses of Difference: An Analysis of Women's Travel Writing and Colonialism* (London: Routledge, 1991)

Mole, Tom, *Romanticism and Celebrity Culture* (Cambridge: Cambridge University Press, 2009)

Monthly Magazine, or British Register vol. LIII (1822)

'A Monument More Durable Than Brass: The Donald and Mary Hyde collection of Samuel Johnson', 2009, Houghton Library, Harvard University. Consulted originally as an online exhibition. Exhibition catalogue (Boston, MA: Harvard University Press, 2010)

Motion, Andrew, *John Keats at Wentworth Place: The Story of Keats House* (London: City of London, Keats House, 2009)

Murray, John, *A Handbook for Travellers in Switzerland, and the Alps of Savoy and Piedmont* (London: John Murray, 1838)

Murray, John, *Handbook for Travellers in Northern Italy: Comprising Turin, Milan, Pavia, Cremona, the Italian Lakes, Bergamo, Brescia, Verona, Mantua, Vicenza, Padua, Venice, Ferrara, Bologna, Ravenna, Rimini, Modena, Parma, Piacenza, Genoa, the Riviera, and the Intermediate Towns and Routes* (London: John Murray, 1877)

Murray-Pepper, Megan, 'The "Tables of Memory": Shakespeare, Cinema and the Writing-Desk', in Judith Buchanan ed., *The Writer on Film: Screening Literary Authorship* Basingstoke: Palgrave Macmillan, 2013), pp. 92–105

Nancy, Jean-Luc, 'Masked Imagination', *The Ground of the Image*, trans. Jeff Fort (New York: Fordham University Press, 2005)

Newnes, George, *Pictorial Knowledge* (London: The Home Library Book Company, 1932), 8 vols

Nichols, Beverley, *Twenty-five: An Autobiography* (1926: London: Penguin Books, 1935)

Nichols, John and George Steevens, *The Genuine Works of William Hogarth: Illustrated with Biographical Anecdotes* (London: Longman, Hurst, Rees and Orme, 1810), 2 vols

Nicolson, Adam, *Sissinghurst Castle Garden* (National Trust, 1979)

Nicolson, Adam, *Sissinghurst: An Unfinished History* (London: Harper Press, 2008)

North, Julian, *The Domestication of Genius: Biography and the Romantic Poet* (Oxford: Oxford University Press, 2009)

Noszlopy, George and Fiona Waterhouse, *Public Sculpture of Staffordshire and the Black Country* (Liverpool: Liverpool University Press, 2005)

Novello, Emma, 'The Tomb of Percy Bysshe Shelley in the Protestant Cemetery at Rome' (1851)

Ocker, J.W., *Poe-land: The Hallowed Haunts of Edgar Allan Poe* (The Countryman Press, 2014)

'On the annual meeting of some Gentlemen to celebrate SHAKESPEARE'S BIRTHDAY', *London Magazine* vol. XXIV (1755), p. 244

Pascoe, Judith, *The Hummingbird Cabinet: A Rare and Curious History of Romantic Collectors* (Ithaca, NY and London: Cornell University Press, 2006)

Payling, Catherine, *Keats and Italy: A History of the Keats-Shelley House in Italy* (The Museum Collection, 2005)

Peacocke, Emma, *Romanticism and the Museum* (Basingstoke: Palgrave Macmillan, 2015)

Pilli, Elena et al., 'Ancient DNA and the Forensics Genetics: The Case of Francesco Petrarca', *Forensic Science International: Genetics Supplement Series*, 1:1 (August 2008), pp. 469–70

Piper, Andrew, 'The Werther Effect: Topologies of Literary Fame' unpublished paper, September 2014

Pittock, Murray and Christopher A. Whatley, 'Poems and Festivals, Art and Artefact and the Commemoration of Robert Burns c. 1844–c. 1896', *Scottish Historical Review*, XCIII, 1:236 (April 2014), pp. 56–79

Plath, Sylvia, *The Unabridged Journals of Sylvia Plath*, ed. Karen V. Kukil (London: Faber and Faber, 2000)

Pocock, Douglas, 'Haworth: The Experience of a Literary Place', in W.E. Mallory and P. Simpson-Housley eds., *Geography and Literature: A Meeting of the Disciplines* (Syracuse, NY: Syracuse University Press, 1987)

Poe, Edgar Allan, *The Poetical Works of Edgar Allan Poe. Together with his Essays on The Poetic Principle and The Philosophy of Composition and a Critical Memoir. With illustrations…* (London: Ward, Lock & Co, 1882)

Pointon, Marcia, 'Casts, Imprints, and the Deathliness of Things: Artifacts at the Edge', *The Art Bulletin*, 96:2 (July 2014), pp. 170–95

Poliquin, Rachel, *The Breathless Zoo: Taxidermy and the Cultures of Longing* (Philadelphia, PA: Penn State University Press, 2012)

Pope, Alexander, *Letters of Alexander Pope*, Selected and with an Introduction by John Butt (London: Oxford University Press, 1960)

Pottle, Frederick A. and Charles H. Bennett eds., *Boswell's Journal of A Tour to the Hebrides with Samuel Johnson LL.D*, (New York: The Viking Press; London: William Heinemann, Ltd, 1936)

Prendergast, Thomas A., *Poetical Dust: Poets' Corner and the Making of Britain* (Philadelphia, PA: University of Pennsylvania Press, 2015)

Propp, Vladimir, *Morphology of the Folktale* (Austin, TX: University of Texas Press, 1968)

Putnam, James, *Art and Artifact: The Museum as Medium* (London: Thames and Hudson, 2001)

Quérard, Joseph Marie, *La France Littérraire, ou Dictionnaire bibliographique des savants…* (Paris: chez Firmin Didot Frères, Libraires, 1836)

Quigley, Christine, *The Corpse: A History* (Jefferson, NC; London: McFarland, 1996)

'Rachel Johnson meets A.L. Kennedy', BBC Radio 4 broadcast Monday 24 April 2017, 13.45pm

Rachlin, Harvey, *Lucy's Bones, Sacred Stones, and Einstein's Brain* (New York: Henry Holt and Co, 1996)

Ratcliffe, Derek, *The Raven: A Natural History in Britain and Ireland* (London: Poyser, 1997)

'Rhymes on Panes', *Chambers' Journal of Popular Literature, Science, and Art*, 5th series, February 1887

Ribieiro, Aileen, 'In Search of Carlyle's Hat', *Costume*, 30:1 (April 2017), pp. 85–9

Richardson, Judith, *Possessions: The History and Uses of Hauntings in the Hudson Valley* (Cambridge, MA: Harvard University Press, 2003)

Rigney, Ann, 'Portable Monuments: Literature, Cultural Memory, and the Case of Jeanie Deans', *Poetics Today*, 25:2 (Summer 2004), pp. 361–96

Rigney, Ann, *The Afterlives of Walter Scott: Memory on the Move* (Oxford: Oxford University Press, 2012)

Rigney, James, 'Worse than Malone or Sacrilege: The Exhumation of Shakespeare's Remains', *Critical Survey*, 9:3 (1997), pp. 78–90

Ripley, N.B., 'A Visit to the Old Manse', *The Book News Monthly*, 28 (1909)

Ritvo, Harriet, *The Animal Estate: The English and Other Creatures in the Victorian Age* (Cambridge, MA: Harvard University Press, 1987)

Roberson, Jessica, 'Shelley's Grave, Botanical Souvenirs, and Handling Literary Afterlives', *Victoriographies*, 6:3 (October 2016), pp. 276–94

Robinson, Mike and Hans Christian Andersen eds., *Literature and Tourism: Essays in the Reading and Writing of Tourism* (London: Thomson, 2003)

Rogers, Samuel, *Italy: A Poem* (London: printed for Longman, Hurst, Rees, Orme, and Brown, 1822)

Roscoe, Thomas, *The Tourist in Switzerland and Italy* (London: Robert Jennings, 1830)

Rosen, Michael, *Fantastic Mr Dahl* (London: Puffin, 2012)

Rousseau, Jean Jacques, *Eloisa, or, a series of original letters collected and published by J. J. Rousseau*. Translated from the French in four volumes by William Kenrick (Dublin: Printed for James Hunter, 1791)

Rousseau, Jean Jacques, *The Confessions of Jean Jacques Rousseau*, trans. and introd. S.W. Orson (London: Privately printed for members of the Aldus Society, 1903)

Rowe, David, *Dylan Thomas: The Boat House and Laugharne* (Llandysul: Gomer, 2003)

Rushworth, Jennifer, *Petrarch and the Literary Culture of Nineteenth-Century France: Translation, Appropriation, Transformation* (Woodbridge: The Boydell Press, 2017)

Russell, Francis, *Portraits of Sir Walter Scott: A Study of Romantic Portraiture* (London: Russell, 1987)

Saddeth, Elizabeth A., Carlyle Tarr, Roy Clayton, and George Ross, eds. *The G. Ross Roy Collection of Robert Burns: An Illustrated Catalogue* (Columbia, SC: University of South Carolina Press, 2009)

Sancho, Ignatius, *The Letters of the late Ignatius Sancho, an African* (London: J. Nichols et al., 1782)

Santesso, Aaron, 'The Birth of the Birthplace: Bread St and Literary Tourism Before Stratford', *English History*, 71:2 (Summer 2004), pp. 377–403

Savage, F.G., *The Flora and Folk Lore of Shakespeare* (London: E.J. Burrow, 1923)

Schoch, Richard, 'The Birth of Shakespeare's Birthplace', *Theatre Survey*, 53:2 (2012), pp. 181–201

Schoenbaum, Samuel, *Shakespeare's Lives* (Oxford: Clarendon Press, 1970)

Schrieber, Mary Suzanne, *Writing Home: American Women Abroad 1830–1920* (Charlottesville, VA and London: University Press of Virginia, 1997)

Scots Magazine and Edinburgh Literary Miscellany, vol. LXXIX (May 1817)

Scott, Mary Monica Maxwell, *Abbotsford: The Personal Relics and Antiquarian Treasures of Sir Walter Scott* (London: Adam & Charles Black, 1893)

Scott, Walter, *The Antiquary* (Edinburgh: Printed by James Ballantyne and Co. for Archibald Constable and Co. Edinburgh; and Longman, Hurst, Rees, Orme, and Brown, London, 1816), 3 vols

Scott, Walter, *The Journal of Walter Scott*, ed. and introd. by W.E.K. Anderson (Edinburgh: Canongate, 1998)

Scott, Walter, *Reliquiae Trotcosienses, or The Gabions of The Late Jonathan Oldbuck, esq. of Monkbarns*, ed. Gerard Carruthers and Alison Lumsden, with an Introduction by David Hewitt (Cambridge: Edinburgh University Press in association with the Abbotsford Library Project Trust, 2004)

Searle, John, *A Plan of Mr Pope's Garden As It was Left at his Death with a Plan and Perspective View of the Grotto* (London, 1745)

'Secret History: Shakespeare's Tomb', broadcast on Channel 4 television, March 2016

Shakespeare, William, *The Complete Works*, Stanley Wells and Gary Taylor eds., 2nd edn. (Oxford: Clarendon Press, 2005)

Shelley, Percy Bysshe, *Essays, Letters from Abroad, Translations and Fragments*, ed. Mrs Shelley (London: Edward Moxon, 1852), 2 vols

Shone, Richard, *Virginia Woolf & Monk's House* (National Trust, 1970)

Shorto, Russell, *Descartes' Bones: A Skeletal History of the Conflict between Faith and Reason* (London: Abacus, 2013)

Simond, Louis, *Switzerland; or, A Journal of a Tour and Residence in that Country, in the years 1817, 1818, and 1819: followed by An Historical Sketch on the manners of Ancient and Modern Helvetia in which the events of our own time are fully detailed, together with the causes to which they may be referred* (London: John Murray, 1822), 2 vols

Simonsen, Peter, *Wordsworth and Word-Preserving Acts: Typographic Inscription, Ekphrasis and Posterity in the Later Work* (Basingstoke: Palgrave Macmillan, 2007)

Singer, Rita, 'Leisure, Refuge, and Solidarity: Messages in Visitors' Books as Microforms of Travel Writing', *Studies in Travel Writing* 20:4 (2017), pp. 392–408

Smith, Graham, 'The Holy Stone Where Dante Sat: Memory and Oblivion', in Aida Audeh and Nick Haveley eds., *Dante in the Long Nineteenth Century: Nationality, Identity, and Appropriation* (Oxford: Oxford University Press, 2012), pp. 89–110.

Smith, Margaret, ed. *Selected Letters of Charlotte Brontë* (Oxford: Oxford University Press, 2010)

Sontag, Susan, *On Photography* (London: Penguin, 2008)

Squire, S., 'The Cultural Values of Literary Tourism', *Annals of Tourism Research*, 21 (1994), pp. 103–20

Stabler, Jane, 'Leigh Hunt's Aesthetics of Intimacy', in Nicholas Roe ed., *Leigh Hunt: Life, Poetics, Politics* (London: Routledge, 2003)

Steele, Richard, *Tatler*, no. 254 (1710)

Sterling, Robin ed., *People and Things from the Walker County Alabama Jasper Mountain Eagle 1910–1913* (New York: Lulu, 2016)

Sterne, *Laurence, The Florida Edition of the Works of Laurence Sterne*, Melvyn New and W. G. Day eds. (Gainesville, Tallahassee, FL: University Press of Florida, 2002), 8 vols

Stewart, Susan, *On Longing: Narratives of the Miniature, the Gigantic, the Souvenir, the Collection* (Durham, NC and London: Duke University Press, 1993)

Stoddard, Richard Henry, *Poet's Homes: Pen and Pencil Sketches of American Poets and Their Homes* (Boston, MA: D. Lothrop, 1871)

Stolberg, Friedrich Leopold, *Travels through Germany, Switzerland, Italy and Sicily*, trans. Thomas Holcroft (London, 1796–7), 2 vols

Stowe, Beecher, *Our Young Folks: An Illustrated Magazine for Young Boys and Girls*, 2:6 (June 1866) (Boston, MA: Ticknor and Fields, 1866)

Stowe, Harriet Beecher, *Sunny Memories of Foreign Lands* (London; Sampson Low, Son and Co., 1854), 2 vols

Stowe, William W., *Going Abroad: European Travel in Nineteenth-Century American Culture* (Princeton, NJ: Princeton University Press, 1994)

Strong, Roy, *The Quest for Shakespeare's Garden* (London: Thames and Hudson, 2016)

Susannah Walker, *The Life of Stuff: Possessions, obsessions and the mess we leave behind* (London: Doubleday, 2018)

Sutherland, John, *The Life of Sir Walter Scott: A Critical Biography* (Oxford: Blackwell, 1995)

Taylor, Charles, *The Ethics of Authenticity* (London: Harvard University Press, 1992)

Tearle, Christian, *Rambles with an American* (London: Mills and Boon, c. 1910)

Tennant, Charles, *A Tour through parts of The Netherlands, Holland, Germany, Switzerland, Savoy, and France, in the year 1821–2. Including a description of the Rhine Voyage in the Middle of Autumn, and the Stupendous Scenery of the Alps in the depth of Winter…*, (London: Longman, Hurst, Rees, Orme, Brown and Green, 1824), 2 vols

The Letters and Prose Writings of William Cowper, ed. James King and Charles Ryskamp (Oxford: Clarendon Press, 1981), 3 vols

Thomas, Dylan, *Collected Poems 1934–1952* (London: J.M. Dent & Sons Ltd, 1952)

Thomas, Julia, *Shakespeare's Shrine: The Bard's Birthplace and the Invention of Stratford-upon-Avon* (Philadelphia, PA: University of Pennsylvania Press, 2012)

Thomas, Keith, *Man and the Natural World: Changing Attitudes in England 1500–1800* (London: Allen Lane, 1983)

Thoreau, Henry David, *Walden; or, Life in the Woods* (London: Macmillan Collector's Library, 2016)

Thoreau, Henry, *Walden and Other Writings by Henry David Thoreau*, ed. William Howarth (New York: The Modern Library, 1981)

Tomalin, Claire, 'Writer's Rooms: Jane Austen', *The Guardian*, Saturday 12 July 2008

Traveller's Guide to Switzerland, The, 3rd edn (London: M.A. Leigh & Son, 1835)

Trubek, Anne, *A Skeptic's Guide to Writers' Houses* (Philadelphia, PA, Oxford: University of Pennsylvania Press, 2011)

Twain, Mark [Samuel Langhorn Clemens], *The Adventures of Tom Sawyer*, John C. Gerber, Paul Baender, and Terry Firkins eds. (1876: Berkeley, Los Angeles, CA; London: University of California Press, 1980)

Twain, Mark, 'Old Times on the Mississippi' (1874–5), repr. within *Life on the Mississippi* (Boston, MA: James R. Osgood & Co., 1883)

Twain, Mark, *Mark Twain's Letters*, Michael B Frank and Harriet Elinor Smith eds. (Berkeley, CA: University of California Press, 2002), 6 vols

Valéry, M., *Historical, Literary and Artistical Travels in Italy*, trans. C.E. Clifton 2nd edn (Paris: Baudry's European Library, 1839)

'Victor Hugo at Home', *Every Saturday: A Journal of Choice Reading*, 7:162 (6 February 1869) (Boston, MA: Ticknor and Fields, 1869)

Velten, Hannah, *Beastly London: A History of Animals in the City* (London: Reaktion Books, 2013)

'VisitEngland: Year of Literary Heroes', *Survey Report 2017*

Wagner, Sigismond [Sigmund von Wagner], *L'Île Saint-Pierre ou L'Île de Rousseau* (Berne: G. Lory et C. Rheiner, 1815)

Wagner, Sigismond [Sigmund von Wagner], *L'Île Saint-Pierre ou L'Île de Rousseau* with an Introduction by Pierre Kohler (Lausanne: Éditions SPESS, 1926)

Wainwright, Clive, *The Romantic Interior: The British Collector at Home*, 2nd edn (London: Palgrave, 1989)

Walpole, Horace, *A Description of the Villa of Horace Walpole at Strawberry Hill* (Twickenham: Printed by Thomas Kirkgate, 1774)

Walpole, Horace, *A Description of the Villa of Horace Walpole* (Twickenham: Printed by Thomas Kirkgate, 1774, revised and enlarged 1784)

Walpole, Horace, *Anecdotes of Painting in England...* (London: for J. Dodsley, 1782), 4 vols

Walsh, Claire, 'Shop Design and the Display of Goods in Eighteenth-Century London', *Journal of Design History*, 8:3 (1995), pp. 157–76

Warner, Marina, *20 Maresfield Gardens: A Guide to the Freud Museum London* (London: Serpent's Tail, 1998)

Watson, Nicola J., *The Literary Tourist: Readers and Places in Romantic and Victorian Britain* (Basingstoke: Palgrave Macmillan, 2006)

Watson, Nicola J., 'Shakespeare on the Tourist Trail', in Robert Shaughnessy ed., *The Cambridge Companion to Shakespeare in Popular Culture* (Cambridge: Cambridge University Press, 2007), pp. 208–11

Watson, Nicola J., 'Rambles in Literary London', in Nicola J. Watson ed., *Literary Tourism and Nineteenth-Century Culture* (Basingstoke: Palgrave Macmillan, 2009)

Watson, Nicola J. ed., *Literary Tourism and Nineteenth-Century Culture* (Basingstoke: Palgrave Macmillan, 2009)

Watson, Nicola J., 'Austen Exhibited', *Exhibiting Literature*, Katerina Kroucheva and Barbara Schaff eds., *Kafkas Gabel: Uberlegungen zum Ausstellen von Literatur* (Bielefeld: transcript Verlag, 2013), pp. 227–50

Watson, Nicola J., 'Gardening with Shakespeare', in Clara Calvo and Coppélia Kahn eds., *Commemorating Shakespeare* (Cambridge: Cambridge University Press, 2015)

Watson, Nicola J., 'At Juliet's Tomb: Anglophone Travel-Writing and Shakespeare's Verona, 1814–1914', in Silvia Bigliazzi and Lisanna Calvi eds., *Shakespeare, Romeo and Juliet and Civic Life* (London: Routledge, 2016), pp. 224–37

Watson, Nicola J., 'Melrose Abbey', in Michael Carter, Peter N. Lindfield, and Dale Townshend eds., *Writing Britain's Ruins* (London: British Library, 2017)

Weatherhead, George Hume, *A Pedestrian Tour through France and Italy* (London, 1834)

Welland, Freydis Jane, 'The History of Jane Austen's Writing-Desk', *Persuasions*, 30 (2008), pp. 125–8

Westover, Paul, *Necromanticism: Traveling to Meet the Dead, 1750–1860* (Basingstoke; New York: Palgrave Macmillan, 2012)

Westover, Paul and Ann Wierda Rowland eds., *Transatlantic Literature and Author Love in the Nineteenth Century* (Basingstoke: Palgrave Macmillan, 2016)

Williams, Bransby, *Bransby Williams by Himself* (London: Hutchinson, 1954)

Williams, Helen Maria, *Letters written in France* (London: printed for T. Cadell, 1790), 2 vols

Winterson, Jeannette, 'Monk's House, Rodmell, E. Sussex', in Kate Marsh ed., *Writers and their Houses: A Guide to the Writers' Houses of England, Scotland, Wales and Ireland* (London: Hamish Hamilton, 1993)

Wise, John R., *Shakspere: His Birthplace and Its Neighbourhood* (London: Smith, Elder and Co., 1861)

Wolfe, Theodore F., *Literary Shrines: The Haunts of Some Famous American Authors* (Philadelphia, PA: Lippincott Company, 1895)

Wolfe, Theodore F., *A Literary Pilgrimage Among the Haunts of Famous British Authors* (Philadelphia, PA: J.B. Lippincott, 1895)

Woodhouse, Anna, 'Looking Through Glass: Windows, Lenses and Spectacles in American Literature and Culture, 1900–1960', PhD thesis (2011), University of Leeds

Woodhouse, Anna, 'Windows to the Soul', BBC Radio 4, Four Thought Series 4, 29 May 2013

Woodward, G.M., 'Familiar Verses from the Ghost of Willy Shakespeare to Sammy Ireland', *The Comic Works in Prose and Poetry of G.M. Woodward* (London: Thomas Tegg, 1808)

Woolf, Virginia, 'Haworth, November 1904', *The Guardian*, 21 December 1904

Woolf, Virginia, 'The Mark on the Wall' in David Bradshaw, ed., *The Mark on the Wall, and Other Short Fiction* (Oxford: Oxford World's Classics, 2008)

Woolf, Virginia, *The Common Reader* (London: Hogarth Press, 1925)

Wordsworth, Dorothy, *Grasmere Journals*, ed. Pamela Woof (Oxford: Clarendon Press, 1991)

Wordsworth, William, *The Prose Works of William Wordsworth*, ed. W.J.B. Owen and Jane Worthington Smyser (Oxford: Clarendon Press, 1974), 3 vols

Workman, Liz, *Dr Johnson's Doorknob—And Other Significant Parts of Great Men's Houses* (New York: Rizzoli International Publications, 2007)

Wright, Emily, *Casting Presence: Death Masks and Portraiture in the Eighteenth to Nineteenth Centuries*, MSt dissertation (2012), University of Oxford

Wright, George R., *France Illustrated* (London: Fisher, Son & Co. 1845–7), 4 vols in 2

Young, Alan R., *Punch and Shakespeare in the Victorian Era* (Bern, New York: Peter Lang, 2007)

Young, Linda, 'Writers' House Museums: English Literature in the Heart and on the Ground', in LuAnn McCracken Fletcher ed., *Literary Tourism and the British Isles: History, Imagination, and the Politics of Place* (Lanham, MD, Boulder, CO, New York, London: Lexington Books, 2019), pp. 165–90

Youth's Companion, The, vol. XXVIII (1854)

Zemgulys, Andrea, *Modernism and the Locations of Literary Heritage* (Cambridge: Cambridge University Press, 2008)

WEB BIBLIOGRAPHY

Alvi, Kiran, 'Edgar Allan Poe's Cottage Reopens', *The Bronx Times* (October 2011) http://www.bronx.com/news/local/1799.html, last accessed 24/01/2017

Anonymous, 'The Real Face of Robert Burns Revealed', *The Scotsman* (January 2013) http://www.Scotsman.com/heritage/people-places/th, last accessed 09/07/2017

Arbis, Emily, 'Alabaster Urn with a Fragment of Shelley's Jaw Bone', *Treasure of the Month*(October 2014), https://view.officeapps.live.com/op/view.aspx?src=http%3A%2F%2Fwww.keats-shelley-house.org%2Fsystem%2Fresources%2F0000%2F0100%2FTOTM_December_2014.docx, last accessed 05/07/2017

Atlas Obscura, 'Walter Benjamin's Memorial' (2017), http://www.atlasobscura.com/places/walter-benjamin-memorial, last accessed 09/05/2017

Bannerjee, Jacqueline, http://www.victorianweb.org/sculpture/lucas/3f.jpg, last accessed 8 April 2015

Basinski, Michael, 'The James Joyce Collection: Its History and Future', University of Buffalo (November 2008), http://library.buffalo.edu/pl/collections/jamesjoyce/collection/history-future.php, last accessed 09/07/2017

BBC News, 'Charlotte Brontë's desk Will Go on Show at the Parsonage Museum from Tuesday 31 May' (May 2011), http://www.bbc.co.uk/news/uk-england-leeds-13524136, last accessed 26/06/2017

BBC News, 'George Eliot Writing Desk Stolen from Nuneaton Museum' (November 2012), http://www.bbc.co.uk/news/uk-england-coventry-war-wickshire-20339748, last accessed 09/07/2017

Bell, Maureen, 'A Brief History of Mason Croft', Shakespeare Institute, Birmingham University (2011), http://www.birmingham.ac.uk/schools/edacs/departments/shakespeare/about/mason-croft-history.aspx, last accessed 09/07/2017

Berlowitz, Jill, 'Mind's Eye Tree Sculpture Unveiled' (2016), http://www.jillberelowitz.com/press/minds-eye-tree-sculpture-unveiled-at-shakespeares-new-place, last accessed 02/07/2017

Blackriverrosi (pseud.), 'Emily Seen in Her Belongings', Brontë Family Blog, http://brontefamilyblog.blogspot.co.uk/2010/03/emily-seen-in-her-belongings.html, last accessed 09/07/2017

Bosi, R., 'Return to Stratford Upon Avon England for UNBOSI', United Nations Board Of Significant Inspiration (April 2016), http://www.unbosi.org/unbosi-announce-return-to-stratford-upon-avon-england, last accessed 21/06/2017

Braun, Rebecca, 'The Author and the World', http://www.authorsandtheworld.com

Brontë Country, 'Brontë Chair', Eagle Intermedia Publishing (1997–2015). http://bronte-country.com/bronte-chair.html, last accessed 07/01/2019

Bulgakov Memorial House, https://discover-ukraine.info/places/kyiv/kyiv/875, last accessed 17/10/2018

Burns' Scotland, Cast, Perth Burns Club, http://www.burnsscotland.com/items/p/plaster-cast-of-the-skull-of-robert-burns.aspx, last accessed 11/11/2015

Burns' Scotland, Cast, Robert Burns Centre, Dumfries and Galloway, http://www.burnsscotland.com/items/c/cast-of-robert-burns-skull.aspx, last accessed 11/11/2015

Burns' Scotland, Cast, Writers' Museum in Edinburgh, http://www.burnsscotland.com/items/p/plaster-cast-of-the-skull-of-robert-burns.aspx, last accessed 11/11/2015

Burns' Scotland, Cast, Irvine Burns Club, http://www.cobbler.plus.com/wbc/news;etter/0003/0300_burns_skull.htm, last accessed 11/11/2015

Césari, Dominique, 'Ermenonville', The most famous Anglo-Chinese gardens of France (July 2000), http://parcsafabriques.org/erm/dErm1e.htm, last accessed 19/06/2017

Clack, Allan, https://cdn.shopify.com/s/files/1/0925/3888/files/Dickenss-Dream-Key1.pdf?1189502324387921879, last accessed 09/07/2017

Colman, Penny, 'A Poet's Pocket: Emily Dickinson's Dress' (April 2013), http://pennycolman.com/a-poets-pocket-emily-dickinsons-dress, last accessed 09/07/2017

Combe, George, 'Notes', Four Views of the Skull of Robert Burns (1834), http://www.nls.uk/collections/rarebooks/acquisitions/singlebook.cfm/idfind/866, last accessed 09/07/2017

Concord Museum, 'The Henry David Thoreau Collection', http://www.concord-museum.org/henry-david-thoreau-collection.php, last accessed 09/07/2017

Cornell University (2017) 'Vitrine', Intypes, https://intypes.cornell.edu/expanded.cfm?erID=204, last accessed 10/05/2017

Cox, Maddie, 'On the Trail of Mary Hornby', Finding Shakespeare (October 2015), http://findingshakespeare.co.uk/trail-mary-hornby, last accessed 09/07/2017

Cunliffe, Lynne, 'The Hidden Charlotte Brontë', The Hathaways of Haworth (April 2013), https://hathawaysofhaworth.wordpress.com/2013/04/14/the-hidden-charlotte-bronte, last accessed 09/07/2017

Dart, Tom, 'Derek Walcott Museum Closes Amid Row Over Caribbean Tourist Developments', https://www.theguardian.com/books/2017/jun/21/derek-walcott-museum-st-lucia-caribbean-tourism, last accessed 08/01/2019

Elephant House, http://www.elephanthouse.biz (2008–17), last accessed 17/05/2017

Elizabeth Gaskell's House, https://www.elizabethgaskellhouse.co.uk/house/manchester-historic-buildings-trust, last accessed 09/07/2017

Fields, Helen, 'Museum Tourist: Charles Dickens Museum', Blogosphere (6 February 2014), http://heyhelen.com/2014/02/museum-tourist-charles-dickens-museum, last accessed 04/07/2017

Fildes, Sir Samuel Luke, 'The Empty Chair' (1870), http://www.victorianweb.org/painting/fildes/drawings/7.html, last accessed 07/01/2019

Fletcher, Chris, 'Charlotte Brontë's Writing Desk' (2010), http://www.bl.uk/onlinegallery/features/chpverse/news.html, last accessed 10/01/2015

Frederick, Michael, (2015) www.thoreausociety.org, last accessed 09/07/2017

George Borrow's house, Norfolk, http://www.literarynorfolk.co.uk/Norwich/george_borrow.htm, last accessed 08/01/2019

Guernsey Museums and Galleries, 'Hauteville House', http://museums.gov.gg/hauteville, last accessed 24/05/2017

Hendrix, Harald, 'Literary Heritage Sites Across Europe: A Tour d'Horizon' in 'Ce que le musée fait à la littérature', Interferences Litteraires No. 16, June 2015, http://www.interferenceslitteraires.be/en/node/481, last accessed 13/12/2017

Herbert, Shiranikha, 'Shakespeare's Skull to Stay in Vault', *Church Times* (November 2015), https://www.churchtimes.co.uk/articles/2015/6-november/news/uk/shakespeare-s-skull-to-stay-in-vault, last accessed 09/07/2017

Hewitt, Peter, 'Shakespeare's Signet-Ring', https://www.shakespeare.org.uk/explore-shakespeare/blogs/shakespeare-100-objects-shakespearessignetring, last accessed 07/01/2019

Hinshelwood, Emily, 'A Postcard to Dylan Thomas' (2014), http://doozie.org.uk/projects/a-postcard-to-dylan-thomas-emily-hinshelwood, last accessed 09/07/2017

Houses, Peter, 'Francesco Petrarca', Sociology of Italian Lifestyle (2017), http://www.peterhouses.com/italian-great-people-of-the-past/francesco-petrarca, last accessed 09/07/2017

Hovasse, Jean-Marc, 'La Table aux Quatre Encriers', http://euromanticism.org, last accessed 09/01/2019

ICOM, http://network.icom.museum/iclm/what-we-do/what-is-a-literary-museum, last accessed 30/08/2019

Jack, Claire, 'The Haunting of Trevor Burk', Writing on the Margins (October 2015), http://bashabifraser.com/2015/10/24/the-haunting-of-trevor-burk, last accessed 12/01/2016

Jamaica Inn, 'Daphne Du Maurier', http://www.jamaicainn.co.uk/daphne-du-maurier' (2014), last accessed 22/06/2017

'Jane Austen in 41 Objects', https://www.jane-austens-house-museum.org.uk/6-muslin-shawl, last accessed 31/01/2018

Jones, Cindy, 'I Met Jane Austen's Writing Table', First Draft (August 2010), cindysjones.wordpress.com/2010/08/24/i-met-jane-austens-writing-table, last accessed 09/07/2017

J.R.R. Tolkien exhibition at the Bodleian Library, Oxford, 1 June to 28 October 2018, https://tolkien.bodleian.ox.ac.uk, last accessed 18/12/2018

Kearney, Martha, Helen Oyeyemi, and Lucy Mangan, 'Being the Brontës' (2016), http://www.bbc.co.uk/programmes/p03n0wsy/p03n0r4n, last accessed 09/07/2017

Keats-Shelley House, 'Scallop-Shell Reliquary', Treasure of the Month (February 2015), http://www.keats-shelley-house.org/en/events/treasure-of-the-month-100.html, last accessed 09/07/2017

Kellaway, K., 'A Dish of Tea with Dr Johnson: Review', *The Guardian*, http://www.theguardian.com/stage/2011/sep/11/dr-johnson-boswell-arts-theatre, last accessed 23/03/2016

Kennedy, Robert E, https://www.nytimes.com/learning/general/onthisday/harp/10003.html, last accessed 13/11/2015

Kyle, Francis (since 1978), http://www.franciskylegallery.com/sites/Fshr.htm, last accessed 22/06/2017

Larkin, Philip, http://philiplarkin.com/larkin-with-toads, last accessed 20/12/2018

Larkin, Philip, https://www.bbc.co.uk/news/uk-england-humber-33833813, last accessed 20/12/2018

Lerner, Elissa, 'What's on View at the New York Public Library Centennial Exhibit?' (May 2011), http://www.newyorker.com/books/page-turner/whats-on-view-at-the-n-y-p-l-s-centennial-exhibit-slide-show, last accessed 09/07/2017

Linda (mouseski58), 'A Virtual Visit to Salem's House of the Seven Gables', The Distracted Wanderer (December 2011), http://www.thedistractedwanderer.com/2011/12/virtual-visit-to-salems-house-of-seven.html, last accessed 09/07/2017

London Remembers, 'Dickens' relief', http://www.londonremembers.com/memorials/charles-dickens-relief (2017), last accessed 09/07/2017

McCluskey, Michael, 'Afterlives of Dickens Objects' (May 2012), http://www.autopsiesgroup.com/dickenss-desks.html, last accessed 22/06/2017

'Maison de Balzac', http://www.literarytraveler.com/articles/honore-de-balzac-paris, last accessed 30/06/2017

Mashhadi, Lynne, 'Visiting Greenway: Agatha Christie's House', In Plymouth (2004–17), http://inplymouth.com/visiting-greenway-agatha-christies-house, last accessed 26/06/2017

'Mason Croft', http://www.birmingham.ac.uk/schools/edacs/departments/shakespeare/about/mason-croft-history.aspx, last accessed 03/07/2017

Mathison, Hamish, 'Robert Burns and Tradition', The Association for Scottish Literary Studies (2007), http://asls.arts.gla.ac.uk/Hamish_Mathison.html, last accessed 21/06/2017

Memoirs of Thomas Jones, https://www.llgc.org.uk/pencerrig/thjones_s_003.htm, last accessed 15/08/2017

Miladysboudoir (October 2016), https://miladysboudoir.net/tag/edith-wharton, last accessed 09/07/2017

Milton's Cottage, http://www.miltonscottage.org

Morris, Sylvia, 'Early American Visitors to Stratford-upon-Avon', The Shakespeare Blog (April 2014), http://theshakespeareblog.com/2014/08/shakespeare-and-americans-early-visitors-to-stratford, last accessed 26/06/2017

Morris, Sylvia, 'Henry Wallis: A Pre-Raphaelite's Views of Shakespeare's Stratford', The Shakespeare Blog (May 2015), http://theshakespeareblog.com/2015/05/henry-wallis-a-pre-raphaelites-views-of-shakespeares-stratford, last accessed 04/05/2017

Morris, Sylvia, 'Unearthing Shakespeare: Good Friend for Jesus Sake Forbear', The Shakespeare Blog (June 2011), http://theshakespeareblog.com/2011/06/unearthing-shakespeare-good-friend-for-jesus-sake-forbear, last accessed 13/11/2015

Moss, Richard, 'Brontë Society and National Portrait Gallery Combine for Brontë200 celebrations', *Culture 24* (January 2016), http://www.culture24.org.uk/history-and-heritage/literary-history/art543485-bronte-society-and-national-portrait-gallery-combine-for-bronte200-, last accessed 09/07/2017

Naomi, Katrina, http://www.katrinanaomi.co.uk/poetry, last accessed 31/01/2018

Neale, Stephen, *Genre* (London: British Film Institute, 1980), pp. 22–3 cited Daniel Chandler, 'An Introduction to Genre Theory' (1997), http://www.aber.ac.uk/media/Documents/intgenre/intgenre.html, last accessed 11/08/2017

New York Times, http://www.nytimes.com/1970/05/28/archives/col-richard-gimbel-dies-at-71-flier-was-yale-library-curator-donor.html, last accessed 09/07/2017

Nisbet, Gary, 'John Steell's Sculpture', Glasgow City of Culture, http://www.glasgowsculpture.com/pg_biography.php?sub=steell_j, last accessed 09/07/2017

Nospam, David, 'Dumfries Mausoleum and Statue', Robert Burns and Tradition, http://www.robertburns.plus.com/MonumentsDumfries.htm, last accessed 14/01/2016

O'Regan, Eilish, 'Portrait of the Artist in a New Light', *Irish Independent* (16 December 2011), http://www.independent.ie/lifestyle/health/portrait-of-the-artist-in-a-new-light-james-joyce-was-farsighted-26802665.html, last accessed 09/05/2017

Oxford Times, 'Narnia Bench Uncovered' (May 2006), http://www.oxfordtimes.co.uk/news/750113._Narnia__bench_uncovered, last accessed 09/07/2017

Pine Street Carpenters (October 2011), http://www.pinestreetcarpenters.com/news.aspx?prid=3, last accessed 09/07/2017

Pitt Rivers Museum, 'Object Biographies', http://web.prm.ox.ac.uk/rpr/index.php/objectbiographies/index.html

Pointon, Marcia, 'Accessories as Portraits and Portraits as Accessories' (2016), https://www.researchgate.net/profile/Marcia_Pointon/publication/311705617_Accessories_as_Portraits_and_Portraits_as_Accessories/links/5856990108ae8f695558a0d8/Accessories-as-Portraits-and-Portraits-as-Accessories.pdf?origin=publication_detail, last accessed 20/12/2018

Pottermore, 'It's Been 10 Years Since J.K. Rowling Finished Writing Deathly Hallows', *Pottermore News* (January 2017), https://www.pottermore.com/news/10-years-since-jk-rowling-finished-writing-deathly-hallows, last accessed 10/06/2017

Princeton University Library, Cast, Princeton University, http://library.princeton.edu, last accessed 09/07/2017

Robertson, Travis, The Raven Society, https://aig.alumni.virginia.edu/raven, last accessed 09/07/2017

Sanchez-Garcia, Jesus Angel, 'Ivory Towers as Writers' Refuges', https://www.researchgate.net/publication/326368597_Ivory_Towers_as_Creative_Refuges_for_Writers_EAHN_Conference_Tallinn_2018, last accessed 08/01/2019

Saunders, Max, http://www.ego-media.org/projects/imagining-the-future, last accessed 18/12/2018

Schiller, Friedrich, 'On Naïve and Sentimental Poetry', 1795, https://archive.schillerinstitute.com/transl/Schiller_essays/naive_sentimental-1.html, last accessed 18/12/2018

Searle, Adrian, Exhibition Review: 'Rachel Whiteread at Tate Britain', (11 September 2017), https://www.theguardian.com/artanddesign/2017/sep/11/rachel-whiteread-exhibition-review-tate-britain

Shakespeare Birthplace Trust, 'A Garden of Curious A-Muse-ments', https://www.shakespeare.org.uk/about-us/news-media/press-releases/garden-curious-amusements, last accessed 09/07/2017

Shakespeare Birthplace Trust, 'David Garrick's Chair', Shakespeare Birthplace Trust Archive, Ref. No. STRSTSBT1868-31392 (1769), http://collections.shakespeare.org.uk/search/museum/strst-sbt-1868-3392-david-garricks-chair/search/everywhere:david-garrick/page/1/view_as/grid, last accessed 09/07/2017

Shakespeare Birthplace Trust, 'Falcon Chair', Shakespeare Birthplace Trust Archive, Ref. STRST186831392 (1630), http://collections.shakespeare.org.uk/search/museum/strst-sbt-1865-5-the-falcon-inn-chair/page/1, last accessed 26/06/2017

Shakespeare Birthplace Trust, 'Shakespeare's House, The Library 17101', Shakespeare Birthplace Trust Archive, Ref. No. SC4/18/32 (1885), http://collections.shakespeare.org.uk/search/archive/sc41832-henley-street-shakespeares-birthplace-library-c-1885-item/search/everywhere:library-69719/page/1/view_as/grid, last accessed 09/07/2017

Shakespeare Birthplace Trust, http://collections.shakespeare.org.uk/search/museum/strst-sbt-1971-121-various-locks-of-human-hair/search/everywhere:locks-of-human-hair/page/1/view_as/grid, last accessed 29/06/2017

Shakespeare's Schoolroom, http://www.shakespearesschoolroom.org/shakespeares-schoolroom, last accessed 30/06/2017

Singer, R.C. (2016). doi: 10.1080/13645145.2016.1259606 https://research.bangor.ac.uk/portal/files/18160973/2017_Leisure_refuge_and_solidarity_messages_in_visitors_books_as_microforms_of_travel_writing.pdf, last accessed 08/03/2019

Smith, Madelaine, 'Jane Austen's Writing Table', Jane Austen in 41 Objects (2014), https://www.jane-austens-house-museum.org.uk/1-jane-austens-writing-table, last accessed 04/07/2017

Solender, Elsa A., 'News, Views and Titbits', Antique Boxes at the Sign of the Hygra, http://www.hygra.com/uk/wb2/WB469/Jane%20Austens%20Writing%20Box.htm, republished from http://www.jasa.net.au/newsdc99.htm, last accessed 09/07/2017

Stewart, Doug, 'To Be...Or Not: The Greatest Shakespeare Forgery' (June 2010), *The Smithsonian Magazine*, http://www.smithsonianmag.com/history/to-beor-not-the-greatest-shakespeare-forgery-136201, last accessed 09/07/2017

Tate Gallery, http://www.tate.org.uk/art/artworks/wallis-the-room-in-which-shakespeare-was-born-t00042, last accessed 06/12/2017

Taylor, Jo, 'Postcards from Newstead Abbey', Placing the Author (August 2016), https://placingtheauthor.wordpress.com/2016/08/31/breathtaking-sarahs-postcard-from-newstead-abbey, last accessed 29/05/2015

'Tea and Coffee in the Age of Dr Johnson', http://www.drjohnsonshouse.org/gifts/html, last accessed 22/03/2016

Tennyson's Museum, https://www.theguardian.com/artanddesign/2009/aug/06/tennyson-museum-bicentenary-poet, last accessed 30/08/2019

Trustees of William Cullen Bryant Homestead, 'About William Cullen Bryant Homestead', http://www.thetrustees.org/places-to-visit/pioneer-valley/bryant-homestead.html, last accessed 09/01/2019

Trustees of Amherst College, 'Emily Dickinson's White Dress', Emily Dickinson Museum (2009), https://www.emilydickinsonmuseum.org/white_dress, last accessed 09/07/2017

Tyler Arboretum, www.tylerarboretum.org, last accessed 09/07/2017

Viva la Violette, 'Weeping at a House Museum', My History Fix (August 2015), http://myhistoryfix.com/inaroundnewengland/weeping-at-a-house-museum, last accessed 09/07/2017

Walden Pond State Reservation, http://www.mass.gov/eea/docs/dcr/parks/pdf/walden-pond.pdf, last accessed 19/06/2017

Watson, Nicola J., Rousseau's trapdoor, *Romantic Europe, the Virtual Exhibition*, https://www.euromanticism.org/rousseaus-trapdoor, last accessed 09/01/2019

Watson, Nicola J., 'The Literary Tourist' Blog, http://www.open.ac.uk/blogs/literarytourist, last accessed 21/06/2017

Wells, Stanley, 'Digging Up Shakespeare', The Shakespeare Blog, 30 June 2011, http://bloggingshakespeare.com/digging-up-shakespeare-by-stanlet-wells, last accessed 13/11/2015

Whittier Birthplace, http://www.johngreenleafwhittier.com, last accessed 27/06/2017

William Culler Bryant Homestead, http://www.thetrustees.org/places-to-visit/pioneer-valley/bryant-homestead.html, last accessed 27/06/2017

Williams, Hannah, 'Why Do We Care about Molière's Armchair?', http://hannah-will.blogspot.com/2021/01/why-do-we-care-about-molieres-chair.html, last accessed 15/06/2019

Woodhouse, Anna, 'Windows to the Soul', Four Thought, Series 4, BBC Radio 4 (29 May 2013), http://www.bbc.co.uk/programmes/b01snbm0, last accessed 09/05/2017; downloads.bbc.co.uk ...fourthought_20130529-2059a.mp3, last accessed 09/07/2017

Youde, Kate, 'Victorian Novelist Elizabeth Gaskell's Home to Re-Open to the Public', The *Independent* (September 2014), http://www.independent.co.uk/arts-entertainment/books/news/victorian-novelist-elizabeth-gaskells-home-to-re-open-to-the-public-9759694.html, last accessed 09/07/2017

Index

Note: Figures are indicated by an italic "*f*" following the page number.

For the benefit of digital users, indexed terms that span two pages (e.g., 52–53) may, on occasion, appear on only one of those pages.

Printed and bound by CPI Group (UK) Ltd, Croydon, CR0 4YY